THE IMITATION OF THE SACRED HEART OF JESUS

by

REV. PETER J. ARNOUDT, S.J.

TAN BOOKS AND PUBLISHERS, INC.
Rockford, Illinois 61105

NIHIL OBSTAT:
Remy Lafort
Censor Liborum

✠ IMPRIMATUR:
John M. Farley
Archbishop of New York
March 30, 1904

Library of Congress Catalog Card Number:
79-112463

ISBN: 0-8955-012-1

Reprinted by TAN Books and Publishers, Inc. in
1974, 1978, 1980, 1982, 1986, 1992 and 2001.

Cover Illustration courtesy of the Discalced
Carmelite Nuns, Danvers, Massachusetts. Cover
design by Peter Massari.

Printed and bound in the United States of America.

TAN BOOKS AND PUBLISHERS, INC.
P.O. Box 424
Rockford, Illinois 61105
1974

CONTENTS.

THE FIRST BOOK.

ADMONITIONS USEFUL FOR PURIFYING THE HEART.

CHAPTER I.

CHAPTER II.

CHAPTER III.

CHAPTER IV.

3

CONTENTS.

CONTENTS.

THE SECOND BOOK.

ADMONITIONS USEFUL FOR THE IMITATION OF THE MOST SACRED HEART OF JESUS IN HIS ACTIVE LIFE.

CHAPTER VI.

CHAPTER VII.

CHAPTER VIII.

CHAPTER IX.

CHAPTER X.

CHAPTER XI.

CHAPTER XII.

CHAPTER XIII.

THE THIRD BOOK.

ADMONITIONS USEFUL TO IMITATE THE MOST SACRED HEART OF JESUS, IN HIS LIFE OF SUFFERING.

CHAPTER III.

CHAPTER IV.

CHAPTER V.

CHAPTER VI.

CHAPTER VII.

CHAPTER VIII.

CHAPTER IX.

CHAPTER X.

CHAPTER XI.

CHAPTER XII.

CHAPTER XIII.

CHAPTER XIV.

CHAPTER XV.

CHAPTER XVI.

CHAPTER XVII.

CHAPTER XVIII.

CHAPTER XIX.

CHAPTER XX.

CHAPTER XXI.

CHAPTER XXII.

CHAPTER XXIII.

CHAPTER XXIV.

CHAPTER XXV.

CHAPTER XXVI.

THE FOURTH BOOK.

ADMONITIONS HELPFUL TOWARD UNITING ONE'S SELF WITH THE HEART OF JESUS IN BLISS.

CHAPTER I.

CHAPTER II.

CHAPTER III.

CHAPTER IV.

CHAPTER V.

CHAPTER VI.

CHAPTER VII.

CHAPTER VIII.

CHAPTER XVI.

CHAPTER XVII.

CHAPTER XVIII.

CHAPTER XIX.

CHAPTER XX.

CHAPTER XXI.

CHAPTER XXII.

CHAPTER XXIII.

CHAPTER XXIV.

CHAPTER XXV.

CHAPTER XXVI.

APPENDIX.

TESTIMONY

OF THOSE THAT HAVE OFFICIALLY GIVEN THEIR OPINION OF THIS WORK.

Opinion of the Very Rev. Father Roothaan, General of the Society of Jesus.

(From a letter of his Paternity to the Author.)

Rev. Father in Christ. P. C.—

Some time since I received the manuscript (bearing date 1846) of a work written by your Reverence, and entitled, "THE IMITATION OF THE SACRED HEART OF JESUS." I was highly delighted with the subject of the Book, and the zeal of your Reverence to promote a devotion so useful and so much recommended. . . . I hope that this work of your Reverence will be printed for the good of the faithful.

Opinions of the Censors in America.

1. "I have examined the little work entitled, 'THE IMITATION OF THE SACRED HEART OF JESUS.' It pleases me very much, and appears well fitted to enkindle in the hearts of the Faithful a love for the Sacred Heart of Jesus, to supply abundant matter for meditation, and point out the path to every kind of virtue and perfection. Nor do I judge that anything hinders it from being published, much less do I think that there is in it aught contrary to Faith or good morals."—*First Cens. Prof. of Mor. Theol.*

2. "I have read the work entitled, THE IMITATION OF THE SACRED HEART OF JESUS,' in four books. And first, the Author's subject—which may furnish abundant fruit to the person that reads it, or meditates thereon—pleases me. Again, the manner in which the author follows up his subject, is complete. Thirdly, the style itself shows a natural simplicity, which is agreeable. Nor do I see what more can be desired in this little work. Neither did I discover anything which may offend against Faith, or sound and pure morals."—*Second Cens. Prof. of Dogm. Theol.*

3. "I have read the book entitled, 'THE IMITATION OF THE SACRED HEART OF JESUS,' and find it very well adapted to awaken the desire of perfection, and, at the same time, such as to direct the reader how to walk without stumbling in the way of perfection."—*Third Cens. D. D.*

4. "Let this work be printed; it will lead souls to sanctity."—*Fourth Cens. Sup.*

TRANSLATOR'S PREFACE.

The Book, which is here presented to the English-speaking public, is one of those works which possess a merit of their own. The general favor with which it has been received throughout Europe, and the high commendations bestowed upon it, leave no room for doubt that it will be equally welcomed in America, where it was originally composed. The circumstances under which it was begun are incidentally alluded to by the author, in the Epilogue.

If care, study and meditation are indispensable in the production of a solid work, the author has added to these even more than the advice of the Roman bard: "nonumque prematur in annum," since it was finished so long ago as 1846. No wonder, then, if it is a Book of rare merit, and worthy of keeping company with the immortal "Following of Christ," of the venerable *à Kempis*. This work it resembles in teaching the highest practical truths, but it differs from the same, in that it is more regular in plan; more complete, actual, definite.

To appreciate the "Imitation of the Sacred Heart of Jesus," it should not merely be read once and again: it should be used as a constant and cherished guide to point out to us how, in every circumstance of life, we may learn to avail ourselves of God's favors and dispensations, to lay up treasures in heaven.

To understand this we need only refer to the general design of the work. It takes a person at the beginning, lays down before him the groundwork of the interior, the spiritual life; and proceeds methodically to lead him, step by step, through its mysterious pathways, until it brings him to the very summit of Christian perfection. Nor is this done by simply inculcating abstract theories and sublime teachings: our Lord is, throughout, introduced, placing before us the living example of His Heart, and applying, practically and in detail, His own lessons.

The very soul, so to speak, of the work is the love of the Heart of Jesus. Other virtues form, as it were, the body. Certain leading principles, like so many veins pervading all, complete the whole. These leading principles are the mainspring of the spiritual life. The chief among them may be said to be: a great purity of heart and horror of sin—avoiding, however, a false delicacy, or scrupulousness of conscience,—an unfeigned esteem of genuine virtue, a generous spirit of self-denial, an ardent affection for prayer, a perfect resignation to the divine Will, a true idea and appreciation of the Church and her mission upon earth, and, consequently, a sincere, a childlike devotion to her; in fine, a real zeal for the salvation of others and for all the interests of Jesus, with whom the soul has, in some manner, become identified. But, in order to realize all this, the reader should give proper attention to the Directory, placed before each of the four Books. This is an essential portion of the work, and exceedingly well adapted to enable us to reap from it the intended spiritual profit.

Whence it appears that the work possesses no ordinary solidity; and, in truth, for directors of souls, for religious, yea, for every Christian—who desires to make progress in virtue and perfection—it should become an inseparable companion.

As regards its English dress, the translator would state, that it has been his principal aim to give, as far as possible, the exact meaning of the author, preferring this to elegance of style and diction—as more useful and appropriate. If he contribute, in any wise, to increase among Christians the knowledge, the honor, the love of the Sacred Heart of Jesus, he will deem his labors amply rewarded.

PROLOGUE.

————

1. THE most ancient special devotion of Christians is doubtless that of the Sacred Heart of Jesus, the Son of God. The holy Sacraments and the other objects of devotion did not yet exist, when the Blessed Virgin Mary found her delight in worshiping the most Sweet Heart of her Jesus; already did Holy Joseph clasp that Heart to his bosom; even then were the Shepherds and the Magi, Simeon and Anna, the Apostles and the Disciples attracted to It and by It: they longed to show to It the affection and love of their hearts. But after Jesus had called upon all men to learn, "that He is meek and humble of Heart;" after He had drawn from the treasury of His heart that best of all gifts, the Sacrament of the Most Blessed Eucharist; lastly, after He had willed that, upon the cross, His Heart should be opened, and continue open, as a place of refuge for all; then was devotion to His divine Heart wonderfully increased. The Apostles now spread it throughout the world as a special worship. Thenceforth, the Fathers of the Church themselves practiced it most tenderly, and commended it most carefully to others. The Saints of every after age became devoted disciples of the Heart of Jesus. But when came the fullness of time, at which He had decreed to pour forth

all the riches of His Heart, the goodness and kindness
of the Saviour were made manifest, and Himself revealed His wish that, thereafter, this devotion should
be a most especial one; since He declared and promised that He would lavish the abundance of His graces
upon all who should consecrate themselves to the worship of His Heart.

2. The object of this worship is the Heart Itself of
Jesus. And since in Jesus Christ there are two natures,
the divine and the human, and only one person, the
divine Person; the Heart of Jesus Christ is the Heart
of the divine Person, the Heart of the Word Incarnate.
And because the divine Person is to be honored with
the highest worship; the worship to be paid to the
Sacred Heart of Jesus, which can neither be separated
nor taken away from the divine Person, is likewise
supreme. This is a Catholic truth, which has pre
vailed over all contrary errors.

3. The end of this devotion is threefold. The first,
to make Jesus a return for that boundless love, of which
His Heart is the symbol, that made Him do so much
and suffer so immeasurably for our sake; and induced
Him to bestow upon us that sweetest and most precious of all gifts, the Sacrament of the Eucharist. The
second, that, through the fervor of our piety, we may,
as far as we can, make amends for all the insults which
have been, or are even now offered to His most Sacred
Heart, which He exhibits to us as the throne of His
affections. The third, that imitating what we worship,
we may be inspired with the same affections, the same
sentiments that animated His Heart during His life of
toil and suffering, and still animate It in His blissful
and Sacramental life.

4. From its antiquity, object, and manifold end, it

is plain that this devotion is most excellent, most profit-able, most solid, and most consoling. But since to imitate what we worship is the abridgment of religion, and since the other ends are contained and reduced to practice in a true Imitation; therefore, in order to insist on this Imitation, and, as far as it is allowed, to direct the same, this little volume is presented to all.

5. This work, which contains a summary of As-cetic Theology, and embraces the doctrine, as well as the practice, of the spiritual and interior life, will sup-ply ample matter for daily meditation, throughout the whole year. In this manner the reader will be enabled to repeat it every year, to examine it more closely, and to impress it more deeply on his mind and heart. He can, if it so pleases, start from the beginning and con-tinue to the end of the work; or he may, whilst going on from the beginning, occasionally break off this or-der, either when some necessity or advantage invites him to some portion specially adapted to his present feelings; or when, on the days on which he approaches holy Communion, his devotion suggests the last Book as better suited to his actual circumstances.

6. For very weighty reasons, things are not pro-posed here in general and in common, as is usually done in books for meditation, but everything is laid down specially and in particular, both in regard to the evil to be avoided, and the good to be practiced. First, that the reader may not be left in uncertainty or beating the air, aiming and grasping at whatever presents itself by the way, and yet gain, or secure nothing. Secondly, that having assiduously before his eyes something determinate, he may direct his strength and efforts, as well in time of prayer and meditation as during self-examination and the per-

formance of good works, to this, that he subdue what is to be subdued, that he acquire what is to be acquired. Lastly, that by destroying separately those things which are the causes, or, as it were, the roots of other evils, he may the more easily and the more efficaciously demolish the rest; and that, by learning and acquiring separately those capital virtues of which, in the lowliness and charity of His Heart, Jesus has given us the example, he may the more readily and the more certainly obtain all other virtues.

7. What regards the manner of writing, although it is most true, that the testimony of Christ must not be announced in loftiness of speech or wisdom, since the kingdom of God consists not in speech but in virtue; yet, it seemed proper to attend carefully to two things: first, that the style should everywhere be suited to the subject; secondly, that the diction should be sufficiently pure.

8. Finally, it must be observed, that the character of this little work is such, as to require, not that it should be read in public to others, but that every one, who desires to use it, may read it privately to himself alone. For its form, its reasoning demand that, in order to relish it, you should, in some manner, converse alone with Jesus, face to face, heart to heart.

DIRECTORY FOR THE FIRST BOOK.

————

1. WHOEVER desires to gather for himself the whole fruit of this work, must rightly understand the aim of each Book, properly apply the means proposed, and diligently strive to surmount the obstacles to the attainment of this aim. Wherefore, in regard to these things, we shall briefly and clearly lay down before every Book that which may serve to direct you with safety.

2. The aim of the first Book is, to teach you how to free the heart, first, from the stains of sin, afterwards from the love of a corrupt world, and lastly, from the inordinate affection for self. And this may be understood in three ways, and reached through as many degrees.

And first, it is required that you free your soul from every mortal sin, and from the love of the world and every ill-regulated affection for yourself, so far as actually to prefer God, your Creator and Saviour, before all things; and consequently, to be unwilling, for anything whatsoever, to offend mortally the Divine Majesty.

Secondly, that you cleanse your heart from every deliberate venial sin, and from the love of the world and the ill-regulated affection for self, so that not even to obtain all things created, nor even to preserve life itself, you would commit any deliberate venial sin.

Thirdly, that you purify yourself from those imperfections which a great fidelity to divine grace may enable you to avoid; and that you so dispose yourself as to abhor the world, and to detest every inordinate affection for self.

Whence it follows that all, they that begin, they that are advanced, yea the perfect themselves, may profitably make use of this book and go over it again and again. For, "Believe me," says St. Bernard, "things cut off sprout forth again, what is driven off returns, what is put out is again enkindled, and what lies slumbering is again awakened. It is therefore but little to have pruned once, the pruning-knife should be applied, yea, if possible, always; if you are in earnest, you will always find something which needs pruning."

Here it must carefully be observed, that a perfect cleansing of the heart is a matter of the utmost importance, whereon almost everything in the spiritual life depends. The chief reason why there are so few who find the path of virtue easy and pleasant; so few who continue to advance readily and perseveringly; so few who attain to the divine union; so few, in fine, who even in this life enjoy the good things which the Lord has here promised to the clean of heart,—is because so few do perfectly cleanse their interior Many there are who labor much and make little progress: they are often obliged to begin anew; they scarcely, or almost never, taste the sweetness of virtue they carry the cross, but do not experience its unction. And, although they may at last be saved, yet for all eternity, they deprive God of a great glory, and themselves of an immense bliss, which they could easily have merited, had they cleansed themselves perfectly. Wherefore, there is hardly anything which the demon strives more to hinder than a complete cleansing of the heart. He suffers us quietly enough to practice virtues, and even to apply ourselves to perfection, provided we neglect purity of heart. For he knows, that in this way we will fall into delusions, and never acquire genuine and solid virtues, much less true perfection. Now, this is the common illusion, against which souls, that are not yet well purified, should especially be on their guard: They desire namely, after a superficial cleansing of the heart, forthwith to deal on terms of intimacy in the interior life with Jesus, to be entertained with Him amid the flowers of virtues, and to taste the most delicious fruits: or, which is still more dangerous, neglecting perfect purity of heart, they aspire to the enjoyment of internal union with Jesus, so full of love and sweetness. There are other illusions, to which souls that enter upon the spiritual life are exposed; for example: they practice external mortification even to excess; they wish,—with a mind in some manner interiorly stubborn, and through a certain violence,—to be freed from something that is irksome to them, or to acquire that for which they long; they keep up fear, even unto down-heartedness. But these things, although dangerous, are not so common nor baneful, as that whereby a person is induced to overlook interior purity.

3. To this, therefore, you must direct all your endeavors. First, having well understood that you are called to true bliss everlasting, learn, as perfectly as possible, all the malice and all the evil of sin, and feel, in some manner, in your soul all the deformity caused in you by sin; secondly, acquire as perfect a knowledge

as possible of the vanity and wickedness of the world, and comprehend most intimately the lamentable fate of those that suffer themselves, of their own accord, to be forever utterly destroyed by the world; thirdly, have a true knowledge of your own self,—what you have made yourself through your offenses, how miserable you are of yourself, and to what you tend of yourself.

To attain to all this, it is not enough to read the Book in a hasty manner, but you should meditate with attention and diligence on what is said, and reduce it to practice. For, in this work things are not so much unfolded as pointed out: first, in order that you may reflect thereon, and endeavor to develop and apply the same to yourself; secondly, that you may stir up the affections of your heart, and ask of the Lord whatever you may need, according to the state of your soul; lastly, that you may secure an inward relish and gather more abundant fruit. For, by thus meditating, by pious desires, by earnest prayer, you shall understand the matter more clearly, and apply it with more profit; and, in return, the Lord, according to the generosity of His Heart, will reward your endeavors, and bless them with His grace. All which is to be understood as referring not to the first Book only, but to the others likewise.

4. There are two methods of using this first Book: each of which is perfectly safe and easy, as is proved by the experience of very many, even uneducated persons, who are wont to spend whole hours in meditation, without weariness and with much fruit.

The first method is mainly suitable for beginners, who, not yet accustomed to mental prayer, cannot keep up a continuous reasoning; nothing, however, hinders others from employing this same method, particularly when they do not feel themselves properly disposed to make deeper reflections.

First, therefore, recite a preparatory prayer, which may always be the same, and as follows: "Gather unto Thee, Lord Jesus, all my senses; cleanse my heart from all evil and unbecoming thoughts; enlighten my understanding, inflame my heart, that, during this prayer, I may employ attentively and devoutly the senses of my body and the powers of my soul, for Thy glory and my salvation; and that, through Thy most Sacred Heart, I may deserve to be heard in the sight of Thy Divine Majesty. Amen. Lord Jesus, in unison with that divine intention of Thy Heart, whereby Thou didst pay to God the tribute of Thy praise, I offer to Thee this prayer." After which, place yourself before the Lord, in some appropriate mystery, or as dwelling in the holy Tabernacle. Finally, beg fervently of Him the fruit of the prayer which you are about to make. These three things constitute the beginning or introduction of the meditation, in whichsoever manner it is made.

Next, if you make use of the first method of prayer, first, read slowly and attentively one or more verses, according as you may find it necessary or useful; secondly, consider how true that is which you have just now read; how true all the Saints deemed it, as well as all they that were anxious to deliver their souls from everlasting perdition, and to save them for eternity; how true you yourself will think it at the moment of death; thirdly, examine yourself, endeavoring to discover what has hitherto been, in practice, your conduct concerning it; if good, return thanks to the Lord, and ascribe to Him all the glory, and do not neglect to beg for grace to be enabled to persevere in well-doing, yea, to act even better and more perfectly; if, on the contrary, evil, grieve, excite an act of contrition, ask pardon; fourthly, form a good resolution of correcting yourself, or making progress for the better: select means adapted to this purpose, and ask for grace to execute your resolve. This being done, if the allotted time for meditation is not elapsed, pass over to other verses, following the same order.

But if you make use of the second method of meditation, after the aforesaid introduction, 1, exercise your memory, either by reading or recalling to mind the matter of the meditation; 2, exercise the understanding, first, by reasoning on the subject of the meditation, proceeding through causes and effects; secondly, by investigating what practical applications can be drawn therefrom; thirdly, what reasons or incitements urge you to this; fourthly, how you have acted till now; fifthly, what is to be done for the future; sixthly, what obstacles should be removed; seventhly, what means must be chosen; 3, exercise the will, first, by stirring up pious and appropriate affections and making internal acts; secondly, by forming good specific resolutions, adapted to the present state of your soul; thirdly, by earnestly imploring grace for yourself and for others.

Lastly, 1, a colloquy is made with Jesus by an outpouring of heart; 2, the concluding prayer is recited after this manner: "Lord Jesus Christ, who didst deign, by a new favor to Thy Church, to disclose the unspeakable riches of Thy Heart, grant, I beseech Thee, that I may be able to correspond to the love of this most Sacred Heart, make atonement by worthy homage for the insults offered by thankless men to Thy most afflicted Heart, and be inspired in all things with the sentiments of the same Heart; who livest and reignest with God the Father in the unity of the Holy Ghost, God world without end. Amen"; 3, finish by recommending yourself to the Most Blessed Virgin Mary, to your Angel Guardian and your holy Patrons. These three things form the end or close of every kind of meditation.

Since experience proves that the examples of the Saints exercise a wonderful and saving influence, on the hearts of sinners as well as of the just, they are frequently brought forward. But, to meditate on these with more fruit, you should consider some particular Saint or Saints, whom you choose for Patron, or to whom you entertain a special devotion. For different persons are edified and moved by different examples: thus a religious is wont to know better, and to study more, the lives of the Saints of his Order; and they that live in the world and strive to serve God, feel more devotion to those Saints whose example seems better adapted to themselves. When, therefore, the Saints are said to have done something after the example of the Heart of Jesus, or to have been distinguished in some specialty, you ought to select in your mind some particular Saint, and see what he did, and how he acted; implore his intercession with God, and recommend yourself to him. And if no Saint occurs to you at the time, you can always recall the example of the most Blessed Virgin Mary, and beg her intercession and protection.

5. Then, in order to guard against, or overcome the obstacles which the enemy of your everlasting happiness throws in your way, and which are wont to relate to conscience; you should, first, rightly under-

stand what is meant by conscience. Now, conscience is the dictate presented through reason, which inwardly warns, or shows us, in particular cases, what is to be done or omitted, and this either under pain of sin, because it is a matter of precept; or, on account of an increase of merit, or the greater good-pleasure of God, because it is only a matter of counsel. It is called a dictate presented through reason; because it is a practical conclusion deduced from principles, known to reason, either by the light of nature, or of grace or faith. For example: My conscience tells me, that to-day (Sunday) I am obliged to hear Mass. This is deduced from these implied premises: On Sundays there is an obligation of hearing Mass: but to-day is a Sunday; therefore, to-day there is an obligation of hearing Mass. But it must be remarked that an inference of this kind is secretly drawn, and presented to man, even in spite of himself: as is made manifest in those who are unwilling to listen to the voice of conscience, lest they be deterred from things wherein they unlawfully indulge, or lest they be disturbed in them. For it is altogether against their will that they hear, that conscience forbids something and condemns them. Hence it appears that conscience, when really such, is independent of man and superior to him.

He that is too prone to timidity or scrupulousness, should here carefully observe and learn, that conscience is not an agitation of the nerves, nor a representation of the fancy, nor a vague fear, nor, finally, the possibility of a case. On the other hand, he that is too inclined to laxity or to rashness, should observe, that a desire of the will, the propensity or aversion of nature, that some passion, or, lastly, some subtle artifice, is not conscience. But let them both remember, that conscience is the dictate presented through reason, or the voice of the Spirit of God, who speaks to us inwardly by reason, as an interior organ, and makes known to us, in particular cases, His Will that commands, or His good-pleasure that counsels.

Conscience is true or right. A right conscience is that one, which shows things as they are in reality; as commanded or obliging, what is commanded; as dangerous, what is dangerous; as counseled or better, what belongs to counsel or perfection. This conscience, if we follow it in such a manner that, from a holy fear of God, — whereby like good children we dread to offend God,—we avoid sins which destroy His friendship, or His paternal good-will towards us, is called a fair conscience. But, if we are so faithful that, at its bidding, we guard against every voluntary defect, and are obedient to the same in all things, it is called a delicate conscience.

Again, conscience may be false or erroneous. Such is that one which shows things falsely or differently from what they are in truth. This happens, for the most part, through the fault of man, who viciates the instrument of which the Spirit of God makes use, so that it does not transmit the divine voice. Ignorance, the habit of sin, every inordinate passion, spoils it more or less. Or, to speak more plainly, ignorance, the habit of sin, every inordinate passion, have, each by itself, the effect of causing something false or trifling, to be assumed as one of the principles from which a practical inference, or conscience, is deduced. Whence it happens, that such a conscience is the voice, not of the Spirit of God; but of another spirit, that uses passion, or any of those other causes, to speak to man's interior.

If conscience errs by our voluntary fault, it is styled vincibly erroneous, and makes us guilty of the errors. Now, it is vincibly erroneous, through our voluntary fault, if, when we put an act, or the cause of an act, a knowledge or a doubt of an error occurs to the mind, and the obligation of avoiding the error is noticed, and when, over and above, ordinary diligence to know the truth is neglected. But, if conscience errs without such a fault on our part, it is called invincibly erroneous, and does not make us guilty in the sight of God.

To erroneous conscience belong likewise, both the scrupulous and the lax conscience, being the opposite extremes. A scrupulous conscience is that which believes it sees, and even when corrected, persists in believing, that it sees, sin where there is no sin; it errs for the most part, because a soul gives in to the imagination, to the obstinacy of her own judgment, or some passion which fetters the heart; whence, being inwardly agitated and perplexed, she sees objects differently from what they really are, or confounds one thing with another, precepts with counsels, things probable with possible, sin and its danger with the appearance or semblance of sin and danger.

A lax conscience, on the other hand, is the conscience of a soul that persuades herself that she does not see—and, even when warned, continues to persuade herself that she does not see—sin, or the danger of sin, where it really exists. An individual falls into this error because he has a mind which labors under culpable ignorance, or a sin to which he is habitually addicted; or because he indulges a passion by which he covets or abhors something inordinately. Whence it happens, that he who has such a conscience is blamable; because he can guard against errors by removing their cause; which he must certainly do when he sufficiently perceives the obligation of removing the same.

We should guard, with the greatest care, as well against a scrupulous, as against a lax, conscience. Both are not only dangerous, but destructive: the one, as well as the other, hinders perfection, and renders it impossible: and, what is more to be dreaded, both are wont to expose salvation itself to the danger of perdition. Wherefore, let every one be careful to have a right conscience.

But, to commit a formal sin, or a sin by which God is offended and man becomes guilty, it is necessary, first, that the act, whether internal or external, by which sin is committed, either through commission or omission, be evil or unlawful, or is considered as evil or unlawful by conscience; secondly, that his mind, when he does the act, or puts the cause of the act, advert to the moral evil of the act, or see that the act is unlawful; thirdly, that the will, whilst he possesses the internal liberty of choosing between consent and dissent, knowing that the act is evil or unlawful, freely consent thereto. For, if he does an internal or external act, the moral evil of which he does not notice, either when he does the act, or puts the cause of the act; he indeed wills or can will the act, but not as morally evil, while he does not see that the same is unlawful. For nothing is willed that is not known. Wherefore, by willing, or doing, such an act, he commits only a material sin, which is nothing else than an error of a conscience, invincibly erroneous whereby God is not offended and man not rendered guilty

To commit a mortal sin, it is required, as not only the theologians, but the Saints also teach, first, that the internal or external act be grievously evil, or deemed grievously evil by conscience; secondly, that, when he does the act or puts the cause of the act, the mind do fully advert to the grievous evil of the act; thirdly, that the will, knowingly and freely, give its consent. If one of these three things be wanting, the sin, which would otherwise be mortal, is venial.

No one commits a formal sin in spite of his will: for man cannot sin, formally, except by his own free will. He can, however, if he so wills, through an abuse of his free will, think evil or that which is unlawful; propose or imagine it to himself, give his consent thereto, and commit sin. Moreover, the demon can, with the Divine permission, and really does, cause in him thoughts and imaginations, evil ones too, that he may entice him to give the consent of the will; but he can never force him to consent. Finally, God Himself, His good and blessed Spirits are wont to suggest thoughts, and to propose objects, but always to induce man to good: they assist his will to do good, but they never force him.

Whence it appears, that in man there is a triple kind of thoughts and emotions; the first, springing from the free will of man himself; the second, thrown in from without by the demon, the evil spirit; the third, also suggested from without, but by the good Spirit. Now then, "By their reasonings we shall know them: and the suggestion itself will make known which spirit it is that speaks" (St. Bern.)—The following rules, which the Saints lay down for the discernment of Spirits, will help you to understand this matter:

I.   To them that easily sin mortally, the evil spirit is commonly wont to suggest, or propose the seeming delights of the flesh, sensual pleasures; that thereby he may hold them more securely in his service, and plunge them deeper into sins and vices.

Towards such persons the good Spirit pursues the opposite course: he continually stings and disturbs their conscience; that he may render them conscious of the unhappy state of their soul, may deter them from sin, and convert them.

II.   By deceitful counsel and cunning, the evil spirit endeavors to lead man to an inordinate love and greediness for riches, or the superfluity of possessions, that, afterwards, he may cause him to fall more easily into sin.

But the good Spirit whispers, that the heart should be kept free from the inordinate love and eagerness for earthly possessions, lest it be entangled by them.

III.   The evil spirit allures, presses, persists, in order to induce man to aspire to vain honors.

The good Spirit places before him, and teaches, generous humility, the true and safe glory of man.

IV.   To them that perceive the needfulness of their devoting themselves to their everlasting salvation, and who begin seriously to think of securing the same, the evil spirit is wont to suggest a certain shame. or human respect, that he may check these good beginnings.

The good Spirit encourages and stimulates them,

that, spurning all human considerations, they may bravely go forward.

V. To those who are sincerely careful to cleanse themselves from faults and vices, and who advance more and more in the desire of serving God, the evil spirit suggests molestations, scruples, sadness, false reasonings, and other annoyances of this kind, that thereby he may hinder their progress.

The good Spirit, on the contrary, is wont to supply strength and courage to those that act rightly or endeavor to do well, to enlighten their mind, to pour in consolation, to give peace and tranquillity, that they may ever the more readily and cheerfully by means of good works, continue to make further progress.

VI. With all his might does the evil spirit strive that the soul, which he desires to deceive and to lead to ruin, do keep secret his wily suggestions. He exerts himself, as much as he is able, that his attempts be not made known to a spiritual director; since he knows that, in this event, he fails in them.

But the good Spirit loves light and order, because he acts fairly, and his works are good.

VII. The evil spirit is accustomed to conduct himself like a commander in war. For as this one examines the arrangements, and reconnoitres the strength of the citadel which he desires to take, and assails it on the weakest side; so the evil spirit explores our disposition and all our virtues, both theological and moral, and at whatever point he finds us weaker, there he is wont to attack and try to take us by storm.

VIII. The evil spirit, the tempter, is wont to lose, altogether, his courage and strength, whenever

he sees his spiritual antagonist, struggling with a
bold front and unterrified heart against temptations.
but, on the contrary, if he perceives that he trembles, and, as it were, loses courage, there is no wild
beast on earth more fierce or headstrong against
man than this same enemy, in order to accomplish
the desire of his wicked and perverse mind.

ST. IGNAT., ST. THOM., ST. TERES'

THE FIRST BOOK.

ADMONITIONS USEFUL FOR PURIFYING THE HEART.

CHAPTER I.

THE FOUNDATION.

1. *The voice of Jesus.*—Learn of Me because I am meek and humble of Heart; and ye shall find rest for your souls.

The voice of the Disciple.—These are the words of Jesus Christ, whereby we are commanded to learn and imitate the Virtues of His Heart, that we may be set free from all misery of soul, and be made truly happy.

This is His doctrine. this is the method of learning, this is the fruit, this is the end.

The first inducement to learn is the excellence of the Master. What is there more excellent than the Son of God, who alone is our Master, appointed by His eternal Father, in whom also are all the treasures of the wisdom and knowledge of God?

His doctrine is the truth, surpassing all the arts and sciences of this world: it smooths the way not to some perishable wealth, some passing pleasures, or a short-lived renown: but to boundless riches, that cease not to last, to unuttered delights, that are constant, to honors supreme, that endure forever.

Whatever He taught us to do, He reduced to one lesson: Learn of Me because I am meek and humble of Heart: this He adapted to all men, this He gives to all, that all may learn the same, the little as well as the great; knowing full well that in this precept, if rightly understood and kept, are contained all things necessary.

His whole life was the application of this doctrine, which He began to practice, before He taught it to others.

2. Let us learn this short lesson, and we shall be wise enough, and sufficiently instructed; nor shall we have to look for any thing more.

The method of learning consists in action, which is performed in two ways: by studying and by practicing.

But first, in order to understand what we strive to learn, and reduce to practice what we have understood, we must pray earnestly.

Afterwards, we must diligently revolve in our mind the depth, the hight, the breadth of the lesson; keeping unceasingly before our eyes the divine likeness of our Master, and examining what we ought to amend, what to avoid, what to hold, and to what to aspire.

Lastly, since it is not enough to know, but we must also practice, the lesson, as it wholly consists in action, and can only be perfectly learnt by acting; we must, as soon as we begin to learn, also begin to practice, showing ourselves before

God and men, meek and humble of heart in thought, word and deed.

And, whilst we progress in understanding and practice, we should so labor that the spirit of the lesson unfold itself ever more perfectly in the plan of our life, in our inmost feelings, in our conversations, in our every action, yea, in the very modifications of the same.

3. If, after this manner, we learn what our Lord has given us to learn, we shall reap the fruit, whereby our zeal and toil shall most certainly be rewarded, according to the promise of Him who cannot possibly deceive nor be deceived.

Which is that promised fruit? Of all—the most desirable. Ye shall find rest, says He. And what is it, to find rest?

Nothing less than to find that with which we may repose, filled and satisfied; without any need to seek for aught more, and without fear of ever losing it, against our will.

Whoever shall have found this rest, will be truly calm and happy: but he that finds it not, whatever else he may possess, shall ever be restless and unhappy; because in his heart he is not satisfied, is obliged to seek for more, and is ever in danger of losing, even against his will, what he has acquired.

We are all so framed that, by nature, we are compelled to covet a blissful repose; neither have we it in our power not to desire the same.

A great blessing it doubtless was, that the Lord placed within us this awakening desire, this urging power; for, more firmly in action, more gently in manner, do we by its means, pursue that which is to make us happy.

And although, by the freedom of our will, we
are enabled to seek rest in a variety of things; yet
will this longing of ours, this power, importune and
drive us onward, until we find the object for the
seeking and attaining of which this faculty has
been given to us.

Christ the Lord, our God, who implanted this
faculty in our souls, and who would not have given
us this irresistible faculty without an object, nor
have given it without the ability of attaining the
same,—shows us here where we should seek, and
how we may find the true object.

Learn of Me because I am meek and humble of
Heart, and ye shall find rest. He makes no distinction, no exception: we shall then find true
rest, unalloyed happiness.

For although our rest, our soul's happiness, as long
as we dwell here below, cannot be every way complete,
yet it will be real; such as the Lord promises and
such as has been experienced by numberless Saints,
who were meek and humble Disciples of the meek
and humble Jesus.

We shall truly enjoy that peace, which no outward enemy can disturb: we shall delight in that
repose, which no inward agitation can disquiet:
lastly, we shall possess that divine likeness and
union, wherein is contained supreme happiness,
yea, every good here upon earth, and of which no
one can deprive us, against our will.

4. Whilst we gather this fruit, we shall, at the
same time, secure our end, the everlasting bliss of
our souls. For He says: Ye shall find rest for your
souls.

If our souls are ours, they are not ours because

we created them, since He Himself created us, and not we ourselves: but they are ours because He gave them to us. In giving them to us, He gave them for an end worthy of Himself, that we,—after He had done what He ought, which He always does, since He is infinitely perfect,—might act jointly with Him, and thus gain for our souls a blissful and abiding tranquillity.

This then is the end: everlasting beatitude of the soul, intimately connected with the glory of the Lord, who, in creating her, had this end in view.

For if God is full of glory in all His works, how glorified must He be, in so great a work as that of the salvation of souls exulting forever in triumph, and praising Him without ceasing!

To attain this end, He helps and strengthens us in a thousand ways and by countless means: for this He goes before us, as a good father before his children, as a guide and companion, pointing out a safe and pleasant way, whilst, at the same time, He relieves and refreshes us.

5. This being so, let us joyously follow so great and so good a leader. What can be more honorable for us? Is it not a great glory to follow the Lord? is it not supreme honor, to be the beloved Disciples of His Heart?

What worldly honor can be imagined, which does not become mere emptiness, when compared with such a dignity?

Nor is there anything more useful, since on it depends our soul's rest: our happiness both in time and in eternity. Now, this is a matter of such importance, that alone it deserves our attention; because without it, all other things are useless and delusive

Lastly, it is sweet and easy; for His commands are not heavy; since He enjoins such things, as with the means which He affords, we cannot only perform, but from the fulfillment of which no enemy of our salvation, no obstacles can hinder us.

And, if we learn of the very Heart of the Saviour, we draw from the sweetest fountain of love; so that we either do not feel the labor, or if we do, we so cherish it as to find it easy and delightful.

O Jesus, meek and humble of Heart! receive me, I pray Thee, as Thy Disciple, the Disciple of Thy Heart, and grant me to learn diligently of Thee to be meek and lowly of heart, that thus I may find rest for my soul, to Thy everlasting glory.

CHAPTER II.

THAT NO OBJECT IN THIS WORLD CAN SET OUR HEART TRULY AT REST, OR MAKE IT TRULY CONTENTED.

1. *The voice of Jesus.*—My Child, thou art created for happiness. This experience affirms, this reason proves, this faith teaches.

Thou seekest incessantly for happiness, and thou dost well. But leave off seeking thy happiness in things created; in them thou shalt not find it.

No object of this world can satisfy the longings of thy heart; even shouldst thou alone possess at once all things created, thy heart should still be empty and wretched.

Things of this earth awaken the thirst of the

heart, they cannot allay it; yea, the more thou dost possess, the more eagerly shalt thou thirst.

How canst thou find in creatures that which exists not in them? can any one give what he does not possess?

2. Shalt thou obtain what no mortal was ever able to obtain? Behold, the wisest of men abounded in all good things, he was affluent with ever-fresh delights, he astonished nations with his boundless wealth, he had filled the uttermost lands with the renown of his glory.

Yet, on account of the void of his heart, he is forced to exclaim: Vanity of vanities, and all is vanity.

Grant that thou possess whatever thy heart may long for in this world: that thou be lord of the whole earth: that all men do thee honor: try all things; and thou shalt find that thou hast as yet found nothing, except vanity and affliction of spirit.

3 Do not wonder at this, My Child: thy heart is not made for this world. Therefore, whatever this world contains is unworthy of thy noble destiny and of thy heart's affection.

Thou art created for greater things, thou art born for things everlasting, thou art destined to things without limit. Do not then give thyself up to what is low and mean, since thou art made to rule forever.

What could it avail thee to gain the whole world, if thou shouldst lose thy soul? Surely, thou wouldst be twice unhappy: here, on account of the wicked state of thy conscience, thou wouldst suffer a torturing agony; hereafter, thou wouldst have to undergo misery everlasting.

Blessed, therefore, is he who spurns whatever

may mislead the heart; who nobly casts aside every obstacle to true felicity; who, mindful of his noble destiny, seeks happiness above all in his Creator.

4. *The voice of the Disciple.* — My God, my Saviour, Thou didst create me for happiness; hitherto I have not ceased to seek it, still I have never yet tasted, nor have I ever yet found happiness.

My passions were ever and anon crying to me: here it is, or there. In my madness, I believed them, and, blinded by my unruly desires, I ran hither and thither; but, instead of the sought-for bliss, I found wretchedness, and tasted its bitterness.

Ah, wretched me! created for happiness in Thee my God! I toiled in vain, whilst I sought it in creatures outside of Thee; and behold! I strayed still further away from the bliss for which I was created, and I found wretchedness, for which I was not made, and perished therein.

God, my Saviour! open my eyes, that now I may distinctly see this great mistake of mine; and grant that, free from error, I may effectually seek in Thee that beatitude which I cannot find in creatures.

CHAPTER III.

THAT IN THE HEART OF JESUS OUR HEART MAY FIND TRUE REST, UNALLOYED FELICITY.

1. *The voice of Jesus.* — My Child, if thou desirest to attain true felicity, render thy whole heart similar and conformable to My Heart

In My Heart thou shalt find peace and tranquillity, which the world cannot give nor take away.

If once thou hadst entered perfectly into the interior of My Heart, thou wouldst thence behold all things earthly, such as they are in themselves, not as they are esteemed by the foolish worshipers of the world.

Then thou wouldst free thyself from the irksome and unnecessary care of creatures, and think nothing worthy of itself, except what is truly good.

2. Now, thy heart, subject to continual fluctuation, changes seven times a day, so that at one time it is glad, at another sad; now calm, then troubled, again inflamed with the love of creatures, and again wearied with the emptiness of them; sometimes it glows with fervor, and next it falls into lukewarmness, and thus, like the sea, it is ever changing.

But, if thy heart were united with Mine, a great and enduring calm would suddenly ensue.

For, safe in thy union with My Heart, as in a harbor of protection, thou shouldst be enabled to remain ever the same and unshaken; secure against change, whether the winds of adversity or of prosperity were blowing.

If thou art sheltered in My Heart, no enemy shall hurt thee. The devil, indeed, runs about, seeking whom he may destroy; and many does he drag into destruction; but thee he shall not approach, nor shall he disturb thy peace.

3. Oh! if thou wouldst acknowledge the divine gift! Oh! if thou wert willing to know what good things lie hidden therein! It does truly contain all that is needed for thy felicity.

Continual peace, undisturbed security, true joy

of heart is the portion of all those that love My Heart, and make their abode within the same.

Of what avail are riches, honor, yea the greatest delights, if the heart be not satisfied and at rest? And what can the whole world give, except restlessness and sickliness of heart?

Wretched therefore shalt thou be, whatever thou mayst possess, until thou shalt rest in Me, who alone can give thee all.

4. *The voice of the Disciple.*—Experience has taught me this, O Lord; for in all things have I sought peace, and nothing have I found except trouble upon trouble.

Thou didst assuredly will, for Thy own sake, as well as for ours, that our heart should find peace in Thee alone. For Thou, O Lord, didst make our heart for Thyself: and restless and unhappy must it be, until it repose in Thee.

O Heart of Jesus most sweet! O Thou the delight of the most Holy Trinity! O Thou the joy of the Angels and Saints! O most blissful Paradise of souls! what can I wish outside of Thee, since in Thee is all that I can and must desire?

In Thee, heaven has its beatitude; in Thee, the earth its felicity: since, then, Thou art the bliss of all, why shouldst Thou not also be mine?

Yes, indeed, O sweetest Heart of My Jesus! Thou art my repose, Thou art my bliss for evermore.

CHAPTER IV.

THAT IT IS NECESSARY FOR SALVATION, TO IMI-
TATE THE HEART OF JESUS.

1. *The voice of Jesus.*—My Child, one thing
above all others is necessary, to save thy soul.
For if she is lost, all is lost; but if she is saved, all
else is saved.

Yet, thou shalt not attain thy eternal salvation,
if thou do not imitate My Heart.

For those whom God did foreknow, He also did
predestinate to be conformed to the image of His
Son.

Which is this image of the Son of God, where-
unto all those that will be saved are to be conformed, if it be not My Heart?

It is not given to every one, to imitate My outward actions; nor does it depend on man to do the
wonderful works, which I have wrought.

Besides, by reason of the diversity of men's conditions in life, all cannot follow My exterior manner of living; but the interior dispositions of My
Heart can be imitated by all, the great and the
small, the learned and the ignorant, in whatever
condition they may live.

If then thou desirest to be saved, be conformed
to My Heart; and do thou reproduce in thy heart,
whatever sentiments animate Mine.

2. Though thou shouldst distribute thy possessions
among the poor; though thou shouldst give up thy
body to the greatest penances; though thou shouldst
understand all mysteries; though thou shouldst work
astonishing miracles; if thy heart be not after the

likeness of Mine, thou art nothing, and all those things shall avail thee nothing forever.

By the likeness of thy heart to Mine art thou to be judged, and thence is thy eternal state to be determined.

But, at the judgment, many will say: Lord, have we not in Thy name prophesied? have we not cast out devils? have we not wrought many wonders? And I will say to them: I know you not: do ye see the wounds which ye have inflicted? Do ye recognize the Side, which ye have pierced, and which for your sake remained open; yet ye would not enter into the same?

Whatever, therefore, thou mayst do, it avails thee nothing, unless thou do it according to My Heart.

3. Not the outward appearance of piety, but a devoted heart makes a man truly good, and dear to Me.

Thou wilt place thy salvation in security, in proportion as thou dost conform thy heart to My Heart.

Do for thy salvation whatever thou art capable of doing: no zeal can be too great, when an eternity is at stake.

When thou art about to die, thou shalt find that everything is lost, whatsoever thou mayst have done; unless thou didst direct it to Me, and to thy salvation.

If, then, thy everlasting salvation is of the greatest importance, remember, as much as thy salvation is worth, so much is the Imitation of My Heart to be prized.

4. *The voice of the Disciple.*—O eternal salvation of the soul! important affair, thou alone art to me

supremely necessary! Why am I in this world if not to save my soul? Why was I redeemed, why furnished with so many means, why loaded with divine favors, if it was not that I might, with more ease and pleasure, secure my soul's salvation?

But alas! I did not yet begin earnestly, that for which I am placed in this world. Ransomed as I was, I sold myself again into a more disgraceful slavery, and perished by misusing the very means and blessings, whereby I might so easily have secured my salvation and my happiness.

O Lord my God! Thou couldst most justly have permitted that I should perish forever, and suffer that never-ending destruction, which my wickedness and the wasting of Thy gifts have deserved for me.

Yet, since the infinite goodness of Thy Heart did not allow this; nay more, since by a new and exceedingly great blessing, Thou hast induced me to value and love the salvation of my soul; I will no longer be ungrateful, I will no longer expose my soul to everlasting ruin.

I resolve and promise to co-operate with Thy Heart's most sweet designs of saving my soul, and rendering her forever happy.

CHAPTER V.

THAT ALL OUR PERFECTION CONSISTS IN IMITATING THE HEART OF JESUS.

1. *The voice of Jesus.*—My Child, all thy perfection consists in thy resemblance to My Divine Heart

For My Heart, which is the Heart of the Word of God, is the standard of all virtues, is holiness itself.

Whoever, therefore, imitates my Heart, imitates God, his Saviour, perfection itself.

Now, since My Heart is the model of sanctity and the source of every grace, thou shalt learn of My Heart, what it behooves thee to do, that thou mayst render thyself holy; and thou shalt draw thence the necessary strength to effect this.

If, then, thou wilt become perfect, imitate My Heart: the more conformed thou art to It, the more perfect shalt thou be.

2. My Heart is humble: humility is the foundation of true sanctity.

If thou do not learn humility of My Heart, thou shalt never possess this virtue; nor shalt thou know aught of it except the name.

And if thou build the structure of perfection upon aught else, it cannot be solid; and it shall be overthrown by the least breath of wind, and great shall be the fall thereof.

Moreover, My Heart is meek, full of charity now, charity is the perfection of holiness.

But thy heart shall never be inflamed with charity, unless it be enkindled by that fire of love wherewith My Own is burning.

Woe to thee, if thou enkindlest thy heart with any strange fire! thou wilt indeed burn, but for thy destruction.

3. Thou shalt never acquire solid virtues, nor attain true sanctity, except by imitating My Heart.

Whatever signs of virtue thou mayst display, how devout soever thou mayest appear: so long as thy heart does not imitate Mine, all thy piety shall be nothing more, than a mask thrown over thy features.

There is no hope of perfection, unless thou propose to thyself My Heart as a pattern of perfection.

4. So it has been from the beginning of the world. For, in the Old Law, it was foretold and known of what sort My Heart would be; and no one was numbered with the Elect, unless he had foreshadowed in his heart the qualities of My future Heart.

And from the beginning of the Church to the present time, My Heart was ever the sanctification of the Apostles, the fortitude of Martyrs, the constancy of Confessors, the purity of Virgins, the perseverance of the Just; in short, the perfection of all the Saints.

Therefore, take courage, My Child, follow My Heart, whithersoever I may lead thee: the more closely thou shalt follow the same, the nearer thou shalt come to complete perfection.

On the Imitation of My Heart depends the entire fulfillment of the Law, all sanctity.

The constant endeavor of imitating My Heart, is a sure sign of predestination.

5. *The voice of the Disciple.*—O sweet Jesus, fountain of life and grace! arouse me, help me to understand and imitate Thy Heart, the standard of virtue, the pattern of sanctity.

Free my heart from every illusion, from every obstacle: grant, that with a guileless and pure heart, I may seek Thee; that I may make Thy interior thoughts, the feelings of Thy Heart, my own; that I may make myself inwardly similar to Thee.

Alas! O Lord, how unlike in heart am I to Thee! How little have I hitherto labored to portray the life of Thy Heart by my own!

Would that I had not struggled to estrange my heart and turn it away from Thine! O blindness! O madness of my soul!

Have Thou pity on me, Lord Jesus! have pity on me, according to the great mercy of Thy Heart.

How many there are, who have not lived so long, nor had so many means, and yet have sanctified themselves by becoming fervent Disciples of Thy Heart! And I have not yet begun to be holy: I am still a sinner!

It is time, O Lord, it is time to begin the work of my sanctification, which I have so long neglected.

This arouses me, this spurs me on, that I can yet be made holy, that I can yet become the Disciple of Thy Heart, that I can yet be marked with that most joyous sign of predestination.

Cheer me up, Jesus most kind, give help, give courage: behold, now I begin.

CHAPTER VI.

THAT WHOEVER DESIRES TO IMITATE THE HEART OF JESUS, MUST PURIFY HIS OWN HEART.

1. *The voice of Jesus.*—My Child, if thou wilt enter into the intimacy of My Heart, and taste the unutterable sweetness of Its intercourse, cleanse thy heart from every evil.

For I, thy Well-beloved, am pure and stainless, I delight Myself among the lilies.

How could there exist a union betwixt My Heart and thine, unless thou hadst carefully purified it?

For who shall accuse My Heart of sin? And how canst thou say: My heart is clean; since thy heart itself is conscious of the contrary?

Alas! My Child, what a heart is thine! Born in sin, so long an abode of evil spirits, defiled and disfigured by so many stains, strongly drawn to evil and sadly estranged from supernal good; fostering so many ill-regulated affections, the fruitful sources of sin, full of itself and of the world; accustomed, for the most part, to have itself in all things for its ultimate object.

2. Wonderful indeed is it, that thou darest invite Me to enter into such a heart, and to reside amid such uncleanness.

A wicked heart is to Me an object of abhorrence, but an unclean heart I loathe: how then could it delight Me to dwell therein?

I seek a pure heart, and all My delight is to dwell therein; and to be there entertained among lilies.

Whoever, therefore, loves cleanness of heart, shall enjoy My presence, and shall experience the tenderness, and divine sweetness of My Heart.

3. Be not deceived, My Child, thinking that it is well with thee, provided thou dost outwardly deport thyself in a proper manner, since I look chiefly at the heart.

And what will it avail thee to have been pleasing by thy outward conduct, to all creatures, if, by thy inward dispositions, thou hast been displeasing to Me?

If thy heart is stainless, then shalt thou be wholly pure: since it is from the heart that proceed evil thoughts, uncleanness, fraud, blasphemy and all manner of evil.

Purify thy heart, therefore, and nothing shall hinder thee from being sweetly united to My Heart, and from tasting the fullness of Its delights.

But, if only outwardly thou turn away from evil, if thou do not root out sin from thy heart, thou shalt never be free from vices: they shall sprout forth with ten times greater vigor from within, than thou shalt be able to shun from without; and, whilst thou appearest to stand firm, thou shalt sink beneath the weight of inward evils.

4. Come then, My Child, prepare a neat dwelling-place for Me in thy heart, and I, when I come, will be wholly thine, and thou shalt be wholly Mine; and there shall exist a wonderful intimacy between us, and a union known only to those who have tried it by experience.

Be of good courage, and begin forthwith this all-important work: thou canst feel no true joy, until thou finish it entirely.

Fear of trouble hinders many from perfectly purifying their hearts.

This is a device of the enemy: the wily foe,— knowing that on a true and thorough cleansing of the heart depends not thy salvation and perfection alone, but also that of others, and, above all, My glory,—strives, by every means, to keep thee from this undertaking.

Give no heed to the suggestions of the crafty schemer, who cares not, whether it be by true or false means, that he attains his object.

Do thou pray, ask for divine grace; with this, set about thy work bravely; and thou shalt see that all difficulties vanish before thy greatness of spirit; and, to thy astonishment, thou shalt find, that where thou didst look for the greatest hardships, there shalt thou meet the greatest consolations.

5. *The voice of the Disciple.*—I beg and beseech Thee, Lord, create a clean heart in me, and renew a right spirit in my interior.

My whole heart is defiled with uncleanness: and from the heart, infection has spread over the powers of my soul, and over the senses of my body.   Alas! O Lord! what is there in me without blemish, or altogether pure?

Send forth, I beseech Thee, the light of Thy grace, and illumine my mind; that I may know, and bewail, all the evil I have done, and the good which I have neglected.

O how I regret, sweetest Jesus, that I have dishonored Thy dwelling-place in so unworthy a manner, that I have displeased Thee, that I have saddened Thy Heart! I grieve, O my supreme Good: I lament and abhor all my sins: I avow my malice and my ungratefulness: I implore the mercy of Thy Heart.

Lord, if Thou wilt, Thou canst make me clean: wash me from my iniquity, and cleanse me from my sin.   Yea, from hidden offenses, and from those not my own, purify my heart.

Come, Jesus, enter my heart, and make for Thyself a scourge with the cords of holy fear, of lively gratitude, and of pure love, and drive out all them that defile this Thy dwelling.

Behold, henceforth I will give admittance to none of them: Thy house shall be called a house of prayer: in it, I will worship Thee; in it, I will love Thee; in it, I will occupy myself with Thee alone.

CHAPTER VII.

THAT OUR HEART MUST ESPECIALLY BE CLEAN FROM MORTAL SIN, THE GREATEST OF EVILS.

1. *The voice of Jesus.*—Look thou, My Child, lest in thy heart there be that sin which causeth the death of the soul.

How canst thou love, or darest thou receive, as a guest, into thy heart, thy deadly foe; who, when admitted, will, without doubt, make thee the slave of hell, the most wretched of men; yea, more base than the irrational beings themselves.

How many there are who exclaim: Alas! what evils ravage the earth! Yet sin is the only evil, and there is none other besides.

Avoid sin, and whatever may befall thee, it will turn to thy advantage.

2. It is marvelous, that a being, gifted with reason, should, of its own accord, commit sin, which, in its very nature, is so unbecoming and detestable, that, even were there no heaven nor hell, it ought to be shunned on account of its inherent foulness.

If thou considerest the infinite Majesty of Him that is offended, and the infinite meanness of the one offending; thou wilt understand, that sin is in some sort an infinite evil.

Whoever sins mortally, assails God, and would do away with God Himself, if that were possible: nor is it for want of will, on the part of the sinner, that the God of heaven and earth is not destroyed.

3. So great an evil is sin, that, in order to destroy this hell-born monster, and to satisfy the divine justice, I, the Son of the Most High, must needs come down from My throne of Majesty, and being made man, suffer during life a ceaseless martyrdom, and, at last, writhing in agony, expire upon a cross.

Alas! wretched man, how canst thou love to do that, which has cost Me so much? Or how canst thou be willing, for a moment's pleasure, to renew all My toils, My sufferings, and My most bitter death?

When thou sinnest mortally, thou makest thyself guilty of a far more grievous crime than the Jews, My torturers. For these, had they known Me as the Lord of eternal glory, would never have put Me to death. But thou, thou knowest Me: yea, knowest who, and how good I am, and knowest this by the experience of My favors.

4. Was it not by My charity alone, that I not only created, redeemed, and preserved thee; but that I ever protected, guided, and cherished thee more kindly than the most tender-hearted parent?

Whatever thou art, whatever thou hast, I have given thee, and, over and above all, I have given thee My own Self: and is this the return which thou makest?

Behold, if thou throwest to an animal, devoid of

reason, a morsel of the meanest food, it shows thee gratefulness, as much as it is able. But I have bestowed upon thee boundless favors, and, in return, thou persecutest Me, even unto the death! Reflect, then, what shouldst thou think of thyself?

5. O child of My everlasting love! whom I have loved more than My life, sin thou no more.

If thou lovest Me, yea, if thou lovest thyself, flee from sin.

For, whenever thou committest a mortal sin, thou diest in a supernatural manner; thou losest whatever merits thou didst possess; thou dost forfeit thy right to the heavenly inheritance; thou becomest a co-heir with the devils; thou givest the preference to misery over bliss, to hell over heaven, to Satan over Me.

Meditate upon these things, My Child, that thou mayst learn fully, as far as the human mind can understand, how great an evil sin is; and that thou mayst shun that, which alone can make thee wretched for evermore.

6. *The voice of the Disciple.*—O my soul! behold sin! Truly the greatest of evils, that places man below the brute, blocks up the gates of heaven, throws open the abyss of hell. O monster to be abhorred, a thousand times more frightful than the demon himself!

O my God! I blush to own it, and disown it I cannot, I have become the vilest slave of sin, and by the greatest madness, the greatest ingratitude, the greatest malice; with it, and by it, I have again and again insulted Thy dread Majesty, before which the awe-struck Angels tremble with reverence.

I feel wholly confounded, because I have become

viler than any irrational creature; I have done iniquity which my reason disapproved, and I have misused all the powers of my soul, all the senses of my body.

7. O Lord my God! Thou didst establish in me Thy sweet likeness; and I, after having defiled the same, have substituted in its stead the horrid image of Satan; yea, in various ways, I have rendered myself even more horrible than the devil.

He sinned through pride, when no punishment had yet been inflicted for sin; I sinned knowing, but disregarding Thy vengeance: he was placed in innocence but once; I was restored to it so many times: he rose up against Him who made him—I against Him, who also remade me.

Most wretched sinner that I am; for nothing, yea, for an object baser than nothing, I have voluntarily cast aside Thy friendship, the blissful peace of my soul, the right to eternal beatitude; I have delivered myself up, as a hapless slave, to the devil; thus, sharing from this time his unhappy condition, and ready to partake of his never-ending torments, unless, returning to my senses, I find mercy in Thy Heart.

8. I acknowledge, Lord Jesus, that I am unworthy to find that mercy, which I have so often abused: I am not worthy to serve Thee, since I have become the slave of the devil. If Thou wilt treat me as I deserve, hell must be my abode.

Yet, Jesus, my Saviour! there is infinite mercy in Thy Heart: my very sins show this; for unless Thy mercy were infinite, Thou wouldst never have tolerated the infinite malice of my sins.

O Jesus! have pity on me, according to Thy

great mercy. A suppliant, I implore forgiveness I hope that Thou wilt pardon me, a wretched sinner. I am sincerely sorry for the sins I have committed, and I firmly resolve to serve Thee faithfully henceforth, and to love Thee fervently.

CHAPTER VIII.

THAT OUR HEART MUST ALSO BE FREE FROM THE LEAST SIN.

1. *The voice of Jesus.*—My Child, cleanse thy heart from every fault: and keep thyself carefully from the stain of even the least sin.

There is nothing, there can be nothing, for the sake of which it is allowed to commit a sin, however light.

Wherefore, although thou mightst thereby save the whole world from ruin, it would be unlawful to offend Me, even in the least thing, since I am infinitely more excellent than the whole universe.

Some guard themselves against grievous offenses, but of light faults they render themselves guilty without scruple; a clear sign that they are rather governed by self-love, than by love for Me.

Deluded souls! they will learn, at their cost, how greatly they have deceived themselves.

2. Whoever overlooks little things, will gradually fail in great ones; and, having accustomed himself to think everything little, he will still fancy, that all is well with him; when, without much uneasiness of conscience, he commits great sins.

In his folly, he finds it delightful to walk on the brink of the precipice: yet, it will come to pass, and that justly too, that, at the first slip of his foot, he is thrown headlong into the abyss.

Beware, therefore, of venial trespasses, lest thou fall into mortal sins.

As long as thou yieldest, even to the slightest fault, so long wilt thou expose thy salvation to danger.

3. Many seem heartily to abhor the renewal of My death by mortal sin; and yet, they cease not, by small offenses, to load My Heart with bitterness, and afflict It with continued sorrows.

Ah! My Child, consider again and again, and carefully attend to what thou art doing. For, whilst thou art willing to inflict a small wound on My Heart, perhaps thou shalt mistake, as has happened to many, and thou shalt pierce My Heart with a mortal blow.

O perverseness of the human heart! Many dread more to give offense to the meanest of men, than to Me, their God and Saviour.

4. So long as thou continues to sin, even slightly, thou shalt be ill at ease; nor shalt thou taste true happiness.

If thou hast thy perfection at heart, as it behooves, unless thou avoidest every voluntary sin, thou shalt labor in vain, whatever efforts thou mayst make.

For, venial sin lessens charity, brings on lukewarmness, viciates acts of virtue, obstructs the sources of special grace; and, finally, despoiling, by degrees, the soul of her possessions, leaves her empty.

5. And for what is it, in most cases, that man exposes himself to evils so numerous, and so great? is it not for self-interest, or for self-gratification?

But consider, how great a loss will ensue, and how severely thou shalt have to suffer in purgatory.

There, torments are undergone, which far exceed all the pains of this world, and all the ills of life: nor shalt thou go thence, until thou hast paid the last farthing.

How exceedingly shalt thou then deplore, that thou didst commit even the smallest offense, on account of which thou perceivest, too late, alas! that thou art excluded from heaven, and most sorely tormented?

Do not, My Child, render useless My Heart's desires and endeavors of making thee happy; neither be thou so thoughtless as to choose to be unhappy, in spite of Me.

6. *The voice of the Disciple.*—Venial sin, O Lord, is then no small evil, since it offends Thy divine Majesty, wounds Thy Heart, deprives the soul of special graces and helps, hinders her progress, viciates her good deeds, prepares the way for her destruction, exposes her to the danger of everlasting perdition, and excludes her from heaven.

And evils so great, I have deemed small! O what madness was mine! And, what is worse, I have committed them without number, without measure. My transgressions have exceeded all bounds.

Where are the limits? Behold! as many powers of the soul, and senses of the body as there are in me, so many kinds of sin: as many gifts and favors, so many faults of misuse or ungratefulness: as many species of employments, so many sorts of offenses. Alas! amongst all my actions, even those of religion or of piety, which is the one wherein Thou findest not some short-coming?

O my soul, we commit so many faults through want of attention, by surprise, and through frailty; ought not these to suffice? Should we add greater ones through carelessness, through the abuse of our free-will, through malice?

Is this the return we make to the Lord, by whose goodness we live, to whose love we owe whatever we are and possess?

7. O Lord God, my Saviour! that I have not perished beneath the weight and multitude of my offenses, this I acknowledge is altogether due to the kindness of Thy Heart: yea, to Thy Heart's mercy it is owing, O Lord, that I have not been utterly destroyed.

I have been lowered to the dust: my strength has forsaken me; darkness has overspread me: my heart itself has grown faint within me. Lo! ever deeper have I sunk, and through very weariness, I am now unable to extricate myself. O, how great is my misery!

O! who shall give water to my eyes, and strength to my heart, that I may weep, and move Thee, O Lord, to set me free!

Have pity on me, good Jesus! and deliver me: cleanse and renew me wholly.

Inflame my heart with the love of Thy Heart: with Its divine fire do Thou consume my offenses: nor keep them for the fire of purgatory. Here, I beseech Thee, here let me burn and be cleansed in the fire of Thy sweet love; not there in the fire of avenging flames.

Behold! O most sweet Jesus, love for Thee will now make me do, what fear has hitherto been unable to effect: through love for Thee, I will shun every sin, even the slightest.

———

CHAPTER IX.

THAT THE HEART OF THE SINNER CAN TASTE ONLY THE BITTERNESS OF MISERY.

1. *The voice of Jesus.*—Well-beloved, if thou hast come to this, that thy heart has nothing wherewith to reproach thee, rejoice, yea rejoice, because peace, like a stream of bliss, is thine.

A good heart makes the soul happy, gladdens heaven, terrifies hell. But a wicked heart fills the sinner with wretchedness, moves the Saints with pity, inspires the demons with fiendish joy and exultation.

Picture to thyself all the possible calamities of this world; thou shalt never be able to imagine misfortunes so great, as those which the sinner bears in his heart.

How hard, how abject, is the slavery of the sinner! with how many chains, and how tightly lies he fettered beneath the yoke of the basest masters, the demon and his own tyrannical passions!

His understanding is bound with the chain of a dull ignorance, so that he may not see the truth:

his will is chained with the fetters of an accursed malice, that he may not love goodness.

His senses are riveted with the fetters of concupiscence, that he may not follow righteousness: he is pressed down by the weight of the chains of his passionate desires, that he may not gain the sweet freedom of grace.

2. Who is more foolish than the sinner, who is himself the cause of his deepest degradation?

If, on earth, there be a foretaste of hell, it is surely in the heart of the wicked; who, inflamed with the fire of his passions, suffers all the tortures of an evil conscience.

How can he ever truly rejoice, who knows that were the slender thread of life broken, he should be hurled into the depths of hell?

Verily, I know not how he dares betake himself to his nightly rest, who knows not whether he shall not awake in eternity as a reprobate?

3. The human heart necessarily strives after happiness: but, blindly hurried away by a mind unbridled and unsubdued, the sinner seeks happiness there, where only greater misery can be found.

Some seem to imagine that they may be able to satisfy their passions, by gratifying them completely; and that, when they are sated, then, at last, peace will come. Alas! how great an error!

For who, in order to put out a conflagration, will cast fresh fuel on the fire? Would he not, by so doing, rather increase than extinguish it?

Even so, if a man should sacrifice to his passions the salvation of his soul, and the health of his body, unsated, still, they would exclaim: Thine we are, give us food.

Oh, were the heart of the sinner exposed, what wretchedness, what disgustful objects might be descried therein! Yet all things are open and visible to Me, who cannot err, and whom men cannot deceive.

4. A heart given to evil habits, sometimes goes so far that it no longer fancies, loves, or relishes anything, except what may gratify the passions and, although it knows that it is hurrying on to an abyss of misery, yet it heeds not, but, like a senseless beast, it runs after its lusts, trampling under foot, not the good things of eternity alone, but also decency, and honor, and life itself.

The sinner needs no enemy to hurt or torment him: he himself is his own greatest enemy, and most cruel torturer.

Even from the things with which he seeks to delight and gratify himself, he is wont to receive manifold tortures.

5. How can he enjoy peace, who nourishes within himself the cause of his disturbance? or how can he even once breathe freely, who is the slave of the devil?

How unhappy must he be, who allows Satan to seat himself on the throne of his heart, and to be lord and master therein!

Blessed is he, that has never experienced the slavery of the devil! that has never groaned beneath the weight of the shackles of sin!

My Child, if thou hast never yet felt the wretchedness of the state of sin, rejoice thou with thy whole heart, and never seek to know what it is to serve the devil.

But if, unfortunately, thou art his subject, have

pity on thy soul; eagerly cast off his yoke, burst his chains, enjoy the freedom of the children of God

6 *The voice of the Disciple.*—O Lord! how great is the wretchedness of the state of sin! How truly unhappy is the soul, that languishes in this most pitiful state! what peace, what joy can she possess, when she has Thee, the Almighty and All-knowing One, for an enemy! when she knows herself banished from Thy Heart, her last place of refuge! when she is conscious that at any moment she may be plunged into fire everlasting.

How truly unhappy, when she cannot look up to heaven, without seeing that she has lost all right to the same! when she cannot look around her, without being upbraided, and without being terrified at every accident! when she cannot even cast down her eyes, without being silently reminded, that hell is her dwelling-place!

How truly unhappy, when she cannot turn to her own heart, without finding Satan therein! without being tortured therein as in a hell tasted beforehand, where there is nothing joyous, nothing consoling; but everywhere horror, and darkness, and dread, and torments.

O most wretched soul! how changed from what thou wast, when, adorned with celestial grace, ennobled by divine adoption, thou wast so fair, so great, as to be an object of wonder to the Saints and Angels!

How disfigured by sin! how abject! how base under every aspect!

7. O Jesus! would that I were able, even at the price of my blood, to undo what has unfortunately

been done! would that I had never fallen into so great a wretchedness, but that I had rather lost my life instead of Thy grace!

O blessed are they, that have never lost their innocence! that have never experienced the misery of the state of sin!

Restore to me, I entreat Thee, my first garment: give me back my innocence: and lo! in the newness of life I will so serve Thee, as to preserve it stainless for Thee all my days, even to the end.

CHAPTER X.

THAT THE HEART OF JESUS INVITES ALL, EVEN SINNERS.

1. *The voice of Jesus.*—Come to Me, all ye that labor and are burdened, and I will refresh you.

He that is just, let him come, that he may be made still more just: he that is lukewarm, let him come, that he may become fervent: he that is a sinner, let him come, that he may be cleansed and made holy.

Alas for human frailty! Where is the man, that has not sinned? For, whosoever shall say, that he has no sin, deceives himself, and the truth is not in him.

2. My Child, if thou feelest thyself burdened with sins, or troubled with defects, hasten to My Heart: here shalt thou be made free; here thou shalt breathe again.

Let not the greatness of thy sins hinder thee, nor the grandeur of My Majesty: I came not to call the just to repentance, but sinners.

The greater the miseries to which thou art subject, the greater the pity I feel for thee: and the more thou art ill, the greater need thou hast of a physician.

I am not astonished at thy infirmities; for I know thy frame and thy heart. That thou didst not fall into greater evils, thou owest chiefly to My grace.

But at this I wonder, that, when I present Myself to heal thee, thou art unwilling to be healed; or, if thou art willing, thou seemest to doubt My goodness.

Ah! My Child, do not offer this most bitter insult to My Heart. For My Heart loves to forgive, and does not grow weary with pardoning.

Behold, with what kindness I treat truly repentant sinners, so that I have even been called the friend of sinners.

3. Where is the heart, that loves as My Heart? No man has a greater love, than that he lay down his life for his friends; but I, the Son of God, have a greater one than this, for I laid down My life for My enemies.

Who ever loved Me first? or who ever bestowed his affections upom Me, who did not first experience the effects of my love?

4. Since many lose their innocence, before they understand clearly what innocence is, or how great its price, it is a great glory of My Heart, to triumph also over their hearts; and of sinners to make them Saints.

O didst thou but know the charity of My Heart, thou mightst then be able to understand, how dearly It loves faithful souls, and how sweetly It invites sinners.

Who is suffering, and My Heart is not suffering with him? Who sins, and My Heart is not thereby affected? Who is ill, and My Heart does not afford a remedy? Who is unhappy, and My Heart does not feel it? Who, in fine, is there in the world, to whom My Heart does no good?

5. I am a good Father; and My children, begotten on the cross, I embrace with the love of My Heart—which remains open for them, that, at all times, they may have a place of refuge, nor this a common one, but the very centre of My affections.

Whilst they sleep, My Heart is awake to watch over them; whilst they are watching, It is occupied with their preservation.

So great is the love wherewith My Heart is inflamed for them, that I love and cherish each, as if he were My only one.

And if some one, misled by the enemy, wanders away, My Heart wails over him, as over the death of an only-born. I pursue him with My love, I invite, I press, I promise. But if he be unwilling to hearken to Me, I have patience, I stand at the door of his heart, and knock again and again.

If, at last, he resolves to return to Me; I fly to meet him, I press him to My bosom, whilst My Heart leaps for joy; because I see the child, whom I had bewailed as dead, alive and safely restored to Me.

In My joy, I call together all heaven, that they may congratulate Me, and exult with Me.

6. If, therefore, thou desirest to delight My Heart, to gladden heaven, and to refresh thy soul, be converted to Me with thy whole heart.

It matters not how much, or how little, thou mayst have sinned, come to My Heart, and thou shalt find a cure for all thy ills.

Trust in Me, My Child, and fear nothing: I call thee, not to upbraid thee with thy faults; but that I may wash them away.

Come, Child come: I await thee, with open arms, and a burning Heart.

7. *The voice of the Disciple.*—Behold, most sweet Jesus, behold, I come, aroused and reassured by the exceeding goodness of Thy Heart.

Coming, I beseech and exclaim: Kindly receive Thy prodigal child, returning from a far-off country, squalid with sin, filled with misery.

I am not worthy to be called Thy child, since I left Thee in a manner so unbecoming, dishonored Thee so shamefully, and grieved Thee so much.

I have sinned against heaven and before Thee: guilty as I am, I dare not now throw myself into Thy arms: behold, I prostrate myself in the dust before Thy feet, appealing to Thy paternal Heart, imploring pardon.

Lo, Thou didst recall me when I fled away: Thou didst seek me, when I was lost: Thou didst bear with me, when I was abusing Thy goodness: with wonderful mildness Thou didst induce me to return: when, at last, I come in this pitiful state, Thou dost not only receive me, but, O goodness! Thou dost even embrace me! O Jesus! O never was there such a father!

Let all the Angels and Saints be glad, and rejoice with me: let them praise and extol Thy mercy forever!

Behold, now I am Thine for evermore: ever faithful I will love Thee, O Lord, and, through love for Thee, I will comply with all Thy wishes.

CHAPTER XI.

HOW THE CLEANSING OF THE HEART IS TO BE UN-DERTAKEN.

1. *The voice of the Disciple.* — Numberless, O Lord, are the things which urge me on to free myself entirely from faults. Heaven holds out promises, hell threatens, earth can at any moment hurl me into eternity.

My heart, also, full of thy gifts, impelled by its own wretchedness as well, and drawn by the infinite goodness of Thy Heart, never ceases to incite me.

But, how shall I perform so great an undertaking? For, although I see that I ought to do it, yet, I know not how to accomplish it.

Do Thou, I beseech Thee, good Jesus, teach me the manner of truly amending and reforming myself. All the glory, thence arising, shall belong to Thee, and to Thy most loving Heart.

2. *The voice of Jesus.*—My Child, if thou wishest to cleanse thy heart, and to root out everything vicious, begin the work with a great courage and a generous mind.

Have the good and determined will of correcting

thyself, and c. never ceasing to strive after a complete cleansing; at the same time, cherish a sincere desire of co-operating with the divine grace, and of following its guidance: and thus thy endeavors shall, at last, be crowned with success.

This is the first and chief means on thy part: from it all the rest derives its strength and efficacy, and without it, however powerful it may be, of itself, everything else can hardly effect any good.

This strong determination of ever striving, with God's grace, to cleanse the heart, and to preserve it unsullied, is the first hope of future purity of heart, the first sign of future perfection, the first token whereby future Saints are distinguished, yea, the first characteristic mark of the true Disciples of My Heart.

3. Being made ready for the work, by this disposition of thy soul, take fire, and enkindle thy heart therewith, that thou mayst consume the sins and defects which exist therein.

Understand, Child, what I say. Thou hast to clear a garden, all bristling with noxious plants and weeds, and disfigured with filthy objects; thou shalt succeed, however, if thou usest the proper means, if thou cuttest away all things hurtful, if thou tearest up and carriest out everything useless; but thou shalt not finish thy work, except after a long time, and with hard labor.

But, by applying the fire, without trouble and in a short time, thou shalt see the whole garden cleansed.

Nay, more; by this burning, the garden itself shall become richer, and better suited to produce flowers and fruits.

In like manner, Child, thou wilt cleanse thy
heart, which may be likened to this garden, much
more readily, and more easily, by using the fire of
divine love, rather than by any other means.

Thereby also thou shalt find thy heart better
adapted to produce the flowers of virtue, and the
fruits of sanctity.

4. Now, this fire thou mayst obtain from My
Heart, if thou drawest near to It, through prayer;
if thou prayest, not with the lips alone, but also
with thy mind and heart.

For, if thou weighest properly in thy mind the
sufferings of hell, or of purgatory, which thou hast
so often deserved: if thou considerest attentively
My divine favors bestowed upon thee, and all thy
ungratefulness:

If thou meditatest carefully on My infinite perfections so worthy of all love and honor, and on
thy offenses, so deserving of punishment:

If, moreover, thou viewest Me, exhausted with
toils, through love for thee, and suffering so many
things, for thy transgressions,—hanging on the
Cross, with arms extended, and with My Bosom
opened for thee:

If, in fine, thou enterest into My Heart Itself,
and considerest to what degree that innocent Heart
did suffer for thy sins, and how, for them, it was
spent and consumed:

If, at the same time, through loving desires, and
fervent petitions, thou appliest, as it were, thy heart
to Mine:—

Then, doubtless, in prayer, shall blaze out that
fire, that heat of divine love, of which I am speaking.

5. From this love do thou draw forth contrition: that is, sorrow for sin committed, and a resolve of not sinning again in future.

No one, My Child, obtains the pardon of his sins, unless he bewail them; nor is any one healed of his vices, unless he hate them.

Wherefore, as much as thou art able, do thou hate and detest, in thy heart, thy sins and vices; which thou canst not hate nor detest too much.

The more thou shalt draw this sorrow from the divine love, the more perfect shall thy contrition be, even if thou do not actually feel the same.

And the more sincerely thou shalt bewail and detest thy sins, with an upright heart, the more certain shalt thou be of the pardon of thy offenses, and the more secure against committing new ones.

6. Thou hast a sure mark of sorrow for the sins of the past, if thou abstainest from committing new ones.

Therefore, have thou, and preserve always, a firm resolve of shunning whatever thou knowest to be displeasing to Me; and of suffering rather all the evils of this life, than to commit a voluntary sin.

But, take heed, lest thou deceive thyself, by imagining, that any kind of resolve will be sufficient. For a vague desire is not enough: a resolution made through custom, or for form's sake, is not enough neither does an ineffectual purpose suffice,—when one appears to will and not to will; when, as he fancies, he is willing to sin no more, and yet, he is unwilling effectually to use the means necessary to avoid sin.

It is requisite, My Child, that the resolution be really sincere, settled, and efficacious, that by it thou mayst be induced to employ the means, which may hinder thee from again committing sin.

Now, to keep this resolution ever alive within thee, renew it often, pray frequently, nourish thy devotion by spiritual exercises: and thus obtain for thyself that special grace whereby thou mayst the more easily become constant and persevering.

7. *The Voice of the Disciple.*—My Heart, O Lord, is truly like an abandoned field, wherein many noxious weeds spring up and many useful plants lie spoiled.

It is a great work, to clear the heart of all these, and, of myself, I can do nothing profitable.

But do Thou help me, I beseech Thee, with Thy efficient and powerful grace, that I may be able to finish happily so great an undertaking.

For I desire eagerly to complete, according to Thy direction, a work so necessary, so useful, so holy; and am resolved not to leave it off, before I have finished it in reality.

Do not suffer, O most kind Jesus, that I ever grow slothful or careless, in so important an enterprise. For, I confess, that I am prone to grow weak in courage, and that I am wont, even after I have begun with zeal, by degrees to fall into luke-warmness.

But do Thou arouse, encourage, and stir me up strongly, nor allow me to cease from my labor, until I bring the work to its wished-for completion.

CHAPTER XII.

THAT THE HOLY SACRAMENT OF PENANCE IS AN
EASY AND EFFECTUAL MEANS OF CLEANSING
ONE'S SELF FROM SINS AND VICES.

1. *The voice of Jesus.*—My Child, My Heart,—
knowing that the frailty of mortals is of such a
nature, that, whilst on earth, they cannot live without sin,—has devised a saving means, whereby, if
it is rightly used, they may not only obtain the remission of their sins, but also receive an increase
of grace.

God is faithful, and, according to His word, He
forgives their sins to those that confess them; and
He gives grace to those that pray for it, and seek to
live better.   (I. John i. 9, and v. 14.)

What would become of most men, if there were
no Confession? How few should be saved! And
how many of those who now rejoice in heaven, or
shall possess it hereafter, should be lost!

2. Therefore have I given power to the Church,
that whose sins she shall forgive, they be forgiven
them; and whose sins she shall retain, they be retained. (Matt. xviii. John, xx.)

"If, then, either hatred, or infidelity, or any other
sin, have secretly crept into the heart of any one,
let him not be ashamed to confess the same, to him
that presides, that, through the word of God, and
through wholesome advice, he may be healed by
him." (St. Clement of Rome. I. Century.)

"But, if thou wouldst withdraw thyself from
Confession, meditate in thy heart on hell, which

Confession will extinguish for thee. Therefore, knowing that against hell, after that first safeguard of Baptism, there remains still this second help in Confession, why dost thou abandon thy salvation? Represent first to thyself the greatness of the punishment, and thou wilt not hesitate to take the remedy." (Tertullian. II. Cent.)

"For there is a remission of sins, although a toilsome one, through Penance, when the sinner moistens his couch with his tears, and when he is not ashamed to make known his sins to the priest of God, and to seek a remedy." (Origen. III. Cent.)

"This remedy of Confession is eagerly to be desired by all, since the soul is harassed by greater danger than the body; and the healing for hidden diseases must be applied as soon as possible." (Lactantius. IV. Cent.)

"Confess, then: let all corrupted matter come out, and flow off in Confession: what remains, shall be easily healed. Dost thou fear to confess, when, by not confessing, thou canst not remain concealed? God, who knows all things, requires Confession, that He may free the humble: for this He condemns him that does not confess, that He may punish the proud." (St. Augustine. V. Cent.)

"But confess thou, in such a manner, that thou do not again turn to thy sins: for then is the Confession of sin profitable, when the sinner, who confesses, does no more, what he had wickedly done." (St. Fulgentius. VI. Cent.)

"Man ought to abstain from sin, when he has confessed: Confession goes before, remission follows." (St. Isidore. VII. Cent.)

For "the Church, which is founded on Christ,

has received from Him the power of freeing men from their sins." (Ven. Bede. VIII. Cent.)

"If sinners are unwilling to confess their sins, God Himself, who is now their witness, shall also be their avenger." (Haymo. IX. Cent.)

"Sins should not be repeated publicly: it is sufficient to make known, to the priests alone, by a private confession, the faults of conscience." (Luitprand. X. Cent.)

"Therefore, reason moves, and God impels the sinner to confess." (St. Peter Damian, XI. Cent.)

"Confession is necessary to the sinner; and is no less proper for the just. (St. Bernard. XII. Cent.)

"Confession should be made, in a threefold manner: without palliating, without excusing, without delaying." (St. Bonaventure. XIII. Cent.)

"Let the penitent, therefore, accuse himself before the priest, with a lively feeling of sorrow, with a firm purpose of amendment, and let him perform the works which may be enjoined." (Thauler. XIV. Cent.)

"Penance is a Sacrament, the matter of which consists in the acts of the penitent, which are divided into three parts. The first is contrition of heart: the second is the oral Confession: the third, satisfaction." (Council of Florence. XIV. Cent.)

Behold, Child, how, from the beginning, the faithful of all times, and of all parts of the world, have regarded and esteemed this sweet and saving Sacrament.

3. What can be more advantageous than rightly to confess? Through Confession, man is freed from faults, he returns into favor with Me, he receives peace of heart; so that he who before felt himself

tortured with anguish now finds himself calm and
happy

The Sacrament of Penance is the medicine of the
soul whereby vices are healed, temptations put to
flight, the snares of the devil destroyed, new grace
is imparted, piety increased, virtue rendered more
and more solid.

Through Confession, the soul regains her rights,
which she had lost by committing sin; and recovers
her beauty, which unrighteousness had disfigured.

4. But it sometimes happens that the sinner,
when he approaches this Sacrament of divine mercy,
impelled either by shame or fear, throws himself
into the abyss of sacrilege; so that now he is not
simply a sinner, but becomes a frightful monster
of sin.

Art thou able, wretched man, to hide thyself from
Me? Art thou able to hinder Me from thrusting
thee down into that lowest depth, which thou thyself hast dug?

Dost thou sacrilegiously conceal thy sins from a
Confessor, who, by the strictest laws, human and divine, is bound to an everlasting and complete secrecy? I will make them known before thy face,
not to one man alone, not to one nation, but to
Heaven and Earth, to all that shall ever have existed.

Then, in the excess of thy confusion, thou wilt
call upon the mountains, that, covering thee, they
may screen thee from shame; yea, thou wilt wish
to hide thyself in hell; but thou shalt not be able:
thou shalt stand and undergo, publicly, thy whole
confusion and deserved ignominy.

Foolish man! thou wast not ashamed to sin to

thy disgrace and perdition; why dost thou blush to confess for thy salvation and glory?

But, consider: why shouldst thou hesitate to unfold thy conscience before him who is appointed by Me, and holds My place in thy regard?

When thou presentest thyself, as a penitent, before him, thou oughtest, indeed, to look upon the Confessor even as upon Myself; for he verily represents Me, and possesses My power.

Yet, he also is a man, and has his own miseries; and he, too, as well as thyself, is obliged to make Confession: which is all the harder for him, as, by reason of his elevated condition, he ought to be more perfect.

Thus has it been ordained from heaven in a most wise and holy manner, that all—priests no less than laymen—who desire to be freed from grievous sin, should be obliged to confess: and that it be especially proper that the priests, whose sacred employments demand a greater holiness, should cleanse themselves, by frequent Confession, even from slighter trespasses.

Hence, laymen confess, with greater freedom and confidence, to the priests; and priests learn, by experience, to feel compassion for their miseries, to be weak with them that are weak, and to weep with them that weep.

5. But there are those that confess their sins candidly enough, and yet are not improved. And why? Because they do not strive with a sincere heart to correct themselves.

Some approach the Sacrament of Penance from necessity, others through human respect, others again from a certain custom. Why wonder, then,

·f they that approach in this manner derive from it but little or no fruit?

Do, thou, My Child,—having ever thy own salvation and My good pleasure before thy eyes,—make each Confession, as if it were to be the last of thy life: thus wilt thou experience sweet and wonderful effects.

6. Yet, know thyself, My Child, and learn, that thou shalt often be tempted to do again those things, over which thou hadst wept, and which thou hadst resolved to shun.

Do not, on that account, lose courage, Child, nor be thou saddened overmuch. These will be the effects, not of malice, but of frailty; being involuntary, rather than deliberate transgressions.

Thence, learn thou the goodness of My Heart, ever ready to pardon thee; and, in like manner, the pitiful condition of thy heart, which is ever inclined to evil, and frequently betrays thee.

Beware, however, lest, on account of this thy great frailty, thou neglect Confession: but the weaker thou feelest thyself, the more frequently have thou recourse to it.

7. Some hold Confession in dread, and do not approach it without trembling.

Behold, the greatest sinners, as well as the greatest Saints, find consolation therein: and art thou tormented with anxiety!

There the dead return to life and the living live more fully. Why, then, tremblest thou, as if thou wert going to death, or to the rack?

Thou errest, my Child, thou errest; this most wholesome Sacrament was not instituted for torturing, but for solacing the heart.

8. Cast aside, therefore, all uneasiness and anxiety. I am not a God of agitation, but of peace; I find My delight, not in the commotion, but in the good will of the soul.

Do what thou canst, and confess with as sincere a heart, as thou art able to do: after that, remain in peace, nor be thou disturbed by the suggestions of the enemy, or of thy own imagination.

My Heart is the place of refuge for sinners. As often as any one flies hither with a contrite and humble heart, I will neither cast him off, nor will I despise him.

Do, then, frequently resort to that divine bath, wherein My Heart will wash thy soul with My Blood, and wash her yet more, until she be wholly pure and stainless.*

---

* This may be explained by a truly wonderful and consoling fact related in the life of St. Mary Magdalen of Pazzi. When, on a certain day,—in the Church of her Convent, where Confessions were being heard,—this holy Virgin was pouring forth her heart before our Lord, present in the Tabernacle, and whilst she was rapt up by divine communications, she perceived that the spiritual world became, in some manner, unvailed before her For she saw the souls, such as they were, of each one of the penitents, whilst they were confessing. And, at the moment when the Sacramental absolution was given, she beheld the divine Blood of Jesus mystically poured upon each of them, and washing them, so that they became exceedingly pure and fair. Now, if such be the effect of one Confession, what must be the effect of frequent Confession? If the soul becomes so pure, so beautiful, when washed only once in the Blood of the Heart of Jesus,—which is applied to us in the Sacrament of Penance; how pure, how beautiful must she become, when she is thus cleansed frequently! Brown and soiled linen is not only made clean by frequent washing, but is made as white as snow. Shall not then a soul, often washed in the divine Blood of Jesus, be-

9. *The voice of the Disciple.*—O most benign
Jesus, how wholesome, how consoling a device of
Thy Heart, is the Sacrament of Penance! How
astonishing a condescension, how wonderful a sweetness, that of the Blood of Thy Heart Thou makest
a bath, wherewith Thou mayst cleanse us from our
sins!

Had not Thy Heart found out this secret, so full of
all consolation, who could have thought of it? And
hadst Thou not made it known, what should have
become of us, what of me?

Thanks to Thee, most sweet Jesus! let the Angels, and all the Blessed, let all peoples and tongues,
return thanks to Thee, for that Thou didst institute
this life-giving, this sanctifying Sacrament, whereby
the guilty dwellers of earth are saved, and heaven
is filled with a multitude of Saints.

That, therefore, I may not misuse so great a
blessing, and that I may gather from it every desirable fruit; behold, I will confess not only frequently, but also carefully: as if preparing myself
for death, I will always, before making my Confession, elicit from my heart an act of true sorrow, and
of firm resolve, peacefully indeed, but with the
greatest sincerity as well: I will lay every fault
before my Confessor, with the same candor that I
would use before Thee, were I to behold Thee with
my eyes: at the earliest opportunity I will perform
the penance enjoined: lastly, I will strive to be

come, at last, perfectly pure and unutterably beautiful? This
most pious thought may, at least, serve to increase your love
for the holy Sacrament of Penance; and whilst you receive
it actually, ought sweetly to occupy your mind, and greatly
to console you.

grateful, and to live with a new fervor, and a purer heart.

O Jesus! what consolation, what sweetness is felt, when my soul, in this Sacrament of Thy mercy, is washed and cleansed by the most sacred and pure Blood of Thy Heart! O do Thou wash me frequently, I beseech Thee, and I shall be made wholly clean: wash me yet more, and I shall be made whiter than snow!

CHAPTER XIII.

THAT FOR THE FORGIVENESS OF OUR SINS WE MUST FIRMLY RELY UPON OUR LORD, AFTER WE HAVE SINCERELY DONE WHAT WAS MORALLY IN OUR POWER.

1. *The voice of Jesus.*—As I live, I desire not the death of the sinner, but that he be converted and live.

If the sinner do penance for all the sins which he has committed, and keep all My commands, living, he shall live, and not die.

The ungodliness of the ungodly shall not hurt him, in whatever day he shall turn away from his ungodliness: the sins which has sinned shall not be imputed to him.

Why, then, art thou troubled, My Child, or why fearest thou so immoderately? Am I like a man, that I should lie or change? Did I say it, and shall I not do it? Did I promise, and shall I not make it good? Did I swear, and shall I not keep My word?

Why dost thou doubt, O man of little faith? Amen: heaven and earth shall pass away, but My words shall not pass away.

2. Behold, God, My heavenly Father, who, for thy salvation, did not spare His only Son, but delivered Him up for thee, no less than for the rest: did He not give thee, together with Him, all other things, pardon, perseverance, Paradise, every blessing?

Through Me, therefore, the only-begotten Son of God, thou art become rich in all things, so that thou canst be wanting in no grace. For, where sin abounded, there grace did more abound.

Go then, with confidence, to the throne of grace, that thou mayst obtain those things that are needful to thee.

3. My Child, I came down from heaven, that I might snatch thee from the jaws of hell: all the days of My life, I was in suffering, that thou mightst be happy through all eternity; I was willingly condemned to die, that thou mightst be free from everlasting death: and all these things I did for thee, when thou wast My enemy; what, then, will I not do, or what can I refuse, when thou lovest Me?

If thy sins affrighten thee, know, My Child, that My infinite merits are infinitely more powerful to save thee, if thou art willing, than thy sins to destroy thee, if thou art uneasy.

If, by reason of thy sins, thou standest in dread of My judgment, call to mind, that, I thy Saviour, who, even at the right hand of God, My Father, intercedes for thee, shall be thy Judge.

4. Enlarge, therefore, thy heart in the Holy

Spirit, whom thou didst receive in the Sacrament of divine mercy. That Spirit of love, that consuming fire, will destroy the remnant of thy sins, and cast out all inordinate fear.

Hadst thou been an exceedingly great sinner, like the thief crucified with Me; hadst thou, like Paul, persecuted Me; hadst thou even denied Me, like Peter: behold, if once thou confessest rightly, so as to enjoy the effect of the Sacrament, all thy sins are forgiven thee.

5. Why art thou sad, My Child, and why dost thou disquiet thyself? Thinkest thou that I am a harsh master, whom it is difficult to satisfy?

Thou art mistaken, Child; thou art greatly deceived. For, behold, am I not a Father, whose Heart is goodness itself? Dost thou not know this? Hast thou not experienced it?

Do not then dishonor Me; do not revile Me, by attributing to Me things which are so wrongful.

6. My Child, thou hast not received the spirit of bondage again in fear: but thou hast received the spirit of adoption of the sons of God, whereby thou mayst love and address Me: Abba, Father!

Do not, then, fear, Child; do not, by worrying thyself uselessly, lose the time which thou oughtest to spend happily in loving Me. For I do not require anguish, but love.

Have confidence, My Child, that thy sins have been forgiven thee. Do now strive to love Me the more, the more I have forgiven thee.

7. *The voice of the Disciple.*—O Jesus! O my love! my life! How delightful to me, how sweet are the words thou utterest from Thy Heart!

O Lord, my God! Thou didst wash not my feet,

not my hands, not my head alone, but my soul, my whole self, and that with Thy own blood.

Behold, Thou didst cast my sins into the depth of a sea, into the abyss of the mercy of Thy Heart, where they have disappeared from Thy sight.

O Jesus! how can I ever be unmindful of Thy mercies, whereby Thou hast thus restored me to life!

I will sing Thy mercies, O Lord, forever: I will praise the goodness of Thy heart for evermore.

8. Bless the Lord, O my soul, and let all that is within me bless His Sacred Heart. Yea, bless the Lord, O my soul, and never forget all He has done for thee. Who forgives all thy iniquities: who heals all thy diseases.

He has not dealt with us according to our sins nor has He rewarded us according to our iniquities: but He has blotted them out according to the multitude of the mercies of His Heart.

As a father has pity on his children, so has the Lord had pity on us; because He is good, because His mercy endures forever.

9. Love the Lord, O my soul, love Jesus, love Him much; because He has forgiven thee much.

Let them love less to whom He has forgiven less: but do thou, by the greatness of thy love, strive to make a suitable return for the greatness of His bounty.

Yea, O most sweet Jesus, I will love Thee with all my strength: nor will I henceforward pass my time in vexing my heart, Thy kingdom now; but I will employ it better, more usefully to me, more pleasingly to Thee: Thy love shall ever be my occupation. In peace in the self-same, will I take my rest and repose.

CHAPTER XIV.

HOW WE MUST GUARD AGAINST A RELAPSE.

1. *The voice of Jesus.*—My Child, hast thou fallen into sin? Do not again give thyself up to it; but so guard against the future as not to return to the past.

When the demon has been expelled from a heart, he goes and takes with him seven other spirits more wicked than himself, and, returning, attempts to enter again. If man does not resist, the enemies enter, and the last state of that man becomes worse than the first.

If, therefore, thou desire not to become the prey of hell, thou must, by all means, resist the temptations of the devil.

Do not be afflicted nor sad, My Child, because thou art assailed, against thy will, by various temptations; be rather rejoiced and consoled. For it is a sign that thou art in the state of grace, and that thou followest My standard.

If thou didst adhere to the devil, he would surely not attack what is his own; but because thou standest by Me, therefore does he tempt thee, and endeavor to draw thee over to his ranks.

2. My Child, temptation is not prevarication; yea, so long as it is displeasing to thee, it is meritorious of a divine reward.

Therefore, however loathsome the things which the enemy may suggest, be not uneasy; however violently he may entice thee to evil, think not that thou art forsaken by Me.

Never am I nearer to thee, or more ready to help thee, than when thou sufferest under these trials.

When thou art tempted, Child, I stand by, looking on the struggle, and helping thee, that, being thus encouraged and aided, thou mayst not only withstand the foe, but gloriously triumph over him.

Be, therefore, ready for the combat: no one shall be crowned, unless he has struggled lawfully; and he that shall overcome shall receive the crown of life.

3. As thou dwellest among enemies to the right and to the left, and art exposed to their assaults from within and from without; thou oughtest to be so well armed at all times that they can never find thee defenseless.

Have thy heart lifted up and united to Mine, with a determined and generous resolve, to endure all things, yea, even to die in the struggle, rather than turn thy back upon Me. Otherwise thou shalt not be able fully to withstand the stubbornness of the contest.

4. In this warfare, two kinds of weapons are necessary to thee: the one, defensive, the other, offensive.

Humility will furnish thee weapons to defend thyself. By means of this virtue, place no reliance upon thyself, put all thy trust in Me: and, being convinced of thy own frailty, shun, as much as thou art able, all dangerous occasions.

For it were an inexcusable, and most shameful presumption, to seek them, or to go to meet them, especially if they are of the flesh.

5. If, nevertheless, the foe assails, call upon Me; rely upon My help, confidingly and lovingly.

He that prays amid temptation, as he ought, cannot be overcome; but he that neglects prayer, is usually vanquished.

Resist generously from the very beginning of the temptation, and pray fervently in this, or a similar manner: O, Jesus! hide me within Thy Heart, that I may not be separated from thee. . . O, God! my God! come to my assistance. . . Jesus and Mary! make haste to help me. . . I will rather die, O Lord, than commit sin.

If the enemy continue to tempt, faithfully withdraw thy mind from the object of the temptation; and, having earnestly turned it to other things, either good or indifferent, persevere in prayer, persevere in thus resisting, not with anxiety or impatience, but calmly and steadily: and the foe shall either flee away, or stand abashed.

6. Let it not be enough for thee to repulse Satan; strive, also, to injure him. This thou canst do, if, by means of the weapons which divine love will furnish thee, thou turn the temptations of the enemy against himself.

As often, therefore, as the demon tempts thee, so often use temptation against his aim and object, that thou mayst unite thyself more closely with Me; glorify Me by thy faithfulness, and acquire for thyself greater strength and merit.

So it shall come to pass, that thy adversary, frightened by his defeat, either dares not return, or, if he dares, will secure for thee a more signal victory and a brighter crown.

7. But, if ever thou be so unfortunate as to fall,

arise without delay; fight with more humility and courage; and beware, above all, lest thou surrender and make thyself a slave to the foe.

Many have been lost, because, after having fought bravely,—when they were on the point of gaining the victory,—cast down by the troublesomeness of the temptation, they surrendered disgracefully, and perished miserably.

Up then, My Child; the struggle is short, but the prize everlasting.

Be magnanimous: courage is a great part of the victory. It prepares thee for grace; it raises the heart, increases strength, moderates labor, frightens and weakens the enemy.

For Me, thy God and Saviour, for thy salvation, for an everlasting crown, for the very Kingdom of heaven, fight thou bravely, and display a sight worthy of God, of the Angels, and of men.

8 *The voice of the Disciple.*—Thanks to Thee, most benign Jesus, who thus teachest my hands to fight and my fingers to war.

Behold, Thou also cheerest up my heart, and givest me courage, so that I am ready to put forth my strength, and to act valiantly.

But I know and confess that of myself I am weak and cowardly: if I am left to myself alone, if I rely upon myself alone, what can be looked for, except that I shall shamefully fall away from Thee and perish ignobly?

Give me grace, I entreat Thee, that I may not presume on myself; that, of my own accord, I may not expose myself; but that I may, with prudence, shun every occasion of falling, and, by watchfulness, escape all the snares of my foes.

And at what time Thou shalt see me attacked by
the enemy, or engaged with him, do Thou arise, I
beseech Thee, hasten to my assistance; because
Thou, O Lord, art my strength.

Be thou near me, I pray· set me beside Thee,
and let any man's hand fight against me; with Thee
I will conquer, with Thee I will triumph.

CHAPTER XV.

HOW THE ROOTS OF VICES AND DEFECTS ARE TO BE WHOLLY PLUCKED UP.

1. *The voice of Jesus.*—My Child, to obtain perfect purity of heart, it is not enough to cherish a
good will, to meditate and pray frequently, to confess often and devoutly. These means are very
efficient and necessary, and therefore never to be
omitted, nor neglected.

But, alone, they do not suffice; since they are
not wont to pluck up completely the roots of vices
and defects.

It is necessary, then, to use besides another
means, whereby thou mayst, so to speak, extermi-
nate the noxious roots, and thus render thy heart
perfectly clean.

These sweet and wholesome effects are produced,
in a marvelous manner, by self-examination, an exercise apparently trifling indeed, and a small matter but in itself very efficient, and more deeply
penetrating than any two-edged instrument,—reaching even to the dividing of the soul and the dis-

cerning of spirits, and searching into the thoughts and intentions of the heart.

Nor does it serve merely to root out evil habits and defects; but, what is more wonderful, to acquire solid virtues, and even to attain to perfection.

2. This self-examination is threefold. The first, which is used to collect one's self, consists in this, that, when an opportunity offers, thou turn to thy heart, and inspect it for a short time, observing whence it is moved, with what things it busies itself; or what it has done, and in what manner; what it should do in future, and how.

Opportunities of performing a very short self-examination of this sort, are wont to present themselves frequently. When, for example, thou beginnest any of the more important actions of the day; and when thou hast performed them.

When something is presented to thy senses, or to thy mind, by which thou mayst be allured, or tempted; also, when thou hast fallen into some defect.

When thou meetest with any difficulty which may occasion trouble, or disturb thee: lastly, as often as, during some length of time, thou hast not looked into thy heart.

Now, this can easily be done, at any time, and in any place, even whilst others are present, and without attracting their attention.

In the exercise itself, there is no difficulty whatever. At first, indeed, some attention should be used, but no straining of the mind; and, in a short time, thou shalt begin to acquire a holy and consoling habit, and gather from it the sweetest and most wholesome fruits.

3. The second is a general examination, by which, twice, or at least once, every day, thou devotest a short time, some minutes, exclusively to asking of thyself an account of thy way of living.

Having briefly returned thanks to God, and begged for divine light, inspect and scrutinize, how, since thou didst last examine thyself, thou hast deported thyself, in thy exterior and interior.

Examine thy thoughts, words, and deeds: see wherein thou hast sinned, or failed: then, carefully mark each sin, or defect, at least mentally.

If thou hast already practically learnt something of the interior life, place thy heart near to Mine, compare, and notice the difference between the thoughts, sensations, and actions of both.

After thou hast, in this manner, discovered thy faults and failings, then see and acknowledge thy unthankfulness for My Divine favors; form an act of sorrow, as perfect as possible, beg for grace to amend thyself, and to make better progress.

4. Lastly, the particular examination is that, by means of which thou exertest thyself, to root out, separately, only one vice or defect at a time.

Most wonderful is the power, and incredible the efficacy, of this exercise. Would that thou didst understand it well, My Child, and that thou didst perform it in a proper manner!

There is no habit so deep-rooted, no vice so great, which, by this means, cannot be overcome and subdued.

For, with God's grace, it can, in some manner, do all things. How many sinners have, by its means, been freed from vices, which had grown on them like a second nature! How many souls has it enabled to cleanse themselves thoroughly! How many has it helped to reach perfection!

Whatever defects, then, thou mayst have, be of good cheer, My Child: sure art thou of victory: sure of future freedom, if thou use this means diligently and perseveringly.

Attack, first, that vice or defect which may be a stumbling-block, or a just cause of offense, to thy neighbor; afterwards, the one which seems to be thy chief fault. When the leader is overthrown, the rest are easily overcome.

5. Now, thy method of proceeding shall be this: In the morning, resolve firmly and considerately, that, during the day, thou wilt shun what thou mayst have chosen to be avoided in a particular manner; at the same time, beg for grace, that thou mayst be faithful to thy resolution.

Then, twice, or only once a day, according as thou makest the general self-examination, thou shalt also search thyself and see how often, since the last scrutiny, thou hast failed in thy special re solve; and mark the number of times.

Afterwards, grieve not only for thy faults in general, but also for these defects in particular: and resolve again to be specially on thy guard against them, and for this end implore also special grace.

Meanwhile, My Child, it will help thee very much, if, when thou perceivest thyself growing, in some way, indifferent or careless, thou inflict upon thyself some small punishment; and this as often as thou offendest against thy particular examination.

6. But that thou mayst use rightly and constantly these and other means, thou needest a guide to

direct, to teach, to fashion thee; to keep thee in, or stir thee up, and cheer thee on at all times.

No one, when left to himself, can walk with safety in the path of the spiritual and interior life; for, oftentimes, he will be exposed to the danger of going astray, of losing heart, of falling into the snares of the foe; nay more, of perishing.

Wert thou a Saint, or a chosen Apostle, thou yet wouldst need some guide. Was not Paul, although a Vessel of election to carry My name among the nations, at My command, instructed and directed by Ananias? Were not the Saints trained to holiness, by others that led a holy life?

Pray, therefore, My Child, that thou mayst be worthy to find a guide according to My Heart, either in thy Confessor, thy Superior, or some other person, who possesses authority, skill and experience in spiritual matters, and a practical knowledge of the interior life.

To such a one, My Child, do thou occasionally make known thy heart: at certain times give some account of thyself, that thou mayst know whether thou advancest rightly; what thou must correct, and how it is to be done; on what thou oughtest to insist, and in what manner it is to be accomplished.

The subjects, concerning which this interior manifestation should be made, are usually: the disclosing of the soul's state or habitual feeling, whether it be peaceful or agitated; what longings for a more perfect life thou feelest within thyself; what obstacles embarrass thee; to what practices of devotion and mortification thou art wont to apply thyself.

What method thou hast in prayer and meditation; with what relish and fruit thou advancest by this method; what spiritual books thou readest, and whether they agree with the present degree of thy interior life: whether thou readest in a manner proper and profitable.

In what manner thou approachest the Sacraments; with what preparation, with what feelings of piety, with what thanksgiving, with what results.

How thou makest thy self-examinations; with what painstaking, and with what fruit.

How thou performest the duties of thy state of life, the obligations of thy office, thy ordinary actions,—by what motive or principle, whether of nature or of grace, with what object,—what end thou hast in view.

In what manner thou deportest thyself towards others, with what disposition of heart, with what profit or loss to thyself and to them.

With what fidelity thou obeyest God's inspirations; how thou feelest disposed towards Me; finally, in what degree thou relishest the sentiments of My Heart.

Do thou, My Child, modestly and religiously, with humble candor and docile charity, make known such and similar matters, sometimes one, then another, according as spiritual necessity or usefulness may require.

All this, if thou peform it after this manner, thou shalt find easy, most useful, and full of consolation.*

---

* Purity of heart, being of the greatest importance, it is thought proper to bring together, in this place, the means to

7. The voice of the Disciple.—Lord Jesus, to ex
ecute all those things, greatly, indeed. do I need
light from above,—wherewith to discover my defects,—and divine assistance, to remove them.

For many of them lie hidden from human eyes
nor can I see them myself, neither can any one
point them out to me, unless aided by a supernatural light.

But if, with the brightness of this light. Thou
deignest to illumine my inmost soul, behold! all
things therein, great and small, shall be unvailed.
For even as the sun shining into a chamber reveals

attain it, although they have been given separately. The
first is a settled and constant determination of always trying to improve. The second, stated and repeated mental
and vocal prayer. The third, the pious and frequent use of
the Sacraments. The fourth, the faithful practice of the
three-fold self-examination, especially of the particular examination. The fifth, the candid disclosing of our interior
life; and, on the other hand, a holy guidance. Whoever
makes a right use of these means, will doubtless attain to
as great a purity of heart, as the Lord is ordinarily wont to
require. But if He require something extraordinary, He
Himself will provide the means, for no one is able to make
provision under such circumstances. Yet, as things are
wont to be preserved by the same means that produced them,
you shall preserve interior purity, by the same means that
have been pointed out to attain it. These then are, "the
five loaves of the show-bread, which must be ever new and
fresh before the Lord." Wherefore, these means are always
to be used with the same care. And, lest you grow lukewarm
by degrees, either through frailty or carelessness, examine
yourself from time to time, and make known how you use
them; and if you have in any wise fallen off, do as quickly
as possible strive to regain your former fervor. As long as
you shall employ these means, even with ordinary diligence,
you shall have within yourself the consoling sign, that you
are on the right road, which leads to perfection.

the very atoms that fill its every space, so Thy grace gleaming on my heart, shall bring to view numberless defects, the existence of which I did nowise suspect.

But what shall it avail me to know my defects, if I cannot uproot them? Thy help, therefore, is also necessary to me, who, without it, can effect nothing conducive to salvation.

Lord Jesus, by Thy most Sacred Heart, I beg and beseech Thee, grant me uninterruptedly the plentifulness of this two-fold grace, that thereby I may be enlightened and assisted.

Without this grace, no assiduity of mine, no care of a director, however much he may toil, whatever zeal he may exercise, can aught avail.

Thou, therefore, O Jesus, the eternal Wisdom, the infinite Goodness, Thou art the supreme Director: do Thou, I pray, guide me, through him whom Thou mayst will to hold Thy place, and with whom I am willing to act in all things as with Thyself.

CHAPTER XVI.

THAT HE WHO DESIRES TO FOLLOW THE HEART OF JESUS, MUST ALSO WITHDRAW HIS HEART FROM THE WORLD.

1. *The voice of Jesus.*—Woe to the world, My Child: woe to the heart that clings to its allurements and its vanities!

It is not enough to cast Satan out of thy heart,

thou must also expel the world. If thou inwardly cherish the world, whatever else thou mayst do wholly to amend thyself, shall avail thee little.

For the world will continue to infect thy heart, will doubtless pervert, and finally betray thee into the power of the demon.

2. What is the world, except an inordinate or perverse love of pleasure, riches, honors; whereby its votaries are themselves corrupted and corrupt others?

If thou desirest to know what thou oughtest to think of the world, consider what I Myself have judged of it.

Behold! I passed through life doing good to all; I loved the enemies that persecuted Me; when fastened to the Cross, I prayed for those that crucified me; but for the world I prayed not.

The world is of the devil, is wholly placed in wickedness, and cannot possess My Spirit: even as falsehood cannot be truth, as corruption cannot be purity.

3. The world is itself a proof, not only of the undeniable existence—but even of the necessity of a hell.

What can there be in common between the world and My Heart, since the world, either openly or secretly, favors every vice; whilst My Heart breathes naught, except what is holy?

The world in league with Satan, its prince, seeks for souls to destroy them forever; My Heart longs to save them all.

Thou canst, therefore, not serve the world and Me: for, if thou art the friend of the world, thou becomest the enemy of My Heart.

4. If thou art a votary of the world, thou wilt perish with the world: but if thou followest My Heart, thou wilt go into life everlasting.

If thou drivest the world, and the maxims of the world, from thy heart, so as to offer it wholly to Me, the offering will be pleasing and honorable to Me, and full of glory and merit to thyself. The Angels and the Saints will applaud the deed, and the world itself shall be compelled to admire the lofty heroism of thy mind.

Blessed is he, My Child, who withdraws his affections from the things of the world, and consecrates them to Me alone!

5. What findest thou in the world, on account of which thou wouldst love it? Behold! all that is in the world, is the desire of the flesh, the lust of the eyes, and the pride of life. And the end of all these is death and hell.

If, then, thou lovest the world, or the things which are of the world, thou takest into thy embrace everlasting perdition.

What good has the world done to thee, that thou wouldst devote thy affections to it? It has done, and never will do thee aught but evil. How, then, canst thou give thy heart to it?

Trust not, My Child, to the smiles and blandishments of the world; they show only a covert desire to deceive and destroy thee.

But hearken to the invitings of My Heart, that longs to save thee from the everlasting misfortunes, which the world is preparing for thee.

6. If thou dost not forsake the world, the world will forsake thee, when thou art spent and worn out in its service; yea, it will laugh and mock at thy

destruction; and, when thou standest most in need of help, thou shalt be alone and powerless.

Think frequently, which of the two, when thou art about to go into eternity, thou shalt rather wish to have followed, the world or Me.

Do freely, therefore, and meritoriously now, what without merit, thou shalt be forced to do then.

Apply thyself to draw thy heart from the love of earthly things; and, by a complete disengagement from it, to triumph over the world.

Have confidence, My Child, I have overcome the world: if thou art willing, thou also canst vanquish it. So soon as thou shalt have conquered, I will give thee a most delightful place in My Heart.

7. *The voice of the Disciple.*—O Lord, how foolishly have I acted! how wickedly have I lived! A willing dupe, I have been misled by the false appearances of pleasure, of riches, of honor; I have forsaken Thee, to make myself a slave of the world, Thy enemy.

I have left the fountain of every good, to go down to the pestilential pool of the world. There made I myself drunk with poisonous draughts; I grew senseless, and, in my madness, I cast aside everything.

I became forgetful of Thee, my God and my all; I gave myself wholly to the world; and in its service, I unhallowed Thy gifts, my external senses, and the inward powers of my soul.

Alas! I became exceedingly guilty: my soul was filled with iniquity: I drew myself nigh to hell.

Thy wrath came upon me, and Thy terrors troubled me, so that night and day I was wretched.

8. Alas! good Jesus! even after—seized with a

great dread of Thy judgment and fear of hell—I
had resolved to lead a good life, into what fatal
illusion did I fall! how banefully did I go astray!

I divided my heart between Thee and the world:
I wished, at one and the same time, to serve Thee
and the world.

O! how great an insult did I offer to Thee, when
I placed Thee on an equality with the world! I
pleased neither the world nor Thee: and, meanwhile, I was most wretched, because, not being satisfied with the world, nor with Thee, I found true
happiness in neither.

But now that Thou didst open my eyes, and
move my heart, behold! O Lord Jesus, I will serve
The' 'lone: I give my whole heart to Thee forever.

Take out of my heart, I beseech Thee, all affection for the world: change for me all its apparent
sweets into real bitterness.

So fill me with the delight of Thy love, that the
world, with all its vanities, become tasteless to me.

CHAPTER XVII.

HOW DECEITFUL THE WORLD IS.

1. *The voice of Jesus.*—My Child, the whole
world is made up of deceits, and by its arts and
wiles, it allures to itself the unwary.

It holds out to man pleasures, honors, and riches;
and says, all these things will I give to thee, if
thou serve me.

But attend thou, not to what it promises, but to what it gives.

Through the deceitful hope of pleasant things, it brings its votaries beneath the cruel tyranny of the passions, and thence leads them to the ceaseless tortures of the stings of conscience.

Didst thou ever find a worldling, even the most fortunate, whose heart was every way satisfied? Neither shalt thou find such a one, even if thou searchest the whole earth.

The world, indeed, promises good things; but, in reality, it bestows true evils only; because what it gives, makes man wicked, and hinders him, by no means, from being truly unhappy.

2. *The voice of the Disciple.*—Yet, O Lord, worldlings frequently obtain possession of those things which they covet; and, therefore, they care little for the spiritual distresses of the heart.

The voice of Jesus.—Even so, My Child: grant that they abound in whatever things they may lust after in this world: as they possess them with an inordinate affection, and misuse them, they enjoy them not, except for their present and future unhappiness.

Besides, they appear, indeed, not to care for the interior tortures of the soul; but, My Child, if thou couldst look, as I do, into their hearts, thou shouldst see how many things they suffer within, which they endeavor to hide outwardly, and thou wouldst conclude that the happiness of man consists, not in having an abundance of the things of this world, but rather herein, that he keeps his heart free from every worldly object. and calmly and permanently satisfied in Me.

Moreover, how long shall these things of world-lings last? Behold! yet a little while, and eternity shall summon them to appear. What then shall the plentifulness of delights and other things avail them? They shall leave the world, taking with them nothing, except the load of their sins.

Wouldst thou, then, be willing, for the misuse of the things of time, to lose the use of those of eternity? or, for the false possessions of earth, to forfeit the true riches of heaven?

3. My Child, if thou cleavest to the world, thou ceasest, in fact, to be a Christian, and thou foregoest the possession of all the privileges which belong to that noble name.

For, at thy new birth, in the waters of Baptism, thou didst, by a solemn promise made before heaven and earth, renounce the world and its wickedness; nor would I, without that promise, have adopted thee as My Child

If, after this, thou goest again over to the party of the world, thou art not only faithless, but even worse than the heathen, who made no such promise. For it is better not to promise than not to make good what is promised.

4. Ask the departed, what they think of the world. The Elect will answer, that their happiness began from the time they learnt to despise the things of earth: and the reprobate will reply, that they were deceived and ruined by the world.

Thyself, My Child, shalt, one day, think and experience concerning the world, the one or the other of these things.

Be timely wise, My Child, lest hereafter thou feel sorrow to no purpose: follow the footprints of the

Saints, by withdrawing thy heart from the world, and keeping thy affections from its contagion.

5. Use the things of this world, as if thou didst not use them; and, whilst thou treadest the earth with thy foot, have thy heart in heaven.

The more thou shalt withdraw thyself from creatures, the nearer shalt thou come to the Creator; and the more proper shalt thou be to receive divine gifts.

If thy heart be wholly disengaged from the world, so far from being hurtful to thee, the world itself will be, in many ways, subservient to thy interests.

O, how base the whole world would grow in thy sight, if thou didst truly consider, what awaits thee in eternity!

6. *The voice of the Disciple.*—Truly, O Lord, the world is a deceiver. Such have I experienced it to be, to my own loss.

When it offered me its own favors, madman that I was, I believed that thereby I should be happy. But Oh! how greatly was I deceived! how truly wretched was I, even when, giddy with worldly love, I fancied myself most happy!

The animal man within me made me imagine that I was happy, whilst I was feeding on the husks, which the world threw before me: and in spite of myself, I groaned full often beneath the degradation of my slavery, beneath the burden of my heart's misery.

I fully acknowledge now, that I was myself the author of my own unhappiness; and that I can, with justice, blame no one except myself.

Because I was unwilling to serve Thee with joy and gladness of heart, amid the abundance of all

things, I became a slave to Thy enemy and to mine,—
served him in hunger, and thirst, and every want,
in so far even, that I delighted to fill myself with
the food of the vilest animals.

7. Would, O Lord, that I could blot out from
the number of my years, those during which, estranged from Thee, I served the world!

What fruit do I now reap from them, except bitterness, stings of conscience, anguish of heart, sins
to be atoned for, either in this life by sorrow, or to
be bewailed in vain in the next?

Be gracious to me, O my Saviour! and forgive
me all my offenses, which I committed by following
the world, and which I now detest from my innermost heart.

Suffer no more, I entreat Thee, that my heart
cling again to aught—even the least object—of this
wicked world: withdraw it wholly, with all its
affections, from the false tinseling of earth, which
contains naught except deceit, emptiness, and
affliction of heart.

CHAPTER XVIII.

THAT TO SERVE THE WORLD IS A CRUEL SLAVERY.

1. *The voice of Jesus.*—My Child, he that loves
to serve the world, knows not the world.

The world is a true tyrant: and wretched slaves
are they that serve it.

How many things,—what sacrifices does it not
exact from its votaries, whom, for all their services,
it repays with unceasing evils!

It demands, that its slaves become the base tools of their passions; that they sacrifice body and soul; that they damn themselves without complaint.

And when it has completed their destruction, it forsakes them as useless wretches, fit only for hell-fire.

2. Oh! at how great a cost do worldlings purchase their own ruin! If they did for Me the half of what they do for the world, how happy should they be, and what Saints!

How cruel is the world's slavery! under it, how many interior sufferings must be undergone! what hardships endured! And all this for the hope of obtaining such things as, when once tasted, cause death; or such as will produce tortures, either at present, by the irksome possession of them, or after awhile, by a bitter separation.

Truly, it is an iron yoke which presses on the neck of worldlings, the weight of which no one does fully know, unless he either tried it, or considers it as he stands on the threshold of eternity.

3. Whoever desires to be saved must separate his heart from the world.

There are those who, by their mode of life, having outwardly bidden farewell to the world, inwardly captivated by the world, in most things, govern themselves by worldly sentiments.

There are others, whom their condition in life obliges to live exposed to the dangers of the world; who yet have so divested themselves of every affection for the world, that they never defile themselves with aught that is worldly.

It is, therefore, not the kind of life which he leads, nor the shape of the dress which he wears, that connects a man with the world, or estranges him from it; but the affection of the heart, the disposition of the soul.

Wherefore, he that is farthest separated in heart from the world, and most closely united to Me, he is dearest to My Heart, in whatever state of life he may live.

Wherever, then, My divine Will may have placed thee, there do thou serve Me in holiness. Since, in every state or condition of life, which is good in itself, thou canst live for Me, and sanctify thyself: although it remains true, that a state of life separated from the world, conduces most to secure salvation, and to reach perfection.

4. How many followers of the world there are, who, convinced of the world's wickedness, see the necessity of renouncing it by a change of life; yet, dare not do so, too fearful lest the world may rail at them.

Is this your fortitude, ye friends of the world? Great-souled, forsooth, ye are all, who, through fear of empty talk, dare not do what faith dictates, what reason approves, what your greatest interest demands.

What are words, but sounds passing through the air and disappearing? Can they stir so much as a hair of the head?

5. Shalt thou be so fainthearted, My Child, that, for the sake of such words, thou wouldst draw on thyself ruin in time and in eternity?

Choose, either to serve Me, to be blissful in My service, and to enjoy the enduring delights of heaven hereafter: or, to serve the world, to lead inwardly a wretched life, and, at last, to undergo torments never-ending.

Behold! life and death, good and evil are placed before thee· whatever thou dost prefer, shall be given thee.

6. *The voice of the Disciple.*—O kind Jesus! how could I falter in my choice? Wretched me! how could I ever choose what was to render me so unhappy!

O infinite Goodness, O my God! Thou hast freed me from error, and hast taught me the truth.

Behold! now I am wholly Thine forever, O Jesus, my true beatitude!

Away with thee, deceitful world, most wicked seducer, enemy of God, and of my salvation; thou foe of all that is good, thou defender of all that is evil; O thou, the most cruel of all tyrants!

O world, thou minister of Satan! too late have I known thee: too long have I loved thee. From this hour, farewell to thee, farewell for evermore!

CHAPTER XIX.

THAT THE YOKE OF JESUS IS TRULY SWEET.

1. *The voice of Jesus.*—Come, My Child, take up My yoke upon thee; for My yoke is sweet, and My burden light.

My service, Child, is not that of a tyrant, nor of a harsh master; but of a most loving Father, who is near His children, who are submissive to Him, that He may help and entertain them.

Love is the spirit of My service: and love finds all things easy.

My commands are not heavy; and to those that love, they are exceedingly light and sweet.

Try and taste My Child, how pleasant it is to serve Me; how delightful, to enjoy My sweetness; how good, to gain possession of the very fountain of all good things.

2. If thou seekest delights, thou shalt find the true ones, in My service alone.

All the pleasures of the world, are either empty or pernicious. But My consolations surpass, beyond comparison, all the delights of earth: they ravish hearts by their purity, they satiate them by their truth.

Yea, betimes, they so overwhelm man, that they give him a certain foretaste of those heavenly delights, wherewith the Blessed in Paradise are inebriated.

3. He that serves Me, is not as the slave of the world, who toils to gather for himself treasures on earth, and in the end, finds his hands empty.

But he lays up for himself treasures in heaven, where neither the rust, nor the moth, can destroy; where thieves cannot dig them up, nor carry away.

All the wealth of earth, compared with the treasures of heaven, is only dust and nothingness.

4. If thou aimest to be honored, behold! what greater honor can be desired, than to be with Me, to be approved and distinguished by Me?

The glory of the world, wherewith one man deludes the other, is false and shortlived: but the glory of My service is true, and shall endure forever.

Greater is the least of My servants, than the lord of a kingdom in the world.

5. Was there ever found a man, who, at the hour of death, repented that he had served Me? Yet, at that last moment, how exceedingly do worldlings regret to have been in the service of the world! or if they bewail it not, how much more wretched are they!

Truthful is the saying, My Child, that he, who serves Me faithfully during life, possesses two heavens, the one in time, the other in eternity: and that he, who spends his life in the service of the wicked world, endures two hells, one now, another hereafter.

6. Courage! then, My Child; bend thyself beneath the yoke, which is borne by the Angels in heaven, and the Elect on earth; and beneath which they enjoy true bliss.

Take it up joyously, and bear it cheerfully. Thou servest the same Lord, that is served by the Blessed in heaven. Whilst thou imitatest them in their service, imitate them also in their cheerfulness.

Let the slaves of sin, and of the world, be sad: joy and exultation are the portion of My servants.

Serve Me, then, but serve Me with gladness: let thy heart, for joy, cheer up thy countenance; and, by thy holy gayety, teach the world, what blessedness there is in serving Me.

7. *The voice of the Disciple.*—To serve Thee, O most benign Jesus, is truly sweet for me: what then must it be for those that love Thee! what for those that have centred their heart's affection in Thee!

If I, who only begin to love, find so great a sweetness in Thee; in what sweetness do they delight, who, fondly devoted to Thee, with a generous heart, have long lived for Thee alone; are admitted into the innermost of Thy Heart, and partake of all Thy bliss most plentifully!

O Jesus, unutterable sweetness! what is man that Thou exaltest him thus? or the son of man, that Thou settest Thy heart upon Him?

8. Behold! to live for Thee, to comply with Thy Will, is not to serve, but to reign. In Thy service, no one is a servant, every one is a King, is a Lord: for thou art the King of kings, and the Lord of lords.

In Thy service, no one is a menial, no one is miserable: each one is noble, each one is fortunate; for Thou art the King of glory; honors and riches abound in Thy house.

In Thy service, no one is wicked; and, therefore, no one is unhappy: but all are good, happy all: for Thou art the King of virtues, the peace and joy of hearts.

Blessed, therefore. are the undefiled, who walk in Thy law! their blessedness is ever-during: for Thy kingdom is the kingdom of all ages.

O most sweet Jesus! what is there for me outside of Thee, or what do I desire upon earth beside Thee? God of my heart, Thou art my life, Thou my blessedness, Thou my portion forever.

CHAPTER XX.

THAT, WITHOUT KEEPING ANYTHING FOR OUR-
SELVES, WE SHOULD GIVE OUR WHOLE HEART
TO JESUS.

1. *The voice of Jesus.*—My Child, give Me thy
heart.

To release thy heart from sin, and from the
world, is not enough: thou must, moreover, disengage it from thyself.

As the complete renouncing of sin renders the
friendship of God steadfast, and as the putting away
of the world, and its vanities, prepares the soul for
the interior life; so, the forsaking of one's self,
leads to union with Me.

It is, therefore, necessary to give Me thy whole
heart, without reserving aught for thyself, if thou
desirest to enjoy that blessedness, than which there
is none greater in this life, and by which alone thou
canst be truly happy.

2. Thy heart, Child, is Mine. For, when it had
no being, I created it; when it was lost, I sought
and ransomed it; when it lay an easy prey to the
enemies, that were going to carry it off, I protected
and preserved it. Thus, by giving Me thy heart,
thou dost only give Me what is Mine.

But, on how many accounts do I deserve its
every affection! What good dost thou possess, in
thy body, or in thy soul, whether in the natural or
the supernatural order, which thou didst not receive from My Heart?

How many years ago shouldst thou have been

burning in hell, if I had either dealt with thee according to thy deserts; or had not preserved thee from sins which deserve hell and its just punishments!

But it was my love, Child, that dealt with thee in so sweet and wonderful a manner; the love of My Heart, with which I loved thee from eternity, and with which, even till now, I have never ceased to favor thee.

Thy whole life has been a succession of blessings, on My part, uninterrupted and manifold: nor has there been any point of time which was not marked with some new favor.

3. And what, O Child of My love, do I ask of thee in return for all these thousands of favors? Surely, whatever I might ask of thee, and whatever thou mightest be able to give, would be far below the greatness and the number of My gifts. Yet, one thing only I demand, thy whole heart; it is enough, if thou give Me that.

Thy heart excepted, I care naught for whatever thou mayst give; because, beyond all else, I long for thy heart.

4. Upon whom canst thou bestow thy heart with more advantage? Thou canst not live without loving, and without giving the affections of thy heart to some object.

Wouldst thou give thy heart to the demon, thy sworn and relentless enemy? or to the world, the demon's corrupt and corrupting ally? Woe, My Child, a thousand times woe to thee, if thou givest it to either of these!

Art thou desirous of reserving the affections of thy heart for thyself? But, My Child, if thou lovest thyself only, thou shalt find a requital in thyself alone. Now, what is the reward of self-love? Behold, self-love digs out a hell, and leads to the same.

Give, then, thy heart to Me, Child: I will fill it with peace, and with gladness, and with bliss.

5. Do not desire to reserve for thyself aught of thy affections: for if thou do this, thou shalt neither be admitted into the secrets of My Heart, nor shalt thou ever be able to taste the sweetness of My love: nay more, thou shalt not be able to keep thyself from the danger of being perverted.

Yet it is not unusual for many, even those who wish to be considered good and pious, to keep, through self-love,—under a specious pretext,—an affection for some one or other created object. What is there more frequent? what can be more dangerous? what more baneful?

I wish to possess thy whole heart, Child: I am its Lord; I, a jealous God, am its only end, its sole beatitude.

6. Love, then, My Child: it is given thee to love: to love is necessary: for this thy heart was made but love thou what deserves to be loved; love Me; and, if thou cherish aught else besides, love it for love of Me alone.

When beside Me thou wilt love nothing except for love of Me,—when thou givest entrance into thy heart to nothing except to Me, or for love of Me,—then, at last, shalt thou possess a heart wholly pure.

Wherefore, My Child, give Me thy whole heart, as a burnt-offering, for an odor of sweetness; nor do thou take it back, not even the least portion of the same: for I hate robbery in a holocaust.

Be ever mindful that, whether in prosperity or in adversity, there can be nowhere a better place for thy heart than with Me.

7. *The voice of the Disciple.*—It follows, then, O Lord, that I must also disengage my heart from all self-love, from inordinate affection towards myself; so that I may wholly be filled with Thy love, and may live by Thy Spirit alone.

Alas! my God, here is the labor, here is the difficulty: there exist in my heart so many things ill-regulated, and these I have followed so long, that to live according to them, has become to me, as it were, a second nature.

Hitherto, the natural disposition of my heart, either inclination or aversion, has been almost the sole rule of my life: this I have followed, in my dealings with others, in the undertaking and the execution of my actions: yea, in the very performance of my practices of religion and piety.

Hitherto, with grief I must own it, whatever pleased my natural inclination, I was wont to pursue: whatever displeased it, I abhorred.

Hence, I find my labors, for the most part, void: I see that well-nigh all my actions were those of self-love; and that they have given me, in return, the fruits only of self-love.

And, unless Thou, by the light of Thy grace, hadst showed me these things, I might have continued with them, without ever suspecting them. So much was I blinded by self-love.

But, since, by Thy gracious kindness, Thou hast laid open before my eyes these baleful evils lurking in my heart, grant me, I beseech Thee, a special help to remove them altogether.

I entreat Thee, O Lord, suffer naught, which is not Thine, in my heart: if ever anything foreign appear therein, oblige me forthwith to cast it out or do Thou, even against my will, take it thence.

CHAPTER XXI.

OF WATCHING OVER OUR HEART.

1. *The voice of Jesus.* My Child, with all watchfulness, keep thy heart safe for Me: for from it proceeds either life or death.

The greatest and most pleasing gift thou canst offer, is to present thy whole heart irrevocably to Me; and thou canst have no better, nor more wholesome employment, than, to preserve thy heart faithfully for Me.

In vain dost thou devote thy heart to Me, if thou do not guard it sedulously: for the enemy, even without thy being fully aware of it, will corrupt it and tear it away.

2. A man, loose in heart, and given up to outward things, may, indeed, on occasion of some swift-passing fervor, devote his feelings to Me; but soon when this warmth of devotion disappears, he will fall into a worse than his wonted low estate.

A heart not watched over, is rarely self-present, and more rarely still, mindful of Me: hence, in a short time, it becomes unfeeling, and grows hardened against things spiritual.

It lies open to every one, like a public thorough

fare, through which thoughts, temptations, errors of every sort may freely pass.

All its enemies come and go through it; and, in various ways, disturb, defile, and corrupt it.

A man, given to outward things, never seriously gives heed to this; and, shrinking from the very thought of dwelling within himself, or of busying himself with what goes on in his heart, he endeavors to flee from himself, or to turn away his mind.

And thus the evil grows worse; and, from day to day, the condition of his heart becomes more dangerous.

3. If thou art unwilling to be the victim of miseries so great, remove their causes, and the effects will cease.

By calling to mind the divine Presence, by frequent recourse to Me, check thou all levity, and take heed, lest thou be too indulgent to thy ever-changing nature; which always seeks to go abroad, which is prone to vanity, which seeks to show itself everywhere, which studies continually how it may gratify the senses.

Shun things trifling and useless; shut out all outer things, with which it is not needful to busy thyself; accustom thyself to dwell within thyself, and to live interiorly in such a manner, as if thou wast alone with Me in the world.

Study, always and everywhere, to possess thyself and to be self-collected: to this thou mayst attain by grace, by effort, and by practice, so that it will become, as it were, natural to thee.

And, when thou hast acquired it, this self-presence of the mind will bring its own reward. For it is a boundless treasure to man.

4. The self-collected man keeps watch over all the avenues of the heart; Me, his God and Saviour, he entertains within himself; with Me he deals generously, with Me he converses familiarly.

Everywhere self-possesssed, he peacefully enjoys the Beloved of his soul, and is ever saved from wearisomeness, and from numberless faults.

Whilst inwardly recollected, he makes progress in virtue; and, in spite of every obstacle, he hastens on to perfection.

Wherefore, allow not thy spirit to grow dissipated, My Child; neither on account of the appearance of external objects, nor on account of the varied throng of circumstances, nor on account of the urgency of labor, nor on account of the comfortless inward state of thy soul.

Observe carefully, with what objects thy heart busies itself; by what it is moved, towards what it tends.

Turn thyself wholly to interior things; and, intent on these, preserve inward peace, and rejoice in My presence.

5. *The voice of the Disciple.*—Grant me, I beseech Thee, Lord Jesus, an inward spirit, that I may keep my heart for Thee, that I may watch over its employments.

For I find it ever busy but, by reason of my neglectfulness, it heeds neither place, nor time, nor objects.

Behold! frequently have I surprised it in strange places, pouring out its feelings, whether of love or of aversion, distracted with emotions, becoming stained by the objects which engaged it.

Frequently have I found it to steal away and give

itself up to dissipation. at the hours, yea at the very
moments, which were specially consecrated to Thee;
and when it ought to have been praying to Thee,
praising Thee, loving Thee, enjoying Thee.

How often have I seen it engaged with objects
vain, or even forbidden, when it should have occupied itself with things good or useful!

When unguarded, it slips forthwith away, it runs
to and fro. it is carried towards different objects, according as it is swayed by different impulses of
nature.

It is never at rest: when it escapes from one object, it is entangled in another. It is excited by
curiosity, it is allured by cupidity, it is misled by
vanity, it is defiled by pleasure, it is wasted by sadness, it is tortured by envy, it is disturbed by love
and hatred, it is worried by its own misery, and by
worrying itself it is broken down.

Thus is my heart busied, thus is it defiled, when
I watch not over it, or when I am careless about it.

6. O Lord! how great the need of being vigilant!
How great the need of guarding my heart! It must
not only be made to stay at home in recollection,
but it must also be kept busy, yet only with Thee or
for Thee.

I must examine, then, by what it is impelled,
whether by nature or by grace: how it acts, whether
according to Thy good pleasure, or according to its
own natural likings; what it has ultimately in view,
Thee or itself.

And I must watch constantly, until my heart, in
some manner, has grown accustomed, sweetly and
courageously to follow, for love of Thee. the motion
of grace.

O Jesus! of how great an importance is this work! whatever efforts be needed to accomplish it, behold! I will not cease to pursue the same, until I see it perfected.

If I loved Thee, if I were all captivated with Thy love, how easily, and how speedily should this work be completed! For, if my heart were filled with love for Thee, it would repose in Thee, it would not stray from Thee:—in Thee it would find its happiness; all else it would, of its own accord, drive off or cast away.

O sweetest Jesus! how wonderful is Thy love! Replenish Thou my heart with Thy love and Thy grace, and my heart will gladly stand watch over itself, will zealously reserve itself for Thee.

CHAPTER XXII.

OF THE SHORTNESS OF THIS LIFE.

1. *The voice of Jesus.*—My Child, in all thy works, remember thy last end: and thou shalt never sin.

Whilst thou hast time, do whatever thou canst for eternity, mindful that thy life is exceedingly short. Soon thou must return to the earth, out of which thou wast taken; for dust thou art, and into dust thou shalt return.

What is the life of man upon earth? A vapor, which appears, for a little time, then vanishes away, and leaves not even a vestige behind.

Ever since thou wast born, thou hast not ceased
to hasten on to death; neither is it in thy power to
stay thy steps.

2. Think over the time thou hast lived. Does it
not appear like a dream? Yet know, My Child,
that it shall seem still more so, when death is near,
which thou must meet full soon.

For what is even the longest life? Behold! the
number of man's days are threescore and ten years:
and, if he be among the powerful, fourscore years.
But, compared with eternity, these years are accounted as a drop in the waters of the ocean.

Nay more, the time of this life, placed in comparison with the endless duration of the life hereafter, is only a point. Yet on this point is hung
thy eternity, whether of bliss or of woe.

Yea, hadst thou lived from the beginning of the
world, even to this hour, if thou wert now about to
die, what should this life be worth to thee, when
thou art entering into eternity; in which there are
neither days, nor years, nor ages, but which flows
perpetually onward, through an uninterrupted forever.

3. Wherefore, My Child, understand well the
value of time. Time is the measure of life: as
much as thou squanderest of time, so much dost
thou lose of thy life.

Time exceeds in value all the treasures of this
world. With all the riches of earth, thou couldst
not purchase a second of time: but, with time, everlasting treasures may be secured.

Oh! could the dead return from eternity, thinkest
thou that they would misspend even a moment?
that they would not employ it; some to free them-

selves from punishments, others to increase their merits?

But alas! though nothing is more precious than time, to many there is naught more wearisome.

There are those,—not only among persons that follow the spirit of the world, but even among such as make a profession of piety,—to whom time seems a burden. They complain of its dullness; they love to waste it; they rejoice when they have spent it uselessly, but without irksomeness.

And thus they squander, in dishonoring Me, and in harming themselves, that by means of which they were able and obliged to glorify Me; to help their neighbor; to gather treasures of merit for eternity.

4. Frequently call to mind, My Child, for what purpose thou didst enter into this world. Evidently for none other, except to prepare thyself for eternity. For, what else is the present life, if not a novitiate of eternity?

Whilst this brief career continues, thou hast numberless duties to fulfill. For, there are thy many faults to be atoned for; thy soul to be saved and sanctified; hell to be escaped; Purgatory to be avoided; heaven to be secured; thou hast a neighbor whom thou must edify and help to life ever lasting; lastly, thou hast to honor and glorify Me in a befitting manner, and with all thy powers.

If thou do not this during life, after it, time shall be no more: and, throughout eternity, thou shalt bear the consequences of thy heedlessness and neglect.

Time is Mine, not thine: I have lent it to thee, that thou mayst use it to perform those things, which I demand, or desire of thee.

If thou squanderest it, thou shalt one day be

held to a most strict account: but if thou usest it well, thou canst merit, at every moment, a new degree of grace, and of ever-enduring glory.

5. Hearken, My Child: frequently imagine thyself at that point, when time shall cease, and eternity begin: and weigh, attentively, what thoughts will then occupy thy mind, both concerning all the past, and concerning the whole future.

Behold! eternity is thy dwelling-place: eternity is thy country: eternity is thy lasting home.

Thou art a traveler and a stranger upon earth; fleetly thou passest over it, in search of thy kindred in eternity. Thither, all that have been, that are, and that shall be, must repair. There all, the great and the small, the rich and the poor, the well-formed and the misshapen, shall be without distinction, except such a one as arises from virtue.

Yet a little time, My Child, and thou also shalt be there.

There shalt thou live: yea, live an endless life. Behold! what a lofty thought, My Child! Time shall wing away its flight, ages shall succeed to ages, the world itself shall perish: but thou shalt never cease to be; thou shalt never cease to live. Oh! would, my Child, that thou didst understand this rightly!

6. If thou savest not thyself for eternity, who will save thee? Most certainly, no one: not even I; for, although I created thee without thee, I will not save thee without thee.

And if thou dost not now work out thy salvation and perfection, how wilt thou do it hereafter? The future is a time, which, perhaps, thou shalt not have, and which thou canst, by no means, promise to thyself. But even wert thou to possess it, the matter would grow more difficult from day to day and would induce thee to delay still farther: and thus thou shouldst stand, at the gates of eternity, still unprepared.

Believe every day to be the last, and live each day in such a manner, that, when the Son of man comes, far from fearing, thou mayst be able to rejoice at His coming.

Blessed is he whom, when I come, I shall find thus employed. Verily, I say, I will place him over all My possessions.

7 *The voice of the Disciple.*—O Lord, how short is life, and how many, and what great things have to be done during it! But, alas! how have I spent hitherto the time of my life!

All these things of supreme importance, which Thou gavest me to do for eternity, I have overlooked, as if they were of little or no worth.

O blindness! O wickedness of mine! Although these things deserve to be wept over, with tears of blood, oh! would that they were my worst transgressions! Woe is me! I have employed a great part of the time of my life in tormenting and grieving Thy Heart, in committing and heaping up sins for myself.

Much of it have I wasted in serving the world, in seeking after its empty possessions, in pursuing its fruitless glory, deceitful pleasures, trifles of every kind.

Much of it have I squandered in satisfying myself, in fostering self-love, in gratifying the inclinations of nature, yea, even in things which otherwise were good and pious.

O my Saviour! how wretchedly have I lived! Instead of virtues and merits, I have gathered wood, and straw, and stubble, to feed the fire, and burn myself in the life to come.

Pardon, I entreat Thee, O pardon the evils, I have done: grant me grace to redeem lost time, to repair the past and make it good, by fervently employing what still remains of my life, in those things for the performing of which it was given me.

The source of my misfortunes was that I did not love Thee, Lord Jesus; that I felt indifferent toward Thee; that I was defiled with a corrupt and corrupting love for other objects.

O my God, Thou who hast freed me from so great a curse, I beseech Thee, enkindle my heart with that fire of love with which Thy Heart is burning. This most hallowed flame will utterly destroy my offenses; this will arouse me faithfully to perform whatever is enjoined to secure a blissful eternity.

CHAPTER XXIII.

OF DEATH.

1. *The voice of Jesus.*—My Child, remember, thou must die: because it is appointed for all men once to die.

Do whatever thou wilt, thou canst by no possible effort escape the grasp of death. The Almighty Himself has fixed the bounds, beyond which none can pass. When thou hast reached them, no matter what may be thy condition, thou shalt die the death.

Whilst life endures, there is naught more certain than death: yet there is naught more hidden in uncertainty, than the time of death, and its attendant surroundings.

Thou knowest not, indeed, when thou s`alt die: yet, hold this for certain, that thou shalt die, when thou thinkest not.

Whether thou shalt see the end of this year, or even of this day, of that thou art wholly ignorant.

Many, counting on a long life, and regardless of making preparation for death, dream of much to be done in the future; when suddenly death puts an end to all their plans, and drags them away into eternity.

Whether thou shalt die at home, or abroad, of sickness, or by violence; whether strengthened with the Sacraments, or deprived of their soothing comforts, all this lies hidden in the mysterious unknown.

2. However, My Child, thou shalt die only once: if once thou diest well, thy everlasting bliss is secured; if once thou diest ill, thy destruction is endless and irreparable.

O inconceivable stupidity of the heart of man! Very many fear not to live in a state of damnation; and yet it is certain, that they shall die unexpectedly. The unchangeable declaration remains firm: The Son of man will come, when He is not expected.

For a reason worthy of God's Wisdom, the time of His coming remains hidden, that men may keep themselves in the state of grace—ever ready. But, as many disregard this, it happens that not a few die without being prepared, and in a twinkling are buried in hell.

Woe, therefore, to them whom death shall overtake in a bad state! When they are dead, hope shall be no more; because from a death in time, they fall into the death of eternity, and from finite evils they pass over to those which are infinite.

Most wretched is the death of sinners: frightful is the death of the lukewarm; but precious, and filled with consolation, is the death of them that have sanctified themselves.

Blessed are they who end a saintly life with a holy death! They reach the end of their labors, their afflictions, their trials, and of all dangers, and they enter into a bliss secure and complete.

3. How differently are different persons impressed at the moment of death! some are terror-stricken at the thought of the past, of the present, and of the future; others are filled with comfort· these feel their hearts dilating, those feel them compressed with anguish: but all wish that they had lived piously.

To be well prepared to die, is the greatest consolation of him that sees the near approach of death.

To how great a danger of dying unprepared is he exposed, who thinks of making ready only when death is at the door! then, either time is wanting, or the pangs of sickness hinder the use of the soul's powers, or passions still have their wonted sway, whilst the habit of neglecting to correspond to grace still prevails; and, meanwhile, the devil's assaults are greater than ever before.

Look forward, then, My Child, before the night overta e thee, wherein no one can securely work, but when every one begins to garner what he has sown.

A good life is the best preparation for death. It is generally true, that he that lives well, dies well.

Daily, before retiring to thy nightly rest, put thy soul in order, as if, the same night, thou hadst to set out for eternity.

4. Death is a good counselor, My Child; wherefore, before thou undertakest, or lea est off, au ht of importance, ask advice of death, that thou mayst know, when it calls thee, what thou wouldst like to have done, what thou wouldst regret to have left undone.

By perfect purity of heart thou canst make thy death most safe and consoling.

Take no counsel of the flesh when there is question of securing a happy death; but, even in spite of its murmurings, pursue what is good, that, in the end, thou mayst save both the body and the soul.

After death thy body shall become the food of worms, and whatever remains of it, shall be the prey of corruption.

Yet, thereafter, it shall arise again, whether thou art willing or not, to share the everlasting destiny of the soul.

Let death be most familiar to thee, My Child. If thou be faithful in asking its advice, and in following it, it will be thy solace in adversity, it will keep thee in due bounds in prosperity, it will be useful to thee in all things, it will not cease to d thee good; and, in the end, it will free thee fr this place of exile, and introduce thee into blissful country in heaven.

5. *The voice of the Disciple.*—Is it possed, Lord, that any one will hold himself un when at any moment he may have to meet

My conscience bears me witness, what I shall wish for at the approach of death: then my sole desire shall be that I had led a life of innocence; that for Thee I had kept my heart undefiled; that I had sanctified my soul.

But, alas! should death overtake me now, I should wish for all this in vain; since, as yet, I possess no sign of holiness, but rather many marks of luke-warmness.

O compassionate and merciful Lord, bear with me a little while, that I may weep over my neglect-fulness, and that I may do what I would desire to have performed, when death comes.

6. O my soul, soon time shall be no more. Let others do as they list: let us, whilst yet there is time, devote ourselves to the work of our salvation.

Each one for himself. When death comes no one can take our place; nor can any one, in our stead, go into eternity. Whatever, therefore, others may say or do, let us place our everlasting destiny beyond all danger.

And what means, O Lord Jesus, can be better and safer, than a true love for Thee, disengaged from every thing besides; since this both cleanses us from our faults, and renders us holy?

If I love Thee truly, I will not fear death, nor aught of all that follows thereafter. Thy love will drive away fear: Thy love will enable me to ap-roach Thee with confidence.

Thou, then, O Jesus, my love, be Thou hence-my life. If Thou art my life, to die shall be in.

love of Thee, let me daily die to sin, to the

world, to myself, that I may live for Thee: let me
become free from things created, and be made
wholly pure, so that, when death opens the door, I
may appear before Thee rejoicingly.

CHAPTER XXIV.

OF JUDGMENT.

1. *The voice of Jesus.*—My Child, so soon as thou
hast gone into eternity, thou shalt find thyself before My Judgment-seat, to give an account of thy
life, and to hear the decision of thy lot forever.

I Myself, the Searcher and Knower of hearts,—
to whom all power is given in heaven and on earth,—
I will preside over this judgment.

All and every one, whether they be willing or
not, must make their appearance before Me, the
Judge of the living and the dead, to receive the
final sentence: nor is it possible thereafter to appeal to another tribunal.

What is just, I will judge: neither by gifts nor
by promises will I be conciliated; nor shall the
prayers of any one change My Heart; neither will
I be moved by repentance.

That day shall be a day of justice, not of mercy.
Then shall each one receive according to his works.

2. What shall thy feeling be then, My Child,
when thou shalt stand alone before the infinite
Majesty, with naught except thy works alone, whether
they be good or evil?

Then will the devil arise in judgment against
thee, and accuse thee, ready to drag thee into hell.

Thy Guardian Angel will stand up against thee, to bear witness to the truth of what is brought against thee.

Nay, even thy own conscience will accuse thee, and overwhelm thee with alarm, and dread, and terror.

Thus accused, with none to take thy defense, thou shalt wither away for fear; nor shalt thou dare to open thy mouth.

3. For all things, whether they be known or unknown, are in My sight; nor is there any thing hidden from My eyes.

Yet, searching I will search the heart, from the first dawn of its reason, even to the last breath of its life.

From it will I draw forth every evil, be it public or private: whether its own work, or that of another; whether great or small; whatever thou hast committed by thought, and word, and deed, and omission.

And not only of things evil, but also of those that are vain, or idle, or useless, will I exact an account.

Nay more, justice itself will I judge: I will weigh, in the scales of the sanctuary, even thy good deeds, and see what was wanting in them; either in the motive, in the manner of doing, or in the end intended, scrutinizing whether all was supernatural and perfect.

Then, many things, which, during life, appeared good, shall be found void and evil.

Then, the showy semblances of the virtues of the lukewarm, shall be seen as they are, and shall be cast aside, as dry stubble, fit only to be burnt.

And, searching still further, I will seek out the fruit of all the favors which I bestow, of all the graces, of all the means of salvation and perfection.

Yea, I will summon time itself against thee, and I will thoroughly investigate in what manner thou didst use it.

4. What shalt thou do then, O sinner, when even the just shall hardly be secure?

Above thee thou shalt descry a heaven uncertain; below, the yawning abyss; at thy right, Angels as witnesses; at thy left, demons enraged; before thee, the supreme Arbiter of life and death.

5. Ah! My Child, now act with care, that thou mayst find safety then. Now it is easy, then it shall be impossible.

Follow now the invitings of My mercy, that thou mayst not then feel the severity of My justice.

Now withdraw thyself wholly from a depraved world, that then, with reprobate worldlings, thou mayst not be forced to hear: Depart, ye accursed, into everlasting fire.

Now, untrammeled by aught of earth, follow thou the Saints, that with them, thou mayst be worthy then to hear: Come, ye Blessed of My Father, possess the Kingdom prepared for you from the foundation of the world.

6. *The voice of the Disciple.*—O Lord! how much better it is, here to examine and judge myself strictly, that I may not be condemned before Thy Judgment-seat!

How much better, here to weigh well all my thoughts, and words, and deeds, that I may plainly see whether they are good, whether they are wholly according to Thy will, whether they shall be able to stand Thy searching, and deserve Thy approval!

At present there is still a remedy, then every effort shall prove unavailing: now mercy is still offered me, then justice will thunder forth: Give an account of every thing.

Lord, O Lord! if Thou wilt mark iniquities, who shall endure it? If Thou searchest also things indifferent, yea, even those that are good, who can stand before Thee?

O Jesus! although I am inwardly rejoiced that Thou, and none other, art to be my Judge, yet, when I reflect that I am obliged to give an account of matters so numerous and so dreadful, I tremble with fear.

For, on what can I rely, when even my good deeds must be mistrusted? On what shall I ground my hope? Behold! naught do I find, whereon to place a safe reliance, except on Thy Heart.

In this, therefore, will I hope: for, though It shall then be the Heart of my Judge, yet It will still remain the Heart of my Jesus, of One that loves them that love Him.

O my Jesus! be mindful of Thy word, in which Thou hast given me hope: for Thou hast said: Who loves Me, him also will I love.

If I love Thee, and am loved by Thee, then will I surely not fear to come and appear before Thee.

Lo, therefore, what I will do: I will love Thee, most lovely and most loving Jesus; I will love Thee with my whole heart, and love Thee all the days of my life.

CHAPTER XXV.

OF HELL.

1. *The voice of Jesus.*—My Child, so long as men live, I do, in some manner, love them all; the good I cherish with a divine affection; the wicked I tolerate, because I await their conversion; and I go in search of those that are straying. My Heart, wherein I bear them all written, devises and uses a thousand ways and means to save all.

But, if there are any who disappoint the hopes of My mercy, if they come to judgment laden with the guilt of grievous sin, confirmed in their obstinacy; I will blot them altogether out of My Heart, and, with the thunderbolts of My justice, I will hurl them into the depths of hell.

2. There, they are bereft of heaven and all its delights, and never shall they behold My countenance in the kingdom of My glory.

They endure an infinite punishment: because they have lost an infinite good.

Plunged in a shoreless lake of fire, they burn and suffer for evermore; and the smoke of their tortures mounts up unendingly.

All evils rush upon them. There, every sense of the body, every power of the soul, shall have its own and proper punishment.

In that, whereby each has sinned, shall he be specially tormented: as much as he has delighted in evil, so much is he tortured with pain.

There, the unclean are forever devoured with a burning heat, overwhelmed with intolerable stench, gnawed by never-dying worms.

There, the wickedly rich are oppressed by extreme want; and suffer a most frightful hunger and thirst, nor shall they find relief forever.

There, they that wrongly sought after honors are infinitely debased, and despised and trodden under foot by the very demons.

There, no interruption is felt in torments, not even for a moment; but they continue, and shall continue forever and ever.

There, every one receives according to his deserts.

3. The place, the masters, the company, everything superadds to the punishments, in an inconceivable manner.

What can there be more terrible than the dungeons of hell, where no ray of light, no order, but continued darkness and everlasting horror dwell?

What more cruel than the demons, who exhaust their arts to invent new tortures, and their strength to inflict them?

What more gloomy than that wretched throng of sufferers, howling endlessly, hopelessly? As many companions as there are suffering, so many new torments are experienced.

4. Behold! so shall he be punished, who is unwilling to serve Me, his God, his Creator, his Redeemer, his unwearied Benefactor.

As I live, every knee shall be bent to Me, and all nations shall serve Me.

Whoever does not willingly serve My Goodness in time, shall unwillingly serve My justice in eternity.

Be not amazed, My Child, at the punishment of

the damned: they themselves are not astounded, but confess that they receive things worthy of their deeds.

No one goes to the torments of hell against his will: all the reprobate rush thither of their own free choice; therefore, they complain of no one except themselves.

They confess, that I am infinitely bountiful, and acknowledge, that they are exceedingly wicked.

5. The gate of hell is sin; the paths that lead to the same, whatever allures man to sin.

How many have perished by an unlawful desire for pleasure, by an inordinate love of riches, by a wicked pursuit of honors!

Long thou for naught, My Child, which may entangle thee in its toils, and afterwards hurl thee into the abyss.

Nor is it less dangerous, in all things to seek thyself. How many, alas! there are, who seem to begin well, but who, because they do not abandon s lf, relapse at length—are thrust into deeper evils, and, finally, are miserably lost!

To escape hell, therefore, it is not enough to have begun well, but it is necessary to have persevered in well-doing.

Forsake sin and the world forever, lest thou be in the end forsaken by Me: forsake, moreover, thyself, lest by thy own weight, thou be dragged down to the lowest depths.

Do all, dearly beloved, endure all, that thou mayst avoid never-ending torments. All the labors and afflictions of this life, are as naught, when compared with the sufferings of hell.

Here upon earth, in a short time, there shall be

an end to labors and sorrows: but there is no being redeemed out of hell.

6. *The voice of the Disciple.*—O Lord, our God! how awful is Thy justice in eternity: Nevertheless, Thy judgments are just, yea, acknowledged just by the reprobate themselves.

But, although nothing terrifies me more than hell, yet, I know of nothing better adapted to awaken in my heart a love for Thee.

How, indeed, O Lord Jesus, can I think of the fire of hell, without being inflamed with love for Thee?

What is there, that manifests, in a more sensible manner, the bounty of Thy Heart towards me? what is there, that presses me more forcibly to love Thee in return?

Behold! if Thou shouldst free some reprobate soul from the torments of hell, and if to her, thus restored to this life, Thou shouldst give most plentiful means, whereby she might not only save herself, in an easy manner, but also gain an everlasting throne of glory in heaven: O how would that soul love Thee! Would she think that she could ever be able to show Thee sufficient thankfulness? Could she ever think of hell, without wholly melting with love for Thee? O how pure would she keep her heart for Thee! how saint-like would she live for Thee!

Now, O Lord, I am indebted to Thee for much more than that soul should be. By preserving me from the pains of hell, Thou didst far greater and better things for me. For, is it not a greater and better blessing to be entirely kept from an evil, than to be released from it, after having undergone its pangs?

Yet, these things, so astonishing, so wonderful, so sweet, Thou didst do for me; not once, not twice, not thrice, but as often as I committed mortal sin.

Had I committed no mortal sin, my obligation should still be greater, my debt of gratitude should be increased, as well as my reasons for loving Thee. For I should be infinitely more obliged to Thee.

Had not the infinite goodness of Thy Heart preserved me by grace, how long ago might I have fallen into a sin deserving of hell! For there is no sin which one commits, which another may not also commit, unless Thou prevent him by a special grace.

Whatever, then, I may have been, this O most sweet Jesus, this I owe, first of all, to Thee, that I am not now in hell, that I am still able to gain heaven. Thou hast freed me from destruction; Thou hast freed me, according to the multitude and greatness of the goodness of Thy heart, from the depth of hell, from the hands of them that lay in wait for my soul.

Come ye, therefore, and I will tell you, all ye that fear the Lord, what great things He has done for my soul.

Should I, then, not love Thee, O Jesus, infinite Goodness! Should I not cherish Thee! yea, I love Thee, I love Thee above all things; and I will continue to love Thee thus, as long as I have being, forever and ever. Thou alone shalt possess all my affections: for Thee, O Jesus, will I live, for Thee, alone, to whom I owe my all.

CHAPTER XXVI.

OF HEAVEN.

1. *The voice of Jesus.*—My Child, the eye has not seen, the ear has not heard, nor has the heart of man conceived, what things I have prepared for them, that love and serve Me faithfully to the end

Who can portray for those who have not experienced it, what heaven is,—that blissful abode from which all ills are banished, in which there is an overflowing of all good things?

No labor shall be there, no sorrow, no temptation, no danger: all these things have passed away with mortal life; they have given place to perfect rest, to endless joy, to a peace that cannot be disturbed, to a security that none can take away.

2. There shall be neither cold, nor heat; neither inclemency, nor change of seasons; neither unpleasant days, nor gloomy nights. Those realms of bliss are illumined by My everlasting glory, softened by the divine serenity of My countenance, enlivened by the infinite sweetness of My Heart so hat everything smiles in the purest light, in the newness of a heavenly spring, for evermore.

Blessed are they that dwell therein! They neither hunger, nor thirst; nor are they subject to aught that is unpleasant; nor shall they be weakened in vigor forever.

There they are replenished and inebriated from the torrent of the delights of God; they flourish in perpetual youth, and, immortal, they shine brighter than the sun for all eternity.

3. My Child, there thou shalt behold Me as I

am, and gaze upon Me face to face, in the most entrancing splendors of My Majesty.

There, by the intuition of My infinite perfections, thou shalt be rapt with admiration, and overflow with bliss; in the excess of thy joy thou shalt, of thy own accord, burst forth in boundless praises, and exaltation of My most lovely Attributes.

Then also thou shalt understand the mysteries of faith, and the secrets of nature.

All the science of philosophers is but ignorance, when compared with the knowledge possessed by the least of the Elect.

Then shalt thou view all the display of My everlasting kingdom, its unbounded treasures, its everenduring dignities.

At the contemplation of a loveliness so varied, and so great, thou shalt be inflamed with an ineffable love for Me.

4. Then, My Child, then, wilt thou love Me, in a perfect manner, without any division of thy affections, without remissness, without end.

Now, thou art sometimes in trouble, because thou knowest not whether thou art worthy of love or of hatred: then, to thy unutterable joy, thou shalt know with certainty, that thou lovest Me, and wilt love Me forever; and that, in return, thou art loved, and shalt be loved by Me, throughout eternity.

Then shalt thou repose on My Heart, with perfect security; and thou shalt taste how delightful it is, to love Me, and to melt away in My love.

Thou shalt be inebriated with an exceeding great sweetness, and rapt above thyself; thou shalt swim in an ocean of love, with the Angels and the Saints amid jubilant hymns of love, for evermore.

Thus shalt thou spend ages, and while away eternity, ever wishing, and ever longing, to love; and, at the same time, ever sated, and ever blissful, with love

5. Then, at last, Child, shalt thou possess Me, and enjoy Me forever: which is the completing of beatitude.

Thou shalt be wholly Mine, and I will be wholly thine: thou shalt enjoy Me, in a manner ever new, ever most delightful.

In Me thou shalt possess every good, and have whatever thou canst wish or desire.

Let thy mind conceive, if possible, how beautiful, how wonderful, how charming, all things are there: how rapturous to behold the glory and exquisite adornment of the heavens, to be present among the choirs of the Angels, to exult unceasingly with the Saints, to contemplate and love the most Blessed Virgin, the glorious Queen of the heavenly kingdom; and, in return, to attract Her sweet looks, and gain Her love.

What delightful dwellings, O My Child! what pleasant companionship! what charming beatitude and all to endure forever and ever!

Behold, My Child, behold the exceeding great reward of those that serve Me with their whole heart. Can the world give such things? or even promise them?

Lift up thy eyes, therefore, and see what awaits thee, if thou art faithful to Me even to the end.

Be of good cheer, My Child; and as much as thou art able, with the divine grace and thy own co-operation, cleanse thy heart and preserve it pure. For nothing defiled, be it ever so little, shall enter into heaven.

But the purer thou art here, the more glorious shalt thou be there; and the nearer to Me, and the dearer to My Heart.

6. *The voice of the Disciple.*—O Jesus, how blessed are they, that dwell in heaven with Thee!

O happy mortals they, who serve Thee with a clean heart! what ineffable beatitude shall they enjoy in eternity! yea, who is more happy than they, even in time!

O bliss-creating service of Jesus, which gains such a reward! thou renderest easy and pleasant all things, that lead to so great a glory and blessedness.

O most sweet Jesus, bid me do, bid me suffer, for Thy sake, whatever Thou wilt: willingly and gladly do I embrace everything, that I may please Thee in time, and possess Thee in eternity.

By Thy most Sacred Heart, do I entreat Thee, lead me safe, through whatever way Thou mayst choose, into Thy kingdom; that, with the Angels and Saints, I may behold Thee, love Thee, enjoy Thee, for evermore.   Amen.

DIRECTORY FOR THE SECOND BOOK.

1. The object of the Second Book is, to teach us—after we have become disengaged from our evil and inordinate affections, how we should exert ourselves, that, by the practice of virtue, we may be enabled to make our election sure. In order to do this the more efficaciously, and the more sweetly, at the same time, we should place before our eyes Jesus, with the inward dispositions of His Heart; because, by following Him who is the way, the truth, and the life, we shall proceed, with safety, certainty, and pleasure, from virtue to virtue, and secure our salvation.

The practice of the virtues, by which we may follow the Heart of Jesus, and express His interior life in ourselves, can, in every state and condition of life, be performed in two ways. The first, by practicing those virtues which are of precept, and which the state and condition of every one require. The second, by exercising, according to the divine good pleasure, those virtues also, which are of counsel, whereby our salvation is better secured, and the divine glory and our merits are the more increased. But since both these ways contain limitless degrees, whereby virtue is ever practiced with greater perfection, there is no one, how perfect soever he may be, who cannot here occupy himself profitably, and gather more abundant fruit.

As, however, Jesus willed that, in the imitation of His virtues, we should, above all, be humble and meek of heart, we must diligently attend and take care, both that, whatever virtues we learn and imitate in Him, we place them upon true humility as their groundwork, and perfect them in a meek charity; and again, that, in the very manner of imitating His virtues, we be especially meek and humble of heart.

2. Nowhere can we learn virtues more safely, and more easily, than in the Heart of Jesus. For, as that Heart is the pattern of true virtue, by merely looking upon It with attention, we shall see what virtue is, and what qualities it ought to possess: neither shall we run the risk of erring in a matter which is to us of so much importance, both for time and eternity. Thence shall we learn, to our unspeakable consolation, that virtue is a right affection of the heart for an object, which is, in some manner, good: and we shall perceive, that this good object,—which sometimes we call, figuratively, virtue,—is not in truth virtue itself, but simply the object of virtue. Thence we shall likewise learn, that virtue, in order to be such as it ought to be in every Christian, must not be natural, but supernatural; and we shall clearly distinguish the difference between the two. The affections of the Heart of Jesus, which He reduced to acts, whether internal or external, did not spring from an impulse or motion of His human nature, but from a supernal or divine principle; they were not performed according to the sentiments of His human nature, but according to the divine good pleasure;

they did not tend to some temporal delight of His human nature, but throughout to God, as to their last end.

Whence, if, from the impulse or emotion of mere nature, we strive after what is good; if we act simply according to the feelings of nature, whether of inclination or aversion; if we seek merely a natural end, we have only natural virtue, whereby we shall acquire no Christian perfection in this life,—no fruit of merit in eternity. But, if of the Heart of Jesus, we learn supernatural virtue, and the practice of the same; replenished with graces and merits, we shall lead an interior life, like to His own.

What is the interior life,—for which the life of the Heart of Jesus serves us as a model,—except to begin all our voluntary acts, internal as well as external, by the grace of God, or a supernatural principle; to perform them according to God's Will; to direct them to God and His interests, as to our end; to occupy ourselves in our Heart with God, our Saviour; and to live for Him by love? Now, all this he does, who begins all his voluntary acts by the divine good pleasure; who performs them according to the divine good pleasure; directs them to the divine good pleasure, as his end,—being most constantly occupied internally with the Lord, through love. Behold the truly interior life, by which genuine and solid virtues are acquired; by which we may attain, safely and sweetly, to true sanctity and divine union. This life is fitted for every state and condition; it is adapted, not only to ecclesiastics and religious, but equally to all laics and persons in the world. Did not the first Christians generally lead this life? Does not the Gospel teach this life to all?

Whoever has a good will may lead this sanctifying life, practice supernatural virtue and attain to perfection. For, the acquiring, or not acquiring of virtue, does not depend on temperament, on a mild or passionate character, as many seem to believe: but it depends on the grace of God, and the co-operation of man's will. For, since God gives grace, not in view of natural qualities, but first gratuitously, and afterwards also in consideration of supernatural merits and prayers; and since the human will, whatever be the natural disposition of a man, is truly free to co-operate, or not to co-operate with grace, it is evident, that virtue does not depend on temperament or natural disposition. Wherefore, we acquire virtue the better, and the more perfectly, not in proportion as our natural disposition is yielding, but in proportion as our co-operation is more efficacious: we reach a more pure and more solid virtue, not by reason of the fewness of natural repugnances we feel, but by means of the more generous acts of the will, which we perform, in spite of natural repugnances. This doctrine, so full of consolation,—which the Saints unanimously teach, and which they learned of the very Heart of Jesus,—deserves our whole attention.

In the practice of virtue, we must guard against delusions, among which this one is the chief and most common: That we are satisfied with producing the object of a virtue, whilst we do not practice the virtue itself; or, that we believe that we practice a virtue, when we bring forward the object of virtue through a natural inclination or intention; or even, that we think, we can acquire true and solid virtue, without repeated and generous acts, whereby the emotions of the passions, and the impulses of nature are overcome or denied. They that neglect to cleanse their heart perfectly, are especially wont to fall into this dreadful delusion. Other delusions, which may occasionally occur in the practice of virtue, arise nearly all from the preceding. Such are. on the one hand, to grow despondent in mind, on account of the difficulties or oppositions of nature: to look upon these as obstacles to virtue, not as means,—such as they may be in reality, if they are used with a generous heart,—to acquire true and solid virtue: on the other hand, to deem the good qualities of nature, freedom from vices or temptations, a virtue; or, even, overlooking true and solid virtue, to aspire to divine union. Now, these, and other delusions, you will easily avoid, if, like a true Disciple of the Heart of Jesus, you lead an interior life.

3. When, therefore, you have come to that part of the spiritual life, which the Heart of Jesus teaches in this Book, you should direct your endeavors to this: to know and love Jesus as perfectly as you can, to learn and acquire, ever better and better, in thinking, in speaking, in acting, the dispositions of His Heart. To attain to this, besides the two methods of meditating,—which are given before the first Book, and which you may also employ here, if you find them useful,—what follows will enable you to understand more fully this matter.

4. The proper method of using the second Book is twofold: the one of meditating, the other of con-

templating: both agree entirely with what the Saints have taught us concerning mental prayer.

If you meditate, let the memory represent to you some virtue of the Heart of Jesus, and let it retain the same, after the meditation; so as to put it in practice.

Let the understanding consider the qualities of the virtue proposed; then, let it compare your own heart with the Heart of Jesus, in regard to the virtue considered; afterwards, let it recall your past life, whether and how far you have practiced this virtue; if sufficiently, return thanks, and give honor to God, your Saviour; but, if the contrary, grieve and ask pardon; lastly, let it look forward into the future, considering when, and how, you can improve this virtue.

Let the will embrace the same virtue, excite internal acts of the same; yea, conversing with Jesus Himself, let it utter the sentiments of the heart: for what it is sorry, what it proposes; what it fears, what it hopes; what it dislikes, what it loves; nay, let it devoutly communicate its every desire, and, finally, ask much.

But, if you contemplate, see in the mystery, or in the particular subject which you propose to contemplate, what are the sentiments of the Heart of Jesus, or of Jesus in His Heart, concerning all and each of the things that occur in the subject; what He esteems, and how highly; what He condemns, and how greatly; what He shuns, and what He embraces.

Then, give heed, in this matter, to the words which issue from the Heart of Jesus, and what words are not even thought in His Heart, much less uttered.

Lastly, observe, in the same manner, what kind

of acts proceed from the Heart of Jesus, and with what virtues they are adorned.

And, throughout the whole contemplation, according to your devotion, or your wants, or the motions of grace, indulge and persist in acts, that is, pious affections and petitions.

Learn, in this manner, by contemplation, to feel, and speak, and act, like Jesus Himself.

The acts, specially recommended in this part of the interior life, besides acts of the theological virtues, are frequent acts of that virtue to which you are applying yourself, of generous self-abnegation of your ill-ordered nature, of a noble love of Jesus. Repeat these constantly.

But, whether you meditate, or whether you contemplate, you ought so to consider the mysteries of the life of Jesus, as if you were present at them: which is expressly taught by St. Bonaventure: "If you desire," says he, "to derive fruit from these things, you must, with all the affection of your mind, setting aside all other cares and anxieties, represent yourself as present at what is related to have been spoken or done by the Lord Jesus Christ; in such a manner as if you heard them with your ears, saw them with your eyes."

5. The Saints, who were skilled in the interior ways of the spiritual life, teach us that the demon, the evil spirit, is more wont to tempt, under the appearance of good, those who, leading a life already exempt from sins, exercise themselves in acquiring virtues. Wherefore, to such persons, they recommend the following rules, to enable them to discern between the good and the evil spirit, and between the suggestions of either.

I. In those who are advancing from good to better, the good Spirit moves the soul peacefully, calmly, gently:

The evil spirit moves the soul roughly, confusedly, violently.

But on those who proceed from bad to worse, the said spirits act in a contrary manner. For the good Spirit stings them inwardly, disquiets and arouses them, that he may bring them to conversion.

And the wicked spirit endeavors to make them quiet in sin, caresses, and flatters them, that he may keep and push them onward in evil.

II. It is peculiar to God, as well as to every good Spirit, in His motions, to give to them that act rightly, or use sincere efforts, true joy and spiritual consolation, and to remove the sadness and trouble, which the evil spirit causes.

And it is the characteristic of the evil spirit to fight against such joy and consolation, by adducing specious reasons, subtleties, and various fallacies.

III. The evil spirit observes very much, whether a soul possesses a delicate or a loose conscience: If it is a delicate one, he strives to render it still more delicate, even to scrupulousness and every extreme, so that he may the more easily trouble and overcome her: thus, if he sees that a soul commits no mortal sin, nor venial, nor any voluntary defect, the evil spirit, as he cannot make her fall into some sin, tries to cause her to judge and think that a sin, which is not sin:

But if the soul is of lax conscience, the evil spirit strives to make her still more lax and gross; so

that, if before she made no account of venial
sins, he endeavors to induce her now to make light
of mortal sins; and, if before she cared little for
grievous sins, he uses his efforts to make her now
care much less, or even nothing at all, for them.

IV. A soul that desires to make progress in the
spiritual life, must always proceed in a manner contrary to that by which the evil spirit proceeds.
Wherefore, if he tries to make the soul more lax,
she must take care to render herself more delicate:
in like manner, if he endeavors to make her so delicate, as to lead her to extremes, or to scruples, she
should manage to place herself firmly in the golden
mean, so that she may render and keep herself altogether quiet.

V. It is the characteristic of the evil spirit,
who transforms himself sometimes into an angel of
light, to begin by thrusting in thoughts conformable to the pious soul, and to finish, by suggesting
his own wicked ones.

VI. The soul should rightly attend to the
course of the thoughts suggested: for if the beginning, the middle, and the end are good, and
tend to a good object, it is a sign that the thoughts
suggested come from the good Spirit: but if in the
succession of thoughts, which the spirit suggests,
he ends with something bad,—or which turns away
from a certain good,—or even with a less good
than that which the soul had before resolved to do;
or, if he renders the soul restless, or disturbs her,
by taking away the tranquillity and peace which
she enjoyed before, it is an evident sign, that those
thoughts come from the evil spirit.

VII. When the enemy has been discovered, and

is known by the evil, to which he leads, it is then useful, that the soul consider the course of thoughts suggested to her, under the appearance of good; and that she review from the beginning, how the enemy tried to overthrow, and take away by degrees, her interior peace and tranquillity, until he brought in his own wicked intention. Taught by this experience, the soul will for the future guard more easily against the deceits of the evil spirit.

St. Ignat., St. Bernard, St. Gertrude.

THE SECOND BOOK.

ADMONITIONS USEFUL FOR THE IMITA-
TION OF THE MOST SACRED HEART
OF JESUS IN HIS ACTIVE LIFE.

CHAPTER I.

HOW MUCH WE SHOULD ESTEEM AND CHERISH SANCTIFYING GRACE.

1. *The voice of Jesus.*—My Child, do not disregard grace, but carefully preserve so sacred a deposit, which has been intrusted to thee.

For this is thy treasure, this thy glory, this thy happiness, this thy every good.

This informs thee, the image of God, and renders thee alike to Him.

Know, then, thy dignity, O man, who, by sanctifying grace, art raised even to the likeness of God, and becomest more exalted than the whole world, so that naught of earth can be compared to thee.

What is the splendor of the stars? what the beauty of all creatures, when placed in comparison with the excellence of a soul adorned with divine grace, and thus assimilated to God Himself?

Lift up thyself, therefore, and, mindful of thy dignity, do not defile nor debase thyself.

2. God adopts thee, resplendent with this grace not simply as His child, but as the child of His love and predilection.

Thus, what I possess by nature, thou receivest by adoption; so that thou art not only called, but art in very truth, a child of God.

Understand, if thou art able, what it is, to be a child of God: what it is, to be loved and cherished by such a Father.

In the world, children esteem themselves happy, and glory in having parents who are wise, good, influential—or wealthy, great, illustrious.

But what are the distinctions of all the parents of this earth, when compared with the Attributes of God?

With how much more reason, therefore, shouldst thou glory and rejoice in having for thy Father, God Himself, the Lord of heaven and earth!

Ponder, then, with a true judgment the excellence of this divine adoption. For, when formerly thou wast a castaway, reduced in the lowest depth of degradation, thou becamest, by sanctifying grace, from bond, free; from one disowned, the acknowledged child of God; that, thus ennobled, thou mayst rejoice in the affluence of the good things of the Lord.

Blessed is he who knows the price of sanctifying grace, whereby he was raised to be a child of God; and who so esteems this, the highest nobility, that, on no account, he shows himself degenerate, but ever continues a child worthy of such a Father!

3. If, by grace, thou art a child, by the same thou art also made an heir,—even the heir of God, and co-heir with Me.

Wherefore, My Child, the everlasting kingdom, which is Mine by right of nature, becomes thine in virtue of sanctifying grace.

When thou lookest up to heaven, and viewest, in spirit, the glory, the beatitude, and all the good things of eternity, say to thyself: Behold my possessions, behold my inheritance, if I preserve the title of grace.

My merits obtained, that this grace should confer upon thee a settled right to the possessions of heaven; of which none, except thyself, can deprive thee.

God's promise remains firm; He is faithful to His word: but, if thou losest sanctifying grace, thou throwest aside thy right, and becomest disinherited.

4. Grace, My Child,—which constitutes thee an heir of the heavenly kingdom,—makes thee also a companion of the Angels, a brother of the Saints.

If thou art glad when thou enjoyest the intercourse of distinguished companions, mortal men though they be, and subject to change; if thou art delighted at having brothers according to the flesh, although their number divides and lessens thy earthly inheritance: how great must be thy joy that, by grace, thou hast the blessed Angels for companions, the chosen Saints of God for brothers,— whose countless number neither divides nor lessens thy celestial inheritance, but, on the contrary, increases and multiplies the same!

And what brothers, too, My Child! how innumerable, how illustrious, how mighty, how good!

They are thy elder brothers: celebrated for their triumphs, crowned with the glory of beatitude, secure of themselves, solicitous for thee; they love thee in truth, encourage thee by their example, help thee by their prayers, invite thee by their rewards.

Blissful grace, which makes thee the brother of such heroes! Oh, My Child, would that thou didst fully understand this!

5. Moreover, by an effect of sanctifying grace, thou mayst, even in this life, enjoy true happiness. This grace is the foundation of interior peace: without it, there is no real peace: with it, an undisturbed calm pervades the soul.

Who, that resists sanctifying grace, has ever enjoyed peace? And what happiness can there exist, where there is no peace?

If thou rejoicest in the peace of grace, thou mayst justly and safely be glad amid prosperity, and thou canst easily and usefully find solace in adversity.

Preserve thyself in grace, and thou shalt always be enabled to possess peace and happiness. Witness all the Saints: yea, also they who, when once converted, kept carefully within themselves the grace of God. When they had this, and compared their present feelings with those of their former life, taught by experience, they could say to **Me:** Better is one day in Thy courts, O Lord, than thousands in the dwellings of sinners.

6. Nay more, My Child, if thou livest in sanctifying grace, My kingdom is within thee; so that I repose and reign in thy heart as on My throne.

Now, My kingdom consists in the tranquillity and joy of the Holy Ghost, who is a Spirit of charity and sanctification.

In this kingdom I hold sway, not as a Lord ruling My subjects, but as a Father training My Child, whom I design to reign with Me.

So long, therefore, as thou continuest under this rule of grace, I guide thee specially by My Wisdom, I protect thee by My power, I attend and encompass thee by My love.

Neither hast thou aught to fear, My Child, for this kingdom so governed, so protected, so cherished; unless, indeed, thyself becomest its betrayer.

If thou art faithful, it shall, doubtless, stand firm and endure for evermore: nor can all its enemies combined overthrow, or even weaken the same.

How sweet, how consoling is this thought, O My Child! how well suited to make thee esteem sanctifying grace above everything!

7. See now, My Child, how many, and what great possessions thou hast in this one good alone!

Does not this one good surpass, in excellence, all the riches of this world?

Pray, Child, that thou mayst ever understand better, and more perfectly the value of grace, and prize it in reality as highly as thou shouldst do.

If thou dost understand and appreciate it rightly, thou wilt deem it little, or certainly not too much, to sacrifice for its preservation not only fortune, fame, and all that is dear and pleasing, but even health, and, if it were necessary, life itself.

Did not My holy Martyrs, and all My sainted heroes,—among whom thou beholdest so many children and tender Virgins,—prize it thus? Did not thousands among them, when it was left to their choice, prefer to sacrifice, amid torments, all the blessings of life, yea, life itself, rather than lose the same, for any possession, however great, that was offered?

Thou, therefore, the child of such heroes, use thy every effort, constant watchfulness, and thy greatest care, to preserve grace, the most precious of all gifts; the more so, as the most powerful exertions of thy enemies are directed to despoil thee, and thus to accomplish thy destruction.

For the rest, dearly beloved, be thou strengthened in grace: increase in the same, and, by acts of true virtue, advance thou, even unto perfection.

Didst thou understand all these things, My Child?

8. *The voice of the Disciple.*—Yea, Lord. Would that I had understood all this before! Would I not then, after I had lost Thy grace, have wept and moaned more dolefully than Esau, when he had forfeited his birthright? For greater, beyond comparison, was my loss, and sustained too, for a far baser object.

Oh! had I understood all this, would I, for aught here below, have cast away so great a treasure?

Lord Jesus, would that I had never lost this greatest of all possessions! One thing, however, brings me solace, it is not yet too late; I may still enjoy the privileges of Thy grace, and thereby sanctify myself.

Thanks to thee, most sweet Jesus, for that Thou hast showed so great a mercy to me, so unworthy. The ineffable kindness of Thy Heart, I will not forget forever.

O Jesus! hereafter, grant me sooner to die than to lose Thy grace. By Thy most Sacred Heart, I beg and entreat Thee, hearken graciously to my petition.

Let others seek after silver and gold, honor and distinction, the joys of this world and its consolations: taught by Thee, O Lord, this alone do I desire above all else, to preserve Thy grace, and to increase therein all the days of my life.

CHAPTER II.

WHY THE SON OF GOD WISHED TO BECOME INCARNATE.

1. *The voice of Jesus.*—My Child, God alone is good. He is the supreme Goodness, supreme Wisdom, supreme Power, supreme Perfection.

What, then, can be better, or more perfect, than to follow and imitate God?

But, as God falls not under the senses, and men are inclined to sensible things, it was thought befitting that I, a divine Person, should become man: that thus I might unvail to them an external form to captivate their senses, and induce them, in a more easy and pleasing manner, to imitate God.

The first men aspired after lofty things; they desired and endeavored to be assimilated to God, that, like gods, they might know good and evil, and they fell: they lost the good which they knew, and suffered the evil which they knew not.

But I wished to present Myself before men in such a form, that, without presumption, without danger, they might safely desire so to render themselves like unto God, as to be freed from evil, and to acquire what is good.

2. First of all, men were to be redeemed; and when their debts had been canceled, they were to be made free.

Heavy were those debts which weighed upon them. So greatly had they offended the divine Majesty, that no mere creature, but God alone, having become man, could fully satisfy the divine justice, and truly repair the honor of the divine Majesty.

Miserable slaves of hell, they lay cast down, and groaning, without having in themselves any means of bettering their condition. I pitied the wretched multitude; and came among them, with a Heart overflowing with mercy, to redeem them, and lead them to a sweet and holy freedom.

3. Heaven had been closed by sin, and, among created beings, whether in heaven or upon earth, there was none able to open it again; had not I come down and unlocked it, no mortal could ever have entered heaven.

Before My coming, God was indeed known in Judea, where some few served Him worthily; but only through the grace given to men in view of My future coming. Among the Nations, how very small was the number of those, who, co-operating with this grace, feared God, practiced justice, and were pleasing to Him!

In how great a darkness were the greater part of them heedlessly groping! in how deep, and how measureless an abyss of wickedness were they buried!

Nay more, even now,—after the work of Redemption has been fulfilled,—what kind of life do many men lead, in spite of the countless means of salvation! Through their own fault, ignorant or forgetful of Me, they roam in blindness, and wickedly rush to destruction.

What, then, should have become of the human race, unless I, the Word, had been made flesh? None could have attained to God, to supernatural beatitude.

But, by assuming flesh, I united in Myself the utmost degree of divine greatness to the utmost of human lowliness, in such a manner, that, whosoever was willing, could, through Me, reach God and supernatural beatitude.

4. I came to glorify God, My Father; to make known to men His name and His love.

Of old the name of God, was the holy and dread Name of the Lord: now, the Name of God, is the holy and sweet Name of a Father.

The Old Law, was a Law of fear: the New, is a Law of love. God so loved men, that He gave His only-begotten Son.

And I, through love for My Father and for men, was incarnated by the Holy Ghost, the Spirit of love.

The whole work of the Incarnation, is, therefore, a work of love, but of a gratuitous love, of an infinite love.

5. I came from heaven, and I return to heaven, pointing out to all the way that leads thither, that where I am, they also may be who follow Me in this way.

I am the truth: I appeared shining in the darkness of the world, to enlighten every man that comes into this world, that every one might surely and safely guide his steps on the journey.

I am the life: for this I came into the world, that they who were dead might have life, and have it more abundantly; namely, the life of grace on their way, and the life of glory in their heavenly country.

Yet, behold! even after man was born again to the life of grace, freed from the slavery of death; and after he had been taught by Me the way to his true country, weak and unstrengthened as he was he could not have been able to follow me.

Great were his infirmities, My Child, great his faintness: but greater was the all-powerful Physician, greater the divine remedy, which heals every infirmity, every faintness.

This remedy is manifold grace, the price of My sufferings, the gift of My Heart; which induces every man to long for health; strengthens him when healed, and helps him to follow Me.

When I came upon earth, I might have run My career more swiftly than a giant. But the multitude of those that were suffering so moved My Heart, that, loitering in their midst, I seemed, in some manner, to grow weak with them; and, going before them, I so smoothed the roughness of the way, so helped and cheered up every one, that, were they but willing, they could easily and joyously follow My footprints towards the kingdom of heaven.

6. See now, My Child, how I have loved thee. These things I did for all in general, and for every one in particular as well: therefore, also for thee as if thou wert alone in the world, wretched and forsaken: and, as if I had come down from heaven, to seek thee, to redeem thee, to save thee alone.

Wherefore, since I came down in this manner that I might be thy guide to My everlasting kingdom, follow thou Me.

In whatsoever condition, in whatsoever state thou mayst be, under all circumstances, propose to thyself My life, as the sure and safe way to heaven.

Neither shouldst thou imagine that My outer life only is such, because My inner life is the principal.

My interior is My Heart: therein is found all glory: therein resides the principle of all virtues.

My Child, be not like the Jews, who gazed upon My outward appearance only, and considered not the feelings and dispositions of My Heart.

Do thou enter into the interior of My Heart: carefully examine the same, study It, be wholly busied therewith.

7. If thou feelest grateful towards Me, if thou lovest Me in return, thou wilt diligently search after whatever may be pleasing to My Heart, and thou wilt do it faithfully.

But thou must seek this in prayer, ask it by love, embrace it by love, perform it with love.

My Child, prayer is the key of heaven: nay more, prayer is the key of My Heart. With this key open thou and enjoy all the treasures of My Heart.

8. *The voice of the Disciple.*—Everlasting thanks to Thee, Lord God, Creator and Redeemer of mankind, for Thy gratuitous and exceedingly great charity, whereby Thou didst create us men, in so wonderful a manner, and didst restore us still more wonderfully.

O Christ Jesus! Who, unutterably existing from eternity, as the Son of God, through an excess of

Thy love for us, wast willing to become the Son of man; who will not love Thee in return? Who will not cling inseparably to Thee? Who will not live solely for Thee, to whom he owes his all?

O delightful consolation! O wonderful sweetness! to behold the Son of God, the Son of a Virgin!

I adore thee, O Jesus, Son of the living God, Thee made flesh of Mary! I hope in Thee, O infinite goodness! I love Thee with my whole heart, O most loving and most lovable love! Thou art my way: Thou, my truth: Thou, my life.

CHAPTER III.

THAT OUR HEART, AFTER THE EXAMPLE OF THE MOST SACRED HEART OF JESUS INCARNATE, MUST BE WHOLLY DEVOTED TO GOD.

1. *The voice of Jesus* —My Child, the first act of My Heart, after the Incarnation, was an act of love, whereby I devoted Myself completely to My heavenly Father.

There was in Me nothing which I did not consecrate with all My mind to My Father: nor was there aught in the Will of My Father, which I did not embrace with My whole Heart.

Even then did I practically say, in My inmost Heart: Behold! My Father, I come as the victim of Thy Will: at the head of the book of life it is written of Me, that I would do Thy Will: behold

I have willed it, and the law of Thy good pleasure is in the midst of My Heart.

At the first moment of My life, My Father placed before Me all the toils and hardships, all the humiliations and sorrows, all I was to do and to suffer, even to the last breath of My life.

With a willing and perfectly devoted Heart, I received all and each of them, according to My Father's good pleasure:

And this inward disposition of My Heart, I cherished every moment of My life; by this was I ever pressed onward, so that I always did whatsoever was pleasing to My Father.

2. Behold, My Child, the model of a true devotion, that, taught by it, at the very beginning of thy career, in the way of virtue, thou mayst, in like manner, devote thyself with thy whole heart.

Nothing, perhaps, is of so much importance, in the spiritual life, as a true and entire devotion of heart. For, a heart that is not altogether devoted to Me proves that it lacks perfect purity.

If thou dealest with Me in a sparing manner, I will also deal with thee sparingly: but, if thou art generous toward Me, I will, in return, be generous toward thee, and I will ever excel thee in generosity.

If, with a liberal heart, thou devote thyself, and all thou hast, to Me, so as to embrace effectually My good pleasure in all things; I Myself will lead thee, safely and happily, through whatsoever may befall thee; I will even, in some manner, be obliged to save thee.

3. This perfect self-devotedness has ever been the beginning of holiness in all My Elect.

Those noble and generous souls deemed the greatest sacrifices of life as nothing; so that they consecrated and wholly devoted to Me whatsoever they possessed, whatsoever they were.

Therefore, too, did I show to them such liberality and bountifulness, that often, even during this mortal life,—on account of the exceeding sweetness of consolation,—they burst into tears, and whilst on earth, enjoyed a foretaste of that bliss, wherewith they were hereafter to be inebriated in heaven.

Yet now very many of those that make profession of a great love of piety, are willing to be devoted, but only in things, and under circumstances, which are pleasing to them.

These are assuredly rather devoted to themselves than to Me. Wherefore, they continue to be slaves of self-love, and remain miserable and devoid of inward happiness; neither do they become disposed to the divine union.

Thou, My Child, if thou wilt be truly free and happy, withdraw thy heart from every object except Myself; and give all thy affections to Me alone.

If thou canst keep thy heart perfectly devoted to Me, thou shalt be able to continue calm and undisturbed under all circumstances. For, every agitation of mind arises, not from passing events, but from a heart ill-inclined toward God's good pleasure.

And if thou desirest to attain to an intimate union with Me, thou must be free from all creatures, and wholly devoted to Me, in all things.

4. My Child, let not thy devotion be like that of many others, which is wholly exterior, satisfied

with outward things alone, and, therefore, merely a semblance of devotion, not devotion itself.

Let thy devotion be truly interior, which has its principle in a heart so disposed, that, with the divine grace, thou art ready to resign thyself, unconditionally, to all My wishes, and to sacrifice all thou hast to serve Me.

Thy devotion, however, must pass over to outward things, since thou art a man, and not an Angel. And, as thou possessest a body and a soul, both My gifts, thou must with both honor Me and sanctify thyself.

But let the things, which are outwardly seen in thee, overflow, as it were, from the abundance of the heart: thus shall thy devotion be solid, and thou shalt be a true follower of My Heart.

5. This devotion, My Child, is the effect of supernatural grace, which, enlightening the intellect, and moving the will, makes a person ready to comply, willingly, with everything that belongs to the service of God.

To this devotion thou shalt never attain by any natural means, because it is itself supernatural, and is practiced by supernatural assistance.

Unless, therefore, thou art aided by divine grace, thou shalt labor in vain; even shouldst thou declare thyself devoted to Me, and appear so in thy own estimation.

Pray, then, that thou mayst receive plentiful grace, and obtain the spirit of devotion. Thou shalt obtain it, if thou prayest well. All things are promised to prayer.

With the aid of grace, and the co-operation of thy own endeavors, true devotion,—which to many, guided by self-love, is known by name only or appears a burden,—shall be easy and sweet to thee.

Whether thou hast sensible consolations or not, thou wilt continue, in peace and with fruit, to transact thy affairs, to fulfill thy duties, and to be faithful to thy spiritual practices.

Without anxiety and solicitude, thou wilt repose in the arms of My Providence, as an infant on the bosom of its mother: and thou shalt be calm and contented in the various ways, through which I may lead thee to life everlasting.

6. *The voice of the Disciple.*—Lord Jesus, who for my salvation, didst consume Thyself, and, as an evidence of Thy love, didst leave me Thy Heart, delivered up for love of me: grant me, I beseech Thee, the grace of a perfect devotion, that everything, except Thyself, being withdrawn from my heart, through love of Thee, I may become wholly Thine.

Relying upon the aid of Thy grace, which I humbly implore, I offer myself, with all my heart, to Thee, that I may be thoroughly devoted to Thee, to Thy service, and Thy interests.

O sweetest Jesus! receive me, all I am, and all I possess, as given and consecrated to Thee: grant me the spirit of holy devotion, that it may fill my heart with its unction; make piety tasteful to me, foster my love for Thee, render prayer sweet to me, and dispose me rightly for action.

Enlivened by it, I will continue ever joyous and constant in Thy service; I will gently draw my neighbor to Thee, and gladden the Angels and Saints themselves; yea, what is more excellent than all, I will rejoice Thy Heart, and fill It with delights.

CHAPTER IV.

THAT WE MUST BE TAUGHT BY THE SACRED HEART OF JESUS, NEWLY-BORN, AND BE IMBUED WITH ITS SPIRIT.

1. *The voice of the Disciple.*—Come ye and see, all ye creatures! wonder and be astonished: Behold! God bowed the heavens, and came down, and lo! He dwells with us!

O infant God! O prodigy of love! O delight of the Angels, who came from heaven, to gaze upon Thee reclining in this manger!

O Jesus, Son of God, born of a Virgin! how lovely! how sweet to me art Thou, thus become an Infant!

Wonderful indeed, in the Majesty of Thy Divinity: more wonderful, in the loveliness of Thy littleness.

Supremely worthy of love, in the boundlessness of Thy divine perfections: ravishing all hearts by the excess of Thy childhood's sweetness.

Who, O infinite goodness! can here be satiated with gazing upon Thee, with loving Thee, with inebriating himself with the delightfulness of Thy Heart's love!

How sweet art Thou! O my Jesus! how sweet art Thou, besides what lies hidden within! what then must be Thy inner Spirit? A most exquisite one, assuredly, and sweet above honey.

2. *The voice of Jesus.*—Yea, My Child, it is the Spirit of My Heart, that produces, that quickens these wonderful, these most delightful things.

This Spirit of Mine,—that, by love, drew Me from the bosom of the Father into the bosom of the Virgin; and that, with so much sweetness, brought Me, the Only-begotten of the Father, upon earth,— this Spirit ever pervades, directs, and leads My Heart, that whithersoever the impulse of the Spirit is, thither It may go.

The fullness of this Spirit dwells in My Heart: for, whom God has sent, to Him He does not give the Spirit by measure.

Upon My Heart that Spirit reposes, the Spirit of wisdom and understanding, the Spirit of counsel and fortitude, the Spirit of knowledge and piety, the Spirit of the fear of God, the Spirit of grace and prayer, the Spirit of love.

Such is the Spirit of My Heart; a supernatural, divine Spirit, who is charity, a love embracing all virtues.

This Spirit of My Heart, is love breathing love; gently and strongly leading, He directs to things perfect, moves to make sacrifices, allures to deeds heroic.

3 Blessed is he, My Child, who possesses the divine Spirit of My Heart, and allows himself to be guided, in all things, by the same! For they who are impelled by the Spirit of God, the same are the sons of God.

Not appearance, nor profession, but the Spirit makes thee a true Disciple of My Heart.

What will all else avail thee, if thou dost not possess this Spirit? He that has not My Spirit, is not of Mine.

Without My Spirit, the things which I do, shall have no meaning for thee; thou wilt not rightly understand what I teach; nor wilt thou find a hearty relish, for what I enjoin. Thou canst know, understand, and enjoy the things, which are Mine, only insomuch as thou shalt be possessed of My Spirit.

If thou art endowed with My Spirit, My judgments shall be thy judgments: My sentiments, thy sentiments: the life of My Heart, the life of thy heart.

In this Spirit, every true Disciple of My Heart, views all things: by this alone, he judges of all things: by this alone, he acts, and is impelled.

Be, then, possessed of the Spirit of My Heart, and do whatsoever thou wilt: this Spirit will guide thee safely, and protect thee in all things.

4. This, My Spirit, has influenced all the Saints: Its unction taught them, Its virtues strengthened them, Its holiness shaped them.

See, what It taught the Apostles and Martyrs, the Confessors and Virgins: behold, to what degree It strengthened them: see how It formed them, so that, trampling upon the whole world, and forsaking themselves, some went to the tortures of death, as if they were hastening to a glorious triumph; others endeavored to equal the Angels themselves; others again, trod blamelessly the common walks of life: but all followed Me with cheerfulness, and kept themselves to the end, in My company, amid all the vicissitudes of earth.

What is there, which the Saints, incited by My Spirit, did not undertake? what did they not do, that, whilst sanctifying themselves, they might ever love and glorify Me, more and more, and, as far as they were able, bring all men to love and glorify Me?

These were perfect Disciples of My Heart; filled with My holy Spirit, they drew thence all their thoughts, regulated all their words, directed all their works, and shaped their whole life.

5. My Child, if thou desirest to learn this Spirit of My Heart, study My life, and meditate devotedly thereon; enter into the interior of My Heart, and affectionately examine and weigh Its sentiments: by Its fruits thou shalt know the same everywhere.

Dost thou not find My Spirit working in all, and in every mystery of My life?

What will it avail to know My Spirit, unless thou receivest of Its fullness? Pray then, My Child, pray fervently, that thou mayst be quickened by It, or obtain an increase of Its quickening.

If thou prayest, as it behooves thee, thou wilt doubtless receive It: for I have promised to give My good Spirit to them that ask.

The better, and the more thou prayest, the more thou shalt receive of the same, the more perfectly thou shalt know It, and the more easily thou shalt follow its guidance.

6. *The voice of the Disciple.* O Jesus! of the fullness of whose Spirit, Thy Disciples so receive, as to live thereby, send, I beseech Thee, the Spirit of Thy Heart into my heart, that It may quicken and guide me in all and through all.

Neither, as Eliseus asked Elias, do I beg that Thy twofold Spirit may dwell in me, since my little heart cannot even contain Thy single one; but I entreat Thee, replenish me wholly with Thy Spirit, expel from me forever the spirit of the world, and the spirit of self.

Grant that, in Thy Spirit, my heart may rightly

relish that wherein Thy Heart delights; understand whatever It teaches; taste in a manner affective, as well as effective, whatever It does.

Grant me to live, hereafter, by Thy Spirit, not simply the life of nature, but of grace; not simply a human life, but one, in some manner, god-like, the life of Thy Spirit.

CHAPTER V.

THAT, OF THE MOST SACRED HEART OF JESUS, WHILST AN INFANT, WE MUST LEARN HUMILITY.

1. *The voice of the Disciple.*—How, O Jesus! art Thou born for us a Child, and given to us an Infant! Art not Thou Who Art: is not this Thy name forevermore?

Who shall declare Thy generation! Behold! Thou art from eternity to eternity.

Who shall speak Thy power, or make known Thy other perfections? Through Thee, all things were made: by Thee, all are ruled: Thou fillest the heavens and the earth: and lo! in what a state do I behold Thee here!

O prodigy! O miracle! God, behold! the infinite God, lies here an Infant, in this cave!

He emptied Himself, having become a Child, an exile in the midst of humiliations, unknown and contented.

How, O most sweet Jesus, how, I beseech Thee, wast Thou born a Babe, and given us as a Child?

2. *The voice of Jesus.*—My Child, I came to save

that which was lost. So great was the fall of the human race that its restoration demanded such an humiliation of the Son of God.

Man had sunk into the abyss of pride: in lowliness I came down, and entered the abyss, to snatch him thence.

Before I came into the world, pride had so far darkened and corrupted the minds of nations, that they not only did not acknowledge humility as a virtue; but, on the contrary, deemed it weakness of soul, and were shocked thereat.

For when they knew God, whose light is placed as a seal upon the human heart, they glorified Him not as God; they became vain in their thoughts and their foolish heart was darkened: they grew corrupt and abominable in their desires. Thus, well-nigh all flesh had corrupted its way.

What could be better, and more effective, to free the world from so great and baneful an error, than the example of a God, supremely wise and perfect, abasing Himself unto emptiness, thus confounding all human pride, and refuting forever its false reasonings and pretenses.

3. Pride, My Child, has ever been and will continue to be the source of all evils; but humility is the principle of all good things.

Truth begets humility, which is the virtue of virtues, and charity gives it life and form.

First of all, then, thoroughly know thyself and God, that thou mayst attribute to God the things which are of God, and to thyself what is thy own.

Take care, therefore, My Child, to understand what thou art of thyself. What art thou of thyself? What, except a mere nothing, out of which

God created thee? This nothingness is thy own, but the being which thou art, is of God.

If thou thinkest that thou art something, whereas, of thyself, thou art nothing, thou deceivest, thou misleadest thyself.

What dost thou possess of thyself, by nature, or by grace? In the order of nature, thou hast, indeed, the powers of the soul, the senses of the body, the gifts of the mind, the outward qualities of person. But whence did all these things, of what kind soever they be, come to thee? Whose are they? Take away that which God made, and gave to thee, and what remains, except nothingness? This latter, again, is thy own, the former is of God.

In giving thee these things, He gave them for an end, that thou mightst use them for His glory, and for thy salvation. If thou hast ever made use of all and every one of them, for that end, thou hast done what thou wast obliged to do. If, at any time, thou hast made an ill use of them, behold! beside thy nothingness, thou must claim also as thy own, ungratefulness, frowardness, and the mis-spending of God's favors.

Now, what art thou in the order of grace? My Child, is not this a fathomless abyss? It is certain that of thyself, without the help of grace, thou possessest nothing which can promote thy salvation; thou canst do nothing to save thyself. Whatsoever, therefore, thou hast of the supernatural order; whatever virtues, whatever merits, thou mayst possess; all these are the effects of grace, without which they could not even have been begun, much less brought to perfection. If, then, God rewards these things in thee, He does but crown His own gifts.

It is, indeed, true, My Child, that to acquire these things thou didst co-operate with grace. But this very co-operation, if duly considered, what does it disclose? It is evident, by faith, that thou must one day give a strict account of every grace. For, thou art obliged to cause each grace to produce its fruit by thy co-operation.

Did not this consideration fill the very Saints with the lowliest sentiments? What thoughts, then, must it needs force upon thee, who so often ill co-operatest with grace, nay, even slightest it?

If thou art unable to count the shortcomings of thy co-operation with grace, ponder the number and magnitude of the debts thou hast contracted, by the neglect or ill use of the gifts of God, in addition to thy own nothingness, and powerlessness, in the order of grace.

My Child, if thou rightly considerest the obligation of co-operating with God's grace, and of making a proper use of His gifts, even of thos in the natural order; thou wilt understand, as the Saints understood it, that the more and the greater the favors thou didst receive, the greater reason thou hast tor deeply humbling thyself.

4. But there are things worse and more humiliating hidden from the sight. See and examine thy manifold miseries, offenses, and sins: and weigh well, what thou hast justly deserved thereby.

Hadst thou received what is rightly due to thee, shouldst thou not long since have felt the contempt of all the inhabitants of heaven, of earth, and of hell, and suffered everlasting degradation?

And if, perhaps, thou hast done naught on account of which thou deservest to be cast away, thou

hast no cause to be elated. For, that thou wast
thus kept from grievous faults, is not thy own, but
chiefly the work of grace.

Nay more, by one venial transgression, committed against the infinite Majesty of God, thou didst
deserve greater humiliations than the world can inflict upon thee.

5. What, then, My Child, what art thou? What
compared with all men? Nothing more than a
drop of water compared with all the oceans. And
what are all men viewed in connection with all the
myriads of Angels? Assuredly less than this earth
is to the boundless heavens. And what are all the
angels in comparison with God Himself? Behold!
they are as if they were not; because the difference
is infinite. Now, compared with the infinite God,
what art thou, a puny being, dwelling in a little
corner of this globe?

What art thou, in truth, My Child, or what dost
thou possess, to make thee proud? yea, what hast
thou for which thou shouldst not humble thyself?

I do not say these things to cause thee to blush,
but to give thee warning, thee, well-beloved Child of
My Heart, lest, misled by pride, thou fall away and
perish.

6. To God alone be honor and glory, from every
creature. He alone is truly and exceedingly worthy to receive empire, and power, and benediction
and praise, and supreme worship, forever and ever

All the perfections seen in creatures, how excellent soever they may appear, are only darksome
rays of God's perfections, which are every way absolute and infinite.

Even had God not so commanded, His boundless

perfections should have to be acknowledged and honored by every reason-gifted being.

Nay more, His own glory is so essentially to be referred to God, that He Himself cannot be indifferent in its regard: for He alone is worthy of Himself.

7. Precious, My Child, is the knowledge of God and of thyself, for it reveals a great truth, most fit to humble thee. Yet this knowledge itself is not humility, since virtue consists not in knowledge but in affection.

Neither does the virtue of humility consist in humiliation, but rather in the love of humiliation. For, there is no virtue, unless there be affection, or motion of a good will.

How many there are who humble themselves, or are humbled by others, and yet are not humble! how many do outwardly give signs of humility, and yet keep pride within themselves.

In order that humility be a virtue, such as that of My Disciples ought to be, and that self-abasement be an act of such a virtue, it must receive its life and form from charity, or supernatural affection.

The virtue of humility is that supernatural affection which inclines and moves thee, always so to tend to thy proper place, that thou givest to God the things which belong to God, thanksgiving, honor, glory; and ascribest to thyself whatsoever is thine, nothingness and unworthiness of every kind.

Now, which is thy own proper place? O My Child, how deep, how terrible is that place which thou hast deserved! But see the love of My Heart! To console thee, to exalt thee. I became man, humbled Myself in thy stead, and assigned thee a better and more honorable place. Since that time, thy place is with Me.

But where shalt thou be with Me? where shalt thou find Me? An Infant in the manger, exiled and unknown in Egypt, hidden at Nazareth, toiling and suffering in public, occupying the last place, and dying therein.

8. With Me, Child, thou shalt be far from pride, which is hateful to God and men, begets every sin, corrupts every virtue, despoils of merits, heaps up punishments, despises the example of My Heart, follows the footsteps of the devil.

Happy lowliness! blissful virtue, which makes thee find favor with God and men! For, whilst God resists the proud, He gives His grace to the lowly; and, whilst the proud themselves look down upon the proud, they admire the humble.

Humility is the first of virtues: no virtue is acquired without it. Humility produces all other virtues, nourishes them when produced, and preserves them safe and sound.

A noble virtue is humility, which makes man truly generous and great-souled. By its means he overcomes, not only what is most arduous, but he even conquers himself.

Whilst the proud man, with his narrow heart, fettered by the dread of humiliation, which may, perhaps, befall him, struggles with himself, shrinking back at one time, hesitating at another, whether or not to assail the difficulty placed before him; the humble one, with a great and expanded heart, has already subdued himself, overcome the difficulty, and marches onward rejoicingly.

It is the virtue that inspires courage—disposes the soul for the greatest deeds. For the humble man, overlooking himself, and relying upon God, exchanges his own strength, and puts on the strength of God, upon whom he rests, and in whom he can do all things.

He is an object of terror to the very demons. These enemies dread the humble: no other mortals do they fear so much.

Lastly, it is a solid virtue, because it so strengthens man, that he is neither shaken by the sayings or doings of others, nor cast down by his own faults or miseries.

It is not, therefore, the virtue of humility, but its counterfeit, which renders thee fainthearted, timorous, or in any wise dejected. So noble a virtue does not produce such ignoble effects.

9. My Child, although humility is so just, so useful, so necessary, so excellent, thou shouldst notwithstanding know, that it is not according to human feelings, not to find one's delight in some object, but in all things to refer absolutely the whole glory to God,—to attribute to one's self nothing except unworthiness,—to be contented with Me in the lowest place, to embrace heartily whatever My Heart embraces.

Certainly, if thou consultest nature, it will shrink back from such things, and seek to avoid them. Yet, if thou desirest to be a Disciple of My Heart, thou must not follow nature, but grace: and act, not according to the bent of thy natural feeling, but according to divine love, whereby thou mayst imitate My Heart, even in spite of nature.

If thou dost this, it will be with thee as it was

with the Saints, who tasted a sweetness exceeding nature, in humility, and found by experience that humiliations themselves were full of delight.

Secure for thyself, by prayer and meditation, the powerful help of grace, and, generously co-operating with the same, embrace humility with mind and heart,—exercise thyself in it, until thou art able readily to reduce it to practice in thought, word, and deed.

My Child, be ever mindful of My example, and forget not My words. Behold! I, an Infant, give thee a new command, the command of My Heart: Learn of Me, that I am meek and humble of Heart.

10. *The voice of the Disciple.*—O most sweet Jesus! O Infant God, who didst empty Thyself by humility! Lo! the stable, wherein Thou dwellest, the darkness, wherein Thou art hidden, the very silence, that surrounds Thee, all cry out, how humble of Heart Thou art.

O Thou Teacher of humility! behold me prostrate at Thy feet, that of Thee I may learn that all-important virtue.

Enlightened and enkindled by the flames of Thy Heart, may I ever know Thee, ever know myself, that thus I may always and everywhere ascribe to Thee what is Thine, and to me what is mine!

Hitherto, I own it, I have never rightly understood the meaning of humility. Now I understand, now I see, that by the virtue of humility I am neither debased nor disgraced, but raised and ennobled; since by it I am elevated to the resemblance of Thyself, who alone art eminently noble.

O most kind Jesus! givest Thou me a place near Thee! O Lord! I am not worthy. And yet, how did I ever seek any other place, as if I could find a better place than with Thee! Forgive, O Lord, forgive my ungratefulness, my injustice, my madness.

Henceforth, behold, I am forever with Thee. Let them seek after higher places, who are anxious to be above others: for myself, as much as I am allowed, I will strive for the lowest, convinced that there I shall be with Thee. My only longing is to be with Thee: with Thee I will be contented wherever I may be.

CHAPTER VI.

THAT THE MOST SACRED HEART OF JESUS, BORN IN A STABLE, TEACHES US HOLY POVERTY.

1. *The voice of the Disciple.*—For Thee, Lord Jesus, for Thee, my heart longs: Thee, my soul seeks, whom she loves. Show me, I entreat Thee, where Thou dwellest.

The voice of Jesus.—Come, My Child, and see. This shall be a sign to thee: thou shalt find Me poor, in a stable.

Hearken thou, and give heed to what My Heart may speak to thee.

The foxes have their holes, the birds of the air have their nests: but the Son of man has not where to recline His head.

Yet, My Child, the whole earth is Mine, and the fulness thereof. But, behold! when I was the richest, I became the poorest of all.

From the time I was born needy in the stable,

until I breathed My last destitute upon the cross, I lived ever in perfect poverty, and as I ever loved it as My mother, so I ever honored it as a Son.

And for what reason, thinkest thou, with what design does My Heart so lovingly embrace poverty? Undoubtedly, My Child, because My Heart, filled as It is with humility and charity, cherishes these virtues most tenderly, and desires most ardently, by their means, to draw the hearts of men from things earthly and perishable, and raise them aloft to that which is heavenly and everlasting.

2. Blessed are the poor in spirit, for theirs is the kingdom of heaven: blessed, for that they are free from the greatest obstacles to everlasting salvation: blessed, for that they possess a wholesome opportunity of practicing numberless virtues: blessed, lastly, because in their heart, they are conformed to Me.

My Child, to have nothing, nay, even to be in want, is not the virtue of poverty: but to keep the heart disengaged from the created things of the world; this constitutes the true virtue of poverty. For love of Me, to bid farewell to all things of earth, to possess nothing as one's own, to cling with the heart to no created object, is the perfection of the virtue of poverty.

To this latter all are not called, but to the former all and every one must tend, insomuch, that it is easier for a camel to pass through the eye of a needle, than for any one without it to enter the kingdom of heaven.

For, unless a man renounce, with the heart at least, all things, he cannot be My Disciple.

3. There is nothing more wicked than the love

of money, for this love perverts the judgment, and misleads the heart: and, since all things obey money, he that loves it, blinded by its inordinate desire, sets his own soul for sale, so that he is ready to sell this immortal gift for a perishable object.

The Saints used the things of earth, with a heart free from them; amid the greatest wealth, they were poor in spirit.

Yet, there are not a few who allow the enemy of man's salvation to deceive them, by the appearance of what is good or right. That crafty foe strives to persuade men that riches, or the abundance of the good things of earth,—as they are indifferent in themselves, and may be usefully spent,—can be coveted and sought after without danger.

But, whosoever suffers himself to be so deceived, soon discovers, that he has become entangled in the snares of the devil's artifices, that he is weighed down by troubles, darkness, perverse inclinations; that, whatever his state of life, he is unable to attain to its perfection; and that, finally, he imperils, in no small degree, his everlasting salvation.

4. My Child, if thou hast riches, set not thy heart upon them: for thou art a steward, rather than a master. With a heart disengaged from them, either renounce them altogether, if such be the divine Will, or use them for My glory, and for the real benefit of thy soul.

Thou must be so disposed that, if it be My Will, thou shouldst renounce all things, or, if I suffer thee to be deprived of them, thou do willingly submit thyself to Me.

If thou art poor, rejoice, My Child, and be exceedingly glad: and lose not the fruit of so great a blessing, by suffering, repiningly, the effects of poverty.

Be not ashamed of being in moderate, or even destitute circumstances, for My sake, who was not ashamed of becoming destitute for thee: but rather glory, for that thou possessest what I purchased for Myself, by many and great humiliations.

5. Whether thou art needy, or rich, cherish holy poverty, and practice a virtue so dear to My Heart and so advantageous to thyself.

There is, indeed, no condition of life in which this virtue may and should not be practiced: frequent opportunities daily present themselves everywhere.

This great virtue may be exercised in regard to one's dwelling-place, furniture, food and drink; in short, the whole manner of living.

For, in all these things, either something is wanting, which is not really necessary; or, if not, it is not according to the desires of nature; or something may, without danger, be withdrawn from what is had for nature's convenience.

If thou lovest holy poverty in thy heart, as is proper, thou shalt not want means and opportunities of practicing the same.

How many poor there are who do not gather any merit from their poverty, but use it to make themselves more wretched, and to offend God! Would that they were wise! then, instead of bitterness, they would taste sweetness, and sanctify themselves.

6. The name of the poor in spirit, who love and practice poverty,—whether it arises from necessity

or free choice,—is honorable before Me. With them, I hold fellowship and intercourse; their heart is like a fertile soil, which receives the seed of My words, and brings forth fruit a hundred-fold.

Who is happier than the possessor of holy poverty, who has whatever he desires in this world? Who is richer than he, to whom belongs the kingdom of heaven?

Do not then, My Child, neglect thy sanctification, for the sake of gathering treasures on earth: use thy endeavors principally to sanctify thyself, and thus to lay up treasures in heaven.

Wheresoever the object of thy affections may chance to be, where thy treasure is, there also will be thy heart.

7. True it is, that for man, left to himself, it is very difficult to despise in his heart riches, and to practice poverty in deed, and in affection.

Thou shouldst, therefore, pray fervently, that divine grace may help thee to perform that, which thy own strength does not enable thee to accomplish in a meritorious manner.

If thou perceivest within thyself feelings opposed to poverty, persevere in prayer, and beg the more fervently, even against thy inclinations, that grace may not spare those inordinate feelings, but root them out completely, until thy heart is altogether free, and looks solely to the Will and glory of God.

My Child, if once the affections of thy heart are well-ordered, thou wilt find, through divine grace, the virtue of poverty not only easy, but even full of sweetness.

8. *The voice of the Disciple.*—O sweet Jesus, Son of God! Thou holdest and swayest the whole

universe: Thou didst adorn the heavens with glittering stars: Thou didst embellish the earth with wonderful splendor; and behold! here Thou reclinest in a poor stable, a Babe hardly covered with tattered clothes.

O how marvelous, how salutary are the disposings of Thy Heart! Who will not, after so great an example,—which ravishes the very Angels,—consider poverty lovely and desirable!

Good Jesus, Teacher of the Truth, and model of holy poverty! enlighten my mind, that I may understand the price of this virtue, and tear away my heart, even in spite of itself, from every inordinate affection for things created, lest, busied with various cares and desires, it become estranged from Thee.

Grant, I beseech Thee, that I may look upon all the things of time as speedily vanishing, and upon myself as passing away with them to things everlasting; allow me the use of the possessions of earth, only insomuch as they are means to guide me to heavenly possessions.

Everything is Thine, O Lord: if, then, Thou desirest me to live in opulence, as the steward of Thy possessions, Thy Will be done: if Thou desirest me to be in poverty, a perfect follower of Thy life, again Thy Will be done.

Yet, so far as it is left to me, and as it is pleasing to Thee, I choose rather to be poor with Thee, O Jesus, the Son of God, than to be rich with the world: I prefer to possess the lasting blessings of poverty, rather than undergo the ceaseless dangers of riches.

I offer myself, therefore, to Thee, most benign

Jesus, as a companion of Thy poverty: I implore Thee as such to receive me. If with Thee, I am contented: if I possess Thee, I am rich enough.

CHAPTER VII.

THAT THE MOST SACRED HEART OF JESUS, DWELL-ING IN SOLITUDE AMONG THE ANGELS, TEACHES US HOLY CHASTITY.

1. *The voice of Jesus.*—Come, My Child, come to the solitude of the sacred Cave: here will I speak to thy heart: here will I unvail for thee the secrets of My Heart.

Here look around: attend to what thou perceiv-est: see, what surrounds Me: observe the objects which keep Me company.

The voice of the Disciple.—O Lord, I perceive Thy Virgin Mother, Thy Virgin Foster-father, a multitude of Angels, rejoicing and singing, in Thy presence, hymns of jubilee. I see Thee, O Jesus, most beautiful, the Lamb of God, without blemish! I behold before me innocence far removed from every object that flatters the senses, ravishing heaven and earth by its loveliness.

The voice of Jesus.—Amid these, My Child, My Heart rejoices, and finds Its delight, because It feeds on purity among the lilies.

I am holiness itself. Born of a pure Virgin, nourished by a pure Virgin; I am the most tender lover of all purity, and shrink, with all My Heart, from every object which is hurtful or contrary to this virtue.

2. My Heart is the fountain of holy purity, whence all they draw, who desire to be loved by Me.

From this divine fountain, all the Disciples of My Heart drink in the love of chastity, each one according to his capacity; and by this love, as by a certain mark, are they distinguished.

What is more excellent than chastity, whereby thou offerest to God the Father, who is a Spirit, a spiritual sacrifice most grateful to Him; whereby, honoring thy body, thou honorest My own members; whereby thou payest reverence to the Holy Ghost, whose temple thou art?

This is the virtue which transforms men into Angels; yea, raises them above the heavenly Spirits.

My Child, whosoever is chaste, is an Angel: nay more, in merit, he surpasses the Angel, since, in spite of nature, he becomes through virtue, what the Angel is, without effort, by nature.

This is the glory of the Church, the triumph of grace, the flower of life, the ornament of the body and soul, the fairest picture of heaven.

3. How beautiful is a chaste life! Immortal is the remembrance thereof; because it is known to God, and grateful to men.

A marvelous virtue it is, which imparts its freshness and beauty, not only to the soul but even to the body.

What the lily is among flowers, that purity is among virtues; by its celestial brightness and elegance, it delights and refreshes the very inhabitants of Paradise.

So much does its loveliness captivate all hearts that, even in the world, there is none, unless he has altogether lost his reason, who does not admire its excellence.

4. Man, with a clean heart and chaste body, enters heaven; passes even into the sanctuary of the Divinity, and enjoys the familiar intercourse of God and His Angels.

The carnal man, like a senseless animal wallowing in filth, understands not the things which are of the Spirit, but finds his delight among sensual objects, the fruits of which are alike destructive to soul and body.

How wretched is he that is impure! how debased in the sight of heaven and earth! how like in his interior to the demon, who is called the unclean spirit!

The world, submerged by the Flood, bears witness how this loathsome vice is punished; so does the land of Sodom, laid waste with fire and brimstone from above; so does every unchaste man, delivered up to his reprobate sense; so, above all, does hell.

Purity, on the other hand, saves from the tyranny of the passions, imparts a most delightful peace, fills the whole man with heavenly joys; yea, adorns him with the seal of the Elect.

5. Which, My Child, are the chief delights of My Heart? Are they not pure souls? These are they that by the purity of their love, fill My Heart with most pleasure; these busy themselves more frequently about Me; solicitous to know, how, above all others, they may render themselves agreeable to Me; these, being both inwardly and out-

wardly more holy, long more fervently to live for
Me.

These are they that understand more easily the
secrets of My Heart, enjoy with more relish the
unction of My Spirit, are more glowing with piety,
and are wont to be more generous and faithful.

To these My Heart, in return, communicates Itself more abundantly; upon them, It pours the
streams of more perfect love and consolation; for
them, It reserves more special graces and favors.

Them I admit into the innermost sanctuary of
My Heart: with them I treat in a more intimate
manner; them I keep nearer to Me upon earth, as
well as in heaven.

In whatever condition of life, therefore, thou
mayst be, if thou wishest to be as dear as possible
to My Heart: if thou desirest to experience the
fullness of Its tenderness: if thou longest to taste,
in the most copious manner, Its sweetness, be thou
pure in body and soul.

6. My Child, this treasure thou carriest in a frail
vessel; unless thou proceedest cautiously, thou wilt
easily lose the same. Take heed, however, lest
thou advance too warily; for an excessive fear becomes a source of danger.

Thou must, first of all, guard thy heart, watch
over its inclinations, check its thoughts. For, if
thou allowest thy heart to wander about, it shall
not long continue unstained.

Be never altogether idle: idleness is the dwelling-place of the unclean spirit.

Desire not to be too familiar with any mortal,
even were he a Saint, or a worker of miracles.

Fly dangerous occasions, as thou wouldst a pestilence. How many there are, who, though else-where sufficiently secure, perish here miserably.

7. Turn away thy eyes, lest they behold the seductions of vanity; be modest: without modesty, chastity cannot endure.

Hedge in thy ears with care, lest, through them, the enemy find access to thy heart. For, where there is no hedge, the possession shall be laid waste.

Keep the tongue not only from unclean words, but also from all scurrility, and every kind of language, of which the devil may take advantage to tempt thee or others.

Restrain the taste in such a manner, that thy temperance in food and drink hinder the flesh from rebelling, and endow and strengthen the spirit with vigor.

Mortify the touch assiduously, not only in those things which, when unlawfully touched, may cause thee to die the death, but also in those which, savoring of sensuality, may, by the aid of Satan, arouse the passions.

8 Be persuaded, however, My Child, that, after thou hast done all this, thou art not able to preserve this most precious, most beautiful, yea, most useful and necessary virtue, except with the help of divine grace.

Wherefore, thou shouldst frequently and earnestly ask for this heavenly gift, and beg for it by fervent prayer, through the intercession of My Virgin Mother, My Virginal Foster-father, thy Guardian Angel, and, finally, of all the inhabitants of heaven.

The enemy, knowing that, through purity. men

become associated with the choirs of Angels, and merit among them that place which he, by his uncleanness, has forfeited, raves with envy, and leaves nothing undone, to despoil men of this virtue.

But let not thy heart fear, My Child, nor be disturbed; My grace is sufficient for thee, provided by neglecting the proper means, thou be not wanting to thyself.

9. Be exceedingly careful, lest thou expose thyself rashly to dangers; and, after having overcome temptations, do not ascribe the glory of the victory to thyself: for, since all this springs from pride, it will doubtless be punished with a disgraceful humiliation.

Through grace, thou shalt be the more chaste, the more humble thou art: for it is humility which deserves that chastity be given. My Child, be ever mindful of these words.

If thou wilt be perfect in the virtue of chastity, be inflamed with a god-like love for Me: for no one, unless he be perfect in the love of Jesus, can be perfect in chastity; but whosoever loves Jesus perfectly, shall be perfectly chaste, perfectly pure. Keep this secret in thy memory, keep it in thy heart.

10. *The voice of the Disciple.*—O Jesus, Thou Virgin of Virgins! whose Mother is a Virgin, whose Foster-father is a Virgin, whose inseparable companions are Angels; whom when I approach, I am clean; whom when I love, I am chaste: endless thanks to Thee, for that Thou didst keep my heart free from the love of all carnal pleasure, and didst enkindle it with the love of holy purity.

All they that love Thee, behold! are hastening

after Thee, drawn by the odor of Thy most delightful innocence, and, as closely as they can, they are
following Thee, the Lamb, whithersoever Thou
goest.

O Jesus, Thou lover of chaste souls! grant me,
I implore Thee, for love of Thee, with all the Disciples of Thy Heart, to value supremely, to love most
tenderly this virtue of Angels, and shun with the
greatest abhorrence, all that is contrary thereto.

Sanctify my heart and body with Thy love, that
I may serve Thee with a chaste body, and please
Thee with a clean heart.

O Jesus, my love and my God! who didst create
me in Thy likeness, permit not that I ever sully or
unhallow it by any defilement.

Suffer not, that for a short-lived pleasure,—for
which I must, either now or afterwards, endure
shame and punishment,—I lose that virtue, which
is my present and future glory and felicity.

If ever, O most sweet Jesus, Thy love should
find me insensible to the loveliness and the rewards
of purity; I beseech Thee, let the dread of the
everlasting flames of hell, prevent the flame of vice.

CHAPTER VIII.

THAT FROM THE MANGER THE MOST SACRED HEART
OF JESUS, TEACHES US HOLY OBEDIENCE.

1. *The voice of Jesus.*—Be attentive, My Child:
thou must hear some things which thou hast never
learnt, never sufficiently understood.

Learn once for all of My Heart, and remember what obedience is. Lo! from this moment even to My latest sigh, obedience is My food, My life.

Observe intently and devotedly My example; consider the dispositions of My Heart.

Behold, if they put Me in a rough manger, I remain contented therein: if they lift Me in their arms, I am content to be carried: wheresoever they place Me, there I stay contented.

Whatever be the wish of those whom My heavenly Father has given authority over Me, that do I will likewise: I have no other will than to will or not to will that which they will.

Neither does My Heart ask, why they will Me here or there: the judgment of the authority that wills, is the judgment of Myself who obey.

2. Thus, My Child, did I, the All-knowing and All-powerful Lord, subject Myself most humbly to creatures, that thou, weak in understanding and will, mayst learn to submit thyself to them that hold My place in thy regard.

Be, therefore, obedient to them, with a humble heart, in all things wherein they have authority over thee, whether it be in temporal or in spiritual matters. For all power is from God.

Wherefore, My Child, when thou obeyest thy Superior, thou obeyest Me. For thou art obedient and submissive to the authority communicated to him by Me.

3. If the Superior be devoid of virtue and good qualities, this is no reason why thou shouldst obey him the less. For he does not, on that account, the less possess My authority, and hold My place.

Whenever he enjoins things which are not evidently opposed to Me, heed thou, and perform whatsoever he may say: but thou art not obliged to follow him in his doings.

Be not concerned, My Child, about the qualifications of the one that commands, but attend to that which is commanded: and perform it faithfully, as if commanded by Myself.

Let the Superior be whatever he may; let him act through this motive or that; what matters it to thee? follow thou Me: seek to imitate My Heart, My Will, and be not troubled or uneasy about the rest.

4. The simple performance of another's will is not the virtue of obedience. Do not irrational creatures do so? nay more, even machines made by the hand of man?

It is necessary, when thou dost the will of the Superior, to be willing to perform with a submissive heart, that which he wishes thee to do; that thus thou mayst cheerfully carry out My Will, made known through the Superior.

For, although it may happen that the Superior does command through ill-will or passion, it is yet My Will that, when no evil is commanded, thou perform, with a good heart, what the Superior requires. For the rest, I will judge the motive of the Superior, who commands, and of the inferior, who obeys; and render to each one that which is just.

My Child, do not imitate them who, deceiving themselves, endeavor, by direct or indirect means, to bring over the Superior to their own will. These, although, in this manner, they have the will and consent of the Superior, do not fulfil My Will, but their own: nor do they practice the virtue of obedience, but they obey self-love; nor are they guided by Me, but by themselves.

5. In order that the virtue of obedience be perfect, it is necessary that,—believing that whatever I require of thee through obedience is justly demanded,—thou submit also thy understanding or judgment to My divine authority, represented in the person of the Superior.

The less thou shalt see the reason of the things which are demanded of thee, and the more inconsistent that which is enjoined shall appear to thy manner of judging; so much the nobler shall be thy obedience, and so much the more merit shalt thou have, if thou submit thy understanding, and fulfill with a good will what is commanded.

Cast aside, therefore, without examination, whatsoever the pride of reason, or the repugnance of sense, may object, in the sincere belief that My divine Will, made known to thee through the Superior, rests upon the best and most certain motives, although thou thyself dost not see them.

It happens, frequently, that the inferior does not see, and that the Superior does not know, the true reasons for which, by the Superior's command, I desire such, or such other things to be done by the inferior. Both are not rarely unconscious instruments in the fulfillment of My secret designs.

If thou wert humble of heart, and burning with love for Me, it would not be hard, or difficult, to abandon, for My sake, thy judgment and will; and it would be most consoling and sweet to have thy weak understanding guided by My infinite Wisdom, and thy will, prone to evil, conformed to My divine Will, the rule of all good.

6. A great thing is obedience: a sublime virtue, whereby a person overcomes himself, and so dedicates himself wholly to Me, that he retains for himself nothing of his own, but offers himself entirely to Me, as a holocaust.

Do I desire other sacrifices without this one? Do I not rather require that I be obeyed? Better is obedience than a victim.

Who is stronger than the obedient man? The obedient man shall speak triumphantly; yea, shall triumph under all circumstances. For he aims at naught, except the doing of the divine Will, which he always secures.

What is there, My Child, which the obedient man dares not? He dares everything, when commanded; he brings to a favorable issue many and great things, whilst the disobedient loses courage and fails.

7. Nothing is safer or more secure than obedience. The obedient person is never lost; nor does he perish who submits his will and judgment to authority. But he that disobeys, he that follows his own judgment and will, to the neglect of authority, he is generally lost, and perishes.

The obedient man, certain of the reward of his actions, shall not even be held to an account: they that are placed over him, and direct him, shall be obliged to give the account.

8. Lastly, My Child, so necessary is obedience, that no works, howsoever good they be otherwise, if contrary thereto, can be pleasing to Me; nor can they acquire for thee any merits.

There is no state, no condition, no person on earth, that is not bound to obey. Without obedience, the order which God, who loves order necessarily, has established, could not be preserved.

Wherever thou mayst be placed by obedience, be assured, that thou couldst nowhere be better; and that thou canst do nothing more pleasing to Me, and more useful to thyself, than that which is enjoined by obedience.

Blessed are the obedient! they hasten on toward heaven, with true liberty, in great peace, in permanent security; but the disobedient groan beneath the galling tyranny of their own will: they enjoy no rest of heart, through a wearisome road they wander toward perdition.

9. My Child, whence is wont to arise the difficulty in obeying? Is it not from this, that thou regardest the person of the Superior, his qualifications. his manner of acting, or his motives for commanding? that thou considerest not, in singleness of faith, as thou shouldst, the divine authority and Will alone?

Such an example, My Child, I did not give. Such was not the disposition of My Heart. Although I was wiser and better than all the mortals who exercised authority over Me, yet I was heartily submissive to them, without considering the persons or their qualifications, without judging the motives which made them act or command.

Nay more, I did willingly and faithfully obey, as if it were the manifestation of My Father's Will, the command of Cesar Augustus, a pagan, who issued his decree with an evil-minded will: and, by complying with this order, I did really do My Father's Will—that I should be born in the city of Bethlehem, as the prophets inspired by the Holy Ghost had foretold.

Observe My whole life: thou wilt find it frequently distinguished by similar deeds.

Look, then, My Child, and act according to the example which My Heart has given thee. If thou do this, thou wilt find obedience easy, sweet, and full of consolation.

10. *The voice of the Disciple.*—O Jesus! how holy, how wonderful is Thy Heart! how great and profound the lessons It teaches! how easy It makes everything! Happy he that understands this!

Yea, blessed he that, taught by the example of Thy Heart, fulfills the divine Will with cheerfulness! Behold, such a one is guided by infinite Wisdom, helped by almighty Power, protected by the divine Goodness.

Who, save the obedient man, enjoys these favors? Let them preside and command who have received the power: for me, it is every way sweeter and better to be subject and obedient.

O truly happy me, if I am truly obedient! For the Lord God rules me, and I shall want nothing: set in a place of divine pasture, I roam secure therein; there never-failing streamlets of living waters flow; there Manna is daily showered down from heaven; there do I live for Thee, O Jesus; there do I surely and contentedly merit heaven.

By Thy most holy obedience, O Jesus, most meek and humble of Heart, grant me, I beseech Thee, Thy grace and Thy love, that I may be perfectly obedient, by renouncing my own will and judgment, and by following, in singleness of faith, Thy divine Will and authority, manifested to me through lawful Superiors.

Certainly, if I, blind-born as I am, follow self-love as a guide, what else awaits me, blind in my judgment and inclinations, except to fall into the pit and perish there?

I tremble in every limb, O Lord, when I call to mind that many men, distinguished for deep science and extraordinary human prudence, through want of obedience, have strayed from the way of salvation and become reprobates.

Behold, I devote and intrust myself altogether to Thy most wise, holy, and divine Will. Give me, I entreat Thee, Thy singleness of understanding, Thy readiness of Will: grant me the lowliness and charity of Thy Heart, that I may be like Thee, as an infant that remains contented, wheresoever it may be placed, whithersoever it may be carried; in short, in whatsoever manner it may be treated.

CHAPTER IX.

THAT, AT THE CIRCUMCISION, THE MOST SACRED HEART OF JESUS TEACHES US MORTIFICATION OF HEART.

1. *The voice of the Disciple.*—Scarcely yet art Thou come among us, O Thou the delight of heaven, sweet Jesus! and behold! Thou pourest out Thy Blood! Disclose to me, I pray, what was the design of Thy Heart therein: show me, I entreat Thee, what were then the feelings of Thy Heart. For, whatsoever, Thy Heart feels, I also long to feel.

The voice of Jesus.—My Child, thou oughtest to be so disposed, as not to stop at the things which thou perceivest by the senses; but so as to go forward even unto My very Heart.

Attend then, and consider how mortified is My Heart. I knew well that I was not at all bound by the law of Circumcision; that, by complying therewith, I should be reckoned among sinners, lowered before men; that My Body should undergo sufferings, and My Soul debasement; but My Heart, moved by the divine Will, enkindled by love as with a living flame, overcame all this.

Understand, My Child, the inner sentiments of My Heart, and be mindful of putting on the same.

All things were well-ordered in My Heart; there is naught inordinate in My whole Humanity. Yet, I did never act from a mere inclination of My human nature.

This I either overcame or passed by, and in all things, even those which were natural, I acted ever from a supernatural principle.

Whether the things, to be done or undergone, were pleasing or displeasing to the feelings of human nature; this was never the cause, or reason, why I did either embrace or shun them.

I was ever moved by the divine Will to do and suffer, with a willing Heart, all things that were according to the divine good pleasure.

2. Behold, My Child, the example which thou must follow, if thou desirest to be a true Disciple of My Heart.

If thou lookest well into thy heart, thou shalt find it divided, as it were, into two parts, each of which is anxious to sway it.

One of these, a sensual propensity, is called the inferior; the other, a rational inclination, the superior part. The former is especially vitiated by original sin: the latter is still guided by a supernal ray.

With the first, the spirit of evil is wont to harmonize; the good Spirit, on the other hand, espouses the cause of the second.

The inferior part struggles to extend its sway over the whole heart, and maintain it by means of pride and self-love, the leaders of all other vices.

The superior part, through humility and charity —which preside over the whole host of virtues— desires, with perfect justice, to rule, to conquer and subdue, as its foe, the part opposed.

3. These two parts, My Child, are the two domestic enemies that hardly ever cease to war against each other, whose aims are opposite,—that can be put down and subjugated, but never destroyed or exterminated.

The superior part, through the divine favor, by the freedom of its will, possesses such strength that not only the inferior part, but the whole world and all hell united, cannot force it to a surrender.

Therefore, the inferior part, together with the evil spirit, endeavors, by every possible means, to encompass, to disturb, to deceive, to worry the same. It tries every artifice: at one time violence, at another caresses; now perverseness, then uprightness; sometimes it shows itself an enemy, at others a friend.

Unless thou do carefully attend, thou wilt hardly be able to distinguish between them. Yet it is necessary to know them distinctly. For on this discernment depends the right governing of the heart; by it illusions are avoided, vain fears are made to disappear, inward peace is preserved and retained, even amid the greatest afflcitions.

The more one part is mortified and subdued, the more the other is made to live and triumph.

4. The first thing, therefore, to be deadened in thy heart is that inferior part, the inordinate craving of nature, which is also called selfishness, or the spirit of nature. Against this thou must never cease to fight.

If, at any time, this enemy, frightened by thy bravery, be put to flight, or forced to conceal himself—until a more favorable opportunity presents itself—do thou diligently seek him out, and, when found, strike him down with fresh ardor.

Thou wilt know him by this mark, that he ever aims immoderately at what is either too high or too low, being ever carried off by an inordinate liking, or dislike, beyond the order which divine Providence has established.

On the one hand, proud and wandering beyond his sphere, and relying on his own powers, he would fain search and look into the insearchable counsels of the Diety; and, although he does not fully comprehend aught of what is beneath him, yet, he would measure, by his own dullness and imbecility, the Wisdom, Power, and other perfections of God, which, in their very nature, are incomprehensible.

He struggles against admitting, what he does not both see and love.

He is ashamed and unwilling to own that he has erred: if it is proved, he grows stubborn.

He seeks to be prominent; he shrinks from the thought of being surpassed, or brought under in anything.

He takes for granted that he can do everything: if he has brought something to a prosperous issue, he is wonderfully self-pleased, and boasts as if he had performed a miracle: has he done aught unsuccessfully? he murmurs, excuses himself, or throws the blame upon others.

He is not concerned about what he is in reality, but about what he may appear to be before others: he seeks to be esteemed: he is anxious that others should speak of him: he longs to possess the affection of men.

He gains enough, if he is praised: if no one praise him, he himself makes up the deficiency.

In himself, he either sees no faults, or he disguises them: in his neighbor, he descries them everywhere.

He is prone to despise others; to suspect many things, and to twist them into evil.

Hence, on the other hand, he is ever inclined to what is low: what pleases the flesh, what flatters the senses, what savors of the world, he loves, he relishes.

He judges matters according to his own propensity, not according to the reality of the things themselves.

As he has himself for an end, he seeks in everything his own convenience or pleasure: he even endeavors betimes to adapt things divine to himself. For he undertakes occasionally to serve Me, whilst he desires to gratify himself.

Wherefore, he easily gives admittance to the

angel of darkness, who, taking the shape of an angel of light, suggests to him many things apparently pious, beautifully thought, tenderly felt: all which increases his pride, and keeps up his self-love.

5. My Child, if this spirit of nature triumphs over the heart, it effects the ruin of the heart.

It behooves thee, therefore, to deaden this part of the heart, by resisting it, by going counter thereto, and by unceasingly repressing the same, as long as it remains vitiated or ill-ordered.

Do not think this hard, My Child: it is incomparably more easy and pleasant to subdue the same, and govern it when subdued, than to be ruled and tormented thereby.

6. But, since natural reason cannot, by itself, attain to a supernatural end, thou must likewise, by mortification, purify and elevate the superior part of the heart.

For, if thou actest from natural reason alone, thou canst thence gather no merit for life everlasting; nor wilt thou be called a Disciple of My Heart.

Thou must, then, mortify the whole heart, and subject it to grace; so that, in all things, it obeys the divine good pleasure.

In thoughts, in words, in deeds, in sufferings, thou shouldst be moved by divine grace, guided by a supernatural reason, directed to Me as thy end.

Nowhere suffer thyself to be hurried into any act, by the mere motion or impulse of nature; but follow grace, act according to My Spirit.

Use the powers of nature, not as causes or principles, but as means or instruments for things supernatural.

7. This mortification of the heart—which is the rule of the interior life, and the spirit of the Saints—is that more useful and necessary mortification, whereby the roots of vices are plucked up, the dangers of temptations avoided, the very causes of inward troubles removed.

This holy mortification is to be practiced, not with fretfulness, harshness or anxiety, but with a tranquil and generous heart.

Now, My Child, in thy heart there are things so great and numerous to be mortified, and they lie so hidden from thee, that, unless enlightened by grace, thou couldst not so much as see them; and when thou seest them, unless strengthened by grace, thou mightst be overpowered by the sight of them.

Wherefore, thou must have recourse to prayer without intermission, that thou mayst obtain light and strength from above.

Then will I—knowing that, as yet, thou art unable to bear the knowledge of all the imperfections of thy heart—so gently order things, that thou mayst know and overcome them by degrees, since I will proportion the grace of strength to the grace of light.

And thou, My Child, must unremittingly be on thy guard, lest thou shut thy eyes to this light sent from above, or neglect to co-operate with this heaven-given strength. For this might be the beginning of thy downfall.

Be faithful: allow thyself to be led by grace in all and to all; and thou wilt experience such things as the Saints have experienced, whereby thou wilt doubtless come to My Heart, and God shall be exalted, and thou shalt be made holy; the more perfectly, the more closely thou shalt become assimilated to My Heart.

8. *The voice of the Disciple.*—O most kind and sweet Jesus! how great is the goodness of Thy Heart! Even to me unworthy, Thou hast made known the way of the interior life, wherein all the Saints walk with Thee.

Behold! my heart is ready to follow Thee in this holy way: guide me in truth, and teach me to do Thy good pleasure.

Too long have I followed the motion of nature: too long have I acted by natural propensity or aversion: I have led altogether too much of a natural life.

Grant me, I beseech Thee, Lord, to live henceforth by grace; to follow Thy Spirit in whatever I may have to do or suffer.

Grant that my heart, created by Thee, ransomed by the price of the Blood of Thy Heart, endowed by Thee, at its every pulsation, with new favors—may at last, disengaged from creatures, soar to Thee, live for Thee alone, love Thee alone above all else.

CHAPTER X.

THAT, AFTER THE EXAMPLE OF THE MOST SACRED HEART OF JESUS, ADORED BY THE MAGI, WE SHOULD OVERCOME ALL HUMAN RESPECT.

1. *The voice of Jesus.*—Behold! My Child, the Magi had come from the East: and, entering the Cave, they found Me, an Infant, with Mary, My Virgin Mother.

Observe My Heart, and imitate Its disposition.

Such as It was in the presence of My own, such It
is before strangers; as It was before shepherds of
the lowest estate, so It is before Magi of the highest rank: I was not ashamed of the lowliness of
My Birth, the obscurity of My condition, the practice of every virtue.

In this, My Heart does not regard the judgments
of men, but, setting aside human respect, It pursues
the things that please My Father.

2. Happy he, that imitates this fortitude of My
Heart; that, with his heart undaunted, overcomes
human respect!

For as My heavenly Father confessed Me, because I confessed Him; so, whosoever shall confess Me before men, him also will I confess before
My Father.

But woe to him, that shall be ashamed before
men of Me, of My teaching, of My example! of
him will I also be ashamed before My Father, the
Angels, and men themselves, when I shall come in
Majesty to judge.

3. What fearest thou, O man? Does not reason
itself tell thee, that honor is due to virtue, dishonor
to vice? why then dost thou dread to practice virtue, as if thou thoughtest it a disgrace?

Behold! beside God, none witness thy actions
except Angels and men. Now, pray then, which
of these shouldst thou mind?

The good Angels—if thou boldly avowest thyself My servant—will joyfully extol thy greatness
of soul, and pray for the continuance of thy fortitude. And men, as well as the Saints in heaven, as
the wise and good upon earth, feeling similarly disposed in thy regard, will act in like manner.

Yea, the reprobate angels, and foolish and wicked men, will admire thee, at least inwardly, in spite of themselves, although outwardly they speak against thee, to hide their own faint-heartedness and cowardice. Oughtest thou to heed the false judgments and idle talk of these? Wouldst thou be reckoned among these, and become a partaker of their lot?

Were all men to talk about thee, wouldst thou be different from what thou art? Thou art just what thou art before Me, My Child; nor can the tongues of all creatures make thee greater or smaller.

4. Who is he that can be pleasing to all? None; neither could I Myself obtain this. Do not, then, attempt what is impossible.

Strive to please Me, as much as thou art able; and, in this holy endeavor, care not for what the world may think concerning thee.

If thou art still guided by a regard for men; it is plain that thou hast not yet learnt humility and charity of My Heart.

Whosoever is humble of heart, and impelled by divine love, desires not to please men; nor fears he to displease them, when he cannot otherwise satisfy Me.

Neither stands he in dread of the judgments and scoffs of the world, but he keeps his countenance, and goes his way; and, if My honor requires it, he utters his opinion with a holy freedom.

He does nothing that he may be seen, he omits nothing through fear of being seen: he cares naught whether he be praised or blamed by a foolish world; whether he be esteemed much or little.

The world is for him, as if it were not: Me alone he has in view, since he knows that to Me everything is due; to Me he loves to refer all, by whom alone he can and will be approved and rewarded as he deserves.

But it is no wonder, that whosoever gratifies pride and self-love, becomes the slave of human respect.

For surely none is more a slave, than he that is swayed by human respect; since he has as many masters, as he sees men.

Meanwhile such a one will do nothing worthy of Me—worthy of his own perfection.

5. My Child, wheresoever thou mayst be, whether living in the world, or secluded from the world, beware of human respect. This vice is met everywhere, not only among people of the world, but even among religious: from the world it enters into the sanctuary, and there it stands an abomination in the Holy of Holies.

Many, deceiving themselves, under the semblance of charity or prudence, yield to human respect: and were they to look properly into themselves, they would discover, that it is not the virtue of charity or prudence, but the vail of timid pride and self-love.

The voice of the Disciple.—Yet, Lord, is it proper always and everywhere, publicly to proclaim virtue, and to profess it openly? If so, I pray Thee, how is this to be done? if not, what rule should be followed?

The voice of Jesus.—Sometimes, My Child, it is not expedient rashly to expose piety; but never, and nowhere is it allowed to betray piety.

In the practice of virtue, it is a sure and safe rule, to consider not one's own, but the divine honor; not to neglect the open profession of virtue, simply to avoid thy own confusion; but to omit its open profession, when My honor or glory might suffer in consequence.

6. In general, My Child, in whatever place thou mayst be, if, inasmuch as this rule allows, thou beginnest at once openly to practice virtue, it will not only give Me great honor, but also prove very advantageous to thyself. For thus the good and the wicked, as well as the fervent and the lukewarm, shall know thee; the first will seek thy company, and sustain thee: the last will let thee alone, and not ensnare thee.

If any there be who do find fault with thy conscientiously free and noble-souled deportment, be not, therefore, troubled or cast down; but call to mind, that if, to the injury of thy conscience, thou didst still seek to please men, thou shouldst not be the servant of God, nor a Disciple of My Heart.

Besides, what would it avail, to be blamed by none, and to be pleasing to all? Couldst thou in the end be defended by mortal man, when I will be thy Judge? or couldst thou be saved, whilst I condemn thee?

What will be the feelings, after death, before Me, their Judge, of those cowardly souls, that, through human respect, placed during life the opinions of a foolish world before My judgments, and betrayed My cause?

Alas! how many reprobates has human respect made, whose lot, had they spurned it, should now be among the Saints!

7. Believe me, Child, it is every way better to regard My judgments, rather than those of men: if thou art pleasing to Me, that is enough for thee; to please men alone, is simple vanity, mere mockery.

Cheer up thy courage, My Child, look down upon the false sayings of men, that fly through the air, and only reach those who grasp them for themselves.

If thou dost once fully learn to raise thysel: above every human respect, thou wilt hardly be again annoyed by it, and, thyself consistent, thou wilt pity the madness of the world, and the silliness of men, who suffer themselves, in so slavish a manner, to be dragged to destruction.

And when thou hast come to this, that thou art no longer moved by any human respect, then, freed from a very great hindrance to salvation and perfection, thou shalt safely advance in the way of virtue.

8. *The voice of the Disciple.*—How true, how holy a doctrine Thou teachest, good Master, sweet Jesus! Help me, I entreat Thee, to reduce it to practice.

I am justly ashamed, Lord, of my past cowardice, my faint-heartedness. Often did I blush or fear to do what my heart approved as good and worthy of honor: on the other hand, I did not blush to give way to human respect, which it acknowledged to be evil and unbecoming.

From a base fear of men's opinions, I have frequently betrayed Thy interests and Thy holy service, and thus rendered myself deserving of great shame and punishment.

Have mercy on me, my God, and forgive my

offenses, whereby, through human respect, I have turned away from Thy Will, and chosen rather, despite my conscience, to follow the opinion of the world.

But now, mercifully recalled and taught by Thee, behold! I am resolved to follow Thee, the sole guide to eternal blessedness.

Let worldlings continue to call good, evil, and evil, good: let them still estimate honor by the changeable and worthless opinion of deluded men: let them still feed on vanity; from Thee I know, and hold with certainty, that to cleave to Thee, is unchangeably good; that to follow Thee, is truly honorable; that to enjoy Thee, most sweet Jesus, the fountain of life and of all good things, does really constitute bliss.

CHAPTER XI.

THAT OF THE MOST SACRED HEART OF JESUS, PRE-SENTED IN THE TEMPLE, WE SHOULD LEARN TO HAVE, IN ALL THINGS, A RIGHT INTENTION.

1. *The voice of Jesus.*—My Child, when the days were accomplished, that they should present Me to the Lord, I offered Myself and all I had, to My heavenly Father, with a pure desire of pleasing Him.

Although, at My Incarnation, I had forever consecrated Myself and My whole life to My Father yet, I never omitted to dedicate to Him every particular action of My life, and keep in view His good pleasure.

But, since a good intention is a matter of such importance in the interior life, that no one can be a true Disciple of My Heart without it, My Heart did not cease to show, teach, inculcate this by Its example.

Look at My life from its beginning unto the end: did My Heart anywhere please Itself? did It seek the glory of the world?

In all My life, Child, can be found no act arising from the mere impulse of human nature, none from mere custom, none from mere necessity, none, finally, whether great or small, which did not spring from the motive of fulfilling the divine Will, of pleasing the divine Majesty.

2. How happy he that has put on this sentiment of My Heart! he is ever useful to himself, ever dear to Me, his Saviour-God.

What is that which is acceptable to Me? the inward affection, rather than the outward act; the intentions of the heart, rather than the fulfillment of the work. What do I reward forever? the fruit of grace, whereby thou art moved to act, and wherewith thou co-operatest, not the effect of nature—whereby thou art stirred up, or which thou followest.

My grace moves the Will to do whatsoever things are by Me directly or indirectly commanded or desired. These I wish to be so done, that they be supernaturally good and meritorious: wherefore, to do them, I give an actual grace, without which they could not be supernaturally good and meritorious. If, then, thou art induced to act by My Will or good pleasure, know, that thou art moved by grace, a supernatural principle.

But the end or intention of thy will forms the species of the act. Such as is thy intention, such will be the act that follows.

If thou hast a right intention, thou wilt, before and above all, intend and seek My good pleasure, Me—thy end and supreme Good.

It sometimes happens, that the primary intention of an action is right, but that a wrong secondary intention creeps in. When this occurs, the goodness of the action indeed is not wholly destroyed, but is lessened in part: and the actor becomes guilty of so much, as there has been of ill-regulated or evil will, in the vitiated intention.

Behold! My Child, I am Alpha and Omega, the beginning and the end: therefore, all things must be derived from Me—be referred to Me.

If, then, thou wouldst be blamed, when thou dost not refer them to Me; how much more so, if thou turnest them aside to thyself, or to My enemy the world?

3. A precious thing, a wonderful virtue, My Child, is a right intention, whereby actions, although natural and indifferent in themselves, when done by means of grace, become supernatural and meritorious. A marvellous secret, whereby lead, and brass, and other metals, are changed into pure gold.

Beware, however, lest thou fall into that quite common delusion which makes men fancy that, by substituting a good intention, they can render meritorious a work or action undertaken, not by grace, or by My Will, but from the sole motive of nature, aversion or inclination, or from self-will alone.

Follow thou, with a right aim, everything begun according to My good pleasure.

Of what avail is a work, how great or praiseworthy soever it may outwardly appear, to him that does it without a right intention?

On the other hand, that which is done with a pure intention, how little and lowly soever it may seem, becomes excellent, and altogether beneficial.

4. Would that men knew and practiced this art of acting rightly! how easily could they merit a bright crown in heaven!

There are those who work much and gain little; who busy themselves about everything; who attempt many and various things, but, in the end, find themselves with almost empty hands; because, like irrational creatures, they act without an end, or pursue an end ill-ordered and unworthy.

How many there are, who exchange the fruit of their labors for an empty breath of praise or admiration; wherewith they ever long to feed their weary and hungry heart!

Behold! how many there are, who make so much of the smoke of vain glory, that they buy it at a price by which they might purchase for themselves the kingdom of endless glory.

Is there not an endless number of such madmen? Take heed, My Child, lest thou be reckoned among them.

There are others who appear to be doing little, and yet deserve to become very holy; these are they who think, that he does enough, who does the Will of God.

5. My Child, when thou devotest thyself to Me
in exercises of piety, thou must place, even above
these practices themselves, the intention of doing
My good pleasure. Thus, whether thou feelest
consolation or desolation, thou shalt remain calm,
gather certain fruit, and honor Me.

If thou art engaged in works of duty or charity
toward thy neighbor, let Me be the end of those
works; for thus it will happen, that thou shalt
never fail of thy reward, and that thou shalt lose
nothing of thy peace—whether thy neighbor be
or be not improved.

If thou hast in view no other object except My sole
good pleasure, thou shalt be contented and happy
in every event; because thou knowest that I do not
demand of thee, and will not crown in thee, aught
save only thy good efficacious will; and that success depends upon Me, who order all things according to infinite Wisdom.

By means of a pure intention, thou art enabled
to remain undisturbed and tranquil amid hardships,
distresses, yea amid temptations themselves; for,
since purity of intention raises thee before Me above
sensible things, thou needest not to be annoyed by
what thou feelest against thy will.

Finally, My Child, whether thou art in action or
at rest, whether thou laborest or divertest thyself,
whether thou art watching or sleeping, whether
thou eatest or drinkest; whether, in short, thou art
doing aught else, do all things, to follow My good
pleasure, to be acceptable to Me; and, behold! a
great and ever-increasing amount of merits will ac-
crue to thee.

6. In the morning, thou must daily make a gene-

ral intention, whereby everything to be done or suffered during that day, is directed to this last end, that, for love of Me, thou mayst accomplish My Will, and thus please Me. This good, this holy intention, will give life to all things that follow, and will virtually continue to add vigor to them.

It is also of the greatest importance to renew, during the day, thy good intention before every action; nay more, when it can be done conveniently, to renew the same during the action.

But to do all things with a right end, it will be of very great help, to foresee occasions of meriting, dangers of losing—virtues to be practiced, snares of pride and self-love to be avoided.

One and the same action may be directed to several and different proximate ends, which, directly or indirectly, tend to the salvation of thy own soul, or of thy neighbor, or to My honor. Whence thou mayst acquire a great treasure of merits, of which they, who act with no aim of this kind, are deprived.

Moreover, every action may be made up of several virtues: as thou practicest as many virtues as thou intendest, and as to every act of virtue corresponds a new degree of present grace and future glory, it is easy to see how important a matter is this holy intention.

But, My Child, thou must take care that these things be not done with anxiety, with injury to inward freedom, or with the loss of peace: for, so far from being useful, they would, on the contrary, be hurtful.

Remember, lastly, that, inspired by the spirit of

the same intention that animated Me, thou oughtest to unite all thy actions and sufferings with Mine,
if, as a Disciple of My Heart, thou art desirous of
acting in a manner worthy of so high a vocation.

7. My Child, vain self-love is so subtle that it
can easily assume any shape, and thrust itself into
all things.

Whence it will happen, that, unless thou be cau-
tious, thou mayst be animated and led by that spirit
of self, rather than by My own. Nor does human
light or prudence suffice to distinguish this, since
neither can, of itself, discern things supernatural;
but a light from above, and the divine assistance
are needed.

Wherefore, thou must pray without ceasing, that
thou mayst be enlightened from heaven; and beg
fervently that thou mayst be helped by grace,
whereby thou art enabled to tend, rightly and
singly, above all things to Me.

8. *The voice of the Disciple.*—I pray and beseech Thee, Lord Jesus, Author of all good, give
Thou light to my mind, love to my heart, strength
to my whole being, that I may ever rightly accomplish what is pleasing to Thee.

Grant me true earnestness, a holy intention, that,
in all things, I may do Thy good pleasure, without turning to the right or to the left.

Suffer not that, henceforth, I be so foolish as to
lose the merit of my actions, for the sake of grasping an airy phantom; nor so undutiful as to snatch
away the glory which belongs to Thee!

Pour into my heart, I implore Thee, the purity
of Thy Heart, that I may, above all else, direct my
thoughts to Thee, find Thee, and repose in Thee

my God, my beginning and my end, the centre and rest of my soul.

CHAPTER XII.

OF THE FREEDOM OF HEART, WHICH THE MOST SACRED HEART OF JESUS, IN HIS FLIGHT INTO EGYPT, TEACHES US.

1. *The voice of Jesus.*—Behold, My Child, king Herod sought Me, a Child, that he might put Me to death. But Joseph, warned by an Angel, took Me and My Mother, by night, and retired into Egypt.

The unseasonable hour of the night, My tender age, the condition of My parents, the abandoning of My native land, the dwelling in a foreign coun‑ try, the tarrying among infidels, whose manners were contrary to Mine, the poverty and obscureness of My life, drudgery and hardship, everything in fine, was suited to render the heart cheerless.

Yet, amid all this, My Heart remained so free, that neither time, nor place, nor men, nor any cre‑ ated objects whatsoever could render It captive.

2. My Child, strive, by every means in thy power, to imitate this holy freedom of My Heart.

My Heart, elevated above the reach of all else, was restrained by the good pleasure of My Father alone. So also should thy heart, raised above all created objects, be held by the divine Will alone.

The greatest freedom to which the heart of man

can aspire is this, to be dependent upon no one, except its God.

This is that true, that perfect liberty, whereby man is nobly exalted, and elevated above his very Superiors, through whom, as the organs of God, he is pleased to have My Will made known.

Whosoever possesses this freedom is raised above every created power, above all the whims and fickleness of men—above all the casual events of times, places, and circumstances; in so much, that, unless he betray himself, he can be enslaved by no created object.

But none can gain this privilege, unless he wholly devote to Me his heart, disengaged from every creature.

For, so long as thou inordinately desirest or fearest aught, so long will thy heart be fettered and embarrassed.

Thy heart will be a slave, so long as it follows its natural inclination in either direction, or seeks in anything, even in what is good, itself as its end.

There are those who, released from sin and the world, endeavor to be also released from themselves, that they may freely live for Me: who yet sigh in My service, as under a heavy yoke; because they suffer themselves to be insnared by a delusion, whereby they fancy Me a troublesome ruler, or a harsh master, ever bent on discovering something to punish.

These, assuredly, do Me great injustice, deter their neighbors from My service, and render themselves wretched to no purpose.

3. Am I not a Father? Where is there a father's heart like Mine? who then is so much a father, as

I am? A Father infinitely wise, who knows every-thing—what is useful, what is hurtful to My chil-dren: infinitely powerful, against whose Will no enemies, whether visible or invisible, can do the least harm to My children: infinitely good, who love My children with a Heart burning with a divine love, and long to turn all things, evil as well as good, to their advantage.

Wherefore, show in My service that thou art the worthy child of such a Father: and do not, by a most unseemly crime, conduct thyself as the servant of an overbearing master.

Do but keep the good will, of shunning whatso-ever thou knowest is displeasing, and of doing what-soever thou understandest is agreeable to Me: and then expand thy heart—not, indeed, to the false freedom, the hard yoke of the children of the world, but to the true freedom, the sweet privilege of the children of My Heart.

4. This do I love, that My children enjoy a holy freedom; and I consider Myself greatly honored thereby.

Use, therefore, a becoming diligence to please Me, and be not anxious to know, whether in reality thou art pleasing to Me: but, setting aside all sub-tlety of the understanding, and all uneasiness of the will, throw thyself with confidence on My Heart. It cannot be otherwise than that, so far from being offended, I will rather be delighted with this free-dom of heart, inspired by a pure and generous love.

Under My guidance, under My protection, under My divine care, be thou free from all inordinate-ness; neither do thou excessively fear hell, the world, nor thyself. For although, of thyself, thou art able to do nothing, thou canst do much in Me, in whom thou believest, in whom thou hopest, whom thou lovest.

If, at any time thou fallest into faults, do not conduct thyself like a menial servant, who, full of alarm, stands in dread of stripes, and is desirous either of running away, or of cowardly hiding himself: but act like a child that loves his father, and forthwith endeavors to make up for his guilt— who runs to his father, with so much the more freedom, the greater the goodness which he knows him to possess.

As often, therefore, as thou sadly fallest, do thou return to Me in a child-like manner—ask forgiveness, and renew thy resolve of being faithful: nor suffer thou the peace of thy heart to be disturbed, or thy freedom lessened.

5. Neither should the means of perfection fetter thy heart; for even these, if they took away the holy freedom of thy heart, would be obstacles rather than means.

Wherefore, so soon as I make known to thee My Will, thou must freely overlook everything else, and be solely dependent on My bidding.

Take heed, however, My Child, lest, under pretense of a holy freedom, thou indulge the fickleness of the heart—as they do who allow themselves to be guided by feeling, not by principle.

To them, that which a little before was pleasing, now becomes irksome: in the glow of fervor, they assume spiritual practices, and soon afterwards leave them off again, or perform them with distaste; they live now in one way, and, in a short time, wearied therewith, they try another; now, they mortify hemselves severely, as if they were wholly spiritual; and, soon again, having become really sensual, they flatter nature.

This, surely, is not to be a child of freedom, but the sport of fickleness, the slave of feeling.

6. My Child, be thou more steadfast in regard to thy freedom. If thou art busied with any employments, do not give thyself up to them—merely lend thyself to them—lest, instead of thyself being their master, they perchance rule thee.

As often as thou feelest thyself impelled by nature, either to undertake or to perform something, do thou forthwith check thy ardor: otherwise thou shalt soon perceive that thy heart is being fettered, and that the matter itself is less rightly done.

Let no place on earth hold thy heart bound to itself: keep it free everywhere, knowing that I, thy God, am found in all places; that My children are everywhere cherished by My Spirit; finally, that where My Spirit is, there is true freedom.

Wherever, therefore, thou mayst be, be master of thyself: in all things whatsoever, whether internal or external, whether spiritual or temporal, whether lofty or lowly, keep thy heart free, united above everything with the divine Will.

7. My Child, thou shouldst so cherish and guard the freedom of thy heart, that no one—neither thy inferior, nor an equal, nor even thy Superior—can take it away.

Wherefore, thou oughtest to judge of nothing, nor strive after it, according to the semblance of things, the opinion of men, or thy own feeling. In all things, let the standard of thy judgment be the truth, which thou wilt find, by examining how My

Heart has judged them: and let My Will be the rule of thy desiring. This truth will free thee, and thou shalt be free indeed: this divine Will shall guide thee, and keep thee free.

The more glorious this holy freedom of heart is to Me—the more useful to thyself and to thy neighbor—with the more care is it to be fostered, the more resolutely is it to be defended against thy foes.

Beside the demon and the world, nature will also frequently rise up against it. Pride, with many reasonings, and self-love, in various ways, will prey upon it, to cause it to yield, at least in some or other matter.

But thou wilt frustrate and overcome the assaults and stratagems of thy enemies, if thou goest boldly counter to what these foes suggest, and if thou simply followest My Will.

Whosoever wills everything according to My divine good pleasure—whosoever lives by this, and seeks his happiness therein—enjoys a true and holy freedom, which I desire every Disciple of My Heart to possess, and which neither hell, nor the world, nor any creature, can take away.

8. *The voice of the Disciple.*—Holy freedom! how sweet a name! but sweeter far its possession: most sweet its fruit. Would, O good Jesus, that I might enjoy it!

But alas, wretched me! of how many things am I still the slave! blushing with shame, I confess to Thee, O Lord, that my heart is full often captivated and held by various things, yea, the most trifling or imaginary.

Give me, I entreat Thee, give me light to know

and strength to burst asunder all my chains, that at last I may be free in truth and holiness.

Mercifully grant, most benign Jesus, that, to preserve holy freedom of heart, I may stand with a heart firm and undaunted, amid all the temptations of hell; that I be unconquered and unshaken by the good and evil things, the sayings and doings of the world; that, above all which is of self, I may repose and persevere in Thy most holy, most delightful good pleasure.

CHAPTER XIII.

THAT THE MOST SACRED HEART OF JESUS, GOING UP INTO THE TEMPLE, TEACHES US TO PRAY.

1. *The voice of Jesus.*—Attend, My Child, and see how solicitous My Heart was, that, in public as well as in private, It might teach, by example, the ways of salvation and perfection.

From My Childhood, I was wont, not only frequently to pray alone, but also to go up to Jerusalem, and to pray publicly in the Temple, and this according to custom.

My Child, what was My whole life, if not a prayer, from which My Heart never ceased, with which It was always and everywhere occupied?

Where did Mary, My Mother, and Joseph find Me when I was lost, if not in the Temple, the house of prayer? Where My Disciples and friends—except returning from prayer, with My Heart still praying? Where, in fine, My enemies—except praying in the solitude of Gethsemane?

Examine carefully every day of My life; behold! the very dawn found Me at prayer, and, even at that time, sanctifying the labors of the day.

When the toils of day were over, lo! when all nature was at rest, the darkness of the night beheld Me praying, and pouring forth My Heart before My Father—with the Angels alone as My witnesses.

But even amidst the very labors of the day, how often did I withdraw a little from the multitude! how often, whilst in the midst of the multitude, and during My labors, did I raise My Heart to My Father!

2. My Child, strive thou with special care and diligence, to acquire this Spirit of prayer, this holy habit of praying.

All the Saints, and followers of the Saints, all the Disciples of My Heart, learned this holy and sanctifying use of prayer. They prayed at stated times, not merely with their lips, but also with their mind and heart: again, wherever they were, under every circumstance of fortune, they had inwardly recourse to Me by prayer—making known to My Heart their joy and gratefulness, amid prosperity; imploring My help and comfort, in adversity; asking counsel, in their doubts.

So shouldst thou also do, My Child, if thou wilt aspire to holiness; yea, if thou art desirous of securing thy salvation.

3. Meditate devoutly, every day. But beware lest thy meditation prove a musing, rather than a prayer; a pious study, rather than a divine intercourse.

Let the mind reason and reflect, as much as is necessary; but let the heart elicit acts, sometimes of faith, hope, charity; sometimes of sorrow, humility, self-denial; again, of fortitude, of good and firm resolve; again, of thanksgiving, of joy and exultation of heart with the Angels and Saints; now of resignation, of conformity to the divine Will, of pure love, reposing in God's good pleasure; or of any other virtue whatsoever; then let it fervently petition much for itself, and also for others: —for the Church and her ministers, for the perfection of the Saints dwelling on earth, for the perseverance of the just, for the conversion of all sinners, heretics, and infidels.

In proportion as thou advancest in the interior life, and attainest to a more perfect degree in the same, thou shouldst shorten thy reasonings, and give freer scope to the affections, so that thou treatest with Me in thy heart, by means of acts and petitions, and, at last, by the mere occupation of divine union.

Meditate and pray in this manner, My Child, and remember that, whether thou prayest orally or mentally, the heart must be foremost, in order that every prayer and supplication may be performed in an attentive and devout manner.

Although thou mayst not be able to pray so well as thou desirest, do not think little of thy prayer, or neglect it. Verily, I Myself, do neither deem it of little importance, nor do I overlook the same.

Do with a good will whatever thou art able; by so doing, be convinced that thou prayest well and meritoriously, and that thou wilt make progress in virtue, as well as in prayer.

4. Let it not be sufficient for thee to pray at certain times: for it behooves thee to pray always, and not to grow faint. Behold My sweet command, according to which thou canst approach Me at all times, and, as a child, converse with Me.

Everywhere there are obstacles, within and without: temptations from every side, both open and secret: always dangers, lest the crown promised to perseverance be lost. Exceedingly necessary, therefore, is grace, which, however, is not wont to be given, in a special manner, except to them that pray.

Almost everything, then, depends on prayer: without prayer, evil things find no remedy, good things become dangerous; but to him who prays, both good and evil will prove advantageous.

Nowhere, My Child, except in prayer, wilt thou acquire a true knowledge of Me and of thyself: therefore, without prayer, thou wilt never attain to true humility and charity.

Without prayer, thou wilt never fully understand My Heart, nor possess Its Spirit. Without prayer, thou wilt, in many things, not seize the sentiments of My Heart; and, what is more dangerous, thou wilt measure My Heart by thy own.

If in thy concerns thou hast recourse to prayer, it will not rarely happen, that thou judgest differently of them, from what thou didst before; because the light of divine grace, which is wont to be poured into the soul during prayer, is infinitely purer than the light of human reason.

What thou didst think to have sprung from grace, thou shalt often find to be the offspring of nature: what thou didst fancy a virtue, thou shalt sometimes perceive to be self-love: what thou didst judge to be for My greater glory, thou shalt often understand to be the effect of thy hidden pride.

5. The interior man, amid his troubles, has first recourse to Me, and begs for help: therefore, he is relieved, and obtains frequently extraordinary favors; whereas, he that has first recourse to human means, so far from being disburdened, increases his difficulties; until, entering into himself, he comes to Me, without whose aid human endeavors are of no avail to the suffering heart.

My Child, if thou comest to My Heart whenever thou art in affliction, there will be no need to look for human consolations: thou shalt find one drop of My consolation sweeter and more effectual than all the flood of men's consoling words.

If, betimes, for My honor and for thy advantage, I give thee no sensible consolation to taste; thou shalt still ever find true comfort in My Heart, both by resigning thyself to My good pleasure, and by receiving My assistance.

This holy resignation, although, on the one hand, it is contrary to the feelings, and, therefore, bitter; yet, on the other, by means of grace, becomes so sweet, in spite of the feelings, that no one, unless he has experienced it, can fully understand the same.

6. When the man of prayer is tempted, he becomes more united with Me; he is not cast down but raised; he is not saddened but cheered up; he is not shaken but rendered more firm.

If, at any time, thou art overtaken by the storm, or even wrapt up in its thick darkness, turn thyself to Me—who am ever present—and, with thy heart, cling to Me confidingly: thou shalt be secure amid the very rage and gloom of the tempest; and, sometimes, thou shalt be illumined with a ray of softest light from above, that thereby thou mayst see, that what thou thoughtest certain destruction, was either a mere nothing, or even an advantage.

When thou art desirous of saying or doing something, and a doubt or perplexity presents itself, whether or not it be lawful; entering into thyself, hearken to My Spirit, and if, by having frequently recourse to Me, thou hast learned to distinguish My whisperings, thou wilt perceive a clear decision—which thou mayst follow with safety.

A soul accustomed to have recourse to Me, has everywhere with her a protector, a counsellor and comforter, whom—not only when she is alone, but also whilst dealing with her neighbor—she knows, and loves to call upon in her heart, to consult, and to entertain.

7. After this do thou strive, My Child, for this do thou leave naught undone, that thou mayst acquire this pious habit of having recourse to My Heart, of tending towards Me as thy centre, of busying thyself inwardly with Me, of dealing with Me by means of prayer. This is that Spirit of prayer, which, if thou secure it for thyself, will lovingly entertain thee in solitude, will guard thee in public, will solace thee in adversity, will check thee in prosperity, will protect thee in dangers, and, everywhere at thy service, will guide thee to holiness.

The voice of the Disciple.—This, O Lord, this is a great good, exceedingly to be desired: yea, it seems that this alone is one of the main secrets of the interior life. But, by what means, I pray, shall I acquire this pious habit?

The voice of Jesus.—First of all, My Child, thou oughtest frequently to beg for the gift of prayer, of all gifts the best—which embraces every gift: by prayer, as other things, so, especially, is the gift of prayer obtained.

Next, it is a good counsel—well-suited to acquire for thyself the habit of prayer—as much as possible, so to arrange thy occupations, that no long interval ever intervene, during which thou dost not for sometime—or at least for a few moments—confer with Me by means of some spiritual practice.

Then, thou must make use of both inward and outward temptations and troubles, as of so many warnings, to turn thyself to Me, for the sake of evincing thy love, imploring grace, and renewing thy resolve of being faithful.

Lastly, thou shouldst persist in thy repeated efforts, until thou art accustomed to make use of prayer, until thou hast recourse to Me under every circumstance, like a child to its parent—not by the power of reason and reflection, but by a spontaneous instinct.

8. Cheer up, My Child, spare neither care nor diligence to acquire this science of the Elect, this object of the longing of all the Disciples of My Heart. It is worth all that and more.

In prayer thou hast a support in thy wants; amends for thy shortcomings, means for progress; a safe hope of perseverance; whatsoever it is profitable to possess.

Prayer is the refreshment of them that hunger

and thirst after justice: prayer is the delight of pure souls: prayer, to sum up all, is the employment of the Saints, and their repose as well.

Whilst thou prayest, thou honorest and glorifiest Me, thou performest that upon earth, which the Angels and Saints are doing in heaven, and which must be thy blissful occupation throughout a joyous eternity.

9. *The voice of the Disciple.*—Delightful, indeed, Lord Jesus, are the things which Thou teachest me concerning prayer: they affect the heart by their unction, and fill it with love for that holy exercise.

Behold, Lord, as much as I am able will I pray: I will pray with my mind, I will pray with my heart, I will pray with my lips. Help me with Thy grace.

By Thy most Sacred Heart, I beseech Thee, grant me the spirit of prayer, in order that prayer, which is manifold, may also be my life.

I ask not for extraordinary gifts, not the gift of prophecy, not the gift of miracles: grant these to them, whom, in Thy loving-kindness, Thou choosest: never will I envy them.

But this I beg humbly; this, I entreat Thee, grant Thou me, the gift of prayer—the gift which is above every gift to me.

Through it comes every good: through it I have access to the fountain of all Good: through it I find entrance into Thy very Heart.

CHAPTER XIV.

OF THE LOVE OF SOLITUDE, AFTER THE EXAMPLE OF
THE MOST SACRED HEART OF JESUS, ABIDING AT
NAZARETH.

1. *The voice of Jesus.*—My Child, after I had
been at Jerusalem, engaged in the things which are
My Father's, so long as My Father Himself willed
it; I went down to Nazareth, and there unknown,
I advanced in grace with God and with men.

Understand this My hidden life : study the
sentiments of My Heart, and strive to imitate them
sedulously.

Thou mightst have seen Me, with a serene countenance and a joyous Heart, now at home, intent
on My various duties and occupations: now abroad,
applying Myself to divers labors: always ready for
everything: everywhere obedient: at all times and
in every place, a spectacle full of grace, to God
My Father, to My Virgin Mother, to Joseph, and
to the wondering Angels.

Behold how the Son of God was employed for
so long a time! behold how He grew up, like the
lily of the valleys, hidden indeed from the world,
but prominent and pleasing in the sight of heaven.

2. Wonder not, My Child, that I passed so many
years in retirement, that I did not show Myself to
the world, except after a long time. This example
of Mine, this interior love of solitude, was exceedingly necessary to men.

Without this love of solitude, men, influenced by

corrupt nature, pour themselves out, as it were, into external things: most of them follow self-love, by imaginary and unusual ways and means of salvation and perfection—whereby they are deceived, and led astray from the spirit of their state and vocation; others obey a secret pride, undertake affairs and fill employments, without due preparation, without regularity—seeking not the things which are Mine, but those which are their own.

Whence it happens, that they wander from the right path. And as—on account of the ceaseless bustle, and their applications to external things—they heed not the divine inspirations, they fall from one error into another; they become more and more wrapt up in their delusions, until, at last, they render fruitless to themselves every means of salvation and perfection.

3. The object of the example of My hidden and inward life is two-fold: to teach men to guard against such evils, that they may keep the safe road of salvation; and to show to them, wherein true perfection consists.

Whatever glitters or resounds, whatever awakens in some manner the attention or admiration of men, upon this most men are wont to look, as something more perfect, and better adapted to glorify God, and to shine before their neighbor.

But how great an error! how great a delusion! For it all arises from secret pride, and ends in self-love.

In truth, perfection, as is made evident by the example of My Heart, consists in doing the divine good pleasure with humility and charity.

Without a regard for solitude, man is not wont

to understand, at all times, the divine Will, to guard humility, or to preserve true—not fictitious—charity.

Pray, therefore, My Child, that thou mayst be worthy to acquire and cherish a love for solitude. It is so great a good, that there exists hardly anything so useful, both to act with a right spirit, and to pray with the same spirit.

Examine the lives of the Saints, and thou shalt not find one among them who did not love sacred solitude.

4. The solitude, which the faithful must cherish, is relative to their state and condition of life. Whence it may happen that what is praised in one ought to be blamed in another.

Now, this is a safe rule, the true method for every faithful soul, of all states or conditions: To love solitude in such a manner, that, after having duly performed whatsoever thy duties or employments demand, thou retire with Me from the crowd, and collect thyself near Me, until the divine Will calls thee away.

If thou withdraw thyself from unnecessary company, useless conversation, the idle rumors of the world; in short, from all matters which do not concern thee, thou shalt have sufficient time to deal with Me in solitude.

But when, from the intercourse of men, thou retirest into solitude, do not simply leave men, and yet carry thy cares with thee.

For there are those, who are no less distracted and dissipated in solitude than they were in the company of men, and amid their occupations; because they give free scope to the vagaries of the imagination, to the inquisitiveness of the under-standing, and the fretfulness of the will.

It is necessary, first of all, to arrange thy free time in an orderly manner, so that, to a settled time, be assigned a fixed employment, lest, over-come by disgust, thou wander about, or waste time in discussing how thou shouldst spend it.

Order, in all things, is of the greatest advantage: it drives away idleness and dullness of spirit· it prevents many temptations and difficulties; it affords an opportunity of doing well, and with ease, many things; lastly, it makes thee live for Me.

5. He that is alone with Me in the sight of Angels, either makes amends for the past, or strengthens himself in what is good: and, whilst reflecting on himself and his actions, he is taught many things. For it is not so much length of time, or multiplicity of matters, as the purity of prayer and meditation, which renders a man truly experienced.

He that is collected within himself, away from the turmoil of the world, recovers his peace, if lost, or strengthens it, when preserved: he rejoices in the communication of graces of divers kinds; he rightly arranges beforehand that which he may afterward be able to perform with fruit and merit.

Whence, My Child, does it come, except from union with Me, that interior men—even under the most trying circumstances—continue so self-pos-sessed that they are an object of admiration to the multitude; and are so persevering that they exe-cute, with the greatest fearlessness. whatsoever they have once resolved?

How many defects shalt thou avoid, how many

virtues shalt thou practice, if thou do but cherish solitude!

All the Disciples of My Heart have ever held as certain, that they were so much the nearer to My Heart, the farther they were with their heart removed from creatures.

8. My Child, if thou art truly humble, thou wilt seek after solitude: for, as much as it is able, humility loves to be concealed, and dreads to be noticed. If thou art enkindled with a true and divine love, thou wilt seek after solitude: for the flame of love, exposed to every breath of the world, is easily extinguished, unless it be frequently fed in solitude.

Or what is worse, charity, if always dissipated, becomes, by degrees, a disguised sensuality.

Solitude, when adapted to each one's circumstances, and properly kept, becomes sweeter little by little, and secures numberless advantages.

For it is the safeguard of innocence, the dwelling of peace, the abode of the interior life, the school of holiness, the place of heavenly secrets, the chosen means of divine communication.

If thou art desirous of enjoying these things, love sacred solitude: frequently will I invite thee, frequently will I lead thee into the same, that there I may speak to thy heart.

7. Be not deterred from cherishing sacred solitude—even should men occasionally censure thee, on account of thy love of retirement. Let talkers have their say: for thyself, attend thou to what is good.

If thou desirest to suit thy life to the opinions of others, thou wilt have to assume as many different shapes as thou meetest men: for there are as many opinions as there are minds.

When the divine Will does not make known to thee, that thou shouldst be with men, stay thou alone with Me.

Thus the Saints, unless called forth by the divine Will, would have continued in solitude, even to their dying hour, unknown to men.

Nevertheless, My Child, as often as by My Will —in whatsoever manner it be made known—thou art sent forth by Me, thou shouldst leave thy solitude with the same readiness and freedom of mind with which thou didst enter it.

At My bidding, leave thou as speedily as possible, or rather exchange for the better, whatever useful occupation detains thee—gladly accommodating thyself, without any sign of displeasure, to circumstances which present themselves.

Do not bind thyself to any preconceived method, rather than to My divine Will; do not, through a false exactness, and an ill-regulated strictness, render piety hateful or unlovely.

If thou hast learnt of My Heart a truly interior spirit, thou wilt safely follow a middle course, avoiding both extremes.

Therefore, imitate not those dissipated persons, who—thinking that the time spent in solitude is lost, or perceiving that things interior are distasteful to them—do ever seek pretenses of pouring themselves out upon outward objects, entangle themselves with what does not concern them, frequently neglect what they ought to perform, and do what they should omit.

Neither follow thou the footsteps of those who,

under cover of piety, neglect all things external, and, with all access shut off, so hide themselves in solitude that neither the inviting of My Spirit, nor charity, nor obedience, is able to draw them thence: and who, if, at any time, necessity drives them out, or disturbs them, are indignant, sullen and fretful.

For thyself, My Child, follow the divine Will. love to be with Me in solitude, according to My good pleasure: and, whenever it is My Will that thou shouldst be with creatures, love to be with them, for love of Me.

8. *The voice of the Disciple.*—O sacred solitude! how great and how numberless the blessings wherewith thou overflowest!

Didst thou understand all these things, my soul? frequently, then, hasten away into solitude: thither go thou as much as thou canst: thither do thou often resort, away from all turmoil, were it only for a little while—but more with the heart than with the body.

There do thou breathe freely; there refresh thyself; there advance in grace; there, among the Angels, entertain thyself with thy Beloved.

O Beloved of my heart, most sweet Jesus! give me, I beseech Thee, and nourish in me, the love of sacred solitude, wherein I may find Thee, wherein I may enjoy Thee, wherein I may be happy with Thee.

Thy conversation, unlike that of men, has no bitterness; neither has Thy intercourse any irksomeness; it is all spiritual joy, pure delight, divine sweetness.

CHAPTER XV.

OF THE DIVINE PRESENCE, WHEREIN WE ARE
TAUGHT TO LIVE, BY THE EXAMPLE OF THE MOST
SACRED HEART OF JESUS, BAPTIZED.

1. *The voice of Jesus.*—My Child, beginning
about the age of thirty years, sent by the Will of
My Father, I left Nazareth and came to the Jordan,
to be baptized.

And when I was baptized, coming forthwith out
of the water, I betook Myself to prayer. But lo!
whilst I prayed, and the crowd of men were thronging around Me, the heavens were opened, and the
Holy Spirit, under the form of a dove, came upon
Me; and the voice of My Father was heard, saying: This is My beloved Son, in whom I am well
pleased.

What solemnity, My Child! how glorious! but
not displayed for Me. This voice came not for
Me, but for men, that they might acknowledge Me
as their Saviour, and, believing in Me, hoping in
Me, loving Me, they might have life everlasting.

I needed not this outward display for Myself;
since, what was done visibly at My Baptism, I
enjoyed unseen at all times. Everywhere and
always, the Father and the Holy Spirit were with
Me.

My Heart possessed always every sufficiency in
things internal: in these It rejoiced fully: in these
It found supreme delight.

My Heart united to the Godhead, by act and affection ever present to the same, lived as if ever absorbed therein.

2. My Child, as much as thou canst, imitate this example of My Heart. Concerning which I have to tell thee many things—but agreeable and full of consolation.

Exert thyself, My Child, that thou mayst ever enjoy the divine presence, that thou mayst everywhere live before Me, thy Saviour—God.

If thou lovest Me, thou wilt find thy delight in walking before Me, in enjoying My presence.

Was it ever heard, or has it ever happened, that any one did not find his delight in the presence of him whom he loves?

Behold! I am always and everywhere with thee, inasmuch as I am a divine Person—nowhere do I lose sight of thee.

Nay more, in My sight no creature is unseen. In every place My eyes behold both the good and the wicked, and look into the very heart of each of them.

Who can hide himself from My sight? Whether he conceal himself in darkness, whether he hide in the loneliness of the wilderness, whether he bury himself in the depths of the earth or the sea, whether he goes down even to hell—everywhere My eyes are upon him.

In such a manner, My Child, am I present to all and each one, that, with My all-powerful hand, I can reach every one, both to restrain or punish, to help or reward him.

3. I am also with thee, not only with all the sweetness of My Divinity, but also with that of My Humanity—in the sacred Tabernacle.

Whithersoever, therefore, thou goest, whether to the right or to the left: wheresoever thou mayst be, whether in thy own country, or in the land of the stranger; in every place, where the Most Holy Sacrament reposes, thou hast Me present, not only with My Divinity, but also My Soul and Body.

There thou findest Me present with the same countenance, the same lips, the same ears, the same affections of the Heart, that once were the delight of My Disciples—as they are even now that of the Angels and Saints in heaven.

Understand, My Child, the whole mystery of love. Behold! from out the sacred Tabernacle, I am with thee, in some manner—wherever upon earth thou mayst be—by the love of My Heart. In My Heart, I busy Myself about thee: with My love, I follow thee everywhere.

4. How, then, canst thou be forgetful of Me? how not be taken up with love for Me? how with mind and heart stray away from Me?

Then, My Child, dost thou truly walk before Me, when thy mind thinks actually or virtually on Me; when, in like manner, thy heart is occupied with love of Me as present.

Now, of this divine presence there are certain degrees, which interior souls arrange in their heart, and by which they come ever more closely to Me.

The first is, when man, by virtue of actual attention, or at least of a virtual intention, lives so self-collected that he does everything in a manner worthy of My sight, and, meanwhile, by repeated acts, turns himself to Me.

In the next place, when—with a heart cleansed from every ill-regulated affection, and dedicated to

Me as a special sanctuary—man attends faithfully, listening to what I speak within, and is ever ready to answer to My whisperings.

Lastly, when the interior soul, in some manner absorbed in Me, so lives for Me that she is wont not to be mindful of herself except in Me; not to love herself, except in Me—ever reposing in Me with a certain sweet and divine union, and enjoying My presence more perfectly than the bird enjoys the air wherein he flies, or a healthy man the health that gives him vigor.

This is the completing of divine union, which surpasses all understanding, to which pure souls— that, by generous sacrifices, whether external or internal, have disposed themselves, with a perfect heart leaving all creatures, and even themselves— with the aid of grace are wont to attain.

5. My Child, the remembrance of My presence is the most efficacious means of avoiding sins. For who, if he calls to mind that he stands in the sight of God, could dare to offend Him, who, at the same instant, can hurl both body and soul into hell?

If, with thy own eyes, thou wert to behold Me present to thee, in a sensible form, wouldst thou be willing, My Child, wouldst thou dare to commit sin in My very sight? Wouldst thou not deport thyself in a respectful manner? But, with the eyes of faith, thou seest Me more clearly and more certainly present, than if thou sawest Me with the eyes of the body.

Remember and love Me who am present to thee, and thou shalt not sin forever. What is it that renders sinless the inhabitants of heaven? Is it not the Vision and the love of the Godhead, and that which arises thence?

When, by faith, thy mind beholds thy God, when thy heart loves Him, thou wilt not offend so great a Majesty. Although, by nature, thou art weak and liable to fall; yet this divine Vision will not allow thee to be deceived, nor will this love suffer thee to fall. For whoever abides therein sins not.

Wherefore, My Child, so long as, by faith and love, thou walkest before Me, thou shalt be sinless; not indeed, by thy nature, but by My presence.

Whenever thou didst sin, surely, whilst resolving to sin, thou sawest Me not by faith, neither knewest thou Me by love. For whosoever sins neither sees nor knows his God.

6. What is there more delightful than My presence? what more pleasant? what more useful for everything? Is it not an enduring Paradise? whom the Angels and Saints gaze upon, face to face, whom they truly possess in heaven the same thou beholdest upon earth by faith, the same thou enjoyest by love — whilst thou growest all the while in merits.

Without the practice of the divine presence, solitude is wont to be dangerous, the intercourse of men hurtful. But, by the use of it, both are helped and made holy.

Thou shalt scarcely find any one practice of piety which contains such a number, such a variety, and such a frequency of acts of virtue as this holy exercise of the divine presence.

Be of good cheer, then, My Child: endeavor piously and diligently, to acquire the habit of living in My presence. When once acquired, it will serve thee as a protection amid dangers, as a light in darkness, as a comfort in solitude, as a safeguard in the world—everywhere as a constant practice of virtues, everywhere as a divine fellowship.

7. *The voice of the Disciple.*—But, good Master, most sweet Jesus, in what manner, pray, shall I acquire this sacred habit?

The voice of Jesus.—Before everything else, My Child, thou must often pray, earnestly beg for grace; whereby thou mayst be excited to call to mind, with a lively faith and a confiding love, the divine presence.

The senses, also, are to be kept under strict discipline; and the inordinate desire of perceiving external things is to be mortified.

Then, the internal faculties are to be guarded: not only wicked, but also useless thoughts, are to be kept from the mind, vain and idle occupations from the heart.

Afterwards thou shouldst endeavor to turn thyself frequently to Me by short and fervent aspirations, which will be all the more profitable to thee in proportion as they are more adapted to the state and circumstances of thy soul.

Finally, My Child, in all things seen, thou oughtest to seek Me, the unseen, the Beloved of thy heart.

Do not the very creatures, which surround thee on every side, warn thee of My presence? Lift up thy eyes and behold how all things, each after its own manner, proclaim that I am present.

Do not the serenity of the sky and the very storm proclaim it? do not the fruits and flowers? Do not consolations and afflictions? Do not virtues and the fountains of grace?

My Child, if thou art an interior Disciple of My Heart, all things that present themselves before thee will help thee to be mindful of Me, and to love Me present everywhere.

Everywhere thou shalt find Me; and thou shalt pass over all even unto Me, in whom alone thou shalt find joy and repose.

8. *The voice of the Disciple.*—O Lord, God invisible beholding all things, incomprehensible and present everywhere, whither shall I flee from Thy face?

Behold! if I go up into heaven, Thou art there; if I go down into hell, Thou art present. If I take wings at the dawn, and dwell in the uttermost parts of the sea, there also Thy hands will guide and hold me.

Darkness has no gloom before Thee: night is to Thee as the day. Everywhere am I in Thy sight; within and without am I unvailed before Thy eyes.

9. Lo then, Thou art ever present to me. How sweet a thought! how great a consolation! what reasons for confidence! how great an incitement to love!

But yet, whithersoever I turn, Thy creatures awaken my faith, warn me of Thy presence, of Thy power, of Thy love, of Thy loveliness. If the shadow of the object is so pleasant, so fair, so good, what must be the object itself?

Behold! this creature is pleasing, that other strong; this one is fair, that one good: but incomparably more pleasing, and, at the same time,

stronger, fairer, sweeter, and everywhere better art
Thou, O Beloved, whom my soul loves!

O Jesus, My Saviour God, delightful Paradise
of my heart! grant, I beseech Thee, that always
and everywhere I be mindful of Thee, that I love
Thee always and everywhere present.

Make my heart a pure and holy dwelling, wherein
I may find Thee, possess Thee, enjoy Thee, for the
sanctification of my soul, and the ever-enduring
glory of Thy heart.

CHAPTER XVI

THAT THE MOST SACRED HEART OF JESUS, TEMPTED IN THE DESERT, TEACHES US EVER TO PRESERVE PEACE OF HEART.

1. *The voice of Jesus.*—My Child, when I went
away from the Jordan, I was led by the Spirit into
the desert. Behold a sight, which filled the Angels themselves with admiration.

For, removed from human society, dwelling
among the wild beasts of the wilderness, I passed
My days and nights in fasting and austerity, exposed to all the changes of the weather.

My Heart persevered in divine communings with
My heavenly Father, in sublime contemplation, in
ceaseless prayer.

Meanwhile, forgotten, or even insulted by the
world, I was assailed by Satan in wonderful ways:
yea, I was even seized by him, carried elsewhere,
and variously and exceedingly tempted.

What impelled Me to undergo these things, if not the love of My Heart, that I might console thee My Child, and teach thee by My example?

Taught and encouraged by this, thou needest not wonder, if, in thy condition of life, thou art tempted by the demon, or annoyed by the world: neither shouldst thou, on account of human events, or the devil's assaults, lose thy peace of heart.

Naught of all this world could disturb or disquiet My Heart: but, ever tranquil and at rest, with a firm Will turning Itself away from the objects cast before It, It went on in peace.

2. My Child, do thou with all diligence aspire to this holy peace, and follow it up with all care.

Blessed is the good soul that keeps herself in true peace! In such a one I abide as in My own kingdom: in her heart I find My delight as on a throne.

My Heart loves to communicate Itself to a tranquil heart; because there Its Inspirations are heard, are fostered, and bring forth fruit.

If thou desirest to commit the fewest faults possible, if thou desirest to derive profit from thy very faults, if thou desirest to practice virtues, in a proper manner, keep thy peace of heart.

If thou wishest usefully to resist the temptations of the devil, and to bring to naught the wicked attempts of hell, be in peace, and continue therein.

3. The enemy,—knowing that he can do little against a soul, so long as she keeps herself in this holy peace,—strives in every way to trouble her.

For this purpose, he sets sometimes every power in motion, and stirs it up: he excites the imagination, he calls out the passions, he suggests many things contrary, now to this virtue, then to that; at one time he assails by flattery, at another by fright; sometimes he persists stubbornly.

If things of this kind befall thee, My Child, be not uneasy, do not lose thy peace. So long as thou continuest in a holy peace, all is safe: but if thou beginnest to be troubled, thou beginnest also to be in danger: and although, by divine grace, thou withholdest thyself from a wilful consent, yet the enemy has gained enough to be satisfied for the present.

He does not think that he can overthrow thee in the first assault, but that, by degrees, if he be able to disturb thy heart, he may worry thee, weaken thee, and so at last destroy thee.

Beware, therefore, that thou be not disturbed, by whatsoever temptation, or for how long soever a time, thou mayst be assailed.

4. My Child, let not thy heart be troubled, whatever may happen. The peace of the heart is not to be lost for aught of this world.

Although thou mayst have rendered thyself guilty of some defect or sin, even then be thou not disturbed in heart. For, if thou troublest thyself after committing a fault, dost thou thereby afford any remedy to the evil? On the contrary, thou committest a fault more dangerous than the first.

Wherefore, after an offense has been unhappily committed, be not annoyed by troubles, nor lose thou courage: but, by an act of humble love, throw thyself with a contrite heart upon My Heart, that thy fault may be consumed by this divine fire, and thy heart be made clean.

Above all, My Child, a firm and unruffled peace of heart is necessary, when, for the greater glory of My Heart, and thy own greater good, thou art suffered to be oppressed by inward desolateness; whereby the understanding is wrapped in darkness, and the will feels itself pushed on to evil, so that sometimes thou seemest abandoned to thyself alone, and to a stubborn enemy.

If in that state thou givest thyself up to mental perturbation, thou wilt render vain the intention of My Heart, and run great risk—not only of depriving thyself of the proffered treasure of merits, and a sublime degree of holiness,—but also of going astray, and of falling.

But if, with a quiet and undaunted heart, thou goest obediently onward, whithersoever My Spirit may lead thee; and instead and despite of thy own feeling, thou followest His guidance, thou shalt pass through the ordeal unhurt, and come out of it more perfect.

5. In exterior things also, much will occur to move and trouble thy heart, unless it be well established in peace.

It will happen, that thou findest men unfaithful, nay more, at times, opposed to thee,—even those that are bound to thee by the obligation of gratitude, friendship, station or office.

If thy peace rests upon the dispositions or doings of mortals, or depends thereon, it will be exposed to sad vicissitudes.

Many judge accordingly as their heart is affected: therefore, it is to be expected that they will not rarely think ill of thee, will find fault with thy doings, will condemn thy eager pursuit of an interior life; in short, will try thy virtue in various ways.

When these things happen, My Child, suffer not thy heart to be troubled: but remain in peace, and allow everything to pass, precisely as thou allowest the clouds to pass over thy head.

And truly, of what avail would it be to thee to be troubled by these matters? Shouldst thou not add a burden, and reap bitterness as the fruit of thy toil?

Accustom thyself to bear patiently things adverse, to hear in silence what is unpleasant, to be quiet among the boisterous, to remain tranquil whilst the world is blustering.

6. *The voice of the Disciple.*—But, O Lord Jesus, how hard it seems in practice, when temptations annoy me inwardly, whilst I long to serve Thee faithfully; or when the torments of adverse circumstances and men assail me, whilst I mean well; not to feel them, not to be troubled by them! Verily, O Lord, this seems impossible to me.

The voice of Jesus.—My Child, it is no evil to feel things which are burthensome, or capable of disturbing the heart: thou must needs feel them to be able to resist them.

It is certainly impossible not to feel them, how pious soever thou mayst be. For piety does neither destroy nor blunt the powers of the soul; but, on the contrary, it renders them more pure and perfect.

Neither is it possible that the inferior part of the heart be not sometimes affected thereby. But these emotions, unless they be consented to by the superior part, can by no means harm thee: nay more, they may be useful to establish thy peace the more solidly; since, the more victories thou gainest over the inferior part, the more subject and tranquil thou wilt keep it, and the greater safety thou wilt enjoy.

But yet, it is ever in thy power to preserve thyself in peace. For—since thou possessest freewill, and receivest ever a sufficient grace—neither the malice of hell, nor the wickedness of men, nor any adversity can disturb thy heart, unless itself be willing.

It depends, therefore, on thyself alone, My Child, ever to possess this good, which is so great, that, next to the state of grace, it is the greatest good of this life.

7. *The voice of the Disciple.*—Yea, Lord Jesus, so it is assuredly. Teach me, then, I beseech Thee, the way of holy peace, which Thou didst show me to be so useful and necessary for all things.

The voice of Jesus.—My Child, many there are who say much about the means of obtaining and preserving peace; but I say: learn ye of Me, because I am meek and humble of Heart, and ye shall find rest—the perfection of peace.

First then, a virtuous heart alone—which, living in grace, strives to imitate the virtues of My Heart —can possess true peace, because there is no peace for the wicked.

Again, a humble heart, which is satisfied with holding an inferior place among men, and which, distrustful of self, has, in every difficulty, recourse to Me—can alone preserve an undisturbed peace.

Finally, a heart enlivened by charity, which is united, or at least resigned, to the divine Will, can alone enjoy, without interruption, the sweetness of holy peace, and persevere securely therein.

If thou art perfectly imbued with the sentiments

of My Heart, so that, for love of a more complete resemblance to Me, and a proof of a more disinterested love, thou choosest, according to the divine good pleasure, to suffer with Me in this world: then, My Child, wilt thou overflow with the plenty of a most delightful peace, enjoy a continued tranquillity, in spite of all the changes of sensible things; and thou wilt be ever jubilant with a cheerful heart; because the very source, whence the heart is wont to be troubled, shall strengthen it in thee.

Behold, My Child, the way to true peace, which leads up by degrees even to perfection. Blessed are they that walk therein. Outside of it can be found no real, no solid, no lasting peace.

If thou possessest not a virtuous heart, resigned to the divine Will by humility and love, do whatsoever thou wilt, go whithersoever thou choosest, nowhere shalt thou find the happiness of peace.

When the heart is not well-disposed within, neither the shunning of occasions, nor the change of places, nor the loneliness of living, nor spiritual books, nor, in fine, the counseling of men can give true peace.

8. Remember, My Child, that the causes of inward trouble do not lie in objects outside of thee; but within thee, in the ill-ordered dispositions of the heart. Whenever thou dost no longer allow these causes to exist within thyself, outward objects will cease to be an occasion of trouble.

Now, there are as many causes that can make thee lose thy peace as there are ill-regulated affections of the heart. And not only do the affections of evil or vain things belong to this class, but also those for good and holy objects, if indulged in contrary to the divine good pleasure.

Wherefore, so soon as thou detectest aught inordinate within thyself, thou shouldst persist in the use of prayer, special self-examination, and other fit remedies, that thou mayst, quietly and effectually, cast it out of thy heart.

How many, even virtuous souls, there are that anxiously seek after peace—using for this purpose various means, and these no bad means—and yet find only greater uneasiness; because they proceed in an unorderly manner, longing too much or too eagerly for the end of the trouble which they feel, or for the obtaining of rest after which they sigh, or because they annoy themselves in the use of the means, or desire to experience a sensible peace!

Seek thou peace in a peaceful manner; and, as it is to be found in the superior part of the heart —where the rational will presides, under faith and grace—possess and preserve it there.

Thus, My Child, thou shalt be able to enjoy constantly a holy peace, My peace, which is the privilege of every true Disciple of My Heart, the seasoning of prosperity, the soother of adversity, the chief of all blessings; in short, the sweet and necessary means of perfection and holiness.

9. *The voice of the Disciple.*—O Jesus, God of peace, and Father of all consolation! Oh! how I desire, how I long for peace, Thy peace, so sweet and holy!

Let others, who wish for them, possess the other good things of life; to me, I beseech Thee, give Thou peace, for me the greatest good of this life, embracing all I desire.

Grant me kindly, to make a proper use of the means appointed, that thus I may become a true Disciple of Thy Heart,—ever peaceful in meekness and humbleness of heart.

O Prince of peace, most sweet Jesus! Whose delight it is to reign in a pure and quiet heart; so establish Thy kingdom in my heart that it be never disturbed, but constantly strengthened more and more until Thou admittest me to rule with Thee in heavenly bliss, where, with the Angels and Saints, Thou reignest in peace everlasting.

CHAPTER XVII.

THAT THE MOST SACRED HEART OF JESUS, ENTERING UPON HIS PUBLIC LIFE, TEACHES US ZEAL FOR SOULS.

1. *The voice of Jesus.*—My Child, God sent His Son into the world, that the world may be saved by Him.

Do not then wonder, if zeal for souls was ever pressing and incessantly urging on My Heart, that It might spread the kingdom of divine love over the hearts of men, by every means which My heavenly Father had placed at Its disposal.

Hitherto I had remained hidden in solitude, as it were to prepare Myself for the work, and to teach all the Disciples of My Heart that they must first have an ardent zeal for themselves before they can profitably exhibit zeal for their neighbor.

Behold! whilst I was sanctifying Myself for the salvation of souls, how often, and with how great a fervor of Heart, was I wont to pray for them, that they might live for the Lord their God, do no evil, and make progress in virtue!

I also associated with Me Disciples and Apostles, whom, filled with the Spirit of My zeal, I cheered on; to whom I communicated My intentions; upon whom I looked rejoiced in Heart, because they applied themselves strenuously to the salvation of souls.

I went around, teaching, and speaking of the kingdom of God,—seizing every opportunity, in private and in public, to induce men to do better.

The example of My life shone forth, like a light that had risen for a people seated in darkness. For I went about doing good to all, and manifesting to every one the humility and charity of My Heart.

How greatly they were edified and moved when they beheld Me toiling all day for their advantage and salvation; and, in the mean time, frequently withdrawing from the multitude, that, for a little while, I might pray alone! When they learned that, after the labors and journeys of the day—whilst My wearied Apostles refreshed themselves by nightly slumbers—I Myself was wont to spend the night in prayer!

Finally, since all power in heaven and on earth had been given to Me, I employed the same for the exercise of the zeal of My Heart, for the divine glory, for the gaining of souls; and I wrought as many miracles as were necessary and proper in the salvation of all.

Behold, My Child, the means which the zeal of My Heart employed to win souls Are not the same means at thy disposal, in whatever state of life thou mayst be? use them, therefore, earnestly for My glory and the salvation of souls

2. Do thou frequently pray; and, in the spirit of prayer, offer some mortifications—little and light though they be—some works of piety and mercy, thy spiritual exercises, and even thy ordinary occupations for this, that My straying children—who are miserably pining away in the far-off country, either of infidelity, heresy, or sin—making, at last, a better use of their freedom, may rejoice My Heart by their happy return; moreover, that the good may advance in virtue, may strive after better gifts, and continue to aspire to perfection.

O, if thou didst know how powerful prayer is for the salvation of souls! How many interior persons there are, and they too secluded from intercourse with the world, who, individually, by prayer alone, have snatched thousands of souls from infidelity, heresy or sin, and raised them to bliss everlasting! Understand, then, My Child, what thou mayst effect by prayer.

Try to inspire some persons with zeal; they thus become thy disciples and apostles, whom thou sendest in quest of souls.

Thus thou wilt perform many things, not by thyself alone, but also through others; who, in turn, will animate and send others; and, in this manner, transmit them from generation to generation.

Be eager to speak frequently on subjects that breathe piety; which promote edification, and render virtue attractive. How many are there now in heaven who owe the occasion of their everlasting felicity to some pious conversation?

It is, indeed, true, My Child, that thou shouldst not be importunate; so as to deter thy neighbor from virtue, rather than draw him to it; but a genuine and fervent zeal knows how to employ a holy dexterity, to produce and employ fit opportunities of conversing on subjects of piety.

Wonderfully effective is good example. It gives life and power to all other outward means. Take this away, and what can all the rest effect? It may cause a noise to the senses, it cannot move the heart.

By the example of thy life, therefore, do thou show forth the incomparable delights of My love; prove to thy neighbor that he, who lovingly serves Me, is, even in this world, most happy. Thus thou shalt, in some manner, force thy neighbor to taste and experience how pleasant is the service of My Heart—the service of My love.

If thou canst not work miracles, so as to suspend the laws of the universe, thou canst, by co-operating with divine grace, perform wonders. Why? is it not wonderful, nay prodigious, that, for pure love of Me, thou overlookest thy own interest, that thou mayst have a care of that of others? thou returnest good for evil? esteemest thyself blissful with Me, in the midst of humiliations?

These and the like prodigies of grace, My Child, have sometimes moved hearts that had resisted all other means, and induced them to pursue a better course.

3. In every place, and at all times, My Child, be thou full of zeal for souls; so that whosoever ap-

proaches thee may feel an incentive to virtue or perfection.

Do not believe that thou art a true Disciple of My Heart, if thou hast no zeal, no efficacious will for the salvation and perfection of souls. But if thou art desirous of proving in deed, that thou really lovest and followest My Heart, foster an ardent zeal.

What canst thou do more pleasing to My Heart than to labor at the salvation and perfection of souls—created to love and glorify Me for evermore?

If thou sendest only one soul to heaven, thou givest Me more glory than all men together, on earth, have ever given Me, or can ever procure for Me. For, whatever glory mortals, on earth, give Me, is limited by the number of acts which are at last finished: but the glory which a blessed soul, in heaven, gives Me—since it is ever-enduring—is equivalent to a number of acts to which there shall be no end forever.

Consider, My Child, how greatly I valued the salvation of souls, since for this object I came down from heaven; sought it through incessant and arduous labors and hardships; and, lastly, sacrificed My very life for the same.

Oh, if thou didst know the worth of a soul, with how great a zeal for her salvation wouldst thou be inflamed! Learn what she is worth, by the price at which I ransomed her.

Save a soul, and behold! thou shalt have performed a deed incomparably more precious than if thou hadst gained this whole world, with all its possessions.

My Child, if thou savest the soul of thy neighbor, thou freest thy own: for he that shall cause a sinner to turn from the error of his way, thall save his own soul from death, and cover a multitude of sins.

How great a joy shall it be to thee, My Child, after this life, to behold in heaven the Elect, who, after grace, owe to thee—some their heavenly bliss, others the hight of their sanctity, and a corresponding everlasting glory; and who will repay thee with a thousand thanksgivings forever !

Verily, the help in the salvation and perfection of souls is not only the most excellent of all things human, but even the most godlike of all things divine.

4. Pray frequently, that thy heart may be endowed with a true zeal — one which humility supports, charity stimulates, science shapes, discretion guides and perseverance strengthens.

Take heed, lest thou suffer thyself to be animated with a zeal which springs, not from grace in a meek and humble heart, but from nature, under the influence of some passion. He that is lcd by this zeal, whilst he endeavors to root out sins, multiplies them; and whilst he burns to make others better in deed, renders them worse in heart.

Strive, as much as thou morally canst, everywhere to correct what is evil, and to promote what is good. But, whilst thou art doing what is in thy power, endure patiently whatsoever thou art unable to correct or improve—intrusting all things to My divine Providence, and praying that all may, at last, serve for My greater glory.

My Child, if the work of thy zeal do not succeed

at the first attempt, try again and again. It happens that men—listening secretly to the evil spirit, or lulled to sleep by lukewarmness—at first scarcely hearken to what is better; but that afterward—when the good Spirit, by means of interior remorse, repeats what they have heard, and exhorts them from within—the zeal of the zealous laborer urging them on, and grace moving them, they turn and surrender.

So long as I wait, so long as I endure a mortal, thou shouldst by no means despair of him. If he is an unbeliever now, how knowest thou whether he will not soon be a believer? If he is a heretic at present, whence knowest thou that he will not soon follow Catholic truth? If a schismatic to-day, he may be united to the Church to-morrow.

Paul was in the morning a persecutor of the Church; in the evening he was a Vessel of election. Magdalen was a sinner in the city on one day; on the following she was a model of every virtue,—a Seraph-like lover of My Heart.

How many there are, who, seemingly lost beyond all hope, in their errors or sins, were yet converted, and found the happy life of grace in this world and the blissful life of glory in the next? Has, then, the power of grace grown less? has man's free-will become extinct?

5. If, in spite of thy endeavors, men be unwilling to be converted, do not lose thy peace of heart.

Imitate the holy Guardian Angels, who, after having done whatever they should and could have done—if the men committed to their charge do not repent nor improve—remain equally peaceful, equally blissful.

If there be any who do not avail themselves of the efforts of thy zeal for the good of their souls, these endeavors shall not be less rewarded; since, with Me, an efficacious will is reputed equal to success.

It is thy duty to water the plants of grace—not to give them increase. Water them, therefore, and labor cheerfully, and, whether or not thou seest an increase, thou shalt never toil without profit to thyself, and honor to Me.

6. Meanwhile, My Child, thou must take heed, lest, whilst thou art laboring to save others, or to make them perfect, thou suffer thyself to become a castaway or a disregarder of thy own perfection.

In thy heart believe that they, to whose spiritual good thou appliest thyself, are already better than thyself, or that they shall be so some day: and how much good soever thou effectest in souls, deem thyself no more than a cymbal, which, without another's aid, cannot give forth a sound.

The more disinterestedly thou shalt have Me for thy aim, and the more humbly thou shalt think concerning thyself, the more fit shalt thou be to promote the salvation and perfection of souls.

For I select weak instruments of this kind—weak in their own eyes—to perform My own great works; that no one may glory in his strength, but that to Me may be given all the honor and glory.

7. *The voice of the Disciple.*—It is not, then, enough, Lord Jesus, that I alone love Thee: it is necessary that others also love Thee; that all serve Thee. For Thou art supremely, Thou art for every reason, worthy of the love of all hearts.

O Jesus! if men knew Thee, would they ever

offend **Thee?** Would they not love **Thee** with their whole heart?

How sweet a labor, to win hearts to Thee! how angelic an employment! how godlike a work!

Who will grant me, to travel over the whole earth, to captivate all hearts, to enkindle them with love for Thee!

Oh would, most sweet Jesus, that I held possession of all hearts, that I might devote them all to Thee, consecrate them to Thy love!

Receive, I beseech Thee, the desire of my heart, whereby I long to be able to secure for Thee, upon earth, as great a love from all men as Thy angels and Saints show Thee in heaven.

Let me become, I entreat Thee, the apostle of Thy Heart, that I may spread Thy love everywhere; that, with a ready and generous heart, I may spend my labor, my pains, my every means, and, over and above, spend myself, for souls that may love and glorify Thee through all eternity.

CHAPTER XVIII.

THAT THE MOST SACRED HEART OF JESUS, PRESENT AT THE MARRIAGE-FEAST IN CANA, TEACHES US SPIRITUAL JOYFULNESS.

1. *The voice of Jesus.*—My Child, as I came for the salvation of all, I became all to all, that I might gain all.

Light is pleasing to all, a source of gladness,

diffusing heat and life. Such was I, the Light of the world: such was My Life, which manifested the joy, the love, the cheerfulness of My Heart.

Search carefully all things, My Child, nowhere shalt thou find Me surly; nowhere shunning, or driving away the people through moroseness: but, everywhere cheerful, gladsomely dealing with men according to the divine good pleasure—animating and sanctifying all things with My Spirit.

Nay rather, behold! when invited, I refused not to be present at the Marriage-feast, together with My Mother and My Disciples; and there to rejoice in a holy manner, availing Myself of every opportunity to gain souls, and to teach virtue and true gladness of heart.

By this example of My Heart, the Saints were taught to entertain a spiritual joyfulness; and thereby to edify their neighbor, and to serve Me with a cheerful heart.

They knew that I am a kind Father, that I love that My children live with their heart expanded—content and happy in the partaking of My blessings.

Ponder these things, My Child: imitate them, that My joy may be within thee.

2. Behold what this spiritual joyfulness does and accomplishes! What is there that gives Me here greater honor than to serve Me with a cheerful heart; to prove, in this manner, to the whole world, that My service is full of sweetness and felicity?

Moreover, the gladness of My Heart adorns virtue, smooths difficulties, softens hardships, brightens the understanding, enlivens the will; in short, makes the whole man well-disposed to everything.

Without joyfulness of heart, all external good

things contribute little to happiness; the powers of the soul are inactive, the body itself languishes, man is wretched—even in the midst of prosperity.

By the practice of spiritual joyfulness, thou wilt render thyself dear to Me, who love him that gives cheerfully; useful to thy neighbor, who will be pleasantly stimulated to that which is good: lastly, beneficial to thy own self, who, by this practice alone, wilt perform several acts of virtue.

What more? Behold! who is the man, that desires life, who loves to see good days? Cheerfulness of heart, this is the life of man; and good days, the best of days, which are passed in God's grace, which is like a Paradise amid blessings.

Now, spiritual joyfulness is a most certain mark of the state of grace.

The joyfulness of the just, therefore, is present felicity, and a presage of everlasting bliss.

3. What is spiritual joyfulness, except the good disposition of the soul—showing that for My sake, she is truly satisfied?

It is not, therefore, founded on nature, but on grace: it does not depend on the peculiarity of one's character, but on the disposition of the heart: it has for its object not sensual, but spiritual things.

Worldly joyfulness is hurtful; it leads to grief and bitter gnawings of the mind: natural joyfulness is inconstant, subject to frequent sadness: but spiritual joyfulness is steady and wholesome.

A heart of good will, together with grace, produces this holy joyfulness; fervent piety gives it expansion: victory over one's natural inclinations makes it solid.

4. The devil, who loves depression of spirits,

knowing how powerfully spiritual cheerfulness acts against him, seeks to assail it by every means, to destroy it by false reasonings, or to diminish it by vain subtleties.

Be on thy guard, My Child, lest thou be caught by him. If thou yieldest to this promoter of sadness, he will not be satisfied with depriving thee of the blessings of holy joyfulness, but, seeing thee disposed according to his wishes, he will attack and tempt thee in the most dangerous manner.

Whatsoever may be suggested, whatsoever may befall thee, give no admittance to gloominess, which depresses the heart. This direful evil dries up the very bones, stupefies reason itself. Wherever it reigns, understanding disappears: yea, wherever sadness of heart prevails, every misfortune is found.

It may come to pass occasionally, My Child, that, without knowing from what cause it proceeds, thou feelest thyself inclined to a certain irksome sadness. When this happens, do thou pray again and again, stir up thy fervor, and employ other suitable means, that thou mayst preserve thy gladness of heart.

5. Often also, contrary or adverse circumstances will present themselves, which will naturally produce their effect upon thee. These, by allowing thyself to be grieved in heart, thou wilt render more burdensome: on the other hand, by preserving a joyful heart, thou wilt make them light. Turn these things, therefore, in the best way thou canst, to the everlasting good of thy soul; and, with thy mind withdrawn from what is unpleasant, rejoice supernaturally over the greatness of thy gain.

But the things which are especially wont to hinder spiritual joyfulness in a virtuous soul are the defects which she commits, and without which she knows full well that she cannot live. Behold here a delusion: behold the deceit of the enemy, whereby he is accustomed to do very great harm to the inexperienced.

It depends on thee alone, My Child, to make these defects—after they have been committed—subservient to thy profit, and, consequently, to the joyfulness of thy heart. For it is a source of great advantage, nay, of great merit, on the one hand, forthwith to repent, through love for Me, of the faults committed; and, on the other, to rejoice in the humiliations which follow these faults, because My honor is thereby repaired.

Finally, My Child, whatever obstacles thou mayst find in thy way, leave nothing that is right untried, to guard against this baneful gloominess. Beware, however, lest, whilst shunning sadness, thou run into it by the other extreme. Wherefore, to avoid it, do not give thyself up to dissipation, to the neglect of thy spiritual exercises, to the pursuit of sensual delights. For, of the end of such a ioy, mourning takes hold.

6. My Child, after the possession of the state of grace, the chief of the means to enjoy spiritual gladness, and to preserve the same, is to be meek and humble of heart, for love of Me.

Be humble, and thou shalt never be cast down: love fervently, and thou shalt ever possess a joyful heart.

If thou followest the propensity or the aversion of nature: if thou art lukewarm or careless in the things which concern My service, even shouldst thou have all the delights of earth, thou canst never taste nor possess true joyfulness of heart.

There are also outward things which contribute to the joy of the heart: holy endeavors to cultivate spiritual gladness, pious jubilations by hymns and canticles, intercourse with those who are spiritually joyous, cheerfulness in action, resignation in suffering, a holy freedom in one's proceeding.

Pray, My Child, and strive to make a right use of these means, and thus shalt thou enjoy true gladness, compared to which all other delight is mere grief—all other gayety, sadness—all other sweetness, bitterness.

This is My joy, wherein rejoice thou always: again, I say, rejoice.

7. *The voice of the Disciple.*—O Jesus! whose Heart is the never-failing fountain of exquisite gladness, whence heaven draws as well as earth; where, save in Thee, shall I find true joyfulness of heart?

O most sweet Jesus! who hast pity in cheerfulness, have pity on me, Thy unworthy Child; fill my heart with holy gladness.

Without Thee, my soul is like a field without water, dry and wretched: Thou alone art true and efficacious refreshment.

When Thy refreshing Spirit is not within me, distasteful is all that creatures can offer: but when Thou cheerest up the heart, my soul leaps for joy; and, in her gladness, bears all things with ease, finds all savory, tastes sweetness even in what is bitter.

Thus do Thou ever, I entreat Thee, gladden my soul. Grant me a humility so solid that I be never dejected: so great a love for Thee, so great a fervor, that ever joyous I may live for Thee.

O Jesus. Beloved of my soul, my whole and sole delight! let me so serve Thee with a cheerful heart that I may honor Thy service, edify my neighbor, sanctify myself, to the everlasting joy of Thy heart.

CHAPTER XIX.

THAT THE MOST SACRED HEART OF JESUS, CONVERSING WITH MEN, TEACHES US TO BEAR WITH THE DEFECTS OF OUR NEIGHBOR.

1. *The voice of Jesus.*—My Child, so long as I was seen upon earth, and conversed with men, I was in the midst of a wicked generation.

How much pride and infidelity, how much uncleanness and iniquity, thinkest thou, did I behold—I the Searcher of hearts—in the hearts of men, to whom naught, save the world; naught, except self-interest, was pleasing!

How was My Heart moved at the sight of men's sinful ignorance, unbridled licentiousness, forgetfulness of the things of heaven, anxiety for those of earth, neglect of virtue, the triumph of vice!

Compare Me, My Child, with such men: My humility with their conceitedness and vanity: My zeal with their indifference and obstinacy: My beneficence with their insensibility and ungratefulness: My charity with their listlessness and disregard: in short, all My virtues with their defects and vices!

Understand, also, what disposition of Heart I displayed before them. Behold! whatsoever they were, I continued to live with them, to converse with them, to stay among them—without complaint or indignation of Heart—yea, to show myself content.

If thou meditatest rightly upon this pattern of life, thou wilt learn to manifest similar sentiments of heart to thy neighbor.

2. Thou, My Child, and all thy neighbors, ye are conjointly children of the same heavenly Father; ye were conjointly ransomed at the same price of My life, ye are all to be united forever in fellowship by the same bond of the love of the Holy Spirit.

Ye are all called to the same kingdom of heaven; that there ye may be made blissful in perfect peace, in the joy of an everlasting union.

See, therefore, that thou agree with them on the way, lest thou be hereafter excluded from the heavenly abode of the Blessed, and delivered up to exterior torturers.

This is My example; nay more, this is My command, that, carrying each other's burdens, ye love one another, as I love you with a supernatural, universal, efficacious love.

If ye love Me, keep My command. If ye keep the same, ye will remain in My love.

He that hates his brother is a murderer: he kills the very soul, and that his own. Whosoever is angry with his brother, shall be answerable before the judgment. He that forgives not, shall not be forgiven. He that forbears not, shall not be forborne. For with what measure ye mete, it shall be measured to you again.

3. Remember, My Child, that thou art living—

not among Angels but among men, who cannot be
here below without failings.

Do not then wonder, if frail mortals err or fall:
but wonder at this, that, whilst thyself thou hast
many failings, with which others must bear, thou
darest sometimes feel indignant at those of others.

If thou bearest not with another's defect, dost
thou not by the very fact commit a fault and show
it, too?

Know that I sometimes suffer well-meaning and
virtuous men to be opposed to each other, that,
without sin, there may be an opportunity of bearing with one another's defects, of practising solid
virtues, and of acquiring merits.

Judge the things of thy neighbor by thy own.
As thou desirest to be dealt with, so deal thou with
others: and do not to others what thou wouldst
not have done to thyself.

Hast thou not many things, My Child, from
which thou wouldst gladly free thyself, and from
which thou knowest, by thy own experience, that
thou art unable to free thyself? What thou sufferest, therefore, in thyself, even against thy will, that
do thou likewise tolerate in others; whom, if thou
hast any humility and charity, thou wilt suppose to
endure their own defects, in spite of themselves.

4. There are they who willingly enough bear
with the defects of friends, and of those whom they
find agreeing with themselves in taste and manners:
but who take easily offense at the failings of all
beside. Now, what virtue is there in this? Do not
the heathen do the same? Nay more, are not the
very animals, devoid of reason, accustomed to act
in the same manner?

How canst thou be My Disciple, if thou hast the feelings of a pagan: or, if thou followest simply an animal instinct?

Be thou animated, My Child, with the supernatural charity of My Heart: whereby I endured, and loved all, enemies as well as friends, even unto death.

Passing, therefore, over every merely natural consideration, endure thou all, love all; make of no one an exception.

Pray for them that persecute and calumniate thee; bless them that revile thee; do good to them that hate thee; overcome evil by good.

Hate the evil which is done: but beware lest thou hate the man who commits the same. How much soever thou mayst detest the sin of a man, thou art bound to love the man himself.

5. The Saints, who followed not nature but grace, did so far clothe themselves with the sentiments of My Heart that they endured and loved—not only all in general, but specially those that were opposed to them.

Yet, My Child, they, too, were men; and, like thyself, had the feelings of nature: but they overcame nature; and, in spite of feeling, in their greatness of soul, emulated My example.

Come, Child, be courageous, and, as is becoming in a Disciple of My Heart, imitate those noble and generous souls.

When thou feelest indignant at the faults of thy neighbor, keep silence; neither suffer thou aught ill-ordered to escape thy lips—whereby thou mayst harm thyself as well as thy neighbor.

Pray for him in thy heart; and steadily refrain thy mind from reflecting on his faults.

Never grow weary of pardoning thy neighbor, of bearing with his faults, of loving him with a supernatural affection; if with thy heart thou desirest to follow My Heart.

If thou hast many and great things to endure in others, remember, Child, that I have undergone more and greater things for thy sake: nay, that I have borne with more and greater things in thee.

Behold! I mercifully forgave thee a debt of ten thousand: shouldst thou not then have pity on thy fellow-servant, as I also had mercy on thee?

Call to mind, My Child, how long, and with how great a goodness of Heart, I have endured thee, and how I do even now endure thee: and learn thence, how and how far thou oughtest to bear with thy neighbor.

6. *The voice of the Disciple.*—O Jesus! how kind and forbearing hast Thou been towards me, yea, art even now! How can I recall this without tears of affection and gratitude!

How wretched soever I may be, I find Thy Heart always open for me: and yet, I own it to my confusion, I do sometimes close mine against my neighbor.

O Jesus, meek and humble of Heart! who knowest that I am less ready to bear with the defects of my neighbor, because I love and esteem myself too much: infuse into my heart, I beseech Thee, the humility and charity of Thy Heart, that, for love of Thee, I may love every neighbor as myself.

Grant me grace, that, as often as I behold the failings of others, I may raise myself above nature; and that, by a supernatural principle, I may be moved to compassion,—not to indignation; to well-wishing,—not to aversion.

Bestow upon us, most loving Jesus, Thy Spirit, the Spirit of charity; that we may love one another, and live united by a holy peace, until we enter the realms of Thy everlasting love.

CHAPTER XX.

THAT THE MOST SACRED HEART OF JESUS, ACTING TOWARD ALL WITH THE GREATEST OPEN-HEART-EDNESS, TEACHES US TO ACT WITH SIMPLICITY IN REGARD TO OUR NEIGHBOR.

1. *The voice of Jesus.*—My Child, when I dwelt among men. they wondered and were astonished, that with each and all of them, I dealt with so great a simplicity.

But it was a secret of My Heart. For My Heart is simple, loves God, and, by the same love, all besides; holding one in all, and all in one.

This simplicity of Heart, which I showed to men, is the image of My Spirit,—charity undivided in itself, busied with many things, itself ever one.

Loving God and men in the same Spirit: contemplating human misery and prosperity; averting evil and promoting good; perfecting various works; supporting the different characters and dispositions of persons; passing, in one and the same manner, through varied and manifold circumstances: and all this in the same Spirit.

By this most pleasing virtue, men were wonder-fully moved. For never had they beheld, nor ever conceived in their mind, so great a simplicity united with so great a dignity: so uniform a kind-ness allied to so wonder-working a power.

In Me there was no duplicity, nothing feigned, no affected loftiness of speech, no artful manner of acting.

The ingenuous frankness of My Soul was apparent to all; My actions reflected, as it were, like a mirror, the sincerity of My Heart.

Hence, My Child, men came to Me of their own accord, and poured out their hearts before Me. Even little children ran to meet Me; and I suffered them to come to Me, so that men wondered; I spoke to them with kindness, I blessed them; I filled them, all joyous as they were, with the love of virtue.

2. By My example, learn to make use of a holy simplicity in regard to thy neighbor,—which consists in drawing thy thoughts, words, and deeds, from one divine charity, and in referring to the same the thoughts, words, and deeds of others.

In My Heart, the centre of charity, is every neighbor to be viewed and loved.

Whoever views his neighbor without My Heart, easily divides his heart among various merely natural affections, or compounds it by means of motives or intentions partly human.

But he that views and loves men in the charity of My Heart, he, with a single eye, sees one in all; he, with a pure affection, loves one in all; he has his heart neither compounded nor divided.

3. Thus, then, be thou simple in viewing or think-

ing that which is thy neighbor's: and do not divide thy heart by rashly judging.

Who has established thee a judge of thy neighbor? Whence thy right to condemn him? how darest thou to cast off, by thy judgment, one whom I shield with My Heart, whom thou art bound to love as a brother, who, in My sight, may be, now or hereafter, better than thyself?

If thou judgest rashly, My Child, thou art inexcusable. For, if thou so condemnest another, dost thou not condemn thyself? By rashly judging him guilty of a fault, thou renderest thyself guilty of a fault.

Do not, however, confound a suggestion with a suspicion, nor a suspicion with a judgment. A suggestion is an evil instigation, which does not depend on man's will, and therefore, unless wilfully indulged in, is blameless. And what is suspicion, except, from some doubtful signs, to think and hold something as probable or truth-like? But judging is, from a sufficient reason, to decide and believe something as certain.

Wherefore, when there is a sufficient reason for suspecting or judging, the suspicion and the judgment are assuredly neither rash nor culpable.

And if a sufficient reason to suspect or judge be wanting, without its being remarked, the error is invincible and guiltless.

If, however, the care of others be committed to thy charge, it is not only lawful, but also necessary, whenever probable signs of evil are given,—that thou have suspicion concerning those who are subject to thee; that thus thou mayst prudently remove the evil, if any be found to exist.

For the rest, My Child, whatsoever sign, word or deed, thou dost observe in thy neighbor, take it ever in good part; if by any means it can be excused in thy mind, do so; but if thou seest that it can in no manner be excused, correct him by a word of charity, or by a sign of disapproval, if prudence allow it, and certain fruit is expected.

O, My Child! the holy simplicity of charity thinks no evil; neither is it grieved because it errs, when innocently it judges well, even of what is evil.

4. Be thou also simple in speech, My Child. Do not divide thy heart by means of the tongue,— as does the world, which, satisfied with outward appearances, boasts foolishly of the art of feigning and dissembling.

Do thou, from the treasury of a virtuous heart, with simplicity present good things to thy neighbor.

Far removed, therefore, from thy conversation be all artfulness, all duplicity, all craftiness; whereby thy neighbor may be misled with fallacies, or rendered distrustful through fear of some concealed untruth, or scandalized by the evidence of implied wrongfulness; or, lastly, be made to suffer harm on account of his credulity.

My Child, whatsoever thy lips utter, let it also be the sentiment of thy heart. Does it, then, behoove thee to express the inordinate emotions of the passions, if thou feelest these within thyself? Beware, lest thou draw such an inference: be far from such a belief; these emotions are not only to be suppressed by the lips, but also by the heart.

Be the same to all; true and holy simplicity is courteous to all, ever agreeable, everywhere uniform.

Whatever be the reasons in thy favor, do not wound the union of charity, for the sake of matters which are indifferent, or do not concern thee. Remember, that one act of charity surpasses infinitely the multitude of all reasonings.

If it happen that, by a word, thou give offense to thy neighbor, humbling thyself in artless simplicity, endeavor, as soon as possible, to give him satisfaction, or an excuse. For humility alone is a reparation of wounded charity.

5. Finally, be also simple in acting. Let there appear in thee no affectation, nor carelessness: be thy whole exterior such, that it may show the candor of thy interior.

Let all things, that regard thy neighbor, be done in charity; which, although it is one and single, yet possesses many and various acts. One and undivided as it is, it knows how to unite many and divided objects; to tolerate equally things unequal, and to preserve and advance those which are united.

My Child, if thou hast truly learnt the simplicity of My Heart, thou wilt, with ease and sincerity, show a yielding charity to all,—becoming honor to every one; being so disposed, as inwardly to give the preference to others, and willing, with one and the same divine love, joyfully to render service to each one, according to his position.

Proceed with simplicity, My Child, go on straightforward, not running to the right nor to the left, in order to speculate about things possible; or to investigate what others may think of thee.

In all things seek Me alone, whom thou shalt undoubtedly find in all, and in whom alone thou shalt possess all.

6. Woe to the double-hearted, who has one thing in his heart, another on his lips; who keeps sweetness on his lips, bitterness in his heart; who outwardly professes sincerity, and inwardly hides deceit!

The heart that enters the path of deceit shall meet no happy issue: it shall find neither the path to My Heart, nor the road to the heart of the neighbor it shall stray to its own confusion.

Duplicity shall one day be unvailed, and the hope of the hypocrite shall perish.

But blessed are the simple; for theirs is secure peace! I say it again: Blessed, because My conversation and familiar intercourse is with the simple

He that walks in simplicity, walks confidingly, and shall be safe.

7. Beware, My Child, lest by following simplicity, thou dash thyself against imprudence. Holy simplicity is artless indeed, because it is holy; but, because it is holy, it is also prudent.

Be, therefore, simple as the dove: but also prudent as the serpent.

Do not lay open thy heart to every one. Do not unvail thy own affairs to thy neighbor, except in so much as well-ordered charity demands.

Whatsoever serves not for common edification, or is not of an ordinary kind, suffer thou to be known to none, except Myself, and to those that hold My place in thy regard.

Let not thy heart be like a broken vessel, which cannot hold what is poured into it.

If thou canst not keep a secret, thou art not only unworthy of the name of a Disciple of My Heart, but even of the confidence of thy neighbor; **very un-**

worthy of the secrets of friends, most unworthy of My own.

Hast thou heard anything whispered against thy neighbor? Let it die within thee: it shall not cause thee to burst, My Child, neither shall it hurt thee in any way.

A tale-bearer shall defile his own soul, and be hateful to others. For he is a doubly envenomed tool of evil.

To say the truth is not always lawful, but to tell a falsehood is never allowed. Prudence, therefore, is necessary, lest, by uttering what is true, or by saying what is false, thou sin against charity and other virtues.

Under such circumstances, My Child, have thou recourse to My Heart: the unction of Its charity will teach thee in what manner thou oughtest to proceed.

Lastly, pray that thou mayst obtain the spirit of holy simplicity, and cultivate a virtue, whereby thou wilt render thy intercourse with thy neighbor grateful and profitable to thyself, as well as to him, and pleasing and honorable to Me.

8. *The voice of the Disciple.*—Thou, Lord, art the model, the pattern of perfect simplicity. Would that I might become like to Thee!

O Jesus, Thou simple love! make Thou my heart single, that I may come as near to Thy simplicity as it can be granted to a creature,—by loving one in all, and all in one.

Render Thou my mind single, by freeing it from the different and false principles of the world and of self-love; and by preserving it from every evil suspicion and rash judgment; that it may be guided by Thee alone,—where things are certain, in truth; and, where they are doubtful, in charity.

Make me wholly single, inwardly and outwardly, that, having become one, I may always and everywhere be uniform,—inferring all things from Thee alone, and referring all to Thee alone, who art the beginning and end of all.

CHAPTER XXI.

THAT THE MOST SACRED HEART OF JESUS, SHOWING TO MEN THE SWEETNESS OF HUMBLE CHARITY, LEFT US A MODEL WHICH WE SHOULD FOLLOW.

1. *The voice of Jesus.*—Hearken, My Child, and receive My words. When of old, by the Prophet, God spoke of His Son, who was to come into the world, He said: Behold My Servant, My Beloved, in whom My soul is well pleased. I will put My Spirit upon Him. He shall not contend, nor cry out. The bruised reed He shall not break, and smoking flax He shall not extinguish. In His name shall the nations hope.

As such I came, My Child; as such I was in this world. I treated men with so great a humility, so great a charity, that I was called the Lamb of God, and known by that name.

See how I lived among men: how I behaved toward them. Although I was their Lord, I was in their midst as one ministering.

From all parts they came hastening to Me, with what ailment soever they might be afflicted; knowing that to Me humility was habitual; mildness, natural,—that goodness was the very essence of My Heart.

And, indeed, the first or the least sigh of any one, who was miserable, moved My Heart, and awakened all Its tenderness.

Did I ever cast off any one? did I ever slight the poorest, or ever the least of all? Did I ever show a sign of dislike to any one? On the contrary, I embraced and cherished all, with the greatest marks of kindness.

Consider, My Child, and reflect, with how great a tender-heartedness I treated little children; with what endearing and even-minded humility I taught the ignorant; with how steadfast and generous a courage I dealt with the troublesome; with how glowing a zeal with worldings; with how feeling a composure with the afflicted; with how great an affability with sinners; with how holy a love with the good; with how humble a charity with all.

This humble charity, the characteristic virtue of My Heart, ravished the hearts of all, to such a degree, that, as the envious murmuringly complained, the whole world went after Me.

Verily, My Child, this humble charity of My Heart overcame the whole world. For whence, thinkest thou, arose so wonderful, so sudden a conversion of the world, if not from the secret unction which moved,—and the well-known goodness of My Heart, which attracted all?

Behold! as the goodness of My Heart became known, men hastened to Me from every place, out of every state of life, under every disposition of body and soul; and, even now, they continue to do so; because they hear that the poor are not spurned by Me; that the afflicted are not forsaken; that sinners are not abhorred; that the weeping Magdalen, the suppliant woman of Canaan, the praying publican, the apostate Disciple returning, the penitent thief, My very torturers, that smote their breasts, are not cut off.

2. My Child, strive thou, with all diligence, to follow this pattern of life, this method of dealing with men, and to realize the same in thy behavior, as a true Disciple of My Heart.

Some Saints, perfectly imbued with the sentiments of My Heart, so behaved, that men could not deal with them, without being led by their very appearance,—as by an exact likeness,—to an affectionate remembrance of Me.

Thou canst not deal with thy neighbor in an indifferent manner: thou wilt produce in him either good or evil.

No one can treat with men without loss, either to himself or to another; except whosoever is willing, with a sincere heart, to humble himself before men.

It is frequently necessary humbly to give up thy opinion, if thou desirest to deal with others without disagreement: nay more, often thou must kindly embrace things unpleasant to nature, if thou wishest to live with them without bitterness.

Whence do dissensions arise among mortals? Is it not from pride, whereby one refuses to yield to another? Whence bitter feelings? Is it not from an inordinate self-love, which corrupts the very heart?

Drive away pride from among men; and behold! with it all human troubles will disappear. Next, expel self-love; and thou shalt see the delights of heaven reigning on earth.

If thou art truly humble, thou shalt captivate thy neighbor; and if thou burnest with a pure charity, thou shalt carry him along, to make him use his efforts to run in the odor of virtues, which breathe forth so sweet a fragrance.

3. Humble charity is mightier than all severity. This, whilst outwardly it may hinder evil, inwardly estranges from good: that on the other hand, corrects evil, and causes good to be loved

Nothing is more easy in directing than severity or laxity But what is there more dangerous for men than the former? or what more injurious to Me than the latter?

They that lead not an interior life, and, therefore, suffer themselves to be guided by nature, rather than by My Spirit,—are wont to fall into the one or the other excess.

My Child, if thou art charged with the care of others, thou shouldst be, before all else, an interior person. Whoever is not such, how is he to be pitied, when placed over others! For he shall doubtless ill perform many things, and do harm to My interests intrusted to him; and of all this he shall give a reckoning

Woe to the religious Community, whose Superior is not an interior person! For behold! it shall languish in spirit, and fall away by degrees; since every Community suffers most dangerously in its head; and hence, the individuals composing the same suffer fatally in the heart, by an ill-ordered affection for creatures,—the most dangerous disease of individuals.

If thou holdest My place in regard to others, thou must guide and govern them by My Spirit, that thou mayst, in them and through them, advance My interests. If thou actest differently, thou mayst, perhaps, promote thy own interests, not Mine,—give satisfaction to thy own nature, and to that of others, but not to My Heart.

If thou art an interior person, animated with My Spirit, thy ways of acting will be strong in deed, but full of sweetness in manner. Thou wilt constantly pursue the objects aimed at, until thou attainest to them,—but with that sweetness of charity, which, whilst it stimulates, never wounds; which, when it urges onward, does not imbitter; which employs a thousand painstakings to win; which finally overcomes, but so overcomes that the conquered one surrenders by a voluntary act, and meritoriously.

Thou wilt so make use of My secret of governing, as not to require the same of all; but, by the same spirit, to gain of each that which, regard being had to talents, strength, and other circumstances, could reasonably be obtained.

Thou wilt know how to take advantage of the character of thy subjects; and to employ the same for its proper effect, and relatively to the greatest usefulness.

Thou wilt take heed, lest, under any pretense, thou estrange subjects, or render them dispirited. And thou wilt strive to treat subjects as I treated My Apostles; so that, full of confidence, they have recourse to thee in every difficulty, and do find thee ever animated by My Spirit, and devoted to them; that thus they may live ever cheerful, and serve Me with a willing mind and a large heart.

Remember, My Child, that there is nothing more difficult than to punish beneficially. Wherefore, if, at any time, it be necessary to punish, see thou do not make the evil worse: take care lest, outwardly thou incrust and whiten the individual, as if he were a sepulchre, and inclose and keep rottenness within.

Never, by word or deed, rebuke another; if either thyself or he be excited with anger. It will be sufficient to restrain, for the present, him that actually commits a formal sin: delay the punishment until thou canst prepare and administer it without passion, and he, being now pacified, may accept and undergo the same with profit.

4. Never needlessly sadden any one: if, at any time, thou art obliged to say or do things unpleasant to others, soften them, for charity's sake, with good reasons, and season them with such a sweetness of manner, that whatever is bitter may be felt as little as possible.

If thou art asked anything which thou canst not grant; show to him that asks, how much thou desirest that thou wert able, and how it grieves thee that thou art unable to comply therewith: and so he will go away satisfied, and more edified, than if he had obtained his request.

Do not, under cover of charity, entertain men with empty flatteries, or deceive them by a certain politic astuteness. This manner of acting is hateful to heaven and earth: for, unless it is grounded on truth, it is not charity but deceit.

5. On the contrary, My Child, do thou so manifest in thyself the character of the humble charity of My Heart, as to be, in every place, the good odor of My example.

So let thy light shine before men, that they may see thy good deeds, and glorify thy Father, who is in heaven.

The voice of the Disciple.—Yet, Lord, didst Thou not recommend to Thy Disciples, that they should shut the door, and keep their own affairs secret?

The voice of Jesus.—Dost thou not understand these things, My Child? Know, then, and give heed. Things which are not required, nor serve for common edification, should be done in private, since they might become a stumbling-block to thy neighbor, and dangerous to thyself: but those which are common or necessary, are to be so performed in public, that the intention remains concealed; that thus, by thy works, thou mayst give good example to thy neighbor; and, for thy intention, whereby thou seekest to please Me alone, thou ever desirest secrecy.

6. If, through divine love, thou exercisest humility and charity toward all, whosoever they may be, thou wilt assuredly be the good odor of My Heart for all who shall see thy example.

And, although others should not profit by thy example, thou shalt be no less dear to My Heart.

Blessed is he, My Child, who by the example of a humble charity, shall so shine before men, as to show that the goodness of My Heart is to be loved and imitated! They that so explain Me, shall have life everlasting.

7. *The voice of the Disciple.* O Lord, meek and lowly Jesus! to perform the things which Thou teachest as drawn from Thy Heart, so full of sweetness, I need a powerful grace. I beseech Thee, help me with Thy most efficacious aid.

I ought, and I desire, to possess a greater humility, and a greater charity as well. For, oftentimes, I own it to my shame, through lack of humility and charity, I offend my neighbor and displease Thee.

Most humble and sweet Jesus, O Thou Magnet of hearts, who, by the divine goodness of Thy Heart, drawest all men, and entertainest them with the inexhaustible sweetness of Thy humble charity; grant, that I may follow Thee; grant me, to be a perfect Disciple of Thy Heart.

Free me from the harshness and bitterness of pride and self-love; render my heart, like Thine, uniformly kind, and ever replenished with humble charity toward all, without limitation of persons.

CHAPTER XXII.

THAT THE MOST SACRED HEART OF JESUS, LIVING IN THE WORLD, TEACHES US SO TO DWELL IN THE WORLD, THAT WE BE NEITHER OF THE WORLD, NOR HARMED BY IT.

1. *The voice of Jesus.*—My Child, so long as I was in the world, I was not of the world: I abode among the good and the wicked: neither had the prince of the world, nor its spirit, anything in Me.

Although I was incapable of sin, yet I made use of such things as might teach My Disciples how they should keep themselves from the defilements of the world.

Inwardly My Heart was so estranged from the world, that It was affected by nothing which is of this world; It so burned with divine love, that, like a flame, It ever rose above all things created.

It was inwardly self-collected, whilst It was busied outwardly: within, It remained united to God, whilst without, It was occupied with men.

But, outwardly, everything was in Me well-ordered: the senses were passionless: My behavior full of discernment.

So prudent and holy was My conversation, that My very enemies went away, saying: Never has man spoken like this one.

Nothing was ever imprudently uttered, nothing was unguarded; no dangerous familiarity, no levity; but a certain placid seriousness, tempered with a wonderful sweetness, distinguished My outward carriage.

In Me, everything was full of dignity, which inspired both respect and love, checked all forwardness, inculcated reserve, recommended virtue.

Withdrawing frequently from men, I betook Myself to prayer; although inwardly I never ceased to pray.

2. My Child, would that thou didst understand these things! Would that thou didst imitate them, that thou mightst abide, without sin or harm, in this wicked world!

To encourage thyself, look at the example of the Saints, who, pressing My footsteps, lived indeed

with their body in the world, but with their heart
uplifted far above the world.

The world harmed them not, because they loved
naught of the world: on the contrary, it was useful
to them; because, the more they perceived the
banefulness of the world, the more highly they
valued the divine friendship, and the more they
cherished the same.

Whatever they beheld in the world, they despised
and rejected as offscourings, that they might enjoy
the blessings of My grace and love.

3. My Child, if thou wilt dwell in the world
without hurt, first of all, let thy heart be well-regu-
lated within. Let it be convinced of the utter
vanity of the world, and abhor it: let it be conscious of the inestimable price of My friendship,
and adhere thereto.

Accustom thyself forthwith to turn inwardly
with thy heart to Me,—so often as anything is offered to thee by the world,—and to utter these,
or similar, aspirations: Besides Thee, what do I
desire upon earth, God of my heart, and my portion forever!

If thy heart be rightly regulated in this manner,
thou shalt be little moved, by whatever thou mayst
see in the world. Nay more, the world, even in
spite of itself, will work with thee unto good; because it will often drive thee to Me,—the centre of
thy felicity; and will make thee understand more
and more fully the unutterable wretchedness of the
world, and the blessedness of My service.

Keep thy heart so disposed, that it be neither
troubled at the greatness of the crimes of others
nor scandalized by the perverseness of the wicked;

nor let it hesitate to continue with Me, in spite of any attempts of hell or of the world.

Know thou, My Child, that the wicked, among whom thou mayst live, can in no way harm thee, if thy heart effectually dissent from them. It is not in the power of the perverse to injure thee, provided thou art unwilling. For no one is harmed except by himself.

4. Notwithstanding, since the flesh is weak, and the heart prone to evil, it may happen that the senses, unless carefully guarded, do, to thy great peril, bring the foe even to thy very heart.

It is, therefore, necessary, in thy intercourse with the world, to guard all the avenues of the senses; if thou do not wish to be exposed to the danger of discovering that, by degrees, thou becomest affected, defiled, corrupted.

The things of the world, which fall under the senses, thou oughtest to see, as if thou didst not see them; to hear, as if thou didst not hear them; in short, to perceive them, by means of the senses, as if thou didst not perceive them.

But thy chief watchfulness ought ever to be exerted over thy heart. For, even should the enemy secretly penetrate within the gates, if thyself thou dost not open thy heart, he shall be unable to enter, or to destroy thee.

Wherefore, preserve with the greatest care the unshaken resolve of cleaving to Me with thy whole heart; of wisely protecting all the approaches to thy heart. After this, attend with confidence to thy affairs, prepared with a resolute mind, in every danger, to have recourse to Me, and to act with fidelity.

5. My Child, thou wilt avoid many dangers, if, at

all times, thou showest a certain dignity,—not indeed an artificial one, but one that springs from virtue, such as is befitting in every Disciple of My Heart.

Wherever, therefore, thou mayst be, so deport thyself that there appear in thee nothing mean, nothing light, nothing either forced or feigned: on the contrary, let there shine forth in thee an easy, sweet decorum, which is well suited to restrain others, and to fill them with respect.

Do not, in act nor in affection, enslave thyself to any creature; always and everywhere keep thyself free.

Neither do thou intrust thyself, and what belongs to thee, to all and every one: but try the spirit. and mistrust the same unless proved. Remember, that many have been deceived by appearances, and destroyed by an imprudent familiarity.

6. It will prove very useful, My Child, to foresee the things to be transacted with the world: to consider carefully, what is to be done, and in what manner; with what persons thou hast to deal, and under what circumstances; in short, what means are to be taken to succeed in the business, as well as to avoid sin.

Thou shouldst, however, rely more upon divine grace than upon thy own industry; thou must, therefore, frequently turn thyself to Me, ask My counsel, and entreat Me.

Yea, My Child, in whatsoever matters thou mayst be engaged; among what men soever thou mayst be; thou oughtest so to behave, so to hold thy heart free from creatures, that thou mayst be able, at the very appearance of sin, with a pious and easy motion, to fly to Me, and hide thyself, far away from every danger, in My Heart.

7. *The voice of the Disciple.*—O most sweet and amiable Jesus! Thou knowest that I am in the world, only because Thou didst will that I should be in the world. I do humbly beseech Thee, preserve me, exposed as I am to the filthy world, that I be not sunk in its mire, nor soiled by its uncleanness.

O My God! the more attentively I look at the world, the viler it grows to me: on the other hand, the more eagerly I meditate upon Thee, the more exceedingly sweet Thou becomest to me: the more good things I find in Thee,—the more and the greater appear those that I see remain to be found.

O Jesus, my supreme Good! keep me near Thyself, and grant that neither the devil, nor his allurements, may carry me off; that the world, or its deceitful vanity, may not beguile me; that corrupt nature may not overcome me; that my unguarded senses may not betray me.

Strengthen me with Thy efficacious grace, that I may lead a blameless life in this world; until Thou takest me from the danger of the world into the secure abode of heaven.

CHAPTER XXIII.

THAT THE MOST SACRED HEART OF JESUS, REQUIRING FAITH IN HIS DISCIPLES, TEACHES US TO LIVE THE LIFE OF FAITH.

1. *The voice of Jesus.*—When the Son of man comes, thinkest thou, that He shall find faith, not of any kind, but a faith lively, active, fervent?

And yet, such a faith I ever required, and do require of My Disciples; because I am ever the same God, ever equally deserving, that they live for Me by faith.

The voice of the Disciple.—Yea Lord, Thou art God, ever the same, ever supremely worthy, that for Thee all things live, that to Thee all be perfectly submissive, wholly devoted.

The voice of Jesus.—Rightly dost thou believe this, My Child, because the universe bears witness that I am God. From the beginning, the Patriarchs and Prophets foretold Me such: as such was I pointed out beforehand by nature, and by the Law, the end whereof I am.

As such did all the elements acknowledge Me: the heavens confessed Me, since, at My birth, they displayed the star: the sea declared Me, since it suffered itself to be trodden by My feet: the earth proclaimed Me, since, at My passion, it quaked: the sun recognized Me, since he hid the rays of his light, and grieved for the expiring author of his being.

The very spirits of hell acknowledged Me as such, since they showed that, without My consent, they could assail not even the vilest animals, and since they gave up the dead whom they were detaining.

The Angels gave testimony of Me, since, at My Incarnation, they announced Me the Son of God; since, at My Nativity, they proclaimed Me to the world as the Saviour; since they ministered to Me during My life; since they showed themselves as witnesses at My Resurrection.

There is another who gave testimony of Me My

Father Himself, since He declared Me repeatedly His own beloved Son.

Moreover, the Holy Spirit also gave testimony of Me, neither does He cease so to do, since, by the enlightening and motion of grace, and the outpouring of His gifts, He draws to Me the hearts of men.

Nay more, My own works also, which I did, give testimony of Me. For behold! it was by My power that the blind were made to see, the lame to walk, the deaf to hear; that the lepers were cleansed, the sick healed, the dead restored to life.

2. Now, all these things, My Child,—and whatsoever else is to be believed to obtain salvation,—by whom are they, infallibly, without danger of error, made known to thee, if not by the Church; by whose mouth I speak more clearly now, than I did of old, by the mouth of the holy Prophets?

Yea truly, this is My mouth, which, when I open, I teach the multitudes: this is the instrument by which I speak exteriorly to men: this is the last rule of the things to be believed, unerring and unalterable: this, finally, is the only Church, wherein is found the faith, by which the just live.

Without faith it is impossible to please Me. Whence it is clear, that every just man who is Mine, lives by the faith, which works through charity.

3. My Child, the life of faith possesses, as it were, certain degrees; the first of which is, when man,—aided by grace from above,—by reason of the divine authority, believes Me, as I speak through the Church, and lives in the state of grace.

My Child, a miracle is God's testimony: a miracle is an evident utterance of God, and the infallible seal of divine truth.

Now, the Church herself is a miracle, an evident miracle, whether thou considerest her origin and prop-agation, since,—established by miracles, without hu-man aid, in spite of hell, in spite of all the powers of the world, in spite of every kind of wickedness of men conspiring by every possible means,—she went forth like lightning from the East, and ap-peared even in the West: or whether thou considerest her preservation and uninterrupted growth, since,—whilst so many of her degenerate children in every age, attacked her anon by fraud, violence, rage; and so many fierce persecutors, at all times, never grew weary with attacking her in open and secret ways,—she herself, amid the ruins of centuries, whilst all the kingdoms of the earth crumbled into dust, stood always more firm, more magnificent, more glorious, crowned with victory, as often as she was assailed.

Wherefore I,—God, speaking by miracles,—speak through this same Church, an ever-enduring miracle.

Blessed he, that hears this Church, One, Holy, Catholic, Apostolic: he that hears her, hears Me, certain that he is in the way of saving truth: he that will not hear her, is like the heathen and pub-lican; neither does he hear Me, nor can he be other-wise than on the road of death-bringing error.

My Child, if thou wilt be safe and secure, cling thou, with heart and mind, to the Church, which I built upon the immovable rock; which I cemented with My Blood; wherein I dwell; which I govern by My Spirit, quicken with My Heart.

Hold thy mind so prepared, that to whatsoever she may teach or command, thou submit thyself humbly and cheerfully: and keep thy heart so disposed, that thou love her affectionately, as thy best Mother, the kind parent of them that are to be saved.

However, faith, to be a saving one, must be enlivened by sanctifying grace. For, without this grace, it neither unites thee to Me, nor does it make thee a living member of the Church, My mystical Body. Wherefore, it has been most truly said, that faith without works is dead; although when grace is lost, by a sin not against faith, faith is not lost at the same time; and the faith which remains is a true faith, even if it is not a living one.

My Child, keep thou with every care, this gift of thy God, divine faith: and make known the life of this faith, by works done in the state of grace.

4. There is a second degree of the life of faith, when all voluntary acts, interior as well as exterior, are animated by the principles of a living faith.

He that has a lively faith guides himself by the everlasting principles of faith; whereby he understands that he is created for a supernatural end, unending beatitude with Me: that all the inferior creatures on earth are made, to help man in the attainment of this end.

But in many persons faith languishes, because they neglect to meditate on the truths of faith,— being too busily engaged with the things that are of the world and the flesh.

For, if these everlasting truths were well considered, and received into the heart, doubtless, the things of God and of salvation would be loved; faith would be vigorous, and bring forth flowers and the richest fruits.

My Child, every Disciple of My Heart possesses
and cherishes this lively faith: by it he lives, cheered
on by hope, and glowing with charity; and he goes
and ascends from virtue to virtue.

5. Many of them whom I call to an uncommon
holiness, I am wont to prepare gradually for a pure
faith. This pure faith is the third degree of the
life of faith. In this degree man leads, by means
of perfect faith, a life altogether supernatural; and,
even in the midst of darkness and temptations,—
following under obedience, blindly as it were, the
torch of faith—he serves Me faithfully, although
he may not see or know whether or not he is serving Me.

My Child, if, by My Spirit, thou art led to this
life, enter upon it with great courage; and follow
with a fearless heart, under obedience, the divine
guidance.

And, when thou art now walking in these interior
ways, where thou shalt see naught, but where thou
shalt perceive on all sides enemies, by whom thou
shalt sometimes think thyself already ensnared;
where thou shalt descry underneath thyself the
yawning abyss, into which thou supposest thyself
ready to fall at every step; where, lastly, thou shalt
deem that heaven above is incensed against thee,
and that thou feelest this; going ever onward,
without knowing by what way or whither, but
supposing that thou art ever coming nearer to thy
destruction: then, My Child, enliven thy faith,
and follow, with a pure faith, even blindly, the
guidance of them that hold My place in thy regard.

Let not thy heart be troubled, My Child: but
cheer up thy courage, and call to mind that thou

art walking in the way wherein the greatest Saints have walked before thee; who, had they not passed through the same, had never sanctified themselves.

When, finally, all secret pride, and self-love have been sufficiently rooted out; when the intended purifying shall have been completed, according to My designs; then the eyes of thy soul shall be opened; and, filled with astonishment, thou shalt find thyself in a new way, which will be like a pledge of life everlasting.

After this, My Child, thou shalt live, as it were, in an uninterrupted serenity: thou shalt behold things not seen before: thou shalt rejoice as thou didst never rejoice before: thou shalt understand, and taste the secrets of My Heart with a new relish: and thou shalt rather fly than walk to perfection.

6. *The voice of the Disciple.*—Being of beings, O God, who canst not deceive nor be deceived! I believe whatsoever Thou proposest to be believed through Thy Holy Catholic Church, whom Thou didst appoint the guardian, witness and interpreter of Thy saving doctrine; whom Thou didst establish the unshaken ground-work of the truth; whom Thou dost so shelter beneath Thy protection, that the gates of hell can never prevail against her.

O Church, One, Holy, Catholic, Apostolic! Virgin Spouse of Jesus, the Son of God,—who abides with Thee all days, even to the consummation of time,—thou that bearest His name upon thy brow, and His divine seal upon thy arms; thou evident and unending miracle! whosoever does not acknowledge thee, is devoid of reason; whoso does not love thee, is truly heartless; whoso does not hear thee, deserves to be considered a heathen.

O Church, One, Holy, Catholic, Apostolic! Mother most loving, Mother most lovely, whosoever has not thee for Mother, has not God for Father! Dear, indeed, is my native land: dear my family: dear my life: but incomparably dearer art thou, my Mother, thou Church divine! O dearest Mother, let my right hand be forgotten, if ever I forget thee! let my heart faint away, if I do not love thee, if I make thee not the beginning of my joy and glory!

O thou Church, One, Holy, Catholic, Apostolic; saving queen of the world, whose everlasting sway is spread over the earth; whose subjects,—the rich and the poor, the European and the American, the Asiatic and the African,—are children of one Mother, brethren of one family, princes all,—all destined to reign for evermore. O thou, upon whom shine the Apostles, glittering luminaries of the world; whose triumphs thousands of Martyrs proclaim; whose wonderful works the armies of Confessors display; whose beauty ever new the Angelic multitudes of Virgins manifest; whose name and splendor all the heroes of virtue adorn; behold! I, together with the thousands of thy children, from the four quarters of the globe,—of all tribes, and peoples, and tongues,—arise and bless thee, uttering with one heart and one voice: Set out with thy comeliness: proceed thou prosperously and reign! Let thy blissful reign be spread even to the boundaries of the earth, that, under it, we mortals, each and all, may, with joyous hearts, together serve God our Saviour, until we draw near to the heavenly City, and the multitude of the many thousands of Angels,—the Church of the first-born,— that are in heaven!

CHAPTER XXIV.

THAT THE MOST SACRED HEART OF JESUS, PROMIS-
ING SALVATION TO THEM THAT PERSEVERE, AND
THE MEANS OF SALVATION TO THEM THAT PRAY
WITH CONFIDENCE, TEACHES US TO LEAD THE
LIFE OF HOPE.

1. *The voice of Jesus.*—Come ye all to Me: have
confidence: him that comes to Me, I will not cast
out.

Hope, therefore, in Me, My Child, and do not
fear; because I, thy Creator, have redeemed thee,
and called thee: thou art Mine; and I am God,
thy Saviour.

My Child, hope is the anchor of life: as the anchor secures the ship at sea, so hope makes the soul
fast in Me.

All things present are done in the hope of things
to come. The hearts of mortals, were hope taken
away, would rest inactive; they would suffer all
things to languish, all things to perish.

Hope is the stimulant of men, it arouses their
hearts, and goads them on to generous efforts.

Worldly hope, wavering and worthless, deceives
and passes away: divine hope, on the contrary,
fixed and immovable, resting upon My infallible
word, sustains him that hopes, and rewards him that
perseveres.

The former is wont to beget rashness or dejection; the latter, a humble and steady greatness of
soul.

This holy hope thou needest, My Child, to strive courageously for the crown, and to bear it off, in spite of opposing difficulties.

Live by hope: cherish reliance on Me, with all thy heart. For in Me is all hope of life, virtue, holiness.

2. The first degree of the life of hope, is when man, with a sure reliance, awaits everlasting beatitude, and the means to attain to the same through the divine assistance.

My Child, since My mercy is infinite, no one, in this life, should despair. A horrible sin is despair: a crime exceedingly insulting to My Heart; besides, what can be more hurtful to man himself? Despair causes him that stands to fall,—does not suffer him that is fallen to rise.

Nor, on the other hand, is it lawful to indulge in presumption. Far, therefore, be it from any one to rely upon himself, and not upon Me, who humble them that presume upon themselves, and protect them that rely upon Me.

Take courage, My Child; act manfully: do not lose confidence, which has a great reward. For to them that hope in Me, and labor valiantly unto the end, life everlasting is mercifully promised by Me, as to My children; and it will be faithfully given to them, according to My promise,—as a reward for their own good works and merits.

3. The second degree of the life of hope is, when, amid casual events and things adverse, a person so trusts in My most wise and loving Providence, that, after having done, with a good and upright will, whatsoever he was able, he confides himself altogether to Me.

My Child, when matters do not proceed according to thy wishes, do not meanly give way to despondency; but cheer up thy spirits, and have recourse to My Heart. This thou shalt ever find the Heart of the best of fathers; in It thou shalt ever meet with sympathy, help, and inexhaustible goodness.

Neither allow thy miseries to lessen thy confidence in Me. The more miserable thou shalt feel, the greater reason thou oughtest to have of mistrusting thyself, and of trusting in Me.

For, distrust in thyself, in order to be good, should beget a firm trust in Me. Wherefore, all distrust, which produces depression of spirits or faint-heartedness, should be cast off as a dangerous temptation.

Throw thyself into the bosom of My Providence, as a child into the bosom of its parent. He shall not perish who is in the arms of such a father as I am.

It should certainly be a miracle,—such a one as never yet has been wrought, nor shall ever be seen,—if My Heart were wanting to them that rely upon Its aid, or if It did not hasten to their assistance.

4. Lastly, the third degree of hope is, when the soul, even amidst great obstacles and arduous difficulties of every kind, trusts in Me with a perfect hope; although she does not perceive, except upon principles of faith, any means of extricating herself.

If thou seest not how thou mayst escape from the troubles that rush upon thee, raise thyself, My Child, above all things human, and, with a pure hope, intrust thyself wholly to Me; rely altogether upon Me, with whom rests both the power to help thee, if I so wish, and the will, if it is for thy good.

The more desperate matters appear, the more firmly thou oughtest to hope in Me. For it is a characteristic of My Heart, to grant more plentiful divine aid to them that are most forsaken, and have recourse to Me with confidence.

Remember, My Child, that I am wont to defend more stoutly those things which are more violently assailed by the demon; and to strengthen most powerfully that which the foe tries most to tear down.

Courage, then, My Child, what fearest thou? Thou hast God with thee. Be valiant, act with confidence, advance boldly.

If, whithersoever thou turnest thyself, thou thinkest ever to perceive a lower deep, keep thyself within My arms; repose upon My Heart, resigned to everything. Then only, when thou shalt be sufficiently free from all self-reliance and expectation,—when, in a human sense, thou shalt deem thyself lost,—thou shalt find, in a marvelous manner, both thyself and Me: thyself saved, and Myself present in person.

Thenceforth, My Child, behold! new things loom up before thee: thy hope will be heroic, at the same time, and delightful: thy confidence in Me full of consolation, with peace ever-enduring.

5. My Child, I know what is advantageous to thee: I can do what thou canst not: suffer Me to act: and, praying and hoping, do thou co-operate with Me.

Many there are who, if they obtain not forthwith whatsoever they hope or ask for, are cast down and become fainthearted.

My Child, whosoever asks with confidence that

which is not contrary to his salvation or to My honor, always receives. For, either he receives what he asks for; or, in its stead, that which I know to be better for him: and so he receives whenever it is good to receive. Sometimes, the objects asked are not refused, but they are delayed, that they may be given at the suitable time.

And, because thou thinkest ofttimes in a human manner, imagining that that would be good for thee which, however, if thou hadst it, would not be good; and, since thou knowest not, in particular, what, or how, things are better for thee: therefore, thou shouldst commit thyself to Me, and persevere quietly in asking and hoping.

There are they who, at first, surrender themselves wholly to Me, and afterward, in certain difficulties, desire to provide for themselves. These, with My permission, are wont to become more entangled in those difficulties; that they may learn, in all things, to mistrust themselves, and to rely upon Me.

6. Who has ever vainly trusted in Me? Who was ever disappointed in the hope which he placed in My Heart?

Behold! by hope My Mother obtained My first public miracle, whereby I changed water into wine. For, although she saw there was scarcely room for expecting the wished-for favor; yet, knowing My Heart, she had confidence, and obtained what she desired.

By hope was the woman, who was troubled with an issue of blood, freed from her long ailment. For she approached Me with so great a confidence that she said: "If I shall touch only His garment, I shall be healed." And so she was made whole.

By hope did the woman of Canaan obtain consolation, and relief in her affliction. Although her confidence and faith were tried, she, increasing in faith, trusted, and prayed the more earnestly, that, pitying, I might help her. She trusted not in vain, she prayed not in vain. For she obtained what she asked.

By hope did Bartimeus, the blind man, receive his sight. For he prayed with confidence, crying out to Me, as I was passing by: and, when rebuked by many, that he should hold his peace, he cried out the more: "Jesus, Son of David, have pity on me." Wherefore, pitying him, I opened his eyes, that he might see.

By hope was the leper cleansed. "Lord," said he, full of faith, "if Thou wilt, Thou canst make me clean." My Heart, thus appealed to, was moved with compassion, and: "I will," said I, "be thou made clean." And forthwith he was cleansed.

By hope did Lazarus—poor and destitute, full of ulcers, cast off by the rich man—persevere with holiness in suffering. For he looked up to his reward: nor in vain. When he died, he was borne by Angels into the bosom of Abraham.

What more? None ever hoped in Me, and was disappointed. Wherefore, My Child, lay aside all fear: lay aside distrust; in life and death give thyself up to My Heart.

7. *The voice of the Disciple.*—O Jesus! how good Thou art! how sweet! Yea, O Jesus, Thou art goodness itself. Thou art very sweetness.

O Jesus, my Saviour! I will deal confidently and not fear, being mindful of Thy Heart; because It is infinitely good, Its mercy endures forever.

Remember, O Jesus meek and humble of Heart, that, in what need soever, no one, who had recourse to Thy most loving Heart, was ever rejected or sent away empty. Animated with such a confidence, O Jesus, I come to Thee: burdened with miseries, I fly to Thee, and, with my miseries, I throw myself on Thy Heart. Do not, O my God, my Father, cast off me, Thy all-unworthy child, but give me admittance, I beseech Thee, into Thy Heart; nor suffer me ever to be separated therefrom. Aid me, I entreat Thee, in all my wants, now and forever, but, above all, at the hour of my death, O most benign! O most compassionate! O most sweet Jesus!

CHAPTER XXV.

THAT THE SACRED HEART OF JESUS, ENJOINING LOVE ON ALL, TEACHES US TO LEAD A LIFE OF DIVINE LOVE.

1. *The voice of Jesus.*—My Child, thou shalt love the Lord thy God with thy whole heart, and with thy whole strength. This is the greatest commandment.

I am thy God and thy Lord. By Me thou wast created: by Me redeemed.

This, then, is My command, that thou love Me. Is it not an easy command? is it not sweet? is it not beneficial? is it not replenished with every good?

What is more easy than to love? Love is the
life of the heart; without love the heart cannot
live. Thus was thy heart constituted from the beginning; I Myself so created, so formed it. For I
made thy heart that it may love: but love Me.

Thou knowest, My Child, who I am, and what
manner of Heart is Mine. Canst thou find on
earth, or even in heaven, a sweeter object of love
than My Heart? Is not My Heart very sweetness?

Ask of them that have experienced it: ask the
Saints who, inebriated with the sweetness of My
love, forgot all worldly things, yea, found that
which was naturally bitter, sweet and full of consolation.

Ask the Angels, who possess My love, and rejoice and exult therein forever.

Canst thou find in any other object so much blissfulness for time and for eternity? What true good
is there, which thou canst not have in My Heart?
Enlarge thy heart, as much as thou mayst wish;
behold! all thy desires shall be filled.

If peace is desired, if consolation, if virtue, if
perfection, if security in life and in death, if any
other good: it is found in My Heart, it is obtained
by loving Me.

Arouse thy heart, My Child; love with thy whole
heart, cherish with thy whole strength: but love,
but cherish Me, thy every good.

Let fear, which contains pain, disappear: let
faintheartedness, which fetters the heart, vanish
away: love thou, My Child, and be free: love thou
and be happy.

Live, henceforth, the life of love, as it behooves
Disciple of My Heart.

2. The first degree of the life of divine love is, so to love Me, with a love of preference, that thou keepest all My commands which oblige under grievous sin; and that thou wouldst, for naught of earth, deliberately transgress any one of them.

He that does not so love Me remains in death. Life and death, divine love and mortal sin, do not dwell together in the same heart.

Deeds are the proof of love. Therefore, whosoever keeps My commands, the same loves Me in truth.

By this, then, thou shalt know whether thou loves Me, if thou keepest My commands.

Now, this degree of love is necessary to all, for salvation; insomuch that, should any one know all mysteries and every science; should he distribute all his possessions to feed the poor; should he give up his body to be burned; should he speak with the tongues of Angels, or should he possess any other powers whatsoever: and have not this degree of divine love, it avails him nothing for life everlasting.

Here eternal salvation is at stake. He that love father or mother; wife or children; brothers or sisters; possessions, or life itself, more than Me, not worthy of Me, nor fit for the kingdom of heaven.

If thou wilt enter into life everlasting, keep the commandments; avoid mortal sin: whatsoever efforts, whatsoever sacrifices it may cost thee.

3. The second degree of the life of divine love is so to love Me, with a love full of affection and generosity, that thou ever seekest effectually to please Me; and wouldst not, for any consideration whatsoever, offend Me—even by a venial sin.

Assuredly, My Child, if thou possessest a heart worthy of My Disciple, thou wilt ever devote to Me thy affections; thou wilt endeavor, before all others, to please Me; and thou wilt carefully avoid whatever thou knowest to be displeasing to Me.

Tell Me what sort of a love that is which, for an empty glory, for a sensual delight, or for any other gratification of corrupt nature, does not hesitate,—not indeed to nail Me again to the cross,—but to mock Me, to wound Me, and to fill Me with bitterness.

If I did not love thee better, if I were not more concerned about thee, what, My Child, should become of thee? If, because such, and such other things, do not utterly destroy thee, I did overlook them, I did not heed them; what shouldst thou have to undergo?

And thou longest for peace? and for My intimate friendship? and for My consolations? and freedom from danger? Behold! even by venial sin, thou destructest the source of all these blessings.

Whence arise thy troubles,—annoyances, anxieties, dangers,—if not from this, that thou art not willing to sacrifice, with a generous heart, those things which the divine love demands of thee?

Thou callest Me thy God: thou speakest to Me thy Father: nay more, thou stylest Me thy Beloved: but, if I am thy God, where is My honor? I am thy Father, where is thy love for Me? if I am thy Beloved, where is thy affection? where thy tenderness?

If, formerly, thou didst so offend: if, formerly, thou wast all along without affection for Me: now at least, be thou zealous for the better gifts; and I will show thee a still more excellent degree.

4. This is the third degree of the life of love;
pure love; whereby thou lovest Me so perfect
that thou dost will and not will the same with M
and art thus in all things conformed to the div
Will.

This, My Child, is the perfection of love: th
is the true union of hearts: this is the life of t
Saints.

This pure love will make thee abhor the san
things that I abhor: it will make thee delight
the same things wherein I delight.

For pure love, true union, consists in an effic
cious agreement of hearts. Whatever be thy ov
sentiments, if thou dost not will and dislike t
same with Me; if thou dost not think the sar
with Me; if, as far as the divine Will requires, th
dost not embrace the same with Me, thy love is n
pure, thy union is not true.

Be not troubled, however, My Child, if th
findest it sometimes so hard to conform to the
vine Will, that thou appearest to do it, as it we
against thy own will. By freely conforming th
self, although with difficulty, thou willest effectua
that which I will. Since, unless thou didst so w
thou wouldst not conform thyself; inasmuch as
one can will against his will. Whence thou p
ceivest that the repugnance, which thou feele
resides in the inferior part of the heart.

5. My Child, pure love directs all things to un
Just as fire changes everything thrown upon it i
itself.

The divine Will is the beginning, and the m
ner, and the end of all things, which it does or suff

It transforms, in some way, all virtues into

self; and ennobles them by its own excellence. Whosoever loves purely, for him every virtue is love,—and love is every virtue.

My Child, if thou hast not actually reached this oneness of love, use thy endeavors; accustom thyself to live by love, to act by love, to suffer by love: thou shalt attain to it afterwards.

6. My Child, love thou this holy love, which alone effects many things replenished with sweetness, and works wonders.

For it bedews what is parched, it heals what is wounded, it bends what is stiff, it warms what is cold, it guides what is gone astray.

It is the light of hearts, the best of consolers, a delightful guest of the soul, a sweet refreshment: it is rest in toil, it is a tempering in heat, it is a comfort in mourning.

It sanctifies and elevates innocent souls in a wonderful manner. Remember John, the beloved Disciple, who, at the Supper, reclined upon My Breast; how,—entranced with love,—he winged his flight as the eagle.

Remember Martha, who ministered to Me; how, inspired with love, like the heliotrope, she was ever turned toward Me; exhaling the fragrance of every virtue.

Remember the holy Virgins consecrated to Me: how, raised by love above all things of the world, they became a spectacle, wherewith God was delighted, at which the Angels rejoiced, whereby the hearts of mortals were moved toward Me.

Nay more, this same love covers a multitude of sins, destroys them; and of very sinners makes Saints. Witness the Magdalen, who, by purity of love, was changed into a new creature, loving with seraphic ardor.

Witness Peter, who, making amends by love for his denial, became the Prince of the chosen Apostles, the Shepherd of My sheep and lambs, the guide of holiness.

Witness Paul, who, transformed by love, glowing with love, ran through the world, like a fire among the dry stubble, and spread the flames of love among all nations.

7. My Child, love is learnt by loving: if thou desirest to make great progress in the art of divine love, love much.

Do not rest satisfied with a dry love, which possesses no unction: cherish a love full of affection. It does not, indeed, depend upon thee to feel a sensible love; but if thou dost cherish it, thou canst always possess an affectionate love.

Thou wilt cherish it by praying devoutly, by asking frequently for the gift, or the increase of the gift, of love; by conversing with Me, more by affection than by reflection, by pouring out the heart rather than by busying the mind before Me.

Thou wilt cherish it by possessing a feeling of gratitude for all the favors thou hast received from Me: life, preservation, all the gifts of nature: redemption, vocation, grace, all the means of salvation; in short, all supernatural favors.

Thou wilt cherish it by having ever present before thy mind how greatly I have loved thee, how much I have done for thee, how much I have suffered for thee: what I have given for thee, what I have prepared for thee in time and eternity: how mercifully, how kindly, how gently, I have so often specially dealt with thee.

Thou wilt cherish it by remembering who and what I am: in whom the Angels and Saints in heaven, and the Elect on earth, ever find their blessedness: who,—as heaven and earth, and all things therein contained, cry out with one consent,—deserve to be loved with thy whole heart, with all thy strength.

8. *The voice of the Disciple.*—O Jesus! O love! what marvelous, what divine, what delightful things dost Thou disclose out of Thy Heart!

O my Saviour God! who am I, and who art Thou? Would it not be much, yea even too much, shouldst Thou merely suffer Thyself to be loved by me?

And,—lest, perhaps, I might doubt, whether it be allowed to me, a wretched creature, to aspire to a place in Thy divine Heart,—Thou hast commanded me to love Thee. O love! O prodigy of love! O delight! O most sweet Jesus!

And shall I not love Thee? shall I not hold Thee supremely dear? Yea, O Jesus, with all my heart will I love Thee: with all my strength will I cherish Thee.

All that I am; all I possess; all Thy gifts and blessings; heaven and earth; all things incite me to love Thee, but naught so much as Thou Thyself, —who art the cause and the end, the object and the reward of love.

O Lord Jesus! I have no other ambition than to excel in love for Thee, than to rival the Angels themselves in their love for Thee.

Let others surpass me in all other things: I will bear it easily, I will suffer it willingly: but how shall I endure this one thing, to be below others in love for Thee? how shall I bear it?

Oh then! Jesus, Beloved of my heart! may I become alike to Thee, all love, all one with Thee by love.

O my Jesus! who shall grant me, that I may enkindle the whole world with Thy love! that I may draw the hearts of all to Thee; inflame them with love for Thee!

Grant, I beseech Thee, that we all may live by love for Thee, and, in Thy love, may spend with Thee a blissful eternity.

CHAPTER XXVI.

THAT THE MOST SACRED HEART OF JESUS TEACHES US TO EXERT OURSELVES TO MAKE PROGRESS IN VIRTUE.

1. *The voice of Jesus.*—Behold, My Child, I have done all things well. The things which were pleasing to My Father, I did always.

Did I ever stand still in those things, so long as I lived? Now, then, whosoever desires to remain with Me, must also walk as I did walk. For, if he stands still, whilst I am walking, how can he remain with Me?

My Child, true virtue stands never still in this life: for, if it neglects to make further progress, it is either a failing or lukewarmness.

Let him who is just, be justified still: and let him who is holy, be still sanctified.

How much soever, therefore, any cne may have advanced in virtue, he must and can advance still further. For, either something better can be done by a person; or the end of his actions can become purer through love, the object of which is infinite: or the different circumstances of the actions may be performed in a manner more excellent.

Hence, My Child, if thou examinest thyself with an upright heart, thou shalt find sufficient matter to humble thyself, when thou findest that thou hast often been deficient in some part; and thou shalt have, at the same time, a powerful incentive to make progress for love of Me,—who lovingly approve, and reward in a liberal manner, whatever is good in thy works; who endure, or even pardon, when asked in a contrite manner, that which is defective.

2. Do not measure thy progress by natural facility, or sensible devotion, or any other natural disposition whatsoever: all these things are unreliable and deceitful.

But do thou measure, reliably and safely, thy progress in virtue, by the efforts which thou makest, generously to overcome or deny thyself for love of Me.

Beware, My Child, lest thou be satisfied with virtues merely natural. For these, since they spring from nature, can neither bear everlasting fruits, nor produce flowers of heaven: and, if they put forth any buds, or bear anything, it is only for time which soon vanishes away.

Every planting which God has not set out; every

plant which does not spring from divine grace,—shall be rooted up.

Advance thou toward things more perfect, by means of solid and supernatural virtues, which, sprung from the principle of grace, become strong and perfect by generous and repeated acts,—blossom, and bear fruit exceedingly, for life everlasting.

That which is more perfect in itself, is not always better for thee: but that is ever more useful to thee which proceeds from the divine Will, and, by means of true virtues, helps thee to reach thy end.

Some there are who place progress in multiplying their practices of piety: others make it consist in performing different things. And all these, so far from making any progress, are not rarely wont to go backward; both because perfection does not consist in these things,—as they are simply means of perfection; and because, being hindered by the multiplicity and unsuitableness of the means, they are unable to reach the goal.

3. Assuredly, My Child, more perfect in My sight is the simple servant-maid,—who, through love for Me, does that which, according to her state and employment, the divine Will requires,—than the religious person, who, neglectful of the duties of her calling and office, passes days and nights in prayer, or in shedding tears, through feelings of devotion.

If thou desirest to perform thy employment properly, first of all, esteem and love it,—not because it suits thy inclination, but because it is the divine Will, which renders even the least things

both excellent and precious. For, unless thou
esteemest the same, thou wilt not long love it: if
thou dost not love it, thou wilt not long discharge
it properly; because,—when the understanding and
will do not help but rather oppose thee,—thou
canst not long act and suffer in a befitting manner.

Again, do not have for object,—nor seek in or
by it,—thyself, or the gratifications of nature: but
Me, and the fulfillment of My Will.

Moreover, perform all the duties of thy employment, firmly indeed in the action,—being intent
on obtaining the end according to the divine good
pleasure;—but gently in the manner, remaining
ever tranquil in the use of the means.

Lastly, accustom thyself to do all things belonging to it for love of Me; who am present, and ready
to direct and help thee in particular circumstances.
Thus thou wilt perform all more easily and securely,
and persevere in so doing.

But whether thou fulfillest the obligations of thy
state, or appliest thyself to spiritual exercises, let
thy chief care be to do all this well.   Here lies
the fruitful field of genuine virtues: here is the
plentiful harvest of true merits.

If thou neglectest this, remember that all other
extraordinary things are deceitful. Neither miracles, nor prophecies, nor ecstasies, nor other gifts
of what kind soever,—shouldst thou possess these,
—are able to sanctify thee.

4. My Child, if thou art really solicitous about
thy progress, thou must will it efficaciously.   For
perfection, and progress therein, after grace, cannot
come, except from a heart that wills it.

If thy heart do not will efficiently, no means shall

ever be able to make thee perfect; thou canst not
come to Me by compulsion, but only by affection.

Call to mind how many Saints, amidst the greatest obstacles, with few outward means, have reached
the very height of virtue; because their heart thirsted
unceasingly for perfection.

Blessed are they that hunger and thirst after
justice; for they shall have their fill! If any one
thirsts after this, let him come to My Heart, and
drink of the fountain of living water, springing up
into life everlasting.

Come, My Child, and taste at this fountain, how
pleasant it is to serve Me by love: and as, after
tasting honey, all other nourishment seems lacking
in sweetness, so, when thou hast once tasted the
sweetness of My divine love, all the food of corrupt
nature will become bitter to thee.

Pray, My Child, pray fervently, that thou mayst
be enlightened from above to understand the exceeding value of perfection; and that thou mayst
be enkindled with a ceaseless longing of attaining
thereto.

Frequently, also, call to mind how many, and
what powerful incentives urge thee on to greater
perfection.

5. *The voice of the Disciple.*—Which are those,
Lord?

The voice of Jesus.—Consider, My Child, who
He is whom thou servest: how lovely, by reason
of His infinite perfections,—which ravish the very
hearts of the inhabitants of heaven; and thou shalt
be aroused to My service, so full of love and sweetness.

Remember the favors of every kind which I

heaped upon thee through pure charity: and, if thy heart has not lost all sense of feeling, thou wilt love Me, in return, with singular gratefulness.

Weigh the enormity and multitude of thy sins, which I pardoned thee, with a Heart so paternal; and wilt thou think, after this, that thou canst ever do enough for Me?

Think on the manifold and continued unhappiness of them that are lying in sin and lukewarmness; and again, on the unuttered felicity of them that serve Me with fervent love.

Look upon the marvelous beauty of virtue, and the unspeakable ugliness of vice: how the former unites men with Angels, and the latter makes them alike to demons.

Meditate on the shortness of this life, and the eternity of the life to come: the certainty of death, and the uncertainty of its hour.

Ponder, with mind and heart, what it is to be in hell without end: what it means to be in heaven throughout all eternity: and remember that the one or the other awaits thee.

My Child, if thou dost frequently and attentively consider these things, so as to keep them ever fresh before thee, thou wilt hasten on to further progress.

6. But in many ways is a person turned away from progress. For the most part, however, he begins to go astray, either because he suffers the love of Me to grow lukewarm in his heart,—by neglecting the fervent practices of an inward life; or because, for the sake of indulging nature, he refuses to overcome or deny himself in some thing.

There are some who do not, indeed, forsake the

road of progress; but who, in various ways, retard their successful career. In this manner do they stand still, who, whilst they should be hastening onward, squander their time, in looking, with self-delight, over the distance which they have already passed.

My Child, forget the things which are behind, being certain to whom thou hast intrusted them: and pass over the remainder of thy journey with unwearied steps.

They, also, are hindered from advancing, who proceed so cautiously, that they appear desirous of examining, at every step, where to set their foot. But, My Child, trust thou rather in Me than in thyself; and, using a reasonable diligence, with a courageous effort of divine love, fly thou forward through every obstacle toward thy end.

They, too, are kept back, who frighten the imagination and fetter the heart by future difficulties, which, perhaps, will never occur; so that, through fear and faintheartedness, they hardly dare or can move. My Child, sufficient for the day is the evil thereof: to-day, therefore, advance thou cheerfully: leave the future to-morrow to Me: I will provide.

7. Remember, My Child, that, by the weight of nature, thou art ever prone to a certain inactivity, or indolent repose. Often, therefore, thou must stir up the will by the fervor of the spirit, and take fresh courage.

If thou yieldest to this natural indolence, if thou givest up the efficacious will of perfection, thou wilt no longer perform anything worthy of a Disciple of My Heart: thou shalt begin to grow sluggish, to fall away, to be filled with miseries, and to experience unhappiness.

A soul possessed of a resolute will, fervent and cheerful, acquires in a few months, that degree of virtue, to which a slothful soul, ever in distress and groaning, cannot attain in many years.

My Child, if thou possessest a determined will of always advancing, thou hast reason to rejoice exceedingly. For a good will of this sort is a manifest proof of the divine friendship. And this is the sweetest and, at the same time, the most solid of all consolations.

8. *The voice of the Disciple.*—O good Master, most sweet Jesus, model of every virtue! I feel wholly confounded, for that I have not yet taken pains to conform myself perfectly to Thee, although I have long made profession of being Thy Disciple.

Have pity on me, Lord; suffer not, I beseech Thee, that I succumb to lukewarmness, yield to natural indolence, or be impeded by any other hindrance: but arouse me, goad me on, impel me by Thy grace.

Give me the fervor of Thy Heart; kindle in my heart the fire, which Thou camest to cast on earth; that I may love Thee more ardently, that I may be more perfectly conformed to Thee, that I may follow Thee more closely.

Renew me wholly, I entreat Thee; take away my slothful and wretched spirit, and enliven me with Thy Spirit,—the Spirit of an everglowing love, ever cheerful,—that never suffers me to grow sluggish, but urges me on strongly and gently to a more perfect Imitation of Thyself,—who alone art the way and the goal of everlasting bliss.

DIRECTORY FOR THE THIRD BOOK.

1. THE aim of the Third Book is to teach us how to tend to that holiness which is called perfection. This holiness is acquired by virtues which are, in some manner, heroic; such as are usually practiced by them that bear their sufferings with the proper disposition of heart. Certain it is, as is proved by the example of all the Saints, that no one ever attained to true sanctity if he did not practice solid, and in some manner heroic, virtues in suffering. And this is not to be understood of those Saints only whom the Church has canonized, but of all those as well, who, although not canonized, strove to acquire that sanctity which Christ Our Lord taught to all by His word and example; and which each one's mode of life may enable him to reach. Of all these noble virtues, whereby sanctity is acquired, Jesus, in His suffering life, furnishes us the most beautiful living examples, full of encouragement and consolation. In His active life the virtues of His Heart do, indeed, shine forth clearly and constantly; and, gently and powerfully at the same time, persuade and allure him, who meditates thereon, to a proper imitation of them: but, in His suffering life, they glitter with all their

perfection and splendor, and do not merely attract the person who meditates, but they also forcibly stimulate and urge him onward. Therefore, it is useful that we should first have meditated on His active life, and become initiated in the virtues of His Heart, when acting; and that we should even have made some progress therein, lest the grandeur and sublimity of the virtues of His suffering Heart might frighten or discourage us.

Now, this sanctity has two degrees: and each degree contains three methods.

In the first degree, all those things which cannot be avoided are religiously endured: according to the first method, they are endured with patience; according to the second, with agreement of our will with that of God; according to the third, with a certain supernatural joy.

In the second degree, all those things are endured which may, in some manner, be avoided; but which, when offered, are accepted with a free will, or are voluntarily sought after and assumed. And, by conformity of our will to the divine Will, all these things are borne; first, through love of Jesus, for some supernatural end; for example, to make amends for the insults offered to Him, for the conversion of sinners, for the perseverance of the just, for the obtaining of this or that good; secondly, through a desire of conformity with Jesus, and of the fruits to be gathered from this conformity so holy and so full of love; thirdly, through the purest love, so that, laying aside, as far as we may, every private consideration, we become uniform with Jesus, and thus well-pleasing to Him.

2. Be persuaded that, in whatsoever state or con-

dition of life you may be, you will really become a Saint if you suffer rightly those things which the Lord will give you to suffer. For, if you merit and make progress by every single act of a common or ordinary virtue, how much more will you gain and advance by acts of heroic virtue;—such as are frequently wont to be performed in times of misfortune!

Remember what it is you merit by every act of an ordinary virtue, when rightly performed in the state of grace: first, a new degree, or increase of sanctifying grace,—which you receive immediately, and whereby you become more perfect in yourself, and dearer to the Lord: again, at the same time, a new and corresponding degree of glory or everlasting bliss,—which you shall receive in heaven, where it is treasured up and awaiting you. And these two you gain *condignly*, that is, according to merit; so that they are justly due to you, according to that promise, by which God has, freely indeed, but truly, obligated Himself. This kind of merit which is strictly called merit, is personal, and not communicated with others.

Moreover, you can merit a certain degree or special help of actual, even efficacious grace,— whereby the understanding is enlightened and directed, and the will encouraged and strengthened to avoid evil, and to do good: and over and above as it were, a part of the great gift of final perseverance. But these two you can only merit *congruously*, or according to propriety,—so that they are never due to you by justice, but simply by a suitableness or becomingness, and by the divine liberality. For to these God has not bound Himself by any promise. As, however, He is supremely liberal, it is befitting in Him, that even so He reward our supernatural acts: neither has He given us any reason for fearing that we shall be disappointed. In this wise you cannot only merit these two for yourself, but also for others.

Now, these degrees, which you merit through virtue, may be greater or smaller,—according as the meritorious acts are more or less perfect. For it may happen, that one heroic act, whereby, with a noble and generous heart, you sacrifice or endure something perfectly, merits more for you than a hundred, a thousand or even more ordinary acts. And, indeed, St. Chrysostom asserts that holy Job, by the one act whereby, amid his misfortunes, he conformed himself to the Will of God, merited more than by all the acts which he performed throughout the whole of his previous life, in the days of his prosperity.

We should be mindful of these things, during our short-lived existence, which has been granted us, that we may gather merits for all eternity. For they will help us to avoid those delusions which are peculiar to this part of the interior life. Of which this one is wont to be the more common: To hearken too much to the feelings or repugnances of nature, thus fixing our attention on the secondary causes of our afflictions, and to decline, under some pretext or other, the sufferings presented to us by Our Lord, or at least bear them with an ill-disposed heart; or even to seek another way than the one through which Jesus Himself walked,— which He smoothed for us, by which He calls us, that with all His Saints we may follow Him with the same disposition of heart with which He has gone before us.

3 Wherefore, when you are occupied with the things treated in this Book, you should assiduously look and aim at this, that you understand, as perfectly as you can, not only the unspeakable afflictions and sorrows of the Son of God; but, especially, the affections and dispositions of His Heart. For here a measureless treasure lies concealed, which a diligent and fervent searcher alone can find and explore. The more attentively and devotedly you shall meditate on the Heart of your suffering Lord, the more perfect things you shall find, and the more possessions you shall acquire.

4. The method of using this Book,—beside the two given before the First Book, and which may also be employed here,—is of two kinds: both of which are placed before the Second Book, and which are here adapted to the meditation or contemplation of the Passion of Jesus Christ.

In meditating, therefore, let the memory propose some virtue, according to the particular period of the Passion of our Lord: and let it remember the same after the meditation, so that you may be able suitably to practice it.

Let the understanding meditate on the virtue,— examining its causes and ends, its modes and its circumstances: considering with what dispositions of Heart Jesus practiced that virtue: then compare the state of your heart in its regard: afterward, look back and examine your past life concerning the same; return thanks, and ask for perseverance, if hitherto you have duly practiced it: if the contrary, make an act of contrition, and, through the suffering Heart of Jesus, ask for pardon: finally, look to the future and see when, and how, you may practice this same virtue.

Let the will embrace the virtue, perform interior acts of it, and resolve to practice it, both inwardly and outwardly, at the proper time; frequently insisting, meanwhile, on pious affections and petitions.

But in contemplating, see what Jesus suffers, and under what circumstances, in this mystery, or particular subject: who He is that thus suffers, from whom, and for whom.

Afterwards, give ear to the words which Jesus there utters; or observe how He is silent, and interiorly pours forth the prayers of His Heart to God the Father.

Lastly, look devoutly and attentively into the Heart of Jesus; see how that Heart is disposed, from which things so heroic proceed. And throughout the contemplation, as much as you can, give yourself up to pious effusions of heart, both by acts and petitions.

The acts in which you employ yourself, during meditation or contemplation, may be various or different; according as you feel affected, or according as you may need, or even according as you may be moved interiorly by the Spirit of God.

You may usefully exercise your faith, and frequently excite lively acts of it, by acknowledging in every mystery Jesus as God, and by adoring Him in His humiliations and sufferings, by which the Divinity, in some manner, hides itself for love of us.

It will also help, often and sweetly, to indulge in hope, being persuaded that if, by a gratuitous love, the Lord did and endured so much in order to save you when every way undeserving; now, that you are willing to co-operate, He will not refuse you what is beyond comparison less, namely, the means of salvation and perfection.

Your heart will, in some manner, spontaneously, be enkindled with love for Jesus, your God and Saviour, when you see how He suffers for love of you. For, since He suffered and died for all and every one, each one can and must truly say: "Jesus loved me, and delivered Himself up for me." (Gal. ii. 20.)

Frequently occupy your heart with abhorrence and detestation of sin; seeing what torments the Son of God endured for it in His most sacred Humanity.

Hatred for the wicked world will spring up in your heart, if you attend to what, and how immensely, Jesus suffered from the same world.

Compassion for Jesus suffering will take wholly possession of you, if you look at Him with a devoted and sympathizing heart.

You will feel a fervent zeal to compensate for the affronts so unworthily offered to Him; for which end you will frequently offer up your own pious desires, good works, and sufferings.

You should, above all, study attentively in each mystery the dispositions and sentiments of the Heart of Jesus suffering, and make the same your own. For, unless you do this, you may indeed meditate on the Passion of Jesus, but you cannot imitate His Heart: you may indeed suffer, but you cannot suffer profitably: you may be burdened with the cross, but you cannot follow Jesus.

The petitions, which it is proper to make, may be various, as well as different. Yea, the objects of the petitions have so wide a scope, that it is not easy to find a limit for them. For you may ask for the gift, or for an increase, of faith, hope, charity; of horror of sin and detestation of the world; of compassion for Jesus and zeal for His honor; lastly, of all virtues and graces; and this not for yourself alone, but also for every one of your neighbors —as was said before the Second Book, and is here repeated, in order to impress deeply on the mind that which cannot be too much inculcated, that the affections or acts of virtues and petitions are of the utmost importance; since from them, after grace, the unction of prayer and its chief fruit are wont to be derived.

5. As regards the discernment of spirits, the following rules, which are here peculiarly appropriate, are given by the Saints.

The first. That is properly called spiritual consolation, when interiorly there is excited some emotion, whereby the soul is enkindled with divine love; whether directly,—as when she is inflamed with the love of God on account of the divine goodness; or whether indirectly, as when she is moved to the divine love by considering the Passion of Jesus Christ, or by sorrow for sins committed against the Lord, or by any other cause whatsoever,— rightly ordered to the service of God. Again, every increase of faith, of hope, of charity, is also a spiritual consolation. Lastly, every inward joy, which stirs up the soul to supernal things, to salvation and perfection, and renders her tranquil in the Lord, is likewise a spiritual consolation.

The second. Whatever is contrary to the things pointed out in the preceding rule, is called spiritual desolateness: as a darkening of the soul, disturbance, or a certain sluggishness; an agitation which moves her to diffidence, which opposes hope or charity; finally, any instigation to the low things of nature, interior sadness,—which makes the mind dejected or restless.

The third. To God alone it belongs to give consolation to the soul, without any preceding cause: since it is peculiar to the Creator to enter His creature, to draw, to turn, to change it wholly to the love of Himself. And then do we say, that no cause precedes, when the consolation is imparted without any previous feeling or thought of any object, whence such a consolation might come to the soul by the acts of her own understanding or will.

The fourth. When a cause of consolation did precede, then the evil as well as the good Spirit can, in some manner, give consolation to the soul, but for contrary ends: the good one, for the advancement of the soul, that she may act rightly, and ascend from good to better; but the evil one, for the opposite, that she may be perverted and ruined.

The fifth. In time of desolateness, no change should ever be made: but we must stand, firmly and manfully, in the intentions and resolves in which we were during the time that preceded this kind of desolateness. Because, as, during spiritual consolation, the good Spirit is more wont to move us, and we also use more readily our natural powers; so, in time of desolateness, the evil spirit does rather stir us up, at whose instigation,—whilst our faculties are more or less impeded,— we can hardly take safe counsels to act rightly.

The sixth. Although, in time of desolateness, we ought not to change our former resolutions, yet it is very useful to change our manner of acting, so that we may fight against the desolateness itself; first, by giving ourselves more to prayer; secondly, by examining ourselves the more, in order to humble and throw ourselves into the divine mercy of the Heart of Jesus; thirdly, by exercising ourselves more in performing works of penance or charity in a prudent manner.

The seventh. He who suffers from desolateness should remember that he is being tried by our Lord, left to his own natural powers with an ordinary grace, and also a special one, although not sensible; that thus, by resisting the various instigations of the enemy, he may display the fidelity of his love. For he is able to resist, with the divine grace, which remains with him,—although he does not sensibly experience the same.

And let him who enjoys consolation consider how he will conduct himself in the desolateness which is about to come upon him: let him gather new strength to bear up against future desolateness: let him strive to humble himself at the thought of how little he is able to do, when not specially and sensibly assisted by our Lord.

Finally, let him who is in desolateness, as well as the one who is in consolation, take care to apply himself to acquire, or to strengthen, solid virtues, and thus sanctify himself.

ST. IGNAT., ST. BONAVENTURE, ST. MARY MAGD. OF PAZZI.

THE THIRD BOOK.

ADMONITIONS USEFUL TO IMITATE THE
MOST SACRED HEART OF JESUS, IN HIS
LIFE OF SUFFERING.

CHAPTER I.

HOW GREATLY WE SHOULD ESTEEM HOLINESS, AND HOW MUCH WE SHOULD STRIVE AFTER IT.

1. *The voice of Jesus.*—Be thou holy, My Child, because I am holy. Whosoever longs to be a perfect Disciple of My Heart, strives to become holy, as I also am holy, by an interior, true, and solid holiness.

Holiness is a great good, it contains all blessings desirable upon earth, and begets everlasting bliss in heaven.

Holiness is the completion of virtue, the guardian of sanctifying grace, the preserver of inward peace, the nurse of the heart's joy, and of ever-enduring happiness.

Holiness is true wisdom, real glory, inexhaustible wealth.

To be the least of the Saints is something incomparably greater than to be the greatest of the whole world.

What is there in this world that can justly be compared with holiness? not science, not dignity, not renown, not the possession of all riches. For all these things are only of earth, they last but for a moment; like vapors in the air, they glisten and soon disappear. But holiness is heaven-born and permanent, it glitters before the inhabitants of heaven like the sun; yea, when the sun fades away, it shall continue to shine for evermore.

Let not, then, the wise man glory in his wisdom, let not the strong man glory in his strength, let not the rich man glory in his wealth: but he that glories, let him glory in this, that he knows and loves Me; that, through love, he follows Me, and thus sanctifies himself.

My Child, if thou understandest not these things at present thou shalt understand them later, even in spite of thyself,—when, at the near approach of death, thou shalt entertain more correct sentiments.

Tell Me, if this day thou hadst to die, which wouldst thou rather desire, to be a Saint, or to have been a king or a Pope? Would to God,—exclaimed, when dying, one who had been a ruler, and had some experience in the matter,—would to God that I had never been a ruler, but, in its stead, the least of God's holy servants! Would, sighed another, that I had not worn the tiara, but had passed my life in the kitchen of some house consecrated to God!

Thou canst not value holiness too highly, since I Myself have held it in such esteem that, to make it possible and easy, I poured out the treasures of My

Heart, multiplied the means at My greatest costs, and ordered all things for the sanctification of the Elect.

Do thou, therefore, aspire to so great a good, My Child: and strive, magnanimously, to become a Saint.

2. *The voice of the Disciple.*—I become a Saint, Lord! Ah me, Lord Jesus! for that, I have sinned too much during my life. And would it not be pride to feel such a presumption? and, moreover, I am so weak that I am unable to perform anything worthy of sanctity.

The voice of Jesus.—Dost thou say these things of Thyself, My Child, or have others suggested it to thee? If of thyself, thou art mistaken: if at the suggestion of others, thou hast been deceived.

And first, if thou hast sinned during thy life, behold! this is a new reason why thou shouldst sanctify thyself, that thus, by the future, thou mayst make amends for the past.

But, My Child, there is no question of what thou hast been, but of what thou oughtest to be hereafter.

How many souls there are that, after having committed sins, have reached, in a shorter time, a higher degree of perfection than others that have ever remained innocent! and this, because they used the remembrance of the sins which they had unfortunately committed, and which had been most mercifully forgiven by Me, as a spur, to urge and goad themselves on to sanctity.

The sins that have been committed are, therefore, not only no hindrances, but, if thou art willing, may be instruments of holiness.

Besides, My Child, to strive after the perfection of virtue, to aspire to sanctity, is not pride nor presumption, but greatness, but nobleness of soul, without which no one is worthy to be a Disciple of My Heart.

These things I say: and take heed which of the two thou wilt believe, Me, or the spirit, thy enemy, who suggests the contrary.

Beware, My Child, lest, after being deluded, thou become fainthearted, and, consequently, incapable of aspiring to those things which alone are most deserving of the aspirations of every noble heart.

Raise thy courage, cast aside all littleness of heart, and cherish sentiments worthy of a Disciple of My Heart.

Lastly, if thou art weak, am not I strong? if thou canst not undergo austerities, art thou unable to love? if thou canst not act, art thou unable to suffer? Now, it is most of all by loving and by suffering that holiness is acquired.

It is not by extraordinary works, not by miracles; but, by love, a patient love, that the sanctification of the soul is chiefly promoted.

Endeavor, for love of Me, to suffer patiently whatsoever I Myself may choose, and give thee to endure: and, behold! thou shalt become a Saint.

If the things which the world calls great could be acquired with as much facility, what worldling would not secure their possession?

3. A constant desire of making progress, a continual striving after holiness, is rightly thought to constitute man's sanctity in this life.

None is perfect in holiness, who does not exert himself to become more perfect: and the more one aims at greater perfection, the more holy does he prove himself to be.

Wherefore, My Child, the perfection of holiness is not the work of a day or a week. Do not, then, imagine that thou shalt be perfect in so short a time. For, by expecting this, and finding thyself afterward disappointed, thou mightest lose heart, or even be dangerously tempted to desist from further attempts.

Perfection is the joint work of divine grace and man's co-operation.

Now, the goodness of My Heart, which wills that thou shouldst be a Saint, is much more inclined bountifully to bestow grace upon thee than thou art to ask for the same: nay, even of Its own accord, It pours grace upon thee.

The more faithfully, therefore, thou co-operatest with grace, the shorter the time in which thou shalt gain possession of sanctity.

4. If thou hast a constant and effectual will of sanctifying thyself, naught can hinder thee from becoming a Saint.

Whatever may be thy natural inclination, thou wilt acquire holiness, not by the disposition of thy character, but by the co-operation with grace through thy free will.

Neither thy character, nor thy state of life, nor thy employment, will hinder thee, if, with a generous fidelity of heart, thou co-operatest with divine grace. Behold! great multitudes, which no one can count, have, by this fidelity, sanctified themselves in the religious state; and millions have become Saints, even in the midst of the world. By this fidelity, a Henry became a Saint in the camp; a

Casimir, at the Court; an Elzear, amid intercourse with the world; an Isidore, in the fields; an Agnes, in the city; a Mary, in the country; a Catharine, in her father's house; a Christiana, in bondage.

Neither does holiness depend on being inscribed in the Catalogue of the Blessed or Saints; because this does not make the Saint, but simply declares to men that he was such. If thou art a Saint in heaven; being perfectly conformed to the divine good pleasure, thou wilt, of thyself, care little whether or not thy name is found on earth registered in the Canon.

Neither, in fine, can temptations and difficulties present an obstacle. For, whatsoever hell can contrive, whatsoever the world may attempt against thee, all this, if thou art willing, shall be made to contribute to thy sanctification.

5. It is indeed true that he who desires to acquire holiness should avoid all, even the slightest, sins: but involuntary faults, which arise from human frailty, are no hindrances to perfection.

Even the greatest Saints were not altogether free from such miseries: and, so long as they lived upon earth, they experienced the frailty of their human nature.

Be not, then, troubled and uneasy about these things, wherein the will does not consciously take any part: a person may be very perfect, although he frequently offends involuntarily.

According to the example of the Saints, lessen involuntary defects as much as thou canst, and, with quiet love, humble thyself thyself before Me for these faults: in this manner thou wilt deprive profit from them for thy progress.

6. This being so, My Child, hearken thou to none who, under some pretense or other, may turn thee from the pursuit of holiness,—neither to thyself, nor to any mortal, nor any spirit whatsoever. But, with a generous mind, that knows not despondency, continue to strive after interior sanctity.

This sanctity is so important a matter, so full of honor, and so grateful to Me, that sometimes one soul, thus sanctifying herself interiorly, glorifies Me more,—is more pleasing to Me, and possesses more influence over My Heart,—than a thousand others, that, although good, rest satisfied with an ordinary virtue.

Know thou, My Child, that holiness, to a certain degree, is really necessary to be admitted into the presence of the divine Majesty; because, without holiness, none shall see God.

If thou dost not attain to this necessary holiness in the present life, thou must be purified with fire unto holiness in the life to come, before thou enterest heaven,—into which naught, except what is holy, can gain admittance.

Yet, for thy consolation, remember, My Child, that, if thou keepest a good and efficacious will of really sanctifying thyself, thou shalt not taste death, until thou hast acquired sanctity.

Meanwhile, never think that thou hast already attained to holiness, or that thou art perfect: but do thou ever advance and pursue the destined prize of thy supernal vocation.

Be of good courage, My Child, dare thou things worthy of a Disciple of My Heart: vie in zeal with the Saints, thy noble brothers and sisters. What thou art, they have been: what they are, thou canst be.

7. *The voice of the Disciple.*—I then, O Lord Jesus, even I, the least of men, must and can become a Saint.

Yea I must; because Thou commandest me so· because I am obliged to correspond to so many singular favors and graces, which Thou hast bestowed upon me; because I am bound to satisfy, as much as I am able, the unutterable obligations, which I owe to Thee, for the mercy shown to me after my many sins; because I must have a care of my salvation, and prepare myself for heaven; but, more than all, because Thou art supremely worthy of all love and honor.

And I can; because Thou givest me abundant and efficacious means; because Thou, ready to supply all the rest, demandest naught, except that I make the attempt with a sincere will; because nothing can hinder me, unless I myself so will it; because all things whatsoever, if I will, can help me and cause me to advance; because, finally, the whole work of my sanctification is simply a labor of love, of love for Thee, of a love which renders all things possible, easy, delightful.

Therefore, I long to be a Saint, not that, on earth, I may be numbered among the Saints, but that, in heaven, I may glorify Thee among the Elect: not so much through fear of pain or hope of reward, as through love for Thee, most kind and sweet Jesus,—that I may the more love Thee, the more honor Thee, now and for evermore.

Behold! O Lord Jesus, I have the will to become a Saint; so long as I draw breath, I shall not cease to will it: I beg and entreat Thee, by Thy most Sacred Heart, help my good will.

CHAPTER II.

THAT IN THIS LIFE NO ONE CAN LIVE WITHOUT SUFFERING.

1. *The voice of Jesus.*—My Child, so long as thou livest upon earth, thou canst not be free from troubles.

What is this whole mortal life except affliction, which man enters weeping, through which he passes amid sufferings, from which he departs groaning?

Since man is born subject to death, it is not possible that he should pass his life without pain; because the source of suffering lies within himself.

The very condition of being subject to death naturally begets many and various miseries, diseases, and sufferings; which cannot cease to exist so long as that fruitful and effective cause remains.

All these things, however, manifold and irksome though they be, are of less importance. For, from the very bottom of corrupt nature worse things spring up,—inordinate and perverse desires, which force man to feel, in spite of himself, that which he would fain not feel.

These are the passions, the sources of so many sufferings, which, inherent in the very heart disturb the peace of many; which excite wars, horrid wars; which, by conflicting emotions, expose the soul to uncounted dangers and sorrows.

2. And how numerous are the torments which befall man from without, and which none can wholly escape!

Cold and heat, the difference of temperature, the thousand inconveniences arising from creatures, and many other effects of physical causes, which although they contribute to the general well-being, yet,— through man's fault, in the state of fallen nature, and in the present order of things,—cannot be brought about without some trouble to individuals.

And, amid all this, what mortal is not ofttimes burdened by labor, without which none can dwell here below, unless he be willing to be burdened still more?

Add and count up, if thou canst, the sorrows and calamities of every kind, which arise from the passions of others: and thou shalt behold on all sides troubles, which, unless thou overcome them, will overwhelm thee.

3. Indeed, My Child, since this mortal life is replete with hardships so numerous and so great, to not a few it would appear almost unbearable, if the spirit of religion did not suggest reasons for patience, and My Heart did not render it smooth, by the unction of grace.

Neither has all the wisdom of this world,—although it has uttered many beautiful sayings concerning endurance and suffering,—ever been able to invent and afford a remedy for them.

How many there have been who, whilst endeavoring to teach others, by discoursing eloquently on the endurance of afflictions, were themselves undone by afflictions!

Hence, what wonder that those, who are devoid of the spirit of religion and strangers to My Heart —whether through unbelief or corruption—should, at last, despair amid their troubles, and their reason being blinded, should wickedly terminate their miseries by the greatest of all—an everlasting misfortune!

But religion renders all troubles both bearable and useful; since it teaches that, through the consoling effect of the wisdom and goodness of My Heart, that which was a just punishment of sin, and a just cause of grief to man, becomes a wholesome remedy against sin, and a plentiful harvest of merits.

The furnace tests metals. Fire hardens clay, but softens wax. The storm throws down the plant, but renders the tree, that is well-rooted, more firm.

So also, My Child, does tribulation try men. Affliction hardens the one, it softens the other. Opposition casts down some, it makes others more solid.

Affliction would lead all to bliss, if all were to receive it properly. If, on its account, any one hastens on to destruction, it is his own fault, since, rightly borne, it would prove a sure road to sanctity, and, consequently, to true happiness.

4. But behold! My Child, every affliction has become much lighter and more consoling, since, by My own afflictions, I sanctified affliction, and walk before those who suffer affliction,—as well by the example of My life, as by the promise of reward, and the aid and consolation of grace.

By My example the Saints learnt the secret of suffering rightly, and the art of converting evil into good.

Hence they learnt, by experience, that afflictions were even sweet to them, and derived such a longing to suffer for love of Me, that they were unwilling to live without suffering, and overflowed with joy in their every tribulation.

Canst not thou also aspire to the like, My Child? Is not this My interest as well as thy own? What fearest thou? Behold! no afflictions can reach thy heart if they have not first passed through Mine: and, by so doing, they lose all their power of hurting, and become imbued with the divine virtue of consolation.

5. Take heed, My Child, lest by the sourness of thy heart thou imbitter afflictions, when they come from My Heart imbued with sweetness.

Suffering is necessary: there is no choice: but whether to suffer well or ill, whether after the manner of the Elect or after that of the reprobate, whether for thy sanctification or for thy condemnation, this is optional with thee, this, My Child, depends upon thy choice.

Prepare thyself: nay, be ready for annoyances, which cease not to occur, and shall never cease.

Do not believe that thou shalt ever have a day without some trouble; since there can never be a day without its supply of malice.

Neither do thou imagine, that with whatsoever efforts thou mayst make, thou shalt be enabled to escape. Even if thou withdraw into the wilderness alone, or cross the sea, or hide thyself in the uttermost boundaries of the earth, misery shall be thy companion everywhere, and shall ever follow thee as its cause or occasion, like a shadow pursues the body.

Wherefore, My Child, if thou art wise, endeavor to make that useful which thou canst not avoid, by bearing the cross of thy affliction with an even and

well-disposed mind, as did the Saints, and by cheerfully following My footsteps.

6. If thou wilt undergo tribulation with ease
and profit, do it for love of Me: this love will take
away the heaviness and bitterness of thy cross, and,
by its virtue, will sanctify thy cross, and thyself
through its means.

Whoso does not suffer his afflictions for love of
Me, will not long carry his cross with alacrity; but
he will soon begin either to drag it along, toiling
and groaning, or, overburdened by it, he will sink
down in his wretchedness.

If thou findest any difficulty in so suffering, My
Child, come thou to My Heart, and pray. Here
thou shalt obtain relief, love, the unction of grace.

My Child, hitherto I have never ceased telling
thee, nor will I cease to repeat it, do thou pray, do
not fail to pray.

For behold! in prayer is everything: by prayer
thou art freed from evils: by prayer thou obtainest
all good things; in prayer thou hast a remedy for
misfortune; by prayer sorrow is soothed; in prayer
thou securest consolation and perseverance.

7. *The voice of the Disciple.*—There is, then, no
escape, Lord Jesus: it is necessary to suffer either
willingly or reluctantly. If I suffer wiliingly, I
shall feel it less: if I suffer with reluctance, I add
a greater burden.

Wherefore, I must hold my heart ready to suffer.
unless I desire to render myself wretched to no
purpose.

Although the necessity of suffering appears sometimes hard, yet its advantage, which will sanctify
me in life, and render me blissful during all eter-

nity, is abundantly sufficient to arouse and stimulate my heart.

But if I love Thee, O most sweet Jesus, the sole thought of Thee will induce me to follow Thee with joy and alacrity, that I may be with Thee, that I may be assimilated to Thee, that I may give a proof of my love, that I may enjoy Thy love.

O Jesus, infinite sweetness! near Thee even bitterness becomes sweet: for behold! by Thy own suffering, Thou didst take away and reserve for Thyself whatever is bitterest in afflictions; and whatsoever of relish or sweetness there is in them Thou didst leave to us.

O Jesus most compassionate, who didst love me so much, I entreat Thee, give me the sentiments of Thy Heart, that I may sanctify all my sufferings and promote, by their means, Thy honor and my own perfection.

CHAPTER III.

HOW THE MOST SACRED HEART OF JESUS FELT DISPOSED IN REGARD TO SUFFERINGS.

1. *The voice of Jesus.*—Consider, My Child, what were the sentiments of My Heart in suffering, and strive to imitate them.

Behold! during My mortal life, My Heart was ever suffering and rejoicing at the same time.

Understand what I say, My Child. I speak not of My divine Will, since it was exempt from suffering, and incapable of it; but of My human will. For by this I practiced virtues: by this I acquired merits: by this I wrought the Redemption of men.

From the first existence of My Humanity, My Heart possessed the fullness of joy, by reason of the Vision of the Divinity hypostatically united to It, which It ever enjoyed, and whereby I was supremely blissful: and, at the same time, by a special dispensation, My Heart was suffering, in view of the cruelty and bitterness of the Passion, which It was to undergo.

Moreover, at the same time, but under a different aspect, My Heart was grieved and rejoiced at Its sorrowful and bitter Passion. It was grieved, inasmuch as the sufferings were painful and disagreeable to My Humanity: It was rejoiced, inasmuch as God had willed and ordained them for the salvation of men.

For My Heart was endowed with a human will, which, although one in itself, was, as it were, twofold in its operation: the one inferior,—which of itself shrunk and fled from things distressful to the human nature: the other superior, which, for loftier motives, deliberately loved and embraced those same painful things.

Both parts, the inferior as well as the superior, were ever upright, never ill-ordered, nor weakened by any defect whatsoever.

The inferior, which regarded and desired the good and advantage of its own nature, and dreaded and shunned the sufferings of nature and death, at the same time, allowed itself to be guided by the superior.

The superior rendered the inferior, as well as itself submissive, and conformed to the divine Will. Hence the supernatural acts of virtues performed: hence merits: hence the plentifulness of the treasures of grace accumulated for men.

Remember, My Child, that thou possessest a similar will, not, indeed, equally perfect and unimpaired, yet truly free: and that in the same thou also findest an inferior and a superior part.

2. My Child, thou dost not always, nor at the same time, know all thou shalt have to suffer. It happens, through a special kindness and mercy that, for the most part, thou dost not see them, except when they come upon thee, that thus thou mayst bear them the more easily one by one.

But My suffering was ever in My sight. Wherever I was, all My future torments were constantly before My eyes.

For at no time was hidden from Me, all that the Prophets had foretold I was to suffer, all that the ancient types and figures had foreshowed, all that the wickedness of the world and of hell was to attempt, all the horrid tortures for which the sins of men were crying out, all that the insulted glory of My heavenly Father required, all that thy own wants, My Child, demanded.

All, and each of these things, were before My eyes, and pressed unceasingly upon My Heart.

But the love of My Heart brought it to pass, that I willingly endured and bore all.

Love rendered everything savory to Me: labors and watchings, insults and mockeries, scourgings and thorns, the cross, and whatsoever things were prepared by the divine Will for the blissfulness of men.

Lo, My Child, the chief disposition of My Heart, love for God and for men. From this source flowed all Its other dispositions.

3. Hence arose that inexhaustible patience of My Heart, whereby I endured, without bitter feeling or complaint, so many things, so cruel and undeserved. For love is patient; charity endures all things.

Hence, amid all My sorrows and afflictions, the resignation of Heart to the divine good pleasure. For, with My Will, conformed by love to the divine Will, I was ready willingly to undergo everything.

Hence My joy amid suffering. For he that loves, and understands the goodness of the object beloved, is glad when he possesses the same. But My Heart understood perfectly the excellence of the divine Will; therefore, too, It delighted to fulfill it, even amid many and various sufferings.

Hence the supernatural longing of My Heart for suffering. For true love desires to testify effectually its sincerity, tenderness, and fidelity; therefore My Heart was forever goaded on by love,—always desiring to consummate that Passion which was for God, and should remain for man, a manifest and ever-enduring proof of the sincerity, the tenderness, the fidelity, yea, of the excess of My love.

4. But, My Child, the love of My Heart went even beyond this. For to ravish the hearts of men, by its excess, and to inflame them with its own fire, this is what It willed, this is what I coveted.

I had come to cast a fire upon the earth, and what did I will, except that it should be kindled?

For this I had the baptism of My Blood, living

and boiling hot, wherewith I was to be baptized. My Passion, I mean, into which I was to be immersed, and plunged completely.

And how was I straitened, until it were accomplished! how was My Heart burning to open that heated bath, which by its wonderful power should cleanse, warm, stimulate, and enkindle the hearts of men!

This bath cleansed and inflamed the Apostles and Martyrs, the holy Confessors and Virgins, who were ready, with a pure heart, to suffer all things, to follow Me through afflictions, mortifications, a thousand torments, a thousand deaths.

And cannot also thy heart be enkindled, My Child? For this did I, all along, love thee so much, that I might inflame thee to love Me in return, that I might gain for Myself thy love.

5. My Child, if thou wouldst more frequently and more attentively consider to what a degree I have loved thee, and how many more reasons thou hast to love Me than I have to love thee, thou wouldst, doubtless, be excited to requite My love with thine.

And, if love do once take possession of thy heart, it will produce therein sentiments, with respect to sufferings, akin to the sentiments of My Heart.

The more thou lovest Me, the better wilt thou feel disposed toward sufferings: and with how much the more willing a heart thou sufferest, the more perfectly wilt thou love Me.

If it happen that thou relishest not the sentiments of My Heart, with respect to afflictions, it is a sign that thy heart is not healthful, nay, that it is ill-affected: and, upon examination, thou shalt find that the cause thereof is that thy heart, devoid of divine warmth, is benumbed by the coldness of a certain indifference, or is feverous with the vitiated fire of self-love.

However, from the very fact that thou art still so ill-disposed, that thou art unable to taste and relish those things which are so worthy of great souls, take thou occasion to bestir and stimulate thyself courageously.

And desire, and covet at least, that thy heart may become animated with the same sentiments that pervade Mine.

6. Pray frequently and fervently, even though nature struggle against it, that thou mayst be enabled to understand the worth of these sentiments, and love the priceless advantage of them.

If, in thus praying, thou art sincere, the eyes of thy mind shall be opened, so as to see clearly that the wisdom of the world,—which abhors the love of wholesome humiliations and mortifications,—is true folly; but that the salutary love, which I Myself, coming down from heaven, taught by word and example, is purest wisdom.

And if thou perseverest in prayer, plentiful grace shall be bestowed upon thee, religiously to embrace tribulations, and to endure them in a holy manner.

Be not, however, satisfied with prayer alone: but endeavor also, according to the amount of grace, and of thy strength, to deny thyself,—to endure afflictions, and to carry the cross with Me.

Blessed is he who relishes sufferings which may sanctify him! he certainly is taught rather by divine unction, than by human skill; he is animated rather by grace, than by nature.

There is nothing, My Child, whereby the true Disciples of My Heart are better distinguished, than by esteem and love of sufferings for My sake.

7. *The voice of the Disciple.*—O good Jesus, how great was the charity of Thy Heart for me! how unselfish Thy love! how great Thy thirst for my felicity!

What things Thou didst suffer, and with how pure a love! and all for me, to redeem me, to teach me, to console me, to unite me with Thee by love!

And can I ever forget Thee? Can I ever love Thee enough? It is little, I own, but meet and just, that I love Thee with my whole heart, that by love I follow Thee even amidst adversity, even unto death.

But, behold! my Saviour God, I feel that I need great grace, to be able to love sufferings, and to follow the sentiments of Thy Heart amid sufferings.

Unless I be helped from above, I cannot with merit deny myself,—neither in great things nor in small,—embrace the cross with joy, overcome the feelings of nature, and accompany Thee throughout, even unto death.

But since Thou invitest, nay even callest me to this: give me abundant grace, I beseech Thee, that thereby I may be enabled to effect what I cannot do of myself.

Widen, therefore, my heart and implant, bountifully and deeply, therein the sentiments of Thy suffering Heart, that I, too, with a meek and humble heart, may love to suffer for love of Thee, whatsoever Thou mayst give me to endure.

CHAPTER IV.

WHAT ADVANTAGES THERE ARE IN SUFFERING WELL.

1 *The voice of Jesus.*—My Child, to thee it is given to understand the secrets of My Heart, to enter devoutly into them, to direct them fully to thy progress.

Hear, then, the secrets which are hidden from the world: learn thou the good things which worldlings understand not.

Behold, walking in the way of the cross, I the Creator have gone before My creatures; I the Redeemer before those whom I had set free; I a Father before My children; and to all men have I made it known, that, whosoever is willing to be a partaker of the unutterable bliss which awaits Me, at the end of the journey, should, with the proper interior disposition of heart, deny himself, and follow Me.

But many hearing this, have said at all times: This is a hard saying, and who can hear it? And, thenceforth, many withdrew and walked with Me no more.

The Saints, however, and all they that were really willing to sanctify themselves, received My invitation with a thankful heart, and judged that their happiness, even upon earth, consisted in being with Me in suffering with Me, and in persevering with Me through every trial unto the end.

2. And, indeed, My Child, what good is there on

earth, which may not be found in suffering with Me?

Here is true glory: a glory which is worthy of the divine approval: a glory which does not pass away with this world: a glory which shall endure and be exalted for evermore.

This is the hidden treasure, wherewith is bought the kingdom of heaven, with its entire unending blessedness.

This is the pure delight, exceeding all the feelings. For if thou arrivest at this, that thou rejoicest in suffering with Me, thou obtainest possession of a spiritual Paradise of delights upon earth.

3. Whilst everything flows on according to nature's inclinations, and whilst no trouble oppresses the heart, a person is wont to cling to creatures, to turn rarely toward Me, and to feel it irksome to busy himself with the things of eternity.

But when he labors under adversity, and is pressed by afflictions, he turns again to his heart; he perceives how vain, how perishable are all the things of this world; he flies for aid to Me, whom he finds, by experience, most of all needed by himself.

Therefore, My Child, the kind Providence of My Heart is wont so to act, that they who are affluent with the possessions of this world, do not enjoy them without inconvenience, in order that thus they may be excited the more easily and effectively to seek the treasures of the life to come.

For, if they possessed a quiet and undisturbed felicity amid worldly riches, they would, perhaps, not even think of laying up heavenly treasures.

It is, then, a merciful dispensation, that evils

abound in the world, lest the world might be loved, and its votaries might perish.

4. As fire consumes rust, and purifies gold, so sufferings exhaust and deaden the passions, and render virtues more pure and precious.

By tribulation properly endured, My Child, thou redeemest thy sins, and thou satisfiest the divine justice, for punishments still due: in so much, that, in this manner, thou canst have here a slight and consoling Purgatory, from which, through the gates of death, thou mayst deserve to wing thy flight to joys everlasting.

What is there that can make thee merit more, than sufferings endured with a proper disposition of heart? For, behold! light and momentary tribulations work out for thee an ever-enduring weight of glory.

Every affliction will add a new jewel to thy heavenly crown, which shall glitter with as many rays as thou hast performed acts of virtue.

In adversity, man is freed from many false notions and errors, and instructed in many ways. Happy he that, in the school of affliction, is taught to be wise in all things!

What does he know, who has never experienced adversity, has never endured aught, either inwardly or outwardly? And wherein can he be useful in counsel or guidance either to himself or to others?

5. Wherefore, Child, do not lose courage, when thou art tried or reproved by Me. For whomsoever I love, him do I lovingly reprove, in order to train him; and, in him, as a father in his son am I well-pleased.

Thou shouldst, therefore, justly be glad amid sufferings, since therein thou mayst have an indication of My esteem for thee, and a token of the fatherly love of My Heart.

There is scarcely aught else to be found which produces a greater confidence in My Heart, or a freer access to It, than to suffer willingly for My sake.

When thou art about to die, My Child, thou wilt rejoice over no circumstance of thy life so securely, nor find so safe a consolation in aught else, as in the most agreeable remembrance of having suffered much with Me.

6. Very many study to shun the way of humiliation and affliction; pleading as an excuse, that they can both better glorify God and help their neighbor, in a more agreeable way.

What a delusion! They do not seek God nor their neighbor, but themselves. For the glory of God and the salvation of the neighbor are not to be promoted according to man's, but according to God's good pleasure.

Now, God indicated to His Son the manner of glorifying on earth His Majesty, and of saving the lost world. And this manner the Son followed by suffering and by suffering He made it known to man.

My Child, do thou follow this path which I Myself have trodden and showed to thee. And that thou mayst be able to keep it, pray thou frequently and fervently.

But whilst praying, ponder thou devoutly all My sorrows of every kind, and the supernatural dispositions of My Heart all the while.

Do not consult merely natural inclinations or purely human feelings; but, by means of supernatural principles, elevate thyself above sensible things, and view tribulations as sent by the divine Will, and, inasmuch as thou art able, embrace them affectionately.

Courage, then, My Child; cheer on thy heart. Behold Me, and all the Saints with Me, cheerfully treading the path of sufferings. Be thou bold to follow. With Me nothing is to be feared; the company is select; the way safe; the goal certain; the reward everlasting.

7. *The voice of the Disciple.*—O Lord Jesus! who will not be roused up to follow Thee? Who does not feel his heart burning within him, whilst Thou utterest these things about the way?

But it is one thing to be enkindled by Thee, and another to follow Thee; it is one thing to meditate and quite a different one to act: yea, it is one thing to know virtue, and another to practice the same.

I acknowledge that the love of sufferings is a most excellent virtue; I admire it in my mind, I do even love it in my heart; but, when an occasion of actually practicing it presents itself, behold! self-love begins forthwith to torment me, secret pride darkens my understanding and forces upon me a thousand excuses, a thousand specious pretenses.

Whilst thus I am miserably struggling with myself, the chance of suffering something for Thy sake flies away, and, I must confess it to my shame, I frequently wish myself joy if I escape unharmed from the struggle.

O most kind Jesus! look Thou graciously, I beseech Thee, upon this my misery, and grant me in

Thy mercy to be able, by Thy grace, to do that which, by my frailty, I cannot effect.

Great is my weakness, great the power of my refractory nature, which shrinks from the very thought of pain or humiliation.

But the reason why I am so weak and sluggish,—so that I dare not go contrary to nature,—is that I do not love Thee sufficiently.

O most sweet Jesus! were I to love Thee, like Thy Saints, how easy, how pleasant even, would it be to triumph over the repugnance of nature!

Grant me, therefore, I pray Thee, this singular grace, that I may love Thee with a more perfect love,—with a love courageous and generous; that it may strongly attract me,—despite the opposition of nature,—through all hardships, to Thee, O Jesus, my life, my delight, my beatitude.

CHAPTER V.

HOW, AFTER THE EXAMPLE OF THE MOST SACRED HEART OF JESUS, WE MUST CONFORM OURSELVES AMIDST AFFLICTIONS TO THE DIVINE WILL.

1. *The voice of Jesus.*—My Child, I had now enlightened the world by My doctrine, enkindled it with My love, and rendered it blissful, to a certain extent, by the perpetual gift of My Whole Self: nothing remained, except to complete all by undergoing the utmost sufferings through an excess of that same love.

Having, therefore, left the Supper-room, I went whither the Will of My Father called Me, whither also the desire of My Heart directed Me: to the mountain of the Olives.

Ponder well, My Child, what were the sentiments of My Heart, whilst I proceeded in the silence of the night, and beheld distinctly rushing upon Me all and each one of the torments of My Passion.

Sorrowful journey! journey filled with unutterable distress and anguish of Heart! Yet, I went on courageously, because I was following the divine good pleasure.

As throughout My life, so now, whilst sorrows were falling upon Me from every side, My Heart united with the divine Will, generously and lovingly embraced adversity, as the gift of My Father's Will.

2. Thus also thou, My Child, when thou art suffering, do not regard the afflictions in themselves; but lift up thy eyes and consider the divine Will, that sends them to thee for thy good, although thyself dost not see that they are for thy advantage.

Indeed, Child, except sin, nothing takes place without the divine Will. But whatsoever happens, sin excepted, is good, not evil, since it proceeds from a Will essentially just, and is a divinely appointed means of sanctifying man.

For the divine Will, which is guided by infinite Wisdom, sustained by infinite Power, moved by infinite Goodness, is indeed able to effect whatsoever it wills, but it can will nothing absolutely for mortals except what is good for them.

And since creatures, whatever they may wickedly attempt, cannot impede the divine Will concerning

thee; so often as anything, which is not sinful in
any manner, befalls thee, it is manifest that it happens by the divine Will, and is for thy good.

Sin, however, as He is infinitely good, God cannot will: but, in His infinite Providence, He may
and does permit it,—both that He may not take
away man's free-will, and that, by a way which will
be understood and admired in the other world, He
may extol His own perfections.

Infinitely perfect as He is, He knows how to
draw good out of evil: and He judged it better to
draw good out of evil, than not to permit that evil
should be possible.

3. My Child, some things happen, which a person cannot avoid, and must endure, whether he
likes it or not.

Happy he that, under these occurrences, resigns
himself to the divine Will, and strives to conform
himself thereto, so that, uniting his own with the
divine Will, he suffers no longer through necessity,
but of his own accord? By this voluntary resignation, tribulations become not only meritorious, but
also lighter.

Would that thou didst well understand this, My
Child, so that, when afflictions of this kind present
themselves, thou do not, through a blameworthy
opposition, lose all merit, and add misery to misery!
For what can be more miserable in this life, than
never to will what shall always be, and ever not to
will what shall ever be?

Other things happen, which one cannot escape
without sin; so that he must either endure them
or incur guilt.

O how unwisely, how unbecomingly do they act,

who, to be free from troubles, do not hesitate to have recourse to unlawful means! Is it proper so to use the portion of My chalice, which is truly a divine gift, and which is never sent, before it has been tasted and seasoned by My Heart?

Lastly, other things again occur, which man may turn aside without guilt. Yet, when no virtue forbids, it is according to the divine good pleasure to embrace the same cordially.

My Child, if thou art a true Disciple of My Heart, thou wilt allow no occasion of this kind to pass by: but, holding thy heart ever in readiness, when an opportunity presents itself of humbling and mortifying thyself without danger, thou wilt accept it as a gift from Me, and embrace it with the greater affection; because, as nature has no share therein, and thy heart is moved solely by My good pleasure, thou art able to display a pure love for Me.

Fervent Disciples of My Heart,—not satisfied with things which present themselves,—often, of their own accord, seek for opportunities of suffering something for Me, and of comforming themselves to Me; for they know that I delight especially in this likeness to Me, as in a perfect evidence of their love.

4. There are they, who, with their mind and heart, ever live in the past, or in the future: who are wholly taken up with thinking over the causes or circumstances of wrongs, which formerly have been done to them, or hail afar off future adversity, whilst they studiously avoid the present.

How greatly are those persons to be pitied! for they are tormented by the past, and deluded by the future.

In imagination they endure much, attempt much: but in reality, they are wonderful self-tormentors, and vain dreamers.

How many of them resolve to endure one day hard things, and meanwhile do not even bear what is easy!

Beware, Child, of an imaginary perfection, which covers self-love, and is altogether an illusion.

Take advantage of the present, seize every opportunity, how little soever, of practicing virtue: great occasions rarely, ordinary ones frequently occur; and a small matter, rightly endured, is a preparation for what is great.

5. My Child, if, in every occurrence, thou beholdest My divine Will, thou wilt heed little, through whom it is that things adverse come upon thee,—whether through a Superior, an equal, or an inferior; whether through one who is good, or one who is wicked:—but thou wilt receive them without distinction, regarding the divine Will alone, which makes use of various instruments for its own most holy ends.

To help thy weakness: first, in suffering adversity, resign thyself, even unto patience: and, although thou neither lovest sufferings, nor art pleased with them, endure what is to be borne, without bitterness of heart, without uttering complaints.

Employ all the means in thy power, and persevere therein, until thou hast become accustomed to be patient, and to be resigned to the divine Will, amidst troubles of ordinary occurrence.

Having attained to the first degree, conform thyself to My Will in every affliction: willing the same because I will it: unwilling to be freed therefrom, so long as I do not will that thou shouldst be free.

To arrive at this, thou oughtest to pray much, tnat thy intellect may be enlightened from above, and that, by the aid of grace, thy will,—for supernatural motives,—may be solidly conformed to Mine, so that thou feelest persuaded, both by faith and love, that there is naught better than the divine Will.

After reaching the second degree, aim thou at the highest. Strive, with all thy strength, so to unite thyself with the divine Will, as not only to be conformed thereto in suffering adversity, but to be the self-same with it.

Then, My Child, shall this union of wills exist between us, when thy heart,—animated with the same sentiments toward the cross that possess Mine,—rejoices, like Mine, in uniformity with the divine good pleasure.

This union of wills is an important matter, is true perfection, solid sanctity. Pure love alone begets this holy union, which cannot exist without elevating and ennobling man, and rendering him blissful.

6. My Child, if thou lovest Me, thou wilt also love My Will. It is enough for him that loves, to know the desire of the one beloved, in order to execute it with a joyful heart.

Come, then, dearly beloved, embrace with thy heart's whole affection the divine good pleasure; and prove, in this manner, that thou art a true Disciple of My Heart,—a lover, not of thyself, but of Me.

So act, so live, that I may find in thee a man according to My Heart,—one who accomplishes all My wishes, as well in adversity as in prosperity.

7. *The voice of the Disciple.*—Most bountiful and sweet Jesus, whose only rule of life was the divine Will, behold! by Thy grace, I resolve to strive ever to follow this most safe and most just rule.

How much soever nature may resist, I am willing to suffer everything Thou mayst permit to befall me, through the means of any creatures whatsoever, whether seen or unseen. Nothing except what is good can proceed from a Heart infinitely bountiful, which loves me more and better than I either do or can love myself.

And I know, O Lord, that I shall have to undergo nothing which has not first passed through Thy Heart, and has thus become sweet.

If my vicious inclination rebel, and attempt to draw Thy Will toward itself, display, I beseech Thee, Thy Power: subdue the insolent foe, that he may not rise up again.

O most loving Jesus! O Thou fire that consumest what is defective, and injurest not what is good: O Thou flame gently burning, and happily destroying! destroy within me every evil and inordinate will: enkindle and nourish in me a good and well-ordered will, that may deem itself blissful, when in all things, even though adverse they be, it follows Thy divine good pleasure.

CHAPTER VI.

THAT THE MOST SACRED HEART OF JESUS TEACHES US IN AFFLICTION TO HAVE RECOURSE TO PRAYER.

1. *The voice of Jesus.*—My Child, when I had now entered the garden of the Olives, whilst the earth was silent all around, behold! there rushed and pressed upon Me, on the one hand, all the sins of the world; on the other, the frightful tortures of My Passion: and with such violence did they crowd upon My Heart, that, although It is the strength of them that are weak, It began to fear, to grow weary, sad, disconsolate.

But when I beheld distinctly, that,—by the great sufferings taken upon Me with so much love, and offered up with so great a mercy for the salvation of all men,—not a few would refuse to be saved, and would, by a willful hard-heartedness, misuse them for their deeper destruction, and return Me at last nothing, except the blackest ingratitude: then, My Child, My Heart, growing faint with anguish, forced Me to exclaim: My soul is sorrowful even unto death!

However, having withdrawn from My Disciples and advanced a little, kneeling down, I prayed.

Meanwhile,—by the struggle between the superior and inferior part of My Heart,—My sorrows increasing to such a degree that My sweat became as drops of blood trickling down upon the ground, I fell upon My face, and, being in an agony, I prayed the longer.

And as My agony, on account of that inward struggle, continued, I persevered in prayer: Father, if Thou wilt, remove this chalice from Me; yet, not My Will but Thine be done. Yea, My Father, Thy Will be done!

Then, Child, sent from heaven, an Angel appeared,—not to take away the chalice of My Passion, which My Father willed Me wholly to drain —but to strengthen Me; that, when joy was set before Me without My Passion, despising the shame, I might voluntarily endure the cross.

Reflect, My Child, how painful a struggle My Heart underwent that night: a struggle, the like whereof is not found: a struggle, on the result of which hung the salvation of the world.

My Heart fought, laboring, wrestling, resisting even unto blood, and overcame: but It conquered in prayer.

2. Behold, My Child, behold a source of varied consolation for thee: My Heart struggling with death and praying: fighting by love, triumphing by love.

For lo! to what extent I felt the hardship of My sufferings, to what an extent I tasted their bitterness. And all this, Child, to teach, to relieve, to encourage thee.

Be not then cast down, nor wonder, when thou feelest a repugnance to suffering. For, if My Heart, although holy and perfect, felt Its pains to such a degree, what wonder if thy heart feels them likewise?

But never shalt thou experience,—never shalt thou feel so much as My Heart felt. Wert thou to endure at once in thy heart whatever thou shalt have to suffer during thy whole life, it would be no more than a little drop of the chalice which My Heart drained in the garden.

Whatever may be the reluctance which thou experiencest in thyself, follow My example; yield not to nature opposing, but go counter thereto.

To this end, in every difficulty, in every anguish, hasten thou without delay to prayer.

3. If, when thou art troubled, thou hast recourse to prayer, distress will ever prove gainful to thee. By prayer thou shalt either be delivered from it with merit, or thou shalt be helped to endure it, for thy good.

Come, then, Child, and with knees bent, or with thy heart at least humbly prostrate, pray thou like Myself: pray that, if it be the divine Will, the cup of thy affliction may pass away; yet not so that thine, but the divine Will be done.

Pray if this chalice may not pass away, that thou obtain grace, to be resigned, to submit thyself to drink it.

Be of good cheer, My Child; under no circumstances shalt thou ever have afflictions which will require thee to struggle so much, in order to be resigned, as I had to contend. Thou shalt never have a contest which will cause thee a bloody sweat.

Whatsoever difficulty thou mayst have, exert thyself, wrestle, fight with thyself, to overcome thy feeling. Struggling again and again, pray, and pray the longer, until thou hast rendered thy heart conformed to the divine Will, and prepared it, in spite of nature, to follow Me through every hardship which may be sent it from above.

4. It is a great misfortune for thee, Child, that thou art wont to have recourse to prayer rather slowly, and first to try human skill; that thou sufferest the unwearied enemy of thy salvation, and the ill-regulated propensity of nature, to obtain too great a sway over thy heart.

Hearken not to the suggestions of the devil, nor of any passion whatsoever. For, by false reasonings, they seek to deceive, to injure thee. Forbidding thyself all reasoning, all intercourse with them, come thou forthwith to My Heart: here is thy counsel, here thy help, here thy comfort.

Even had an Angel visibly to be sent down from heaven, thou shouldst not be left without consoling aid, if thou prayest, as it behooves thee.

And if, despite thy pious efforts, thou continuest to feel an opposition within thyself, be not on that account dejected. Provided thy will be resigned to the divine Will, this repugnance felt, indeed, but not willed, so far from doing thee harm, shall, on the contrary, if thou strugglest against it, be of the greatest advantage to thee.

It is the characteristic of an heroic Disciple of My Heart, to pray and endeavor with all his strength to overcome himself completely,—as well in those things from which nature shrinks, as in those to which it is prone.

5. When thou prayest in affliction, Child, thou oughtest so to pray, that thou art willing to be resigned,—whether thou obtainest relief, or, in its stead, receivest something else, which is better for thee, because more conformable to the divine Will; or whether thou tastest sweetness, or experiencest bitterness.

For that prayer is not the best, in which the greatest consolations are felt! Since what is sweet is not always useful, nor is that which is bitter always hurtful. Nay more, in man's present state sweetness is wont to do harm, bitterness to be advantageous.

That is the best prayer, from which thou goest with greater humility and greater charity, and feelest so disposed, that, in order to do the good pleasure of God, thou art willing to go efficaciously against whatsoever is pleasing to nature, and to embrace whatsoever is displeasing thereto.

How pitiful a sight before God, and Angels and men, to see persons, who daily pray long and much, go thence and carry naught away with them, except faults of negligence and abuse of grace, or a more delicate pride and self-love,—having in no wise become better inclined toward their duties, nor abler to bear the defects of their neighbor, and still unwilling to curb their own inclinations.

Thou, My Son, do thou pray better, as taught by My example. Pray, and overcome nature: pray, and resign and conform thyself to the divine good pleasure.

These arduous efforts shall not long be needed. Yet a little while, and thou shalt not now prepare thyself for tribulations, nor encourage thyself in them: but thou shalt sing glad and glorious triumphs with the Saints, who all have come out of great tribulation, and who now, in their reward, are enraptured by the unbroken excess of rejoicings, and exult for evermore.

6. *The voice of the Disciple.*—Thanks to Thee, most compassionate Jesus, true comforter of them

that are in pain: thanks to Thee; for tnat Thou consolest me so disinterestedly and so gently, amid all the repugnance I am wont to feel in regard to sufferings; and for that, at so great a cost to Thyself, Thou didst open for me a source of remedies in every affliction.

By what Thou didst so mercifully deign to undergo, I see, with the greatest consolation, that natural reluctance can not hurt a good will—which alone Thou regardest, and to which alone Thou grantest peace upon earth.

O Lord, O Thou the consolation of men, and the joy of Angels! who, when afflicted, didst betake Thyself to prayer: grant, I beseech Thee, that, after Thy example, in every tribulation, I may forthwith have recourse to the remedy of prayer; thus to sacrifice the opposition of nature, and to cause myself to be resigned and conformed to the divine Will.

Thy Heart, most benign Jesus, is the open and safe refuge of all them that are miserable: behold, I entreat Thee, my weakness; arouse me, impel me, that in every difficulty, under every circumstance, I may flee to the same—may there find bliss, and derive thence strength and courage.

O sweet Jesus, my love and my every good! I beg and implore Thee, bestow upon me the grace always and everywhere to repose with Thee, in the divine Will, and to continue thus with Thee forever.

CHAPTER VII.

HOW THE MOST SACRED HEART OF JESUS TEACHES
US, AMID TRIBULATION, TO USE THE AID OF
CREATURES.

1. *The voice of Jesus.*—My Child, when I rose
from prayer, following the good pleasure of My
heavenly Father, I came to My Disciples, to teach
thee by My example, as well as to obtain through
them some comfort in My extreme affliction.

But alas! I found them heavy with sadness, and
buried in sleep, so that, when awakened, far from
offering Me any relief, they knew not what to say;
and instead of giving Me comfort, they themselves
needed solace.

It was the bitterest bitterness to My Heart, Child,
to see those very ones—whom I had trained with
more than a father's care, whom I had cherished
with so great a love, whom I had solaced so often,—
now, during My Passion, so indifferent, so heedless,
that they could not even for one hour watch with
Me.

Where are now those promises, lately made, that
they would be faithful to Me, even unto death?
where is now their pledged word? where that constancy so solemnly avowed? All this has van-
ished; but it passed through My Heart; and oh!
how deep a wound did it inflict!

However, since, whilst I was suffering, I did not
go to My Disciples, except by the Will of My
Father, according to the same good pleasure of My

Father, I embraced, with My Heart resigned, the pains which followed My recourse to them.

2. It is not then forbidden, My Child, amid distresses, to resort for comfort to creatures, provided it be done in a befitting manner.

Now, thou wilt do it in this manner, if thou appliest to creatures solely as a means of conforming and uniting thyself more easily and more perfectly to the divine Will.

It is peculiar to the more perfect Disciples of My Heart, to suffer, and to conceal, so far as allowed, their suffering from man; and to lay open and communicate to Me alone the afflictions of their hearts.

But thou, Child, if thou art not yet able to reach so great a height of perfection, go thou, after having first prayed, go thou to some pious and interior person, not indeed to receive sensible comfort from him, but to be relieved and assisted, so as the better to come to My Heart, the fountain of true consolation, and to cling to Me rather than to any other solace whatever.

Indeed, if thou art truly wise, to cleave to Me ought ever to be thy greatest comfort. For, united to Me, even shouldst thou be deprived of all other solace, thou shalt calmly repose upon My Heart. And what can there be more sweet? what more secure?

3. So often as in thy troubles thou needest counsel or guidance, or art exposed to the danger of delusion, do not trust in thyself alone, lest thou err in thy own sense, and be deceived by the appearance of good.

For it is chiefly in these matters that I am wont to lead man by man; both that the order of My divine

Providence may shine forth the more clearly, and that men may love each other the more dearly—when they find, by experience, that they are not sufficient for themselves, but that each needs the assistance of the other.

And they who, under such circumstances, deem themselves too wise to need the direction of others, are wont to have a termination full of dangers.

Sometimes, also, to have recourse to created means is not only a counsel of security, but a precept of obligation.

It has been most wisely and properly established and ordained, that man should be helped by the other creatures, which were made for his real good; that at one time, by abstaining from them, he may practice virtue; at another, that he may be exercised by them for his salvation and perfection; and again, that he may use them as means.

Marvelous is My Providence in all My works. All things serve Me: if thou lovest Me, Child, they shall also serve thee.

4. Now, when it behooves thee to use creatures as a means, this use should be carefully attended to, and the result should so be looked for, that, in whatsoever way the matter may turn out, thou art resigned to the divine Will.

For, after having employed a sufficient diligence, the result, whatever it be, will be to thee a sign of the divine good pleasure.

Sometimes I inspire designs, to the execution whereof I will that men should apply themselves with courage and perseverance; although I do not will their success. In which event they obtain a two-fold advantage; on the one hand, the merit of the labor for a successful execution; on the other, the merit of resignation at the unfavorable result.

If any of thy affairs have an unhappy end, through thy fault, grieve thou for the fault, but accept with patience the pain of the misfortune, and bear it willingly. For the fault is, indeed, contrary to My Will, but the pain consequent on the fault, is according to My Will: therefore, the fault must be grieved for and detested, but the pain should be embraced and lovingly undergone.

And, if any misfortune happen through another's fault, resign thyself even in such an event; neither do thou lose thy patience nor peace of heart.

For, if I permit the successful issue of anything to be hindered by the fault of others, this is itself a sign, that I do not will thou shouldst be successful. And as, whilst permitting the fault, I hate it, and will, at the same time, the unfavorable issue of thy undertaking: so do thou, with a similar disposition of heart, abhor that fault and embrace the unpropitious result.

5. My Child, were thy heart rightly disposed, thou wouldst be resigned under all circumstances; that thus thou mightst gather from each of them a new pearl to adorn thy heavenly crown.

Assuredly, a great and supernatural discernment is required for the right use of creatures: for even if one begins with a good intention to employ them, he may easily become entangled and go wrong.

Thou shouldst pray, therefore. and implore the light and assistance of grace, that thou mayst remain free; and neither fail by the neglect of created means, nor exceed in the use of them.

6. *The voice of the Disciple.*—O Jesus, Thou the first and last refuge of the afflicted heart! what consolation can all creatures together afford, if the unction of Thy Heart's sweetness is wanting.

So often as, in my afflictions, through an ill-ordered inclination, or some reason contrary to Thy Will, I have had recourse to creatures and sought consolation in them, so often did I return from them more deeply afflicted and rendered desolate.

But this happened through the goodness of Thy Heart, that I might be happily pressed, and compelled, in some manner, to return to Thee, infinite sweetness, and pour out my sorrow-stricken heart before Thee,—who art ever near to them that are troubled in heart,—and who alone art mighty to give true consolation.

Thanks to Thee, most benign Jesus, for the great kindness of Thy Heart, whereby Thou didst deal so mercifully and so savingly with me.

O Lord, my light and my salvation! illumine my understanding, that in presence of creatures I may look upon Thee alone: purify my affections, that in the use of them I may ever love Thee; and grant that, disengaged from all, I may repose in Thee alone.

Guide me by Thy Spirit, Lord Jesus, and make me so use creatures, that I be pleasing to Thee; and so pass through the evils of time, that I obtain the good things of eternity.

CHAPTER VIII.

HOW, AFTER THE EXAMPLE OF THE MOST SACRED
HEART OF JESUS, WE SHOULD SUFFER THE OPPO-
SITION AND PERSECUTION OF MEN.

1. *The voice of Jesus.*—Dearly beloved, the hour
had now come when the Son of man would be delivered into the hands of sinners.

Behold, Judas Iscariot, one of the twelve Apostles, and with him a great multitude with lanterns
and tools, with clubs and swords.

And he went before them, as the leader of My
persecutors: and accosting Me with a false heart:
Hail, Rabbi, said he: and forthwith he kissed Me;
and so betrayed Me to them.

But I, knowing all that was to come, was more
intensely grieved, in My innermost Heart, at the
wretched fate of My unhappy Disciple and of the
crowd, than at My own suffering.

Wherefore, I began to try My utmost, and leave
naught undone, to soften and win their hearts.

Disregarding altogether the insult offered, with
a friendly countenance, and a more loving Heart, I
kindly addressed that Apostle: Friend, whereto art
thou come?

His heart remaining insensible to so great a
goodness,—to make him enter into himself, I urged
him gently, and powerfully at the same time, to
cause him to understand that I knew his crime, and
to induce him to reflect on the enormity thereof:
Judas, said I, Judas, betrayest thou the Son of man
with a kiss?

When he heeded not My saving voice, but, on the contrary, hardened his heart, then, at last, I had recourse to My omnipotence, yet so as not to interfere with his free-will.

Behold now, by a miracle, at the mere sound of My voice, as if struck by lightning, I laid prostrate the treacherous Disciple and his whole crowd; and sent, at the same time, a powerful grace to his heart. That unfeeling heart was moved; but he was unwilling to hearken to its emotion; he felt the grace, but he would not yield to the same.

2. My Child, if by meditation thou wert able, to some extent, to understand with how great a love My Heart had, at all times, pursued them, from whom I received such things in return, and how It had ever heaped new favors upon them; thou shouldst comprehend how unutterable were the sorrows which, like torrents, rushed upon and overflowed My Heart.

When thou hast anything similar to suffer, Child, do not lose courage: but let the example, which I gave thee for thy instruction and comfort, animate and console thee.

Verily I say to thee, Child, thou shalt suffer distress in the world: but have confidence and fear not, because I am with thee.

Remember My saying: The servant is not greater than his lord. If they have persecuted Me, what wonder if they also persecute thee? If the world hate thee, call to mind how it hated Me first.

3. Know this, My Child, so long as thou art the Disciple of My Heart,—so as to abhor the world and its sentiments,—that wicked enemy will oppose thee.

Thy manner of acting it will call hypocrisy, singularity, or some other vice.

At one time, it will pretend that it pities thee: at another, it will make a mockery of thee.

When thou withdrawest into solitude, it will accuse thee of melancholy or sourness of temper: if thou appearest in public, it will endeavor to blacken thy virtues; and thy faults it will either exaggerate beyond measure, or flatter thee for them unto thy destruction.

If, according to the zeal of thy charity, thou laborest for the salvation of the world; thou shalt, for the most part, find an unfeeling indifference, or receive in return bitter ungratefulness.

These things, and the like, will the votaries of the world do to thee,—not the open ones alone, but also they that are secretly such; not only they that publicly persecute Virtue, but also they that apparently seem to reverence piety, but, in reality, think hardly otherwise than the very worldlings.

Behold, Child, these things I have foretold thee that when they come to pass thou mayst remember My Word; and, cheered on by My example, remain firm in thy resolve, and be enabled to feel compassion for them that afflict thee, to pray for them, and even to be zealous for their salvation.

Assuredly, such wretched men are deserving of all pity; they injure themselves rather than thee.

4. My Child, thou must expect this during thy lifetime, that thou shalt often experience that men will oppose thee, and that they who once were for thee,—being now unaccountably changed,—will be against thee.

Beware, then, of men; do not rely upon them; whilst they favor thee, nor be thou troubled when they go against thee.

If thou deportest thyself so toward others as to keep thy heart pure and free, thou wilt resign thyself to Me with more ease and profit when they trouble thee, and thou shalt preserve thy peace and gain merit.

Go, Child, dwell among men wheresoever thou wilt: thou shalt find everywhere those that will try thy patience.

Shouldst thou deal with the devout only; shouldst thou live among persons secluded from the world, and with body and soul consecrated to Me, even there thou shalt not be secure against opponents.

If among My twelve Apostles there was one who persecuted Me, wonder not that among them that profess a life of piety, yea, even the religious state, there be found some who oppose thee.

5. Yea, Child, all they that desire to lead an interior life shall suffer persecution. For to an interior and devoted Disciple of My Heart, persecution is never wanting.

And, indeed, persecution is manifold; just as martyrdom is manifold.

For there is persecution from enemies, and from friends: there is persecution from visible foes, and from the invisible as well: there is persecution from the wicked, and also from the good.

So, there is a martyrdom of faith, there is also one of charity: there is a martyrdom of the body, there is also one of the soul; lastly, there is a great martyrdom of the heart.

My Child, if thou desirest to become a perfect Disciple of My Heart, thou must, in some manner or other, be a martyr.

For, as such a Disciple, thou art a companion of the Saints. Gaze, therefore, upon that mighty host which no one can count, standing before the throne of the divine Majesty, with palms in their hands, the symbol of martyrdom.

Although the Saints did not all shed their blood, all did, however, undergo sufferings, that they might obtain the palm of some martyrdom.

6. But observe, My Child, that no one, who is truly a martyr, chooses for himself, by his own will, his own martyrdom; but that he suffers that one which has been inspired, or appointed him from above.

Believe thou, therefore, that to be thy martyrdom, whatsoever has been presented to thee by divine Providence in thy state, employment, or other circumstances, wherein thou art placed.

To obtain an opportunity of suffering martyrdom, it is not necessary to betake thyself to infidel and barbarous nations, or to look for an avowed persecutor of the Church.

The world persecutes thee: man troubles thee: one betrays thee: another mocks and derides thee: this one humbles thee: that one opposes thee: corrupt nature, or an ill-regulated propensity, resists thee: something else is a source of grief to thee: lo, My Child, here is thy persecutor.

Despite the contradiction of men and their opposition; despite their sayings and annoyances, thou keepest bravely and generously the precepts of religion and thy rules, thou practicest virtue, and employest thyself in piety: behold thy martyrdom of faith.

Thou prayest for thy persecutors: thou lovest and helpest, in spite of natural repugnance, thy neighbors who are ill-affected toward thee: thou art zealous for their salvation, and offerest up for them thy prayers, labors, and sufferings: behold thy martyrdom of charity.

Sickness torments thee: thy head, thy breast, thy limbs are aching: hard work is killing thee: behold the martyrdom of the body.

Thou sufferest interior anguish: thou feelest racking temptations: or such things as divine love employs to purify altogether, and to perfect thy soul: behold the martyrdom of the soul, and of the heart.

But remember, My Child, that for those who have attained to the use of reason an unwilling martyrdom, or one which they endure for some cause or reason whatsoever it may be, is of no avail; for it must be undergone willingly, with resignation, or, at least, with patience, for the love of God. It is not enough, then, to suffer, but thou must suffer voluntarily for My love. A martyrdom, not quickened by divine love, is dead and worthless.

Behold! Child, a manifold crown is offered to thee, one which thousands of mortals of every state and condition of life have eagerly sought for, one which so many youths and maidens have exultingly borne off: and art not thou also able and willing to pursue and obtain the same?

Look up to heaven: contemplate the glory of the Saints, and their blessedness; remember that they are thy brothers and sisters: raise thy courage, secure for thyself a crown and palm, that thou mayst be received among them.

7. *The voice of the Disciple.*—O most sweet Jesus, Thou who art the Chief and Crown of Martyrs, the Comforter of mortals! I frequently experience that men are opposed to me, and I feel it deeply.

If, however, I be sincere, I am forced to confess that I have no cause of complaint: for I, the meanest and most ungrateful of men, have followed Judas and his throng against Thee, my Lord and God.

Hence, I own it, I truly deserve to be abhorred by every creature. Hence I am every way unworthy to be loved by Thee, or to be admitted among the sainted Disciples of Thy Heart.

Yet, since Thou hast a Heart so kind that Thou didst desire to admit even Judas, and didst use every endeavor to gain him! how can I distrust or fear! On the contrary, how great a hope and confidence should I not have, that, how wretched soever I may be, Thou wilt not cast me off, when I come to Thee, but wilt mercifully receive and help me!

Relying, therefore, upon the goodness and grace of Thy Heart, I resolve to make atonement for my past infidelity by my persevering love; to undergo for love of Thee the martyrdom graciously offered to me; and thus, finally, to sanctify myself to the everlasting joy and glory of Thy Heart.

CHAPTER IX.

HOW, AFTER THE EXAMPLE OF THE MOST SACRED
HEART OF JESUS, WE SHOULD BEAR TO BE FOR-
SAKEN BY PERSONS WHO ARE SERVICEABLE OR
NEEDFUL TO US.

1. *The voice of Jesus.*—When the crowds had
drawn near, and laid hands on Me, behold! My Disciples all fled, and left Me alone in the midst of My
enemies.

Such are they, My Child, whom I had chosen;
whom I had trained with all the care, solicitude,
and love of My Heart; to whom I had made known
all things whatsoever I had heard of My Father.

These are the very same, that, a little before,
had all, in like manner, protested that, even if it
were necessary to die with Me, they would not deny
Me.

But now, when it was the power of darkness, and
the time of trial, forgetful of Me, their Saviour and
Father, they all became runaways.

Reflect, Child, how grievously this total dereliction on the part of My Disciples wounded My
Heart.

Give heed also, and ponder, with what sentiments
of Heart I bore this affliction.

2. If thou dost truly enter into these sentiments
of My Heart, thou shalt be able to endure calmly
and meritoriously for My sake, to be forsaken by
all men whomsoever.

It happens not rarely, that man is suffered to be

abandoned, even in his distress, by persons very useful or necessary to him, that thus he may be assimilated more perfectly to Me, and be raised higher in sanctity. This shows forth more gloriously the power of My love, which so strengthens weak man, that, though alone, he stands ever firm, even whilst the raging winds and storms of adversity are rushing upon him.

This, too, is oftentimes useful, that man may wholly free himself from creatures, and leave himself completely.

For when, on the one hand, he sees himself forsaken by men, he easily withdraws his heart from them to give it to Me, who abandon no one; and when, on the other hand, he perceives that he is unequal to the troubles which assail him, he comes, as it were of his own accord, to Me, and throws himself, and all he has, into My paternal bosom.

It is, indeed, heroic and worthy of the divine approval, that a person abandoned by all, be equally satisfied with this dereliction,—love the more purely those who forsake him, endure willingly, for My love, the loss of men's affections, and repose, amidst all accidents, in Me alone. This, surely, is the mark of a humble heart, which gives itself wholly to My love.

3. When one possesses the affections of another, —although he may have a good enough object in view,—he frequently allows much to creep in which is ill-regulated, or at least merely human.

But I,—who am a zealous lover of the heart, who do not wish that man's heart should be busied except with Me or for Me,—am wont so to arrange matters, that he is sometimes forsaken or discarded by mortals, even by those who it seems ought to have shared with him his weal or woe till death.

A person must contend much and long with himself, that he may order perfectly the desire of being loved by others.

The voice of the Disciple. — But, O Lord, is it evil, without a bad intention, to desire, or even seek to be loved by others?

The voice of Jesus. — My Child, it is one thing to wish or seek this for thyself, and another to desire, or to seek it, for My sake.

If thou seekest another's affections in order to delight or repose thyself therein: if thou desirest them on account of personal qualities to indulge thy own inclination: finally, if, in any manner, thou so wishest for them, as, either directly or indirectly, to finish with self—some gratification of nature: thou wouldst fain be loved for thy own sake.

If, on the contrary, thou desirest or strivest to gain the love of others in order to devote thyself to My interests, to secure their everlasting salvation, or to promote the perfection of souls,—to extend the kingdom of My love, to win hearts for Me: behold! thou seekest to be loved for My sake.

Now, My Child, if, in a direct or indirect manner, thou aspirest to be loved for thyself; this, although it be done with no evil intention, is inordinate,— since not thou, but I Myself am thy end: therefore, it is imperfect, and, what is more to be dreaded, it is wont not only to lead to sin, but also to entangle men therein.

But, if thou desirest to be loved for My sake, thy love is well-ordered, it is pure, it is love for Me; it is a love with which the Saints have loved, and sought to be loved; by means of which they have accomplished much good, and which thou, Child, shouldst employ in like manner.

4. There is hardly anything in the world, to which the human heart cleaves more feelingly, than to friendship, which—full of change as it is—is wont to be either very advantageous or very prejudicial.

A precious possession hard to find, more difficult to keep, is genuine, pure friendship, whereby one loves another sincerely for love of Me; whereby one seeks the true good of another as his own; whereby, without flattery, without human respect, one takes care to correct the faults of the other, to cheer him on and assist him to acquire virtue and sanctity; whereby one is faithful to the other in adversity and prosperity, in death, yea after death, as well as during life.

My Child, if thou lovest any one, and so lovest him, that thou growest uneasy in consequence, that thou art moved rather frequently to occupy thy mind or heart with him, at proper and improper times; that thou desirest to hold long or frequent conversations with him; that thou givest heed to his outward accomplishments, and entertainest or directest thy affections by them; that thou makest bold to express thy admiration for him or to flatter him in his presence; that thou callest his defects by an honorable name, or excusest them, that thou takest ill that others be loved by him; that thou seemest in some sort inconsolable, or too unhappy, when thou must altogether part with him; then thy love, thy friendship, is not genuine nor pure, even if thou do not observe it, even if thou do not suspect it. But if, on the contrary, thou experiencest none of these things, thou hast a good sign in favor of thy love and friendship.

My Child, if thou hast a true and sincere friend, a rare treasure, deport thyself in a becoming manner in his regard, and so deal with him, that whether he remain faithful or prove faithless, thou never regret to have so acted.

But, although friendship, founded upon love for Me, is of itself good, thou shouldst, however, keep thy heart so free, that, if I so dispose things, thou art willing to possess Me alone, instead of all others, as the friend who suffices for thee.

Thy heart shall never be altogether quiet, nor prepared for an intimate union with Me,—whatsoever else thou mayst do,—unless, soaring beyond every natural affection, it love with My love alone, and repose in the sole love of Me.

Wherefore, Child, centre thy affections on Me; bind thy heart to Mine, that it may neither fall nor shake, if men withdraw themselves.

5. What are men except pliant and frail reeds, whereon thou canst not lean securely, if thou wilt not expose thyself to the risk of reeling or falling?

Even should mortals not depart from thee, thou thyself must in a short time depart from them,— since death separates each and all.

When thou art forsaken by men, thou shalt nowhere find a surer nor greater solace than near Me, —who was, for love of thee, treated in like manner.

Be not exasperated, Child, nor do thou complain, as if thou didst not deserve to be so dealt with, at least by this or by that one.

Ah, My Child! if thou art not willing to suffer,

except from whomso it may please thee, what principle of virtue dost thou possess? And if thou art willing to suffer only what thou hast deserved, what is there great in that? or what therein is worthy of a Disciple of My Heart?

6. If any do, in some manner or other, fall away from thee, show to them by thy friendly disposition, thy mildness, and thy honorable treatment of them, what pure charity is able to do, which,—overlooking all repugnances of natural feeling,—devotes itself rather to their good than to thy own inclination, even after they have rendered themselves unworthy.

It is true, Child, it is difficult so to go against nature: but a humble Disciple of My Heart, one who is animated by love for Me, does not regard the opposition of nature, but the object of his love: and, whilst another, in his coldness and lukewarmness, remains hesitating, he, in his fervor, has already surmounted the difficulty.

Inflame thy heart with the fire of love, wherewith My Heart is burning: glow thou with that fire: love thou with that love: if thou do this, behold! all difficulties will flee before thee and disappear.

7. *The voice of the Disciple.* — Blessed is he who, enkindled and enraptured with love for Thee, follows Thee, O Jesus, love of love, divine charm of the heart! He runs cheerfully through every hardship; and soon, rising above everything of man and self, with heart dilated, on the expanded wings of divine love, is borne aloft with Thee,—securely united to Thee.

O most sweet and bountiful Jesus! grant me, I

beg and entreat Thee, this love so fervent, so efficacious, whereby I may love Thee for Thyself, and
naught beside, save for Thyself: whereby I may
endure it with ease, if Thou sufferest me to be forsaken by men.

Be Thou only forever with me: Thou alone wilt
be enough. Should all, abandoning me, betake
themselves to flight, my heart shall not be troubled,
if Thou art with me.

This alone do I crave, and will not cease to ask,
that they who shun and forsake me, may not shun
nor abandon Thee: but, on the contrary, may cling
to Thee more closely, may love Thee more perfectly.

CHAPTER X.

HOW WE MAY IMITATE THE MOST SACRED HEART OF JESUS MADE A PRISONER.

1. *The voice of Jesus.*—My Child, the soldiers
and the attendants of the Jews, rising from the
ground, rushed upon Me, and having seized Me,
they bound Me.

Behold, Child, behold the Lamb of God in the
hands of the executioners, bound for the sacrifice!
bound, because He willed it; and He willed it because He loved.

For the chains of love pressed My Heart more
tightly than the fetters of My enemies bound My
hands.

And, unless My Heart, led captive by love, had hindered it, My almighty hands could have destroyed My enemies, and broken their chains.

But love endures all things: no humiliation does it think too great, no suffering does it consider excessive: whatsoever it wills, it seizes and holds, and remains itself ever free.

O if thou knewest, My Child, how great a blessedness it is, to be the captive of divine love, assuredly thou wouldst not, wert thou able, even for a moment, desire to be thy own master; but thou wouldst willingly deliver up body and soul, thyself, and all thou hast, that by it thou mightest be bound and held!

2 He that lives under divine love, thinks neither persecutions, nor chains, nor imprisonment, nor death itself, suffered for My sake, anything doleful or unfortunate; but he rather deems it a great gain, an object worthy of a holy ambition, to suffer all this for love of Me.

Why, thinkest thou, does it happen, that some, when, to keep the faith, they must suffer chains or inconveniences, do not remain in the truth, but go after the inventions of men, and fall into the judgment of condemnation? Is it not because they are not impelled by pure love for Me—so as to be willing to lose their life in this world, that they may save it in the next?

Hence, Child, as they are unwilling to be My fellow-captives, they become the prisoners of the devil; and as they desire to save their life in time, they lose it in eternity.

My Child, if ever it be thy lot to undergo chains or imprisonment for virtue, do not fear them that may kill the body, but can do naught beyond; but rather fear Him who can destroy body and soul forever.

3. It is a grace, a happiness, to undergo afflictions for My sake, if thou sufferest them unmeritedly. Whilst partaking of My sufferings, it behooves thee to rejoice, as about to exult in the revelation of My glory.

Let none suffer as a wrong-doer, a scoffer, or a criminal; but, if as My Disciple, let him not be ashamed, let him glorify Me in that name, by enduring courageously and perseveringly — piously and humbly manifesting his joy, for that he is reckoned among them who were deemed worthy to suffer for My sake, and thus to become Saints.

Some of whom were racked; some underwent mockeries and stripes, beside chains and prisons; others were stoned; others were tortured and cut asunder; others again perished by the sword; others, finally, wandered about in sheep-skins, and disguised in other garments, in want, distressed, afflicted; wandering over mountains, in dens, and in caves of the earth.

But to them, of whom the world was not worthy, because they persevered and overcame with Me by suffering—I gave to sit with Me on a throne, as also I, by suffering, persevered and overcame, and am seated on a throne with My Father.

How blissful art thou, My Child, if, for My sake, thou becomest a partner in affliction with these! because whatever there is of everlasting glory and honor, whatever there is of true virtue and holiness, whatever, finally, there is of the Spirit of My Heart, rests upon thee.

4. But not to every one is given an opportunity of suffering chains and tortures for virtue. All they, however, who strive after a perfect Imitation of My Heart, can and must, in some sort, become captives for the sake of virtue.

For who is there that cannot bring the senses of his body into captivity—not merely that they may do no evil nor yield to vanity—but that they may be held within restraint, and exercised in the practice of virtue?

Few, however, preserve their senses within the limits of reason; and fewer still mortify them according to the principles of faith.

My Child, how art thou wont to deal with the senses of thy body? Dost thou not suffer them to be too free? Consider what, in regard to them, is desired for perfection.

5. As to the powers of the soul, canst thou not also, in some manner, bring them into captivity? Thy roaming imagination,—so tenacious of the past, and so inquisitive as to the future,—thou wilt force, by degrees, to be sufficiently subject to thee, if thou recallest her forthwith when she makes her escape; if at home, thou entertainest her constantly with things useful; if thou repressest assiduously her sudden impulses and triflings, until she be accustomed to remain quiet.

Keep thy mind wholly subject, as is proper, in obedience to faith; lest, perchance, becoming a searcher of Majesty, thou be overwhelmed by glory, or a fugitive from truth, thou become a slave of error.

Nay, more subdue thy opinions, and,—unless some other virtue forbid it,—subject the same, for charity's sake, to the judgment of others. By so doing thou shalt gain the more, the more truth-like thy own opinion appears, and the more difficult it is, consequently, to subdue the same.

To be inwardly and outwardly unguarded and dissipated proceeds from the defect of a heart which is a slave, either to its enemies, to its passions, or even to itself.

Thy chief care, therefore, should be to keep thy heart free from the servitude of all things inferior. For only then wilt thou be able to devote it, in its vigor, with all its affections, to pure, supernal charity, and to become My fellow-captive in the chains of divine love.

6. Marvelous is Charity in its workings. If thou servest Charity, behold! all things shall be turned for thee into blessings.

Love Me, Child, thy God and Saviour; by loving thou wilt learn to love Me more perfectly: love is better learnt and perfected by loving than by speculating.

If thy heart is wholly submissive to My love, thou wilt easily and carefully guard against that false freedom of thinking, of speaking, of acting according as thou feelest inclined.

This mad license—not true freedom—what else is it except a cloak of the passions, the bane of virtue, the realm of vice, the misfortune of families, the ruin of cloisters, the plague of society?

And the more widely this evil daily spreads among worldlings, the more plausibly it creeps in among the godly, the more cunningly it enters even among religious; with the more care oughtest thou to put thyself on thy guard, lest it also infect thy heart; and lest, under the appearance of good, it draw the same away from the servitude of humble love, to the freedom of the flesh, which leads to the slavery of hell.

Thou canst not be thy own master, how much so ever thou mayst desire and strive to be so. Thou art bound to love, and, therefore, to devote thyself to some object, even in spite of thyself. But thou canst not give thyself up to anything created, without the most grievous injustice and the basest ingratitude to Me, and without manifold evil to thyself.

Wherefore, Child, be willingly Mine! give thyself up to My love; since, in order that thou mightst be Mine, I was willing to be a captive for thee.

How happy shalt thou be, when bound, inwardly and outwardly, by the same chains of love, that unite with Me the Angels and Saints in heaven!

7. *The voice of the Disciple.*—O most loving Jesus! to what extent didst Thou love me, who didst condescend to become a captive for me,—a captive of sorrows in the hands of Thy enemies, that Thou mightst allure and make me a captive of Thy love!

O Lord, my Saviour! when I call to mind Thy chains, I utterly despise in my heart all worldly freedom—desirous of being Thy fellow-captive in chains.

If the fetters of enemies are wanting to me, behold! I give myself up to the chains of love, that, all the senses of my body and the powers of my soul being seized and made subject, I may be so bound to Thee, as never to be separated from Thee.

Grant, I beseech Thee, Lord Jesus, that these may be no empty wishes, but efficacious resolves, which, with Thy grace, I may fulfill for the consolation of Thy Heart, and the sanctification of my soul,—for which Thou hast so much suffered.

CHAPTER XI.

HOW, AFTER THE EXAMPLE OF THE MOST SACRED HEART OF JESUS, IT BEHOOVES US TO BEAR FALSE ACCUSATIONS.

1. *The voice of Jesus.*—My Child, hereafter thou shalt see the Son of man, although the Supreme Judge of the living and the dead, cited, accused, and condemned by sinners deserving everlasting death.

For behold! they led Me bound to the High-priest, where the other priests, and the Scribes, and Pharisees had assembled.

The chiefs of the priests and the whole council sought false witness against Me, that they might put Me to death.

And many, coming forward, bore false witness against Me.

But the High-priest rising up, said to Me: Answerest Thou nothing to the things which these men bring against Thee?

My Child, what, thinkest thou, did I reply to their false testimony, and to the saying of the High-priest, in order to defend Myself? What say the Scriptures? "But Jesus was silent."

So it is, My Child, I was silent with My tongue, as a man that has no disproof in his mouth; but with My Heart I spoke to My heavenly Father, conforming Myself to His good pleasure, and beseeching Him to have pity on those wretched men; to pour into their hearts the abundant grace of the Holy Spirit, in order to save their unhappy souls.

2. My Child, knowing that it is most painful to be assailed with false accusations; and most difficult to bear them perfectly, I willed that My Heart should be in the highest degree assaulted and overwhelmed with unjust calumnies, that, when thou thyself art falsely accused, thou mayst find some solace in My Heart, which was similarly afflicted, and from Its example receive a secure guidance.

And truly, there is hardly anything more painful to the human heart than to be defamed with false accusations. Hence, some persons are thereby so much disturbed in their reason, that, overcome by feeling, if they could lawfully choose, they would prefer to die rather than to live so dishonored.

My Child, take heed, lest thou suffer thyself to be troubled or be clouded in mind: but, with a calm heart, examine the matter better: act as a worthy Disciple of My Heart.

Remember, that neither the malice of those that defame thee by false reports, nor the error of those that believe falsehood, can make thee different from what thou art, nor take away the virtue of thy greatness of soul, which lifts itself above falsehood uttered and believed.

But, if thou viewest the matter in the light of faith, thou shalt see that its sublime excellence, heavenly honor, everlasting reward, correspond to the greatness of thy humiliation.

And although thou mayst be innocent of the

faults objected to thee, as, however, thou hast, in many things, offended the divine Majesty, thou shouldst willingly embrace the opportunity of satisfying for those things in time, which otherwise may remain to be atoned for in eternity.

Moreover, even shouldst thou prefer to cleanse thyself of thy offenses, and to enter heaven by other means; yet, do thou rather receive these things offered thee by divine Providence, as both more certain and more secure.

How painful soever these things may be to the feelings of nature, suffer them, My Child; undergo them for love of Me; bear them with Me.

And if thy heart almost fail thee for grief, come thou to My Heart, which suffered more painful things for thy sake: here strengthen thy heart, protesting that, in spite of nature, thou art willing, for love of Me, to be resigned.

3. I am absolutely unwilling, My Child, that thou shouldst hate thy neighbor, how much soever he may wrong thee. But, although I gave a command of loving even enemies, yet I insisted on no precept of being silent or of omitting to justify thyself against false accusations: a counsel, however, I give, unless silence be sinful.

He, therefore, who, when falsely accused, speaks with a sincere heart, and in a proper manner, in his own defense, sins not: but he that speaks not, does better.

It is certainly a very great perfection, to endure in silence false accusations: to suffer that men believe about thee whatsoever they may please; to intrust thyself wholly to Me alone, and resignedly to remain with Me.

Behold! herein does grace triumph: this fills the Angels with admiration; this unites thee in fellowship with the Saints; this gives glory to God in the highest; this proves thee truly a humble lover of Me, and a genuine Disciple of My Heart.

This is the great secret of the interior life, drawn out of My Heart, which many hear, and many even admire: but which few relish, and fewer follow.

4. The Saints, however, appreciated this fully, and found it quite to their taste; burning with love for Me, and animated with a desire of following Me, they suffered, with a joyful heart, false testimonies of every kind.

And, when with one word they might have justified themselves and regained their good name,—intrusting the care of their defense to Me,—they preferred to be silent with Me, and to be considered the outcast and offscouring of this world, lest they might be found unlike to Me, and display a doubtful love.

It is most true, My Child, that this is neither easy, according to human feelings; nor does natural reason alone furnish a sufficient incitement thereto: but feeling and reason must be transcended by means of faith and love, which present and press forward abundant and most powerful motives and incentives.

Know, Child, if thou art not willing to act, except from feeling or natural reason, thou shalt not only never be perfect, but not even saved.

Live by faith; act out of love for Me. And if nature resists, because it dreads mortification or humiliation, let this itself be a new recommendation for thee to be silent, that thou mayst overcome ill-ordered nature.

5. Doubtless, the enemy of thy salvation and perfection,—who is ever roaming about seeking whom to insnare,—will draw near to thee, and suggest numerous, troublesome, and plausible things: but do not so much as hearken to his suggestions; yea, turn away thy mind from him, or say to him with scorn: Begone, Satan; for it is better to follow the divine Saviour, who goes before and shows a safe and secure way, than to leave the company of Jesus, to search out another uncertain and dangerous road.

Perhaps, also, some one will ask thee: Answerest thou nothing to the things which are objected to thee by these persons? Neither do thou, My Child, make any reply to this question, but imitate Me, and be in like manner silent.

If they insist: Seest thou not that thy despised name, the edification of thy scandalized neighbor, the honor of insulted virtue, God's glory itself, demand of thee, that thou do justify thyself? Believe them not, Child, it is not so.

If at any time circumstances appeared to require that I should speak in My own justification, it was doubtless then, when I remained silent; they did not, however, require it; for had they so required, I would have spoken.

6. Let the matter rest therefore, My Child, and intrust it wholly to Me, that, in the wisdom and goodness of My Heart, I may do that which is best for Me and for thee.

Do thou, meanwhile, suffer with Me in silence and patience. I know the accuser and the accused, the judge and him that is judged,—him that humbles and him that is humbled:—I Myself will repay, at the proper time, and give to each according to his works.

That thou mayst the better persevere, frequently call to mind, with what feeling of pain I Myself endured greater humiliations; with how courageous a mind, and how generous a Heart I bore them for love of thee: and thou wilt surely not refuse to love Me in return, who loved thee so much; nor to undergo lesser humiliations for the sake of My love.

Do not fear confusion: embrace it with a noble heart; it will not lower thee; it will not harm thee; on the contrary, it will elevate thee, make thee alike to Me;—it will adorn thee with merit and sanctity, it will replenish thee with the sweetest unction of consolation.

7. *The voice of the Disciple.*—O most sweet and loving Jesus! have pity on me and help me. For behold! because I am still lukewarm in Thy love, and imperfect in humility, I find my heart ever ready to grow indignant, and my mouth prepared to justify myself, whenever anything displeasing is laid to my charge.

And what is worse,—nor can I confess it without shame,—often do I find myself inclined to seek excuses for real faults; and, how just soever the imputations may be, I am ever moved to defend, or at least to extenuate, the defects attributed to me.

Hence it appears, O Lord my God, how great a sway the world still exercises over me, since I am more anxious to be approved by men, than to be assimilated to Thee: yea, and how great a perverseness is still lurking within me, since I am desirous of being considered innocent, whilst I know myself to be guilty.

Woe is me! When at last shall I be humble? when shall I begin to love with a generous heart? I beg and beseech Thee, Lord, spare not my pride, however hidden it be: incite me by a fervent love, that, co-operating with Thee, I may root out that curse.

O Jesus so bountiful to me! I indeed am willing to follow Thee, and to bear with Thee, in silence and resignation, false judgments and insults: but for this, weak as I am, I need a powerful grace.

Strengthen me, therefore, with Thy most potent grace; that, for Thy love, I may remain with Thee, silent and patient, unto that end which Thou mayst be willing to appoint.

CHAPTER XII.

THAT THE MOST SACRED HEART OF JESUS TEACHES US, HOW WE OUGHT TO BEAR PERSONAL INSULTS.

1. *The voice of Jesus.*—My Child, when the testimony of them that accused Me did not agree the High-priest, that he might find a plea for condemning Me, addressed Me again, saying: Art Thou the Christ, the Son of the blessed God? I adjure Thee by the living God, that Thou tell us, if Thou art the Christ, the Son of God.

Since all things in heaven, in earth, and under the earth, had borne evident and superabundant witness to My Divinity, there was no need of answering the High-priest, who was tempting Me;

however, to manifest the reverence due to the living and blessed God, My Father; to give testimony to the truth, even at the risk of My life; to move the hearts of these wretches, if, perhaps, they might be willing to hearken to grace, I replied: I am. Nevertheless I say to you: Hereafter ye shall see the Son of man sitting on the right hand of the Power of God, and coming in the clouds of heaven.

My Child, had they heeded these clear and sacredly terrific words, would they not—suddenly changed from judges into suppliants,—have cast themselves at My feet, imploring pardon and mercy?

But the unhappy High-priest, with his council, spurned both the proffered grace, and the salutary warnings. For the wicked man, when he is come into the depth of sins, contemneth.

2. Then the chief of the priests rent his garments, exclaiming: He has blasphemed. Behold! now ye have heard the blasphemy. What think ye? But they all cried out together, that I was guilty of death.

After this iniquitous and cruel insult, at which all heaven was horrified, behold! more atrocious and painful things awaited Me. For, as it was now late, the High-priest and his associates retired to rest, and left Me in the hands of the rabble, to be tortured during the remainder of the night.

Whatsoever thou mayst do, My Child, how intently soever thou mayst meditate, thou canst not fully understand the sufferings of My Heart during that saddest of nights.

Then, Child, they spit in My face,—that face whereon the Angels long to gaze:—and they, that held Me, vied with each other to mock and insult Me.

And, that they might act with more freedom, they covered My face: and, casting aside all restraint, some buffeted Me, others struck My face with the palms of their hands, insolently saying: Prophesy to us, O Christ, who is he that struck Thee? Others, in fine, uttered many other blasphemous things, and heaped many indignities upon Me.

Behold then, behold the Son of God, as it were a worm and no man: the reproach of men, and the outcast of the people!

3. Meanwhile, My Child, I was like a lamb before its shearer, neither opening My mouth, nor showing any sign of revenge, of anger, or impatience.

But, drowning in My Heart the intense sorrows, I displayed, in look and gesture, an invincible meekness, in order that My enemies themselves, struck with so great an example of forbearance, might be converted: and that thou, Child, being thus encouraged, mightst not refuse to imitate Me through love.

For if I, the Son of the living and blessed God, endured, for love of thee, such cruel and incomprehensible tortures, is it too much that, for love of Me, thou shouldst bear some insulting word, some ignominious appellation, or some reproachful action?

If thou art unwilling, for My sake, to undergo similar things,—little, indeed, in comparison of what I suffered for thee,—canst thou believe that thou hast a true love for Me, a love worthy either of Myself or of a Disciple of My Heart?

Ask the Saints. Even the least among them will answer thee by deeds, glorious both to themselves and to Me. Assuredly, those generous hearts would have been ashamed, and would have deemed their love either of no account or false, and thought themselves undeserving of the special affection of My Heart, had they not lovingly undergone the humiliations presented to them by Me.

Do not say, that thou art unable to endure such humiliations, because thou art not a Saint. For thou art able, if thou wilt, with the aid of My grace —which shall not be wanting. If, then, thou dost not undergo them, thou provest by the fact, not indeed that thou art unable, but that thou art not really willing. If thou art not a Saint, act in concert with grace, and willingly suffer humiliations, and behold! thou wilt become a Saint.

4. My Child, whether thou art willing or not, so long as thou livest among mortals, thou canst not be safe from every kind of humiliations; therefore, thou shouldst have thy heart ever in readiness, that, whensoever any do come upon thee, thou mayst forthwith have recourse to Me and implore My help.

Yea, it will happen, and even for thy good, My Child, that men do not only oppose, or overlook thee, but even that, before thy face, they provoke or insult thee. Then, if thou do not come speedily to Me by means of prayer, thou shalt find thyself exposed to great trouble and danger.

They that are still beginners in the interior life, and little advanced in mortification of heart, are easily disturbed by violent affronts; because unsubdued nature, when an opportunity presents itself, rebels, and excites a great dread of humiliation, and a lively feeling of worldly honor.

Yet all worldly honor is mere emptiness: for it rests not upon truth, but depends on the voluble tongues of men, who flatter or speak evil at pleasure.

But to endure, by virtue, the humiliation of an affront, is true glory; because it renders man similar to Me, and deserves an imperishable diadem.

5. The best defense of honor is an heroic generosity of heart. And, with men, is not meekness or clemency of more avail to protect or regain a good reputation, than anger or revenge? The latter betrays a little mind, and openly displays a heart enslaved to the passions: the former proves a great soul, a noble heart, and claims perforce the silent admiration of enemies, in spite of themselves.

Hence, even a pagan said: "To conquer one's self . . . not only to raise an opponent, but even to load him with favors. . . . Whoso does this, him I do not compare to the greatest men, but I judge him most like to God."

Upon these things, however, Child, I will that thou shouldst look as secondary only, and that thou shouldst ascend higher,—to supernatural motives,— lest thou reap no fruit for eternity from thy arduous efforts and painful sufferings.

There are many persons to whom worldly vanity is more palatable than My example; and who prefer to be slaves of their passions, rather than to be assimilated to Me.

Yea, to such a degree do some allow themselves to be carried away by their passions, that, when calumniated, they rather inflict death on their own soul, and expose themselves to the torments of hell; than let the offender go unpunished, or generously to pardon the injury of a moment.

Woe to men endowed with divine faith who live worse than the heathen, guided by reason alone!

Unhappy men! they shall see at last how foolishly, how wickedly they are acting, who,—when an opportunity is given them of appeasing God, of expiating their sins, of gaining merits, instead of so doing,—provoke God to wrath, heap up sins, and aggravate the torments they shall have to undergo.

6. The more courageous any one is to conquer himself, and the more numerous and difficult the victories he gains, the stronger shall he become against himself, and the more easy and fruitful shall he render future victories.

Wherefore, My Child, cheer up thy courage: overcome thyself, that thou mayst ascend to Me, that thou mayst follow Me. By this do thou judge thy virtue, the sincerity of thy love for Me: by this do thou distinguish whether thou art a true Disciple of My Heart.

Mark this well: if, in order to follow the divine Will, thou dost not go counter to the repugnance of nature; even shouldst thou work miracles, shouldst thou daily soar off into ecstasy, know, that all thy piety is nothing more than simple delusion.

Be generous and follow Me, thy Leader, and Protector, and Comforter: care not for what men may do to thee, or what may be the feeling of rebellious nature.

If thy heart does not reproach thee, when, with a meek and lowly heart, thou endurest wrongs done, have thou confidence, My Child; for thou hast a sign of My grace present and abiding in thee. For a representation of fire burns not: neither does a mere simulation of love thus suffer.

7. *The voice of the Disciple.*—O Jesus, God of supreme Majesty! truly incomprehensible is the excess of Thy humiliations: incomprehensible the excess of Thy love.

Every knee bends before Thee in heaven, in earth, and in hell: and behold! Thou art overwhelmed by the insults of fiend-like men, Thou art sated with revilings!

O Jesus, truly meek and humble of Heart! for, like a lamb in the midst of wolves, cruelly torn to pieces, Thou desirest, by a miracle of meekness, to move, convert, save even them! Woe is my heart, if, after such things, it refuses to humble itself, or desires to avenge any wrong whatsoever. For, if it is unwilling to yield to so great an example and to so great a love of its God, so humbled for its sake, what can it expect, if not the rigor of justice?

I entreat Thee, Lord God, righteous Judge and Retributer, enter thou not into judgment with me, but compassionately forgive me whatsoever I have done wrong through anger or revenge.

Behold, now, in Thy presence, most sweet Jesus, I lay aside and offer up forever, in spite of the feelings of nature, every desire of wrathful retribution, of vengeance, of every thing contrary to charity.

By whatsoever is dear to Thee, I beg of Thee, O Lord, favorably accept this sacrifice, which I unite with the sufferings of Thy Heart, and thus offer to Thee: I implore Thee, do Thou unite and bind to Thee forever, by the one bond of Thy divine love, all them that injure me.

CHAPTER XIII.

HOW IT BEHOOVES US TO IMITATE THE MOST
SACRED HEART OF JESUS, SO FAR AS TO BE
WILLING TO BE CONSIDERED AS FOOLS, WITH
HIM AND FOR HIS SAKE.

1. *The voice of Jesus.*—When it was morning,
My Child, behold! all the chiefs of the priests and
the ancients of the people returned to the council;
and soon the whole multitude, dragging Me in
chains through the streets, led Me to Pilate, a heathen, the governor of Judea.

They standing outside, with loud cries, called out
the governor, and began to accuse Me before him
of many and various false crimes.

But Pilate, hearing that I was of the jurisdiction
of Herod, king of Galilee, sent Me to him.

Herod, another heathen, was rejoiced at the sight
of Me: for he had heard much concerning Me, and
hoped to see some miracle performed to gratify his
curiosity.

But to a carnal man, who understands not the
things of God,—although he himself put many
questions, and the Jews were accusing Me unceasingly,—I answered nothing; yet, in My silence, I
displayed so eloquent a modesty and holiness, that
he could perceive that he was receiving a silent and
befitting admonition, and that My example might
move him to conversion.

However, this earthly-minded person, abusing all
these graces, and not able to understand why I did

not defend Myself,—why I did not seek to gain his favor,—attributed My conduct to stupidity and foolishness.

Wherefore Herod with his army despised Me; and put on Me a white garment, as if I were a madman:—thus he mocked and insulted Me.

Then, sending Me back, in the same garment, to Pilate, he exposed Me, as a simpleton, to the city and the world.

2. *The voice of the Disciple.*—O Lord God! that Thou shouldst be looked upon as a simpleton! Spare, O Lord, spare the dignity of Thy divine Person. Why dost Thou not hurl down Thy thunderbolts upon the sacrilegious wretches,—that the vileness of men may not thus profane the divine Majesty?

The voice of Jesus.—O My Child! thou knowest neither My Heart nor thy own. The pride of thy own heart demanded so great a remedy.

For, if thou darest to be proud, after thou hast seen the Son of God treated, for thy sake, as a madman and a simpleton; what wouldst thou not do without so great an example of Mine? Would not self-love, by its subtlety, set aside every precept, and aim at the very summit of pride?

Wherefore, from the greatness of the remedy, learn the grievousness of the disease: and hence measure thou, on the one side, the abyss of thy heart's misery, and on the other, the depth of My Heart's love.

Deep was calling on deep: the love of My Heart heard and willed that I should be humbled to the deep, that I might snatch thee from the abyss.

Notwithstanding I felt an unutterable pang in

My human nature, yet, for thy sake, I underwent. with a willing mind, this depth of humiliation, in the hope of gaining at last, by so great a demonstration of love, thy whole heart, of inflaming it with the same love and of animating it with the same sentiments.

3. An unfathomable mystery it was, Child, that God Himself should appear among men as foolish! a mystery, which love alone did work by its excess, and for which love alone is able to account.

For My Heart, made a captive by love, was urried onward by love, through humiliations, through ignominy, through reproach, through the appearance of madness itself,—feeling most bitterly, all the while, the painfulness of shame, and yet willingly embracing its disgrace.

If any one loves Me, he will keep My Word: the disciple is not above his master: but every one shall be perfect, if he is as his master.

Thou, therefore, My Child, if thou truly lovest Me, wilt not refuse to bear with Me the name of one unsound or foolish in mind,—whensoever I suffer thee to be distinguished by such an appellation.

It is not, indeed, lawful that, of thyself, thou shouldst give cause for aught of the kind: but to suffer that others take occasion so to do; or to desire that, without offending God, an occasion may be given, to be accounted silly or foolish, for My sake, is truly an heroic virtue and a very great perfection.

4. Be ready, Child, to appear, in some manner, foolish to men; for, in whatever condition thou mayst live, thou shalt be sometimes considered

such, if thou art willing to be a perfect Disciple of My Heart.

A life interior and devout, not merely in name, but also in fact, cannot be accounted otherwise than as a kind of folly by the votaries of the world's opinion.

For how, otherwise than foolish, must it appear to them, to despise the present advantages of the world in the hope of future blessings: to love poverty, and keep the affections disengaged from the things of earth; to submit the will and judgment to others, even when inferior to thee in virtue and science; to mortify unceasingly the senses of the body; without necessity, to seek no reparation for injury; to love enemies in sincerity of heart; to love humiliations, and esteem them advantages?

Come, then, My Child, be comforted, and with a great heart and willing mind endure all things with Me.

For behold! by the disposition of My Providence, what thou undertakest will, sometimes, have no success, and this will be attributed to thy silliness; others, however, will meet with success in the same undertaking, and the greater it be, the more silly thou shalt appear.

When accused, reprimanded, or ridiculed, thou wilt be silent, and thou wilt be looked upon as stupid by them that know not the exquisite wisdom of My Heart.

When thou disregardest opportunities of seeking thy own advantage, in order to promote My interests, thou shalt appear to many as devoid of common sense.

If intent on dying to thyself in order to live for

Me alone, thou shalt be censured by some as being feeble-minded through indiscretion, yea, also, through false piety.

These and similar things shall befall thee, Child, not only from them that show themselves votaries of the world, but, sometimes, from those that make profession of a virtuous life, or even of the religious state; and who, as they possess not My interior Spirit, love, indeed, the virtues whereby they may please themselves and others, but relish not My afflictions, My ignominy, My humiliations.

By them to whom the excess of My humiliations is a stumbling-block in practice—thou shalt oft times be treated most harshly, and shalt be made to feel it most keenly.

5. Do not lose courage, nor be thou dejected in heart, My Child, whosoever be the persons by whom thou art dealt with in this manner: on the contrary, cheer up and rejoice: bear it at least with patience, if thou canst not yet do so with gladness.

Is it not better to be considered foolish with Me than to be deemed wise by men alone?

Verily, verily, whosoever is willing, for My sake, to be looked upon as foolish in this world, shall receive in return a hundred-fold blessings in this life, and unfading glory in the life everlasting.

These results did the Saints experience, and they found more and better things than they had understood or had dared to expect. Do thou, also, My Child, make the experiment, and thou shalt meet the same reward.

6. This is the highest wisdom, which the world and its votaries neither do nor can know; but

which the meek and humble Disciples of My Heart understand and relish.

If thou lovest this teaching of My Heart, if thou actest by its spirit; well done, Child, well done; be glad and rejoice; because thou art become most like to Me.

It is certainly a most weighty matter: but do thou lighten it by love; and to cheer thee on, call to mind the speedy end thereof, and the everlasting reward in heaven,—where, after a short time, thou shalt be with Me, and where thou shalt shine with so much the greater honor before the angels and Saints, with how much the heavier weight of humiliations thou hast been pressed down before men.

These things have I spoken, Child of My Heart, that, when they shall come to pass, thou mayst have recourse to Me; that, in Me, thou mayst possess peace and consolation; that, with Me, thou mayst persevere.

7. *The voice of the Disciple.*—I confess to Thee, O Jesus, most kind Father; who hast hidden these things from the wise and prudent of this world, and hast revealed them to the little and lowly Disciples of Thy Heart. Yea, Father; for so has it seemed good in Thy sight.

As much as I can, I embrace them with my heart, desirous, above all things, to know and love Thee, most sweet Jesus, Thee treated, for love of me, as a madman.

Too late, alas! too late have I known this sublime mystery; too late have I embraced this supernal wisdom, which taught and formed the Saints.

Grant me grace, O most compassionate Jesus,

that, as I desire, forgetful of me and mindful of Thee, I may be carried forward after Thee, by love, that I may follow Thee by love, even so as to appear with Thee, if it please Thee so to allow, silly, stupid, foolish.

O Jesus, infinite sweetness! with Thee all becomes sweet! to be like Thee is supreme felicity upon earth, and the most certain pledge of heaven.

CHAPTER XIV.

HOW, AFTER THE EXAMPLE OF THE MOST SACRED HEART OF JESUS, WE SHOULD BE WILLING TO BE PLACED BELOW ALL.

1. *The voice of Jesus.*—Being led back to the residence of the governor, I stood before him, who knew that through envy, I had been delivered up by the priests and Pharisees.

As Pilate had no doubt of My innocence, he was desirous of freeing Me, if he could effect this without displeasing the Jews. Wherefore, he bethought himself of an expedient, which showed the base weakness of his soul, and covered Me with the utmost disgrace.

On the festive day, the governor was accustomed to release to the people one of the prisoners, whomsoever they chose. At that time he held a notorious prisoner who was called Barabbas.

Now, Barabbas was a robber, who, for a sedition raised in the city, and for a murder, had been cast into prison.

Pilate, then,—thinking that I, the benefactor of all, a lover of peace, the restorer of life, should be preferred to this man,—said to the assembled chiefs of the priests, to the magistrates and the people: It is a custom that, at the Passover, I release one to you: which of the two, therefore, will ye that I release to you, Barabbas or Jesus?

But, at the instigation of the chief-priests, the whole multitude exclaimed: Not this one but Barabbas.

Consider, Child, how this struck My Heart: how deeply it affected the same; how it tore It asunder.

Contemplate Me standing behind Barabbas in the sight of all: and see how I am treated by the highest and the lowest, as the least of men.

This disgraceful rejection, although it over-whelmed My Heart with a feeling of pain, I suffered willingly, both that I might save from the everlast-ing rejection of the reprobate, as far as in Me lay, the wretched Barabbas, thyself, My Child, and the whole world; and that I might leave thee an ex-ample full of consolation.

2. Do not, then, take it amiss, but endure it pa-tiently and resignedly with Me, if thou art placed beneath others.

What wonder if thou, who art dust and naught of thyself, sufferest thyself to be placed, for My sake, below others, when I, the Lord and God of all, allowed Myself for thee to be cast beneath the meanest of mortals?

Since the time thou didst sin, even venially, against the divine Majesty, thou didst truly deserve to be placed, not only below men, but even below irrational beings, which have not injured or offended the divine Majesty.

Wherefore, Child, when I permit thee to be put beneath others, be satisfied there, as in a place fit for thee.

And if thou deemest thyself to be placed lower than is just, do not, pray, examine too minutely the merits of others, nor thy own: but consider My example, and descend thou, in thy heart, still lower,—knowing that the nearer thou comest to Me, by humiliations, the nearer also thou shalt be to Me in glory.

How, indeed, couldst thou be a true Disciple of My Heart, if thou desirest to be the first, where I Myself was the last? Should the Disciple go before the Master. Is it not befitting in a Disciple to follow his Master?

Wherefore, follow thou Me, and be willingly the last with Me. Behold! how many there are in the world who are forced to occupy the last place; and because they do it against their will, therefore they do it without comfort, without merit! Thou, My Child, stay cheerfully with Me, and thou shalt have no cause for regret.

3. Happy thou, if, for love of Me, thou art willing, of thy own accord, to be placed behind all! For, if thou sufferest after this manner, thou wilt sanctify thyself by those things which shall doubtless befall thee.

Others shall be sometimes exalted, and placed like lights upon the candlestick: thou shalt be overlooked, and put under the bushel.

What others ask, they shall readily obtain, and they shall be thought to deserve it: what thou

askest shall appear unreasonable, or thou shalt be
deemed undeserving of the object.

What others say shall be looked upon as well-
suited, or even as decisive: what thou sayest shall
seem unsuitable or absurd.

Others shall complain at pleasure, and many will
sympathize with them: thou, when suffering under
pains or hardships, if, forced by necessity, thou
darest to speak, shalt be thought disturbed in thy
imagination.

The defects of others shall be dignified with an
honorable name: thy virtues shall be esteemed as
the effects of a weak mind.

Others they shall humor: but thee they shall put
down; and plead as an excuse, that thou dost not
only deserve this, but that thou standest in need
of it.

Not a few such things, My Child, whereby thou
mayst be placed below others, shall befall thee·
and, when they occur, nature will be grievously afflicted. But strengthen thy courage, and, in spite
of nature, continue with Me, preferring to be the
last with Me, rather than the first without Me.

Do not only gladly suffer that thou be placed
behind others, but wherever thou art, and canst do
so lawfully, take the lowest place for thyself:
there, Child, there thou shalt find Me, there thou
shalt have Me with thee.

If thou do this, He that raises the lowly will
one day say to thee: Friend, go up higher. And then
thou shalt have glory before the Angels and Saints

4. If the dignity of thy state or office elevate thee
above the rest, let the humility of thy heart, in a
becoming manner, place thee, for love of Me. below

the same. Thus thou wilt be enabled to imitate Me,—to whom all power is given,—merit much for thyself, and be more useful to others.

Neither do thou imagine that this kind of conduct is in any wise hurtful to thy authority. For, although it is proper and necessary that a Superior do uphold his authority, he cannot better do this than by that humble charity which does not merely hold the outward man in submission, but which also captivates the heart itself, keeps, and fills it with love, confidence, and every good disposition.

Do not reserve for thyself the greater and more showy performances, and leave to thy subjects what is of less importance, and more humble: on the contrary, as much as possible, reserve the latter for thyself, and assign the former to thy inferiors. Thus thou wilt follow my example, gain the good will of subjects, and stimulate their courage.

By so doing thou shalt better accomplish more things by means of thy subjects than thou canst do by thyself: and whilst thou art placed over others, thou shalt, as their companion, yea as their minister, be seen with Me.

5. As much as it is left to thee, choose rather to be subject than to have command: nay more, wheresoever thou mayst be placed, shun every word and sign which may display thy worth, talents, or other gifts and accomplishments,—none of which things should be made subjects of vanity.

Do not meddle in the affairs of others, as if thou wouldst better or control them: neither do thou show thyself ready, unless virtue demand it, to give advice, as if thou wert skillful.

Suffer willingly that others excel thee in science

and other matters, even in outward virtues: do thou carefully what thou canst, for the rest rely upon the divine good pleasure, and glory with Me in thy humiliations.

Know thou that only then thou hast attained to true holiness, when, for love of Me, thou rejoicest, that, in fact, or by efficacious affection, thou art with Me in the lowest place.

But, if as yet thou art unable to attain to this so perfectly: pray, Child, and use thy endeavors; and thou shalt come to it afterward.

6. *The voice of the Disciple.*—O Lord God, my Saviour, how divine is Thy Life! how sublime the doctrine of Thy Heart's example! Who can understand it fully, except whomso Thou teachest inwardly by the unction of Thy Spirit?

Alas, Lord Jesus! hitherto I have been without understanding: until now I have aspired to the highest place, although I beheld Thee in the lowest.

Wretched me! how greatly have I erred! I left Thee alone in Thy humiliations, and, blind and alone, I withdrew far from Thee: I estranged myself far from Thy Heart.

Vain and wayward, I strove to excel among men, and to make for myself some name, whilst my conscience bore witness, that, on account of my sins,— whereby I placed Thee, O Jesus! not only behind Barabbas, but, by an excess of malice and ungratefulness, behind the very demon,—I deserved to be cast beneath the feet of all, and to be filled with confusion before heaven and earth.

I am unworthy, Lord Jesus, to be with Thee, even in the last place. But since, in the infinite goodness of Thy Heart, Thou hast so mercifully reclaimed me, I trust Thou wilt kindly give me a place near Thee.

Thou hast opened my eyes to see my error, Thou hast moved my heart to make me love Thy company, even amidst humiliations: grant, I beseech Thee, grant me grace, give me courage, that, for love of Thee, I may willingly persevere therein with Thee.

CHAPTER XV.

HOW, BY VOLUNTARY MORTIFICATIONS, IT BEHOOVES US TO FOLLOW THE MOST SACRED HEART OF JESUS SCOURGED.

1. *The voice of Jesus.*—Behold! My Child, Pilate, seeing that, contrary to what he expected, Barabbas was preferred to Me by the Jews, stood amazed; but, believing Me nevertheless innocent, he was still anxious to release Me, and at the same time, to gratify the people.

Seeking to serve two masters,—on the one hand to please men, on the other to satisfy his conscience, —he tried another means, full of injustice and cruelty, in order to rescue Me.

For he resolved to place Me in such a condition that men, if they still possessed human feelings, should not be able to look upon Me, without being moved to commiseration.

I find no cause, said he, in this man: I will, therefore, chastise and release Him. And immediately he ordered Me to be seized and cruelly scourged.

And behold! forthwith the soldiers tied Me to a pillar: and now they lacerate My Flesh with continuous stripes and countless wounds: they vie successively with each other to multiply the blows and increase My torments.

Lo! blood streams on every side; it crimsons everything; it besprinkles the very scourgers. These, mad with rage, exert themselves more fiercely, tear off the flesh with their lashes and scatter it around!

Let us cut Him off, they shout, let us cut Him off from the land of the living, and let His name be remembered no more!

At this heartrending sight, the heavens were moved: the Angels themselves stood astounded at the excessive love of My Heart for men.

2. Thou, My Child, ponder thou attentively and compassionately these torments of Mine; and learn how grievous, how horrifying, are the sins of the flesh, which required such an atonement. Do not these wounds cry aloud upon all, that, at least through pity, they should cease to gratify the desires of the flesh, and not continue to heap up new sorrows?

Learn, also, how great is the love of My Heart, whereby I, the innocent, of My own accord, underwent the punishments of the guilty. Yea, Child, love, the ardent desire of saving all, brought it about, that with all My Heart I gave My immaculate Body to the strikers, and willingly bore the appalling tortures of the scourging.

Learn, too, how thou oughtest to treat that body of thine, which, conceived in sin, grown up amidst its passions, is ever prone to evil.

See, what the Saints did learn: observe, in what

manner they mortified their members, how they afflicted their senses.

How many among them, who never lost their first innocence, yet never ceased to wage a fierce war against their flesh, who subdued their frail body, and, by every kind of mortification, brought it under perfect subjection!

Their hearts were like to My Heart, and, therefore, they produced similar fruits in their body. Neither would they at all have thought themselves happy, unless herein also they had in some way conformed themselves to Me.

3. Wherefore, Child, even if thou art just, mortify thy flesh, both that it may not rise up and destroy thee; and, especially, that thou mayst assimilate thyself to Me, and thus sanctify thyself.

Many there are, lovers of self, sensual men, although unwilling to be considered such, who do not relish the mortifying of the flesh, and who are ever ready with some pretense to exempt themselves from mortification.

Foolish and deluded souls! Verily, verily, unless ye do penance, ye shall all likewise perish. If any one, though he seem a Saint or an Angel, say the contrary, let him be anathema.

Remember what the Spirit says: "They that are Christ's, have crucified their flesh with its vices and concupiscences."

The prudence of the flesh is death: the prudence of the spirit, life, and peace, and joy.

Wherefore, if ye live according to the flesh, ye shall die: but if by the Spirit ye mortify the deeds of the flesh, ye shall live, and enjoy peace and joy of heart.

4. My Child, rouse thyself by the spirit of love, whereby My Heart submitted to the cruel scourging, and thou shalt find mortification easy, and experience its sweet and saving effects.

There is no time when, nor place where, thou canst not, occasionally, practice the mortification of some one of the senses.

Besides, wheresoever thou art, shouldst thou not be more eager to mortify thy body, for the sake of following Me and gaining heaven, than sinners are so to gratify their flesh as to renew My flagellation and to deserve for themselves the pains of hell?

Come then, My Child, have no fear. Voluntary mortification is the way of life, of freedom, of tranquillity, of virtue, of sanctity.

Blessed are they that walk in this way! their happiness is known only to them that have tried the same.

5. He that does not mortify himself in things indifferent and lawful, will hardly mortify himself in those that are necessary and unlawful.

If thou wilt learn to mortify thyself in what is great, constantly mortify thyself in what is small.

Now the curiosity of the eyes, now the eagerness of hearing things new; again the desire of uttering what is useless, again the wish of smelling what is pleasant; then the inclination to experience that which flatters the touch, again the greediness to eat or drink without a sufficient reason; and again the intention of doing that whereby others may be incommoded; these, and similar things, may be a matter of frequent, nay, in some manner, of continual mortification.

These, My Child, will be for thee faithful guardians of innocence: these will be aliments of divine love: these will preserve fervor in thy heart: these will be unceasing sacrifices offered upon the altar of the inner sanctuary, which, united to the sacrifices of My Heart, shall forever mount up before the throne of the Most High as an odor of sweetness.

These things little, but frequently occurring every day, are useful and proper for all, for the young and the old; for the weak and the strong; for those beginning, for those advancing, for those perfect: nor can any one exempt himself from them without the disgraceful mark of lukewarmness.

In these there is no risk of health for any one; for these there is no need of special permission: these are safe and wholesome for all.

6. But all cannot equally undertake great mortifications: for all have not the same need, nor the same bodily strength; nor, in fine, the same vocation.

Wherefore, it is advisable for each one to lay open his circumstances to a spiritual director, to decide with him the measure of mortifications, not to undertake anything extraordinary without consulting him, lest for the appearance of a good he lose a real good, or lest he render himself unfit for what is better.

Among mortifications, those are to be preferred which, by their nature, are thought better suited to subject the senses to the spirit and to grace, and which dispose thee better, courageously to endure hardships, after My example.

But before all others, those should be embraced which are prescribed by Me, by the Church, by Superiors. These are practiced with more holiness and security than those which are undertaken by free choice: these produce more plentiful and more precious fruits, since to mortification the virtue and merit of obedience are added.

My Child, if thou gratefully rememberest, how I was wounded for thee, how I was bruised for thy iniquities, thou wilt apply thyself, with the Apostle, to bear My marks in thy body, and so to live, that My life may be manifest in thine.

7. *The voice of the Disciple.*—O my Jesus and my God! Thou art truly a man of sorrows; for behold, I gaze upon Thee scourged, and I see that Thou hast neither beauty nor comeliness, as a leper, and one stricken, so that there is no sightliness in Thee!

Whence, alas! whence art Thou reduced to this extremity? I, a vile wretch, have cruelly sinned, for which Thou, God Supreme, atonest by stripes so great and countless, by wounds so cruel and numerous.

O what a Heart is Thine, Lord Jesus! how great the excess of Thy love, that Thou didst endure such things for me! O most loving, O most sweet Jesus! how powerful a reason for trusting in Thee, however wretched I may be! how urging an incitement to love Thee in return with my whole heart!

But how monstrous, how horrible were my conduct, if, whilst I am bound to requite Thee with a grateful love for evermore, I were to renew Thy torments by my sins!

It were better a thousand times here to die before Thee, than to become guilty of so unutterable a crime. Yea, Lord, for love of Thee, I choose rather here to expire, than to sin against Thee.

That I may efficaciously avoid this, grant me the grace constantly to keep my body in subjection, and on all occasions to mortify my senses.

Give me, I beseech Thee, a fervent love for Thee: and behold! mortification will be to me the life whereby I live for Thee, follow Thee, unceasingly worship Thee, daily offer to Thee, now a sacrifice of praise, or thankfulness, then a victim of some feeling or inclination, again a burnt-offering of my whole heart.

———

CHAPTER XVI.

HOW, FROM THE EXAMPLE OF THE MOST SACRED HEART OF JESUS, WE SHOULD LEARN TO ENDURE BODILY AILMENTS AND PAINS.

1. *The voice of Jesus.*—My Child, after the scourging, whilst My whole body was dripping with blood, behold the soldiers led Me into the fore-court of the governor's residence, and there gathered together the whole band.

And platting a crown of thorns, they placed the same cruelly upon My head, and a reed in My right hand.

And they came one by one, and bending the knee before Me, they mocked Me: and rising, they took the reed and struck My head with the same, so that the points of the thorns, driven in ever deeper, pierced My head on every side.

Now, Child, had My suffering come to an unutterable excess; and even to My latest sigh, as long as the crown remained, were they to go on with ever-increasing violence.

Behold, I dragged Myself, My limbs broken, My joints bruised, all My senses sickly, weary, and, through the excess of pain, hardly under My control!

From the sole of the foot, even to the top of My head, there was in Me no soundness, neither within nor without.

2. My Child, thou wilt never more perfectly understand these torments of My Passion, than when thou shalt suffer similar ones; when thou feelest thy body writhing with pain, and thy soul undone by afflictions.

When man is despoiled of fortune, reputation, or other external possessions, it is hard, indeed, and distressing to nature: but it is much harder and much more distressful to be tortured by the pains of bodily ailments.

For in these outward things, by greatness of soul, with the aid of grace, a person can raise himself so far as either to forget, or not to heed, the cause and effect of his troubles: but, in bodily ailments, he cannot avoid feeling that which he feels, and, whatsoever he may do, always and everywhere he has his aching self with him.

However, if sickness is the greater pain, it procures also greater advantages for him that suffers rightly.

Wherefore, Child, let it be thy chief care to endure the same with a heart well-disposed, and to follow therein, as much as thou canst, the dispositions of My Heart.

3. And first, when thou feelest any indisposition, accept it as a dispensation of the love of My Heart, and say, at least interiorly: Blessed be the Lord, because He has visited His servant! And although

thou feelest that thou dost so only with difficulty, do not neglect it: for thou wilt thereby more easily overcome reluctant nature, and gain the more merit.

Next, resign thyself to the divine Will, in the best manner thou art able: and renew this holy resignation as frequently as possible, being assured that thou shalt derive thence the greatest strength and comfort.

Afterward, unite thy sufferings with Mine, and this by repeated acts, for various ends, which thy need, advantage, or even thy piety may require.

By this divine union, which overflows with the unction of grace, thy afflictions will be soothed, and will become for thee lighter and sweeter.

Lastly, to help thee to persevere, and to possess thy soul in peace, constantly withdraw, so far as possible, thy attention and even thy thoughts from the causes of thy sufferings, and from the sufferings themselves: and direct thy mind to My example and the unconquerable patience of the Saints and think how boundless, how sweet a reward thou shalt obtain in heaven, unless thou lose it by voluntary impatience.

4. Meanwhile, Child,—since thou needest much grace, and canst of thyself do nothing profitable,—according to thy strength, persist in prayer: especially in short and fervent aspirations, addressing Me in these or similar terms: Behold, Lord, he whom Thou didst love even to the death, is sick. . . . Lord, grant me patience. . . . Give me resignation. . . . Grant me to be united with Thee unto the end.

And, if thy infirmity increases, thou wilt exhibit a conduct most worthy of a Disciple of My Heart, if thou dost actually offer to Me thy body, as a living victim, and accept death, at a time and in the manner, which may be most pleasing to Me.

Know, My Child, that, whatsoever thou mayst do to the contrary, thou shalt occasionally be much inclined to dejection of spirits. Remember that this is the effect of sickly and languishing nature, whereby thou shouldst not at all be made uneasy. Only take care thou do not yield to it, or indulge it of thy own accord. For, by giving scope and indulgence to the same, thou wouldst both increase thy sufferings, and render thy very heart ill-disposed.

If at any time thy suffering and anguish should bring thee so far as to be hardly able to use the powers of thy soul with consciousness, remain thou quietly in My arms; neither do thou endeavor, with violence or anxiety, to excite within thee any acts or affections, but be satisfied with remaining calmly resigned to Me.

Blessed is he that, in sickness, adheres perseveringly to the saving divine Will. For, so long as he is united to the divine good pleasure, he reposes upon My Heart, and all is safe.

My Child, do not be despondent in mind, nor feel distressed on account of the greatness or the length of thy sufferings: remember that several of the Saints dragged out a long life amidst the pains of sickness, and thereby sanctified themselves, because they were resigned: and reflect that, however great and lasting thy pain may be, it is as nothing compared to the unmeasured and ever-enduring joy, whereby thy patience shall be rewarded in heaven.

Call to mind, that My torments and My martyr-

dom lasted as long as My life: and remember that
I endured all this willingly for love of thee. By
these things thou shalt be much assisted to bear
with constancy thy afflictions, for love of Me.

5. Show not thyself voluntarily peevish or impa-
tient toward them that take care of thee. Thy illness will often make them appear to thee careless
or neglectful.

So often as it is needful or useful, thou mayst
freely manifest with humility and charity, whatsoever thou thinkest is necessary or advantageous for
thee. But, meanwhile, thou shouldst feel so disposed, that, whether thy desire be granted or refused, thou do continue calm and resigned.

Do thou patiently bear, as not the least portion
of thy illness, whatsoever thou mayst have to endure from them that have care of thee. For, under
the disagreeable circumstances wherein thou art
placed, this may have great merit.

6. Beware, My Child, lest, under pretense of infirmity, thou indulge the flesh. Herein do many
err, who by sickness are not only not made better,
but rather worse, becoming lovers of the body, and
slaves of their passions.

Give to the body what is due to the body: but
neither in good nor in ill health, neither in life nor
in death, do thou minister food to the inordinate
propensities of the flesh; which, as in health, so
also in sickness are dangerous, and, therefore, to be
mortified.

Do thou, in a spirit of mortification, submit to
unpleasant remedies, and to the use of bitter or unsavory drugs. This mortification is the more precious, and a proof of purer love for me, as it is

more irksome and farther removed from natural inclination.

7. Whilst thou art sick, Child, do not trouble thyself with desires of attending to thy office or employment, of laboring for thyself or others, of performing works of piety; or, in fine, of doing other good things, which are incompatible with thy infirmity.

Such things serve for naught, except to cause thee useless affliction, to disquiet thee to no good purpose, and to displease Me.

Those things I do not now require of thee, My Child; what I demand for the present is, that thou suffer with a good heart, and be resigned to the divine Will.

Do now what I desire of thee; and leave all the rest to My Providence, that knows how to order everything rightly without thee.

8. Look to it, My Child, that, when sick, thou be not anxious to follow thy own guidance. For it is especially at this time that, being blinded, thou wouldst blindly lead thyself into some precipice.

Hearken religiously to thy Superiors, and suffer thyself to be directed by Me through them. Honor the physician for the need thou hast of him, and obey him in simplicity of heart.

Do not harm thyself, through negligence or carelessness, whilst thou art sick: but use remedies in a reasonable manner, praying God, from whom is all healing, that, if it be for thy good, He may deign to heal thee.

Having done so, how serious soever the disease may be, believe that it is something advantageous for thee, since it is the divine Will.

Come, Child, be willingly a martyr to suffering for My love, who, through every excess of pains, am become the Chief of all Martyrs.

Have patience, O Child of My Heart, have patience: behold! still a little while, thy grief shall be turned into joy, and I Myself,—who, for love of thee, was crowned with thorns,—I will crown thee with honor and glory.

9. *The voice of the Disciple.*—Blessed art Thou, O Lord, who didst visit Thy servant, that in time, Thou mayst mercifully prepare me for eternity!

O my God, heavenly Healer of men! behold, to Thy keeping I intrust my body and soul. Thou knowest what is best for me: do with me whatsoever Thou wilt, according to the goodness of Thy Heart.

I suffer much, Lord Jesus; Thou knowest it. Assist me with Thy grace: strengthen me with Thy love. If Thou wilt that my pain be lasting, increase Thy grace, increase my patience.

Whatsoever I endure, I unite with Thy sufferings, so much more painful than mine, and I implore Thee, that Thou direct all to Thy honor and my salvation.

Grant me this great favor, which I humbly beg of Thee, through Thy most benign Heart, that Thou keep me inseparably united with Thee, and thus lead me to the end of my miseries, to bliss everlasting.

CHAPTER XVII.

HOW, AFTER THE EXAMPLE OF THE MOST SACRED
HEART OF JESUS, WE OUGHT TO ACCEPT DEATH.

1. *The voice of Jesus.*—My Child, Pilate led Me
forth, wearing a crown of thorns and a purple garment, and showing Me to all the people, he said:
" Behold the man!"

The Jews seeing Me, were not only not softened,
but, on the contrary, thirsted more eagerly for the
remainder of My Blood; and all shouted with one
accord: Crucify, crucify Him!

Pilate, being again disappointed, and fearing
even more than before, said: " I find no cause in
Him." But they insisted the more, and threatened
him: " If thou releasest this one," they cried,
"thou art not a friend of Cæsar."

Seeing that he could not give freedom to Me
without losing the favor of the people, and, prob-
ably, that of Cæsar, Pilate formed to himself a false
conscience, and thus fell into a fatal delusion. For,
washing his hands before the people, he said: " I
am innocent of the Blood of this Just one: look
ye to it." But they shouted: " His Blood be upon
us and upon our children!"

Then Pilate decided that their request should
be granted, and Me, whom he had again and again
found and declared innocent, he delivered up to
their will, that I might be crucified.

2. Oh! My Child, who shall tell what My
Heart then felt? Behold! I had come down from

heaven to console and save the world: I had struggled in heat and cold, I had endured hunger and thirst, I had spent My life by ceaseless labor and endless suffering; I had, finally, sacrificed everything, to make all men happy: and must I at last receive from them, as a requital, death, yea the death of the Cross!

How great a sorrow rushed upon My Heart at so black an ungratefulness, so horrid an iniquity of men! How great a grief at the obdurateness of the hearts of those, who, spurning felicity, devoted themselves, of their own accord, to destruction! How great a torment at the affliction of My most compassionate Mother, and beloved Disciples, from whom I saw Myself torn away not only cruelly, but also disgracefully!

Nevertheless, the sentence of death I embraced with My Heart resigned, because I regarded not the unheard-of wickedness of those that condemned Me, but considered the good pleasure of My heavenly Father.

For My Father, in IIis infinite Wisdom, wished to draw the greatest good, the Redemption of the world, from the greatest crime, whereof He disapproved, and that they were committing by an abuse of their free will.

Therefore, in spite of the feelings of My suffering human nature, I submitted with a certain supernatural joy to a death, whereby the world was to be saved, heaven opened, the divine Majesty appeased and honored, My Heart Itself loved in return, and exalted for endless eternity.

Study these dispositions of My Heart, Child put on these sentiments: and, as much as thou art able, accept with the same affections the death which thou must undergo.

3. My Heart,—knowing that men naturally shrink from death, and dread it as the most terrific of all things on earth, on account of the past, the present, and the future,—did not suffer them to be without an example, whereby they might rightly be instructed and sweetly comforted.

Be not, then, troubled, nor astonished, My Child, if thou feelest a vehement horror and repugnance of nature when death is approaching, either actually or prospectively. In this there is no harm: it is wholly natural, which, if thou wilt, may prove advantageous to thee.

Only do not yield to the feelings of nature, lest, perchance, they render thee ill-disposed; or hinder thee from being resigned to the divine Will,—to which all things natural and created must be submissive.

Patiently endure every natural repugnance, and use the same as an occasion to practice great virtues, and to gather many merits.

4. My Child, suffer not thy imagination to stray, neither follow thou natural reason in order to investigate the dispensations of divine Providence; nor do thou give in to thy own will, how good or holy soever it may appear, lest thou fall into a dangerous delusion.

But, thy imagination being restrained, subject both thy reason and thy will to Me: thus thou wilt merit not a little, and, at the same time, remain tranquil and secure.

If thou feelest pain or uneasiness, by reason of the objects or persons that death obliges thee to leave behind, let not thy heart be disturbed. For this anxiety could not be of any avail to them, neither to thyself, but it might, on the contrary, be very hurtful.

When thou hast done for them what thou art obliged or able to do, intrust them all to Me, who know thy circumstances, and who, according to the love of My Heart, will have a much better care of thine than thou art able to bestow.

Be mindful of My example, Child; reflect, how I abandoned them that were dear to Me, and committed them to the divine good pleasure. With this do thou occupy thyself, with this be thou comforted.

5. Do not sadden thyself, My Child, because thou thinkest thyself about to depart this life. For what is life upon earth except a continued annoyance? What is it to abide in this world, except to remain in exile? What, in fine, is it to dwell among men, except to sojourn away from Me and My Angels?

If thou lookest rightly at the matter, when I call thee, better is death for thee, than a life of bitterness. For death is the end of the ills of this world; and departure thence to Me, the beginning of blessings, which know neither change nor termination.

The voice of the Disciple.—But, O Lord Jesus, if I knew that, after death, I should be among the Saints with Thee, I would assuredly not be grieved, but I would rejoice indeed; yet, at this I tremble, by this I am tortured, that I know not what is to be, whether I may be judged worthy of love or of hatred: whether, consequently, a happy or an unhappy eternity awaits me.

The voice of Jesus.—Why fearest thou, or why art thou in vain filled with anxiety, My Child? Know thou, that a person who is sincerely willing to be saved and to co-operate, for this purpose, with grace,—from how wicked soever a way of life he may turn himself,—shall not be cast off by Me, who desire that all be saved.

Hold this for certain, that for him who does what he is able to do, I will supply the rest. Do then peacefully what thou canst, and throw thyself upon My Heart: here, Child, here thou shalt never perish.

Be, therefore, quiet, and, as far as thou art able, prepare thyself for thy passage from time into eternity.

6. And first, offer thyself to Me, with a submissive heart, and pray that I may accept thy death in union with Mine, as a sacrifice to atone for all thy offenses, to satisfy for all thy debts, to render due worship to the divine Majesty, and to testify thy love for Me.

Then, with all thy heart, forgive wholly every one of thy enemies, all thy neighbors, who have injured or offended thee in any matter whatsoever.

Next, with all diligence, receive the holy Sacraments, with which the Church, in her motherly solicitude, is careful to strengthen thee, that in the last struggle thou mayst be enabled to obtain victory, and enter heaven in triumph.

Finally, resign thyself altogether into My hands, desirous of dying, not when or in what manner thou mayst wish, but when and in what manner I may prefer. Thou knowest neither the time nor the circumstances which are the best for thee; but I know them, Child, and under these, if thou dost not voluntarily put a hindrance thereto, I will call thee to Me.

Wherefore, resign thyself entirely to Me, by an absolute surrender of thyself into My hands; and be persuaded that thou canst do nothing better than conform thyself wholly to the divine good pleasure and sacrifice thyself as a holocaust of the same. If thou dost this thou wilt be saved.

7. How happy he, My Child, who thus prepares himself for death, and keeps himself in readiness! For him doubtless death is safe and blissful; for him death brings no evil, but, on the contrary, a great and manifold good.

For, behold! thy Father, who is in heaven; thy mother the Queen of heaven; thy companions, the holy Angels; thy Brethren, all the Elect; thy true and permanent country; thy glory and blessedness: all these are in the other life, and, except in the other life, thou canst not enjoy them fully.

Now, Child, death is the only gate through which thou art able to pass from this life into the next. Is it not, then, a happy hour, when I Myself will open for thee the door to such possessions?

Meanwhile, until the time comes, when I will open for thee, act, suffer generously; endure perseveringly: I am with thee in thy toil and tribulation; and, unless by a voluntary act thou set Me aside, I will continue with thee until I introduce thee into My kingdom, into the fellowship of the Saints and Angels.

8. *The voice of the Disciple.*—O most sweet Jesus! how great a consolation dost Thou pour into my soul from Thy affectionate Heart. If the unc-

tion of Thy secret communion is so delightful, what will be the very possession of Thyself in the kingdom of Thy glory!

Yea, Lord, introduce me into Thy kingdom: for I long to be released and to be with Thee.

Draw my soul from her prison, that, from the dungeon of this miserable life, I may pass to the freedom of the heavenly country, from all these misfortunes to bliss never-ending.

O Jesus, my God and my Father! whose child I am, lingering here in the land of the stranger, if,—as I hope from Thy Heart, so infinitely good,—I am to enjoy Thee for evermore, why is not the little remainder of my life engulfed by eternity? Why am I not even now with Thee, to love Thee perfectly, to sing Thy mercies forever, to praise, to extol without end, without measure, the kindness, the love of Thy Heart?

So long as I stay here, I am in danger of losing Thee alike and myself: so long as I carry about this mortal body, I can neither avoid all defects nor love Thee so much as I desire.

O Lord Jesus! when I consider these things, for Thy sake, my soul is weary of life. However, not as I will, but as Thou wilt: Thy will be done as it is in heaven, so also upon earth. For love of Thee, I choose rather to incur that danger, to undergo those bitter things according to Thy Will, than by my own will to escape from them.

Only do Thou remain with me: and keep me resigned to Thee, united with Thee during the rest of this life, unto life everlasting.

O Thou life of the present! O all ye things visible! what are ye when beheld from the threshold of eternity! seen thence, ye appear what ye are, bright and empty vapors.

O eternity! object unutterable! great thoughts do I form concerning thee: but greater are in thee: things infinite are in thee, which eye has not beheld, nor ear heard, nor the human heart conceived.

O everlasting abode of all that have received rational life! soon I shall be in thee: soon I shall behold thy wonders: at any moment, when comes the Bridegroom, whom my soul loves, it may be opened to me: so soon as it is opened, behold! leaning upon the Heart of my Beloved, I enter together with Him. Yea, Lord Jesus, my love forevermore!

CHAPTER XVIII.

WITH WHAT DISPOSITION OF HEART, AFTER THE EXAMPLE OF THE MOST SACRED HEART OF JESUS, WE OUGHT TO FEEL AFFECTED TOWARD THE CROSS.

1. *The voice of Jesus.*—My Child, when the sentence of death had been pronounced against Me, everything was prepared with the utmost dispatch for its execution. Behold, the cross stood already waiting for Me.

Bound, therefore, all covered with blood, torn with stripes and wounds, I was led to the cross: when I beheld it, My Heart warming up, sighed out: Hail, O hail, dear cross, always loved, unceasingly desired, at last prepared for Me! O sacred cross! through thee I will conquer, through thee I will triumph, through thee I will reign.

Then, embracing the cross and pressing it fondly to My Heart, I bedewed it with My tears and My Blood: next I placed it upon My shoulders, in the sight of the world, before the gaze of heaven.

Surrounded by the thousands of Jews and Gentiles, in the holy City, in the full light of mid-day, clad in My own garment, I marched onward carrying My own cross.

Behold, Child, I go to raise the cross upon the mountain, the standard of My kingdom, against the prince of the world: and to paint upon My standard, with My own Blood, the indelible watchword of My own: "The love of Jesus sacrificing Himself for the love of man," in opposition to the watchword of worldlings: "Love of the pleasures, riches, honors of the world."

By this My watchword, by this sign thou wilt conquer, My Child; but the enemies, erring in their watchword and sign, shall fall.

2. Beneath the banner of the cross men will flock together from every nation, and people, and tribe of the earth; and they will be united among themselves with Me.

Under this banner, My Disciples will know Me as their Leader, and, animated with love for Me, they will follow Me cheerfully.

Under this banner all they who are Mine will fight; will triumph over hell, the world, themselves, and bear off the kingdom of heaven itself.

Come, ye, then, come ye all, and what ye shall see me do, do ye also: let each one take up his cross and follow Me, his eyes ever fixed upon Me, marching onward with a great courage and dilated heart, nowhere turning, neither to the right nor to the left.

All ye, that shall have accompanied Me, shall be partakers of an assured victory, of an everlasting reward: but the more closely any one shall have followed Me, and with the greater courage of love he shall have behaved, the more close shall he be to Me in glory, the greater shall he be in My everlasting kingdom.

Let none forget the watchword: let none desert the banner, but let each one be prepared to conquer or to die for the watchword beneath that banner‧ altogether assured, that, if so disposed, whether he live or die, he shall be My companion, and, therefore, the partaker of My most certain victory.

3. I, My Child, never abandoned the cross: but I clung to the cross, I persevered on the cross, I expired on the cross, conquering and triumphing.

Happy the soul, that, animated with My sentiments, lovingly embraces the cross, and keeps to it faithfully! Her does the cross keep near Me; it does not cast down, but it raises up; it does not encumber, but it leads easily to the hight of sanctity, to the final triumph.

Wherefore, Child, thou shouldst remain with Me under the cross, live under the cross, die under the cross, if thou wilt be made like to Me, and one day triumph with Me.

Listen to none, neither to flesh, nor blood, nor spirit, that advises thee to forsake the cross.

Where, Child, where can it be better than under the cross? The cross is the guide to the everlasting kingdom: the cross is the wisdom of the Apostles, the trophy of the Martyrs, the glory of the Confessors, the security of the Virgins, the sanctification of old age, the preservation of youth, the condemnation of worldlings, the mirror of religious, in fine, the refuge and comfort of all the afflicted.

If thou fleest from the cross, whither wilt thou go? Behold! thou shalt fall into the camp of the enemies; where thou shalt have not one cross, but where manifold torments will meet thee from every side, will rush upon thee, will destroy thee.

There My banner, which breathes the love of My Heart, inspires courage and generosity, will not incite or console thee; but the fetters of tyrants, under a showy name, will drag thee through thorny paths; not to happiness but to misfortune; not to joys but to pains; not to glory but to ignominy.

Here, under the cross, Child, thou art with Me, thou hast Me to lead, to guard, to crown thee: here thou art in the midst of all the good, the brave, the generous; here thou art in communion with the Elect and the Saints, who have preceded thee, and who, whilst living, fought, and, when dying, triumphed under the cross: here, in fine, thou formest one fellowship, one army with the Angels themselves, who, thronging to thy side, protect thee, fight along with thee, strive to extend the same kingdom.

Foolishly, therefore, and fatally wouldst thou act, shouldst thou think of forsaking the cross, or imagine that it can anywhere be better for thee, than beneath the cross.

4. However, since the prince of the wicked world and his emissaries are thy enemies, do not

wonder if they allure thee frequently by imaginary advantages; and endeavor, by showy reasons, to induce thee to desert the cross, and to pass over to them.

My Child, do not even cast a glance at their false advantages, nor hearken thou to their wily subtleties: but lift thy heart and eyes to Me, who carry My banner before thee, and protest that it is thy determined will to follow Me to every fortune, even to death itself.

Hence, it will come to pass that the assaults and wiles of thy foes will awaken in thy heart a greater abhorrence of them, and a more firm adherence to Me.

5. But it is not enough for thee, My Child, not to flee from the cross; thou must embrace, thou must carry the cross.

Give heed to this, mark this carefully: do not all the faults which thou committest arise from this, that thou refusest or hesitatest to embrace and carry the cross, which is offered to thee?

When thou woundest charity, what else is the true cause thereof, except that thou declinest to undergo the present cross, some humiliation, the sacrifice of thy own opinion or natural inclination?

Why dost thou offend against holy poverty? Is it not because thou takest not the cross to thyself; because thou art unwilling to subject thyself to the trouble of asking leave, or to expose thyself to a refusal?

Why dost thou trespass against modesty? is it not because thou neglectest mortification; because thou dost not embrace this cross?

Why failest thou in obedience? is it not because

thou lovest not the cross; because thou dost not make the entire sacrifice of thy will and judgment?

Yea, Child, against what virtue soever thou sinnest or offendest, if thou lookest well into it, thou wilt find this to be the cause, that thou dost not take upon thee nor embrace the cross with a willing heart.

Nevertheless, a cross of this kind is small and light: if thou dost not receive lovingly such a one, how wilt thou take up one which is greater and heavier?

Look, Child, lest falling into delusion, thou become worse: like those, who fancy for themselves some great cross, and resolve to carry it at some future time, and, meanwhile, studiously shun every present cross, although less burdensome; and, when placed between the cross and guilt, are wont to embrace the latter rather than the former.

6. What fearest thou? why dreadest thou the cross? Cheer up, My Child: receive the cross, it will receive thee, and reward thee in a wonderful and manifold way: for, behold! it will preserve thee from uneasiness, from trouble of conscience, from anguish of heart, by which others, who prefer guilt to the cross, are wont to be tormented; it will guard for thee peace, it will adorn thee with virtues; in fine, it will console thee by its unction.

Courage, then, My Child; even if thou experiencest difficulty, do not flag in spirit. Behold! I, the guiltless Son of God, carry before thee, for love of thee, the heaviest cross: do not disdain, for love of Me, to carry thy cross after Me. Love, which rendered My bitter cross sweet for Me, will also render thine sweet.

Pray frequently, that thou mayst deserve to love

the cross, together with sanctifying grace, above all the good things of this life,—the cross, a folly, indeed, to them that perish, but divine wisdom to them that are saved: a torment to the enemies, but a consoling pledge of everlasting bliss to the Disciples of My Heart.

Well, then, My Child: come, follow Me: thither leads the way whither I will show thee: if thou abidest with Me, I will dispose unto thee, as My Father has also disposed unto Me, a kingdom.

7. *The voice of the Disciple.*—As the Lord lives: and as lives the Lord, my King, in whatsoever place Thou mayst be, my Lord, whether in death or in life, there will be Thy servant.

Gazing upon Thy standard, and encouraged by its motto, I will follow Thee, my Leader, through all: if any hardship present itself, mindful of Thy watchword, I will repeat: for the love of Jesus, who has sacrificed Himself for love of me, I will overcome this difficulty: despite the feeling of nature, I will remain under His banner.

If armies in camp should stand together against me, my heart shall not fear: if a battle should rise against me, in Thee will I hope.

Come, ye companions, behold! Jesus will be King over us: He will march out before us, He will fight our battles.

Let us go out, bearing His reproach: let us hasten to the contest placed before us, looking on Jesus, the Author and Finisher of our faith; who, having joy set before Him, endured the cross.

Let us go and die with Him: if we die together with Him, with Him we shall also live: if we endure with Him, with Him we shall also reign

CHAPTER XIX.

THAT JESUS CRUCIFIED, BY PRAYING FOR HIS EXE-
CUTIONERS, MANIFESTS THE INFINITE GOODNESS
OF HIS HEART TOWARD SINNERS, AND THAT, BY
GRIEVOUS SIN, THESE CRUCIFY HIM ANEW.

1. *The voice of Jesus.*—My Child, behold! at
last we come in Golgotha, to Mount Calvary. They
lay down the cross forthwith, they push forward
and hurry on everything.

Nor do they, meanwhile, cease to torture Me.
Nay, they even gave Me wine mingled with myrrh
and gall. So great was their cruelty!

And, when they were now ready, raising a shout,
they cruelly fasten Me to the cross, driving in the
nails, with violent and repeated strokes, which the
valley below re-echoed to the sky,—each one of
which pierced the Heart of My Mother, there
present.

Thus, Child, did they dig My hands and My
feet: they counted all My bones, which, by the
stretching of My Body, could be seen distinctly.

Then couldst thou behold the cross ruthlessly
raised, and Myself hanging between heaven and
earth; whilst the Blood flowed from every wound,
washing the earth, and crying to heaven for the
salvation of man.

And, to increase My torments, they raised on the
gallows two thieves, one at My right and one at My
left, so that I was hanging between them.

But behold! so soon as I was elevated on the

cross, darkness overspread the whole earth. The sun and the moon, together in mourning, hid their light, and wrapped the world in doleful grief.

The people stood looking on. They that passed by, shaking their heads, blasphemed Me. But they that stood around mocked Me: in like manner also, the chiefs of the priests, with the Scribes and elders, insulted Me by derisive gestures The soldiers, too, jeered at Me, and, adding insults, they offered Me vinegar. All, in fine, sated Me with reproaches.

And amidst all this, what was I doing. Child? What My Heart? Father! I exclaimed, unfolding My Heart, Father! forgive them; they know not what they do: they know not how enormous is the crime which they are committing.

2. The Angels wept at this spectacle: all nature recoiled with horror, amazed at so great a wickedness of men, awe-struck at the marvelous goodness of My Heart.

Thou alone, wicked sinner, remainest unmoved whilst the universe trembles: thou, whilst heaven and earth are terror-stricken, renewest the tortures of My Passion.

Behold! by sinning again, thou puttest a new cause for My death: thou perpetratest afresh that for which I was nailed to the cross, that for which I also died.

Nay, more, since, by My grace, and by thy own experience, thou knowest Me better, and art bound to requite Me with greater gratitude and a more tender love; if thou dost again deliver Me up by sin, thou hast a greater sin than they that crucified Me: thou superaddest to the painfulness of My

wounds: thou piercest My Heart, not when It is
dead, but whilst It is living: by thy cruelty, as far
as in thee lies, thou slayest Me, the Author of life,
the Judge of thy everlasting destiny.

3. O most wretched of men! does naught of all
this move thy heart? More wicked than Judas
the betrayer, thou sayest to thy vile passions:
What will ye give to me, and I will deliver Him to
you?

And, placed between the passions which allure
thee, and Myself who forbid thee, thou exclaimest:
Not this One, but Barabbas!

And when thy conscience cries out against thee:
What, then, shall I do with Jesus? thou shoutest,
by thy actions: Let Him be crucified! let Him be
crucified!

And, O crime! wishing to gratify thy desires,
with Pilate thou givest Me up to be scoffed at, to be
scourged, to be crucified!

Is this, O man! is this the return thou makest
to Me, who created thee, who redeemed thee, who
preserved thee? Have all My favors, so great and
so numerous, come to this, that for all these things
thou makest again a mockery of Me and nailest
Me to the cross!

4. O if thou didst realize how frightful an evil
thou art committing when thou sinnest in this
manner, how couldst thou venture to do it? how
canst thou have the hardihood?

Dost thou desire to know how a great an evil
grievous sin is? consider, how, in order to atone
for it, I, the only Son of God, did give, not the world,
not heaven, not mankind, not the Angels, but My
Own Self, the Lord of heaven and earth, of men

and Angels, so as to pour out My Blood and lay down My very life, amid torments surpassing all understanding.

Dost thou wish to know it still more clearly? Reflect, with a living faith, how sin renders all the torments of My Passion useless, and renews the same, in a most cruel manner, for thy greater condemnation.

Assuredly, the malice of sin is nowhere seen more evidently than in My Passion: neither could the enormity of sin have ever been known so clearly, if I had not died for it upon the cross.

Weep, then, sinner, weep for thyself and over thy future lot: for if in the green wood, if in Me, the sins of others do produce such an effect: what will thy own sins, so great and so numerous, do in the dry wood, in thee?

If the Angels, when they yielded to pride, were not spared, but were dealt with according to justice; how much greater punishments, thinkest thou, does that man deserve, who tramples upon the Son of God, even after he has crucified Him?

Be not deceived, be not over-confident because thou art not punished on the spot; for now I endure: in time I give way to mercy, because for the exercise of justice I have an eternity.

If thou so wilt, thou canst fill up the measure of the sins which are tolerated in thee. I will not take away thy free will. I desire from men no service extorted by necessity.

Behold! from the treasury of My Heart, I have poured out upon thee abundant grace: if thou wilt co-operate efficaciously I will give thee an incomparable reward: if, on the contrary, thou wilt not, look thou to it; thou shalt bear the consequences.

But lo! I am still thy Saviour, still thy Father, ready to receive thee in My arms: but afterwards thou shalt find Me a just Judge and Retributer.

Have pity on thy soul, while it is yet time; and do not render thyself forever unhappy, by misusing that Passion, whereby thou canst secure for thyself everlasting bliss.

5. Come, O come to the cross: here the kindness of thy Saviour is made manifest: here the greatness of My fatherly affection shines forth: here My wounds do not only move to sorrow and penitence, but, likewise, offer both pardon and grace: here the voice of My Blood, with a loud cry, makes intercession for thee: here, finally, My Heart burns with desire for thy eternal salvation.

Contemplate, gaze upon Me, the Son of God, nailed to the cross and dying for sin: and thou wilt detest the same with thy whole heart, and turn thee again to serve Me with fervor; even as the crowd of those that were present on Calvary, and beheld this spectacle, returned striking their breasts.

If thou art tempted to sin again, fly to the cross; and, looking upon Me hanging thereon, say to thyself: Behold! the Son of God dies upon a cross to save me: shall I crucify Him anew, in order to damn myself? Should I do this, can there be in hell punishments enough to punish, according to its deserts, so great an iniquity?

In every contest with the devil, thou canst contend with him in no more advantageous place than beneath the cross: for here was he despoiled of his sway and strength: here thou shalt easily triumph over him.

6. And thou, My Child, didst thou understand what I said? Didst thou fully comprehend what horrible things the sinner does against Me, when he sins grievously? Canst thou behold unmoved all this? art thou not willing to use thy every effort to hinder such things?

See how important a matter it is to prevent sin, since, by so doing, thou hinderest Me from being again overwhelmed with reproaches, from being again torn to pieces by scourges, from being again crucified, at least in desire, by the sinner.

Wherefore, shouldst thou prevent only one sin, thou wouldst do something greater and better than if thou shouldst preserve thy country from destruction.

Canst thou love Me, and not care to turn away so great an evil from Me? If love do not inflame thee, let compassion at least move thee to take care that I be not again subjected to insults so great and manifold.

Thou makest profession of being a Disciple of My Heart: of thee, therefore, I ask, of thee I desire with My innermost Heart, that, by thyself and by others, whomsoever thou canst induce thereto, thou strive as much as thou canst, always and everywhere, to prevent sin, and to make amends to Me by the fidelity of thy love for the cruel ungratefulness of sinners.

7. *The voice of the Disciple.*—But I also, Lord Jesus, am a sinful person I am not worthy, I confess it to Thee, to be called a Disciple of Thy Heart.

For I have heaped countless insults upon Thee: I, too, have sated Thy Heart with the most bitter sorrows· yea, did I not,—O be merciful to me a sinner! did not I oftentimes crucify Thee?

Eternal thanks to Thee for that infinite goodness of Thy Heart, whereby Thou hast borne with me so patiently, and hast converted me so mercifully.

O most benign and sweet Jesus! I humbly implore Thee, grant me grace to make amends for the great wrongs I have done Thee, and to love Thee, during the remainder of my life, with the more fervor and tenderness the kinder and sweeter Thou hast been to me

---

CHAPTER XX.

THAT JESUS, BY FORGIVING FROM HIS HEART THE THIEF, AND BY PROMISING PARADISE TO HIM, TEACHES US HOW WE SHOULD ENDURE ANXIETY CONCERNING OUR ETERNAL SALVATION.

1. *The voice of Jesus.*—Behold! My Child, while all nature, wrapped in darkness, was mourning for Me, one of the thieves, hanging near Me, began to blaspheme Me: but the other, struck with a saving fear, rebuked him: And dost thou not fear God, said he, seeing that thou art under the same condemnation? And we, indeed, justly; for we receive the reward due to our deeds: but He has done no evil.

Moved by the example of My divine patience, heroic charity,—whereby I had prayed for My very torturers,—the unconquerable meekness of My Heart, My perfect resignation amidst the torments of My Passion, and assisted by a supernal light and grace, he conceived and expressed his faith and hope in Me, as well as his love for Me.

Penitent in heart, he turned himself with affection to Me, and: Lord, he exclaimed, Lord, remember me, when Thou shalt come into Thy kingdom.

Seeing that he co-operated with grace,—which outwardly worked upon him by means of the spectacle presented to his view, and inwardly flowed upon him from My Heart,—I hastened to console him, as he was well-nigh overwhelmed by the weight of his past offenses, and full of anxiety about the future salvation of his soul.

Forthwith of a robber, I made him a Saint; of an avowed evil-doer, a Disciple of My Heart; of the sinful Dismas, a companion and partaker of My kingdom. Such is the goodness of My Heart!

Verily, I said to him, verily, this day thou shalt be with Me in Paradise. He believed, and continuing to weep for his errors, and to love My goodness, he persevered calmly upon his cross, awaiting the blissful hope, and union with Me in My kingdom.

Lo, My Child, how thou shouldst deport thyself amid the troublesome anxieties concerning thy salvation, which torment thee sometimes.

2. *The voice of the Disciple.*—Do not take it amiss, I beseech Thee, O Lord, if I speak. Behold! Thou didst not say to me: Thou shalt be with Me in Paradise. Wert Thou to tell me this, I would, of a certainty, believe it; neither would I

be any longer uneasy about my everlasting salvation. But now, I do not know what may befall me in the end, and for this is my heart tormented.

The voice of Jesus.—Were I to say the same Child, thou couldst not understand it, except in so much as it is compatible with thy free will; for I am ever the same: I made man in the beginning, and left him in the hand of his own counsel: I gave him My commands, and said to him: If thou wilt keep My commands, they will keep thee.

But, thy freedom remaining the while, and being rightly used, I say also to thee: Thou shalt be with Me in Paradise. For I will that thou and all others be saved.

It is true that some vessels are made unto honor, and others unto dishonor: but it is the wickedness of man, not the Providence of God, that makes the vessels unto dishonor. For, if any one, being a vessel unto dishonor, correct himself, he shall be a vessel sanctified unto honor.

3. *The voice of the Disciple.*—Salvation, then, O Lord, depends on man's free will.

The voice of Jesus.—Thou mistakest, My Child: for man, in order to work out his salvation, yea, even to begin to do so, needs grace from above, without which he can neither secure the same, nor even attempt it.

But I give freely this preventing and assisting grace to all men; by the use of which each one can save himself, by its neglect he loses himself.

Therefore, man's salvation comes from Me first; afterward, it depends on his own free co-operation: but his perdition arises in the first place from himself, in the next, from the neglect of grace.

The voice of the Disciple.—Yet, O Lord, it is this possibility of abusing my free will; and the dread that, at some time or other, I will abuse it, which especially disquiets my heart.

The voice of Jesus.—But, My Child, herein lies the virtue, the glory of man, that he has the power to transgress, and yet does not transgress; to do evil, and does not do it. This is, upon earth, a service worthy of Me, honorable to Me: most noble and meritorious for thee.

Yea, thy very anxiety, lest thou mayst, at some future time, abuse thy free will, provided it be kept within proper bounds, will procure thee many advantages.

For nothing is better adapted to keep thee in humility, without which all other virtues are nigh to a fall and to destruction, than to know, yea, in some manner, to feel, that, even if by holiness thou art raised to the third heaven, thou mayst still become a reprobate.

Thence arises, also, a more anxious love for Me, whereby thou exertest thyself to avoid more carefully all dangers and to cling more firmly to Me.

Thou wilt also learn to withdraw thyself more perfectly from the things of this life when thou knowest that no complete security can be found therein.

Lastly, thou wilt sigh more fervently for that immortal life, where thou shalt be safe and secure, not only from danger, but from the fear of danger.

4. It is profitable, My Child, to be solicitous, above everything else, concerning thy everlasting salvation: but thou shouldst be on thy guard lest thou fall into faintheartedness.

There are they who,—seeing that it is possible

for them to be lost, and trembling with fear, lest they may lose in the future the merits which they have acquired by much labor, and fall into an eternity of woe,—become so downhearted that they have neither strength nor courage to serve Me with cheerfulness, but they drag on a life unworthy alike of Me and of themselves.

Whence it happens, that of a possibility they make a reality, by turning a possible into a real danger.

Be thou wiser, My Child: beware lest thou convert that which is for thy good into thy downfall: lest by too great a fear of ruin thou expose thyself to ruin.

Keep faithfully thy good will of doing what morally thou art able; and patiently endure every anxiety, if thou dost experience any that is troublesome, as a precious and wholesome share which thou hast inwardly in My sorrows.

In suffering an affliction of this sort, endeavor on the one hand, never to yield to it, but to remain resigned to the divine Will; and, on the other, be careful not to leave off anything of thy usual works or practices, which are conducive to thy salvation and perfection.

5. Whatever inward sufferings thou mayst feel, be not disturbed thereby, fully persuaded, that to a person of good will,—who does what he can,—troubles cannot arise except from the enemy of salvation; who—unable to lead such a one into sin or destruction—endeavors to lead him by annoyances, anxieties, specious subtleties, under pretense of greater security, to that whereto he cannot bring him by temptation.

Guard diligently against these snares, My Child; nor suffer thyself, by any reasoning whatsoever, to be pushed out of the center of thy peace.

So apply thyself to work out thy salvation, as if its success depended on thy labors; and so have recourse to Me by prayer, as if I alone could make thee not only succeed, but also make thee perform the works themselves; and, lastly, so do thou confide in Me, as to believe that I will hear thy prayer and crown thy labors with a happy result.

6. But behold! My Child, every man is here disquieted in vain: for I desire that none should perish. Now what is it that can cause the perdition of a person except sin? Keep thyself, therefore, free from sin, and thou shalt not perish forever.

Why, then, art thou tormented by anxiety about thy predestination? Behold! if thou wilt be predestined, shun evil and do good perseveringly, and thou shalt be predestined.

Blessed is he, who, setting aside all vain reasonings, by deeds, not by speculations, strives to make his election sure!

7. *The voice of the Disciple.*—O most sweet and loving Jesus! Thou art truly the God of consolation. Thanks to Thee for this great blessing, whereby Thou raisest up and refreshest my downcast heart.

Behold! Thou art hanging on the cross, overwhelmed by sorrows, and Thou forgettest Thyself in order to be mindful of men; Thou securest my salvation not only by suffering but also by consoling. Why, then, should I not calmly intrust to Thee my everlasting destiny?

By Thy grace, which I will never cease to implore, I will do all that I can; all other solicitude I throw upon Thy most tender Heart, which did not suffer even the thief to perish in death.

Remember me, Lord, in Thy kingdom; be mindful of me in my banishment: be especially mindful of me whensoever Thou seest me in danger of losing my soul; remember me in life and in death, that hereafter I may be with Thee in Paradise.

CHAPTER XXI.

HOW GREAT A TENDERNESS OF HEART JESUS MANIFESTED TOWARD US, WHEN HE GAVE US HIS OWN MOTHER AS OUR MOTHER.

1. *The voice of Jesus.*—Behold! My Child, there stood beneath the cross the Virgin Mary, My Mother, whom neither affliction of Heart, nor the insults of the crowd, nor the cruelty of the torturers, nor the danger of death, were able to part from Me.

For she was prepared in her Heart, either to die in My presence or, to be present while I was dying.

There also stood the Disciple, who, by the innocence of his life, was most endeared to Me; and who, at the last Supper, reposing upon My Breast, inebriated himself with the love of My Heart.

When I saw My Virgin Mother and the Virgin Disciple, whom My Heart loved, looking upon My

Mother, I said: Woman, behold thy son. Then to the Disciple, as to the one representing them all: Behold thy Mother. And from that hour the Disciple took her as a Mother.

2. Behold then, My Child, at what time men were incessantly heaping new and more cruel torments upon Me; where the malice of the human heart overflowed, there more than overflowed the love of My Heart.

When about to expire and to go away into My kingdom, I did not wish to leave My Disciples orphans, but, in My love, I resolved to give them a Mother, the best of all mothers, My own Mother herself.

Nay, more, on account of the eminent dignity of My Mother, and My perfect love for her, it was becoming that I should manifest every solicitude and every care for her; that I should provide for her the honor and love which are her due.

For this it was befitting, that, always and everywhere, I and she, being known together, should also be loved together.

And, indeed, even from the beginning of the world, when God promised Me as a Saviour to man groaning beneath the tyranny of the infernal serpent, He promised also My Mother.

This divine promise, so full of all consolation, spread among the whole posterity of the first man, and ever continued to be cherished with a religious reverence. For, although it was obscured among the nations, it was preserved always unchanged among the people of God: and from time to time it was renewed through the Prophets, and unfolded the more clearly, the more nearly the fullness of time was at hand, when God would send His own Son, to be born of the Virgin.

Wherefore, My Child, those whom from eternity, in the counsels of His mercy, God had joined together, whom He had promised together; them also were men expecting, for them together they were longing. For, as often as they did exclaim with a sigh to My Father in heaven: Distill dew, ye heavens, from above; and let the clouds rain down the Just! so often they sighed for My future Mother: Let the earth be opened, and bud forth the Saviour!

3. When, at length, I came into the world as the Saviour, behold! I was seen with My Virgin Mother. From the time I possessed a created Heart, this Heart was inseparably united to the Heart of My Mother.

I ever honored and loved the Virgin, in a manner worthy of her—as My Mother; and she, in return, honored and loved Me, not only as her Son, but also worshiped and cherished Me as her God.

There is no created being upon earth, nor in heaven, that has honored and loved Me, that has worshiped and cherished Me as much as My Virgin Mother. She by herself, she alone, by her worship and love, has incomparably surpassed and excelled all the Saints and Angels together.

Nor is there anywhere a heart, which is so much united, so acceptable to My Heart, as is the Heart of My Virgin Mother.

And should not I honor, should not I love such a Mother? and should not I wish to see her honored and loved always and everywhere? Is it thus My Heart is known?

4. Verily, verily, I say, wheresoever the Gospel shall be preached in the whole world, it will be said: That My Mother has done these things for Me, and that I have been subject to her. Nay, even to the end of time, wheresoever I will be worshiped and loved as a Saviour, there shall Mary be honored and loved as a Mother.

Moreover, in whatsoever place My Religion shall exist, it will ennoble the mind of man, and elevate the condition of woman.

For whence, thinkest thou, has there arisen in the mind of every one of the faithful so great an esteem for innocence, and so humane a feeling for woman, except from My most pure and august Virgin Mother?

Uncivilized barbarism made woman a slave of misery: civilized infidelity made her an idol of the passions; error in religion, an instrument of deceit; the true Religion alone made her truly free and truly estimable; preserves her free and worthy of honor, by ever proposing to her as a model the Virgin Mother of God.

5. Behold, then, My Child, behold thy Mother, who adopted thee beneath the cross, whilst she was suffering with Me. This, thy Mother, thou shalt honor all the days of thy life, remembering what, together with Me, she suffered for thee.

Acknowledge the greatness of the gift which, when dying, My Heart bequeathed to thee, by giving thee such a Mother. What is there better that It could have given to thee? Behold! in all the world, there is naught dearer to My Heart, nothing sweeter for thee, than this best of mothers.

For her maternal Heart overflows with an extraordinary compassion, love, and solicitude; nor can she forget to cherish the children whom, amidst such sorrows, she received from Me, when I was expiring.

Her Heart, modeled after Mine, is opened to all under the sweetest of appellations, the heart of a Mother; so that all they that have recourse to it, are easily admitted, kindly received, and introduced by her to My Heart.

Through the Virgin Mary I came to men; through her also must men come to Me.

Whatsoever graces, therefore, thou desirest to obtain from Me, intrust it to Mary; that My Mother, and thy Mother, may appeal to My Heart in thy favor, and prove that she is a Mother.

She will certainly be heard for the veneration due to her; for it is not becoming that I turn away My face from My Mother, or refuse her anything. A Mother's rights, which she possessed and exercised upon earth, she has not lost in heaven, where she reigns with Me, the Queen of Angels and of all the Saints.

If any one come to Me through My Virgin Mother, he shall not be cast off, but he shall be admitted even into My Heart; and he shall learn by experience, how great is the hight and the depth and the breadth of the power, which My Mother possesses over My Heart.

6. As I, by nature, have God as My Father, and Mary as My Mother; so also, Child, if, by adoption, thou desirest to have God as thy Father, thou must have Mary as thy Mother.

And, if thou art desirous to find Mary thy Mother, show thyself a child, do not sadden her

Heart, by grieving My Heart through sin. For accursed is he that angers his mother.

But a twofold curse, a twofold woe to them that venture to destroy or to diminish the honor and love due to My Mother! for as the praises, so are also the sneers, aimed at My Mother, flung back at Me, her Son.

Therefore, also, shall her enemies be infamous: yea, whosoever shall sin against her, shall hurt his own soul. But they that make her known by duly honoring and loving her, shall have life everlasting.

Do not think that Mary is merely equal to the Saints and Angels, or even that she is the first among them; for she forms an order above all the rest of creatures; so that, far surpassing all the Saints and the heavenly Spirits, she beholds none above her, except Myself with the Father and the Holy Ghost.

Therefore, she must be honored with a special worship, and an affection all her own. Love and honor her, Child, as much as thou art able: thou canst not offend by excess, so long as thou dost not honor and love her as a Divinity.

Above all, learn of Mary to follow My Heart perfectly. For she kept all My words, and all My examples, meditating on them in her Heart: and thus she attained to the teaching of My Heart, whose life, and virtues, and sentiments she showed forth and expressed to perfection in herself.

7. Blessed shalt thou be, My Child, if thou dost so venerate My Virgin Mother. Through her, thou shalt find the way to holiness,—to the interior life,—easy and pleasant: through her, thou shalt

obtain mercy, and grace, and comfort, and every thing else that is necessary or useful to thee: through her, finally, thou shalt be and continue with Me.

To her, therefore, do thou have recourse under all circumstances, at all times. What canst thou fear? thou art a child, she is a Mother. Why shouldst thou hesitate? behold! no one goes to her in vain: all receive through her: the world salvation, the captive redemption, the sinner hope, the just glory, the Angels joy.

8. *The voice of the Disciple.*—O Jesus, my Saviour-God! Thou givest me Thy own Mother as a Mother! Who has ever heard anything like this? Thou alone, O Lord, couldst draw such a gift from the treasury of Thy Heart, and bestow the same upon us sinners.

Thanks to Thee, most loving Jesus! eternal thanks to Thee for so great a gift, so kindly bestowed upon me most unworthy.

Behold! Thy Mother is my Mother! Bear with me, most sweet Jesus, if I repeat: Behold, Thy Mother is my Mother! This is indeed a shout of joy in the heart, this is honey in the mouth, this is sweetest melody in the ear.

O blessed me, who am made the son of the Queen of heaven and earth, of the Mother of my God, my Saviour, my Judge!

Through such a Mother, O my Jesus, I will fly to Thee: through her motherly love I will draw nigh to Thy Heart; through her Immaculate Heart, I will enter into Thy Heart, even unto an intimate union with Thee.

And when I shall have to go to judgment, be-

hold! O sweetest of all consolations! I shall have
an advocate with the Judge, the Mother of the
Judge and mine, a Mother that makes intercession
with her Son for a son, a Mother to whom the
Judge has given all power over His Heart.

Thee, therefore, so great a Mother, O sweet Virgin Mary, I will endeavor and rejoice to honor ever
more and more; I will find it my delight by every
means, to extend thy worship, so long as life endures.

So long as this heart of mine shall be capable
of loving, it will love thee, O Mother of Jesus, and
my Mother! yea, it will burn to influence all hearts
with the same fire of love, that we may all begin
upon earth to love Thee, for the sake of Jesus, and
Jesus for His own dear sake; that thus we may
deserve to be made blissful in heaven, and continue
to love and to cherish throughout joyous and endless ages.

CHAPTER XXII.

THAT JESUS, FORSAKEN UPON THE CROSS, TEACHES
US HOW TO ACT WHEN WE ARE LEFT EXPOSED
TO TEMPTATIONS.

1. *The voice of Jesus.*—My Child, when on the
cross I bore the iniquities of men, for whom I had
given Myself, through love, as a hostage and security; My Father so loved men, that He delivered
Me up for them.

Wherefore, the devil,—who, after the temptation

in the desert, left Me for a time, having returned during My Passion,—now assailed Me more violently, and pressed Me more stubbornly.

Beside his own malice, he made use of the wickedness of men, whom he stirred up both to afflict Me with every torture and a most disgraceful death. and to perpetrate before Me the most horrid crimes.

The demon, with his associates, was exulting, as if enjoying a triumph; and, pressing forward his most wicked assaults, he cried: God has forsaken Him, pursue and take Him.

And I, without any sensible comfort whatsoever, crushed, for the sake of men, in My weakness, was abandoned to enemies, who were outwardly raging against My Body, and inwardly tearing My Heart.

In My loneliness, in the midst of torments so frightful; behold! to the Father, whom I loved infinitely, and by whom I was infinitely loved, I raise My eyes, filled with tears, and well-nigh extinct, as well as My Heart, now reduced to Its utmost agony: My God! My God! why hast Thou forsaken Me?

Lo, Child, the utterance of the unfathomable affliction of My Heart, sunk into an abyss of sorrows, and overwhelmed, as it were, by a deluge of woes.

2. However, I resigned Myself lovingly to the good pleasure of My heavenly Father: and I offered Myself wholly as a sacrifice to Him, who was to console Me at last, according to the greatness of My sorrows.

But, since suffering is the measure of love, I endured and made known this excess of the most painful anguish; that men might thence learn to how great an extent I have loved them.

And, as I remembered others, so was I especially mindful of thee, My Child: yea, for thee did I encounter, with My Heart submissive and contented, the rage of My enemies, and that deep-felt dereliction.

For I knew that, according to My divine Providence, thou couldst not be exempt from the assaults of the demon; neither was I ignorant of the greatness of the affliction which thou shouldst have to undergo in this severe struggle with a most wicked foe: and, therefore, I placed before thee My example, that thence thou mightst derive abundant instruction and comfort.

I know thy frequent and deep groanings, My Child, when thou findest thyself in the midst of relentless foes, whilst thou desirest to live for Me in perfect peace, free from every hindrance.

But consider that I, the only begotten Son of God, the Saint of Saints, was, by a spontaneous love, exposed to the rage of My enemies and there left forsaken: and thou wilt not wonder, nor take it hard, if thou, in many ways a sinful person, art suffered,—even after thou hast been for a long time in My service,—to be exposed, for thy own advantage, to the assaults of the tempter, and to be deprived, during them, of sensible consolation.

For, in this is the divine kindness toward thee made apparent, that it neither takes away the war, without which the enemy is not overcome, and peace secured; nor removes the occasion of the contest, without which there is no triumph, and no crown obtained.

It is an effect of the sincere love of My Heart, if It leaves to thee wherewithal thou mayst become conscious of thy own frailty, when exposed; that thus thou mayst be kept in humility, and, impelled by necessity, mayst continually tend and draw near to Me.

How many there are who, through temptations, persevered and were saved, and who, had they been without these trials,—growing by degrees lukewarm and proud,—would in the end have become reprobates!

Dost thou know even one, among all those that have sanctified themselves, who was free from temptations? Have not the greatest Saints been wont to feel the greatest temptations?

This is the way whereby a more than ordinary purity of heart is obtained: whereby more perfect virtue is acquired: whereby the soul is better prepared for the divine union.

3. Many err in this, that they think temptation a sin. What can there be more dangerous than this error? Hence arise an erroneous conscience, anxiety, faintheartedness, sloth, lack of strength and courage to resist generously, and to triumph.

Believe Me, Child, even should a temptation of any kind whatsoever last a whole lifetime, it could not make thee guilty of any sin, if only it be displeasing to thee.

Cast aside, therefore, so baneful an error; throw off, in like manner, an overgreat dread of being tempted. This dread, born of error, fostered by self-love, becomes an occasion of being the more tempted, and the more dangerously too; since thou art tempted, not so much by a divine permission, as through thy own fault.

This is one of men's misfortunes that they ever

tend to one or another extreme. For, some run great risk, because they fear temptations too much; others, because they do not sufficiently guard against them. Thou, My Child, follow thou the middle course, if thou wilt be safe.

4. *The voice of the Disciple.*—Yet, Lord, should not sins be supremely feared and shunned? Why should I not, then, extremely fear, and shun the dangers and occasions of sin?

The voice of Jesus.—Certainly, My Child, sins should be extremely feared and shunned. But guard against deception: avoid confusion: distinguish correctly. Temptation is one thing; sin is quite another: the danger of temptation is one thing, the danger of sin another: finally, the occasion, on the part of the devil tempting to sin, is one thing; the occasion, on the part of man placing himself proximately near to sin, is altogether different.

Now, the occasion on the part of man, as it is a proximate danger of sin, and, consequently, a sin, thou shouldst carefully shun; the occasion on the part of the devil, as it is simply a danger of temptation, and, therefore, not sinful, thou art not obliged to avoid.

Do not think it strange if the devil tempts thee, since his sole occupation is to roam about, and to tempt. In his insolence he attacks all, uses different ways to tempt; when driven off, he is not ashamed to return; when defeated he does not leave off to come again to the assault.

Wherefore, if thou art tempted, do not suffer thyself to be troubled. It is the malice of the devil, not thine own wickedness.

Thou wouldst act foolishly, and to no purpose, shouldst thou lose thy peace of heart, on account of temptations. For, by so doing, thou wouldst place thy peace in the power of the demon, who, doubtless, would never allow thee to enjoy the same.

My Child, I know thy weakness; I know the malice of the devil: but I know also the power of My grace: I know what of thyself thou art able to effect against the demon, and what thou canst do by grace. And I,—to whom the devil is so much subject that, against My Will, he cannot attack even the vilest animals;—I, to whom thy salvation has cost so much, will not allow that thou be tempted beyond what thou art able to endure, but I will, on the contrary, prepare, together with the temptation, a favorable issue.

5. *The voice of the Disciple.*—Thanks to Thee, good Master, sweet Jesus, for that Thou hast thus showed me how I should act in regard to temptations, before they come or rush upon me: teach me also, I beseech Thee, how I should deport myself, when they are now at hand and assail me.

The voice of Jesus.—Observe, Child, that the devil may assault thee, or approach thy heart in three ways: by the way of the outward senses; by the inward way of the understanding; lastly, by a sort of middle way, that of the imagination.

By whichsoever of these ways thou mayst be tempted, so soon as thou perceivest the temptation, take heed that thou be not agitated or troubled: but, by directing thy attention to Me, who am present, strive to possess thy mind in peace.

If the temptation comes through the senses, suf-

fer them not to be exposed, without sufficient reason, in the direction of the dangerous object: but
quietly, and withal manfully, turn them away, so
that, if possible, thou do no longer perceive the evil
which is presented.

If it assails thee through the understanding, do
not act so as to deal anywise, even mentally, with
the foe; but, how specious soever his reasonings,
how much soever as evident truths his suggestions
may appear; so soon as thou seest them to be contrary to some virtue, submit thyself to Me, without
any reasoning, and behold! thou shalt be victorious.

If the temptation is pressed upon thee, through
the imagination, by means of objects formerly perceived by the senses, or even now made up by the
devil, take diligent care that thou allow not the
imagination to stand still, as if looking at the imag-
inings: but do thou forthwith, and effectually,
turn away the imagination: and represent to it, if
convenient, objects known by faith, such as death or
judgment, hell or purgatory, heaven, or rather the
Son of God hanging on the cross, and looking at thee,
and offering to thee His Heart, as a place of refuge.

But give heed to this, My Child, mark this well,
that, in every temptation whatsoever, it is enough,
simply to turn thy mind away from the temptation
to some other object. Since this is to resist it, even
in a positive manner.

These things having been guarded against, endeavor as much as thou art able, for thy greater
progress, in every temptation, to unite thyself gently
and firmly with Me, by acts of love, be they ever
so short.

I do particularly recommend, My Child, while

thou art wont to live in the state of grace, that, in temptation, thou make use of acts which are not directly opposed to the evil suggested, but which unite thee by love with Me. For thus thou wilt better preserve peace of heart, frustrate more securely the wicked design of the demon, render virtue more solid, and unite thyself more strongly and more perfectly with Me.

However, thou must always rely more upon divine grace than upon thy own strength. Wherefore, thou shouldst pray frequently, in time of peace as well as of war, that, whilst thou art contending, grace may support thee, encourage thee, give thee victory.

If, in this manner, thou yieldest the glory of the victory to Me, who am the first conqueror, and who will not give My glory to another; then, Child, will I protect thee with My shield, and fight for thee, like a strong and invincible warrior: and a thousand shall fall at thy side, and ten thousand before thee: nor shall any foe prevail against thee.

6. *The voice of the Disciple.*—O most loving Jesus! how sweet, how pleasing the things which out of Thy Heart Thou pourest down upon me! Let heaven and earth and all things therein with me, return Thee a thousand thanks!

However, I beseech Thee, teach me still one thing, and it is enough. Behold! it happens, that when I come out of the struggle, I am tormented by a great fear, that my soul has perhaps fallen a prey to the enemy.

O Lord! who hast the words of everlasting life, speak to me the word, whereby my soul may be comforted. This will be a new favor of Thy Heart.

which will in return bind me to Thee by a new and sweet debt of gratitude and love.

The voice of Jesus.—Behold! My Child, if the temptation, while it was upon thee, displeased thee, thou hast a sure sign that thou didst not consent thereto. But in this also thou must distinguish the inferior part of thy heart from the superior, to which it belongs to sin or not to sin.

The inferior part does not always agree with the superior, but frequently in spite of the superior, it takes, in some manner, pleasure in the temptation: yea, it does so much that it causes the superior, although not willing, to feel some pleasure. But feeling does not hurt, where there is no consent.

If thou doubtest whether thou didst merely feel the temptation, or whether thou didst also give consent thereto, observe the difference between feeling and consenting. Thou mayst indeed feel the temptation, although thou dost not love it, with thy free will adverting to its being wrong: but thou canst not consent to the temptation, unless, perceiving that it is a sin or evil, thou love it by thy free will.

But, when thou also doubtest whether or not thou didst love the temptation in this manner, follow the rule of the Saints: A person of a delicate or fair conscience may hold as morally certain that he did not consent, so long as he is not sure that he did consent.

Assuredly, My Child, whosoever is wont to cling to Me, and with a sincere heart dreads to be separated from Me, if at any time he is tempted to sin; in order, knowingly and willingly, to consent thereto, must do great violence to himself, both to resist the saving sting of conscience—which he is in the habit of heeding and following—as well as to turn the will from an object constantly loved, to an object constantly held in abhorrence. All which, surely, no one can do, without clearly distinguishing its malice and without embracing it, if he do so at all, with his knowledge and will.

On the contrary, he that is accustomed to sin through an evil or loose conscience, when, after having been tempted, he doubts whether he gave consent thereto, ought to presume that he did consent. For, since, on principle or by custom, he has contracted a habit suited to sin; when he is tempted to evil, in order to be able to resist, he must likewise offer great violence to himself, not only to obey actually the warning voice of his conscience, which, in a matter of this kind, he was not wont to heed, but also with a strong will, to repel the temptation. Now, all this he cannot do without manifestly perceiving his own pious efforts and his unusual victory.

7. Hence, thou seest, Child, how happy they are who serve Me faithfully, since, in temptations, with which man's life is replete, they may so agreeably console themselves; whereas, they that are negligent, for their shame and correction, are tormented by inward pains and anxieties.

And this is only one of the thousand blessings which I heap upon the Disciples of My Heart. Rejoice, thou, My Child, rejoice in so great a good; and use and enjoy it for the glory of My Heart, and the sanctification of thy soul.

This, however, thou must guard against after temptation, that thou be not desirous of so examining into the matter as to expose thyself to danger, by reviewing in thy mind the temptation or its several circumstances.

As much as circumstances permit, calmly humble thyself, and beg pardon if, perchance, thou hast in anywise rendered thyself guilty of some pride, some inordinate fear, some diffidence, some curiosity, some carelessness. After this, with a renewed love for Me, proceed boldly and cheerfully.

8. Lastly, remember, My Child, that the way of temptations is open to many errors, insomuch that by himself no one can safely pass through it. Wherefore, whosoever thou art, religious or secular, learned or unlearned, thou needest an experienced guide; and, so long as thou dost obediently follow him, I will not permit that obedience lead thee to destruction. I Myself will have a care of thee.

Come, then, Child, cheer up thy courage: be stout-hearted. Let the winds blow; let the storms rage; how canst thou be fearful? behold! I am with thee.

These things have I spoken to thee, My Child, that, in the midst of temptations, thou mayst find relief and comfort; but not, that thou mayst have no temptations, nor feel their irksomeness. Endure them in the right spirit: and, in their own time, they will produce manifold fruit.

Do not grow faint in courage, but be resigned to the divine Will. Up, then, persevere manfully, knowing that he is blessed that endures temptation; because, when he has been proved, he shall receive the crown of life.

9. *The voice of the Disciple.*—O how good art

Thou, my Jesus! how good art Thou! Behold!
O Thou delight of the Saints and Angels, Thou
art forsaken upon the cross, and deprived of every
consolation; yet, meanwhile, Thou dost not abandon me, nor suffer me, every way unworthy as I
am, to be without solace; for, with a marvelous
sweetness, Thyself relievest and rejoicest me.

Willingly do I intrust myself to Thy care; wholly
do I resign myself to Thy Will; do Thou carry out
the designs of Thy Heart in my regard: cleanse
and sanctify me in a way and manner pleasing to
Thee. Only keep me from every sin.

In every temptation, in every danger, assist me
efficaciously; protect me, help me; so keep me
united with Thee, that I may never be separated
from Thee.

CHAPTER XXIII.

THAT JESUS, IN HIS ABANDONMENT, THIRSTING AND
NOT RELIEVED, SHOWS US HOW WE SHOULD DE-
PORT OURSELVES IN SPIRITUAL DESOLATION.

1. *The voice of Jesus.*—O all ye that pass by the
way attend, and see if there be any sorrow like My
sorrow!

Lo! all My persecutors troubled Me taken in the
midst of straits; and there was none to comfort
Me among all them that were dear to Me.

Behold, My Child, My head pierced with thorns,
My face covered with blood and tears, all My
limbs torn, My whole Body lacerated, from the

sole of My feet to the crown of My head all one wound: My Heart weighed down with unutterable sorrows, undone by the hard-heartedness of men, forsaken by My beloved and most loving Father Himself.

Amidst all these sufferings, I was racked by a new torture, a most violent thirst, so that I was forced to exclaim: I thirst!

This thirst was manifold, My Child: a burning thirst even unto death, of refreshing Myself, every way exhausted as I was; a more burning thirst for the salvation, the love and everlasting gratitude of men; lastly, a most ardent thirst for the fulfillment of the good pleasure of My heavenly Father.

But My enemies hearing it, so far from affording Me relief, on the contrary, in My thirst gave Me vinegar to drink.

For the restoration of the divine glory, and for the salvation of men, My Father willed that I should die in the deepest affliction, without any relief.

My Passion ever increased: but apace grew the love of My Heart, whereby, uniting Myself to the divine good pleasure: Yea, Father, I said in My Heart, yea, since thus it is pleasing before Thee.

And thus I wholly resigned Myself to continue, and at last to expire in the uttermost desolateness.

Meditate on these things, My Child: do thou also remember them, when thou art thyself experiencing spiritual desolation.

2. So long as exercises of piety are inwardly relished and please the spiritual taste, it is both easy and pleasant to be engaged therein; but it is hard and disagreeable to perform them faithfully

and exactly when they produce only wearisomeness and disgust.

But because, during that inward consolation, the
human heart is wont to take delight in a sensible
sweetness, and does not purely love Me for Myself,
I do frequently, when he is now able to bear it, deprive a person of all sensible relish.

This is a secret invention of My Heart, that the
soul may learn, even in spite of herself, to seek and
to love, above all things sensible, not My consolations, but Myself.

If thou remainest faithful in spiritual desolation,
thou provest evidently that thou servest Me by pure
love, not in consideration of thy present advantages.

Thou shouldst, therefore, not be uneasy amid
desolation, My Child, but shouldst exert thyself to
act generously and to endure manfully.

3. Continue steadfastly in thy undertaking; and,
in order to overcome weariness or disgust, which
comes upon thee in spiritual desolation, pray more
than usually; carefully examine thy actions, both
interior and exterior; watch more attentively over
thy heart; lastly, mortify thyself in small things
more frequently and more perfectly.

By this constant and solid fervor, thou wilt efficaciously resist languor. Meanwhile, resign thyself
ever more and more; and look upon it as thy greatest consolation, to embrace submissively and lovingly the divine Will.

I do not always desire to console thee in a sensible manner, even when thou hast done whatsoever
thou wast able to obtain the same, lest it prove hurtful to thee, or lest thou ascribe to thyself what
belongs to Me.

But this I do desire, that thou keep thyself in all humility, and love Me in the most disinterested manner. Therefore, I suffer, that thou shouldst intensely feel that it is not in thy power to acquire or to retain consolation, but that it is My gift.

Acknowledge, then, that thou art altogether unable to procure true consolation, yea, that thou art unworthy of receiving even the least; and own that it is the highest favor, far surpassing every sensible consolation, when thou art reckoned by Me among My children, and cherished by the love of My Heart.

4. *The voice of the Disciple.*—Yea, Lord God, it is a very great grace, an incomparable favor, to be Thy Child, to be dear to Thy Heart; but my desolateness does not only cause me wearisomeness, betimes it even does not allow me to perceive that favor.

So long as I possess the moral conviction, that, by sanctifying grace, I am a Child dear to Thy Heart; to lack all consolation, both human and divine,—although it is hard and irksome to nature,—appears bearable; neither does it take away the peace of the heart.

But, Lord Jesus, sometimes desolation takes hold of me, and affects all the powers of my soul to such a degree that it appears to me that I am separated from Thee, and that I cannot persuade myself that I still possess a place in Thy Heart.

O my Saviour! who knowest all things, and needest not that any one tell Thee, Thou knowest the greatness of my sufferings, more painful than 'eath itself. Every other affliction I deem a co..... tion in comparison of this desolateness, upon which I dare not look, and yet from which I cannot turn away my eyes.

O Jesus! by the excess of thy own desolateness upon the cross, I entreat and implore Thee, do not refuse to relieve, or at least to instruct me. I confess that I do not deserve either of these favors, and that Thy example ought to be enough for me; yet unless Thou Thyself appliest it to me, I am such a wretch, that seeing I do not perceive, and hearing I do not understand.

5. *The voice of Jesus.*—My Child, it is one thing to do good, and another to know that thou art doing good. The former makes up the merit; the latter begets enjoyment. Again, Child, it is one thing to live in My grace, and another to be aware that thou art living in My grace. The one constitutes thy true felicity; the other adds nothing to thy felicity, except a sensible delight.

Now, of this agreeable and delightful knowledge, in which there is no merit, I do sometimes affectionately deprive a soul, that she may be manfully trained to sanctity and be made perfect in love for Me. This is the highest purity of love: to struggle for love by means of love, whilst thou feelest not the love through which and for which thou art contending.

Be not anxious, therefore, My Child, to persuade thyself that thou livest in my grace. For thou wouldst labor in vain to obtain for thyself that which, for the present, I do not wish thee to have.

I seek and love thy true good, rather than thy sensible delight; and this privation I know to be truly useful to thee, in order that, when thou findest, in sensible things, no support whereon either to stand or to lean, thou mayst repose, outside of what is sensible, in Me alone, the unchangeable Good.

Wherefore, Child, as much as thou canst, turn thyself to Me, away from the troubles which thou feelest; throw thyself on My Heart, re-affirming ever the same, that, for love of Me, thou art willing to do in all things the good pleasure of My Heart.

After this, perform gently whatsoever thou hast to do, and omit none of thy accustomed good works on account of spiritual desolation.

So long as the desolation besets thee, do not occupy thyself, under any pretense whatsoever, with troublesome reflections about the same; remain quiet; pray; ever resign, ever give thyself up to Me.

Lastly, remember this, that, in this desolation, thou must lean not upon any creature outside of thyself, nor even upon thyself, but upon Me alone. Therefore, the more thou art able to leave thyself, to turn thyself away from thyself, to cling to My Heart, yea, to lose and forget thyself therein, the better it will be for thee.

6. *The voice of the Disciple.*—Benediction, and praise, and glory be to Thy Heart, O Lord, because Its goodness has moved Thee to teach me the way of life in the midst of the shadow of death.

Yet, although I am so unworthy that I do not even deserve to prostrate myself in the dust before Thy feet, suffer me, I beseech Thee, to make known to Thee a still greater desolation, an unutterable torture, whereby the sorrows of hell appear sometimes to come upon me.

For I seem, betimes, in some wonderful manner

to feel persuaded, not merely that I am deprived of Thy grace, but even that I have been cast away by Thee, and, therefore, that hell is my home, which I try in vain to escape.

I should not dare to make known to Thee, Lord God, this great wretchedness of mine, did not my extreme misery compel me to lay open before Thee the abyss, the depth whereof I know not.

7. *The voice of Jesus.*—This is enough, My Child; it shows sufficiently what thou dost experience.

Attend to this above all other things, Child, beware of this beyond everything else, that thou be not discomposed, how great soever may be thy desolateness.

Behold! what thou sufferest, the Saints themselves have suffered, who, having become most perfectly assimilated to Me, have in this manner altogether died to themselves, and, as new creatures, have solely lived for Me.

Believe, and hope, and love purely, My Child: lo! now is the time to practice pure virtues, to elicit heroic acts.

Be not downhearted: that which seems death, is a hidden life; that which now appears destruction will, in the end, be found to be a renewal.

But from what thou sufferest, learn thou, Child, how great is the kindness of My Heart, whereby I preserve thee from experiencing in reality everlasting reprobation; since thou feelest that the mere thought of it exceeds all the sufferings of life.

Hence, also, infer how justly thou art bound to love Me in return without measure, since by Me thou hast been preserved from an immeasurable misfortune.

8. Now, observe, My Child, that it is the demon who, by his suggestions, causes thee to doubt about My truth, when I assert that I will the salvation of all men: that it is the demon who sets thee on to distrust My mercy, in which they that hope shall not be put to confusion, from which they that ask do receive: that it is the demon who stirs thee up not to think kindly of Me, whilst yet, with an infinite love, I ordain all things for thy everlasting happiness.

It is from the devil that come all things which of themselves are evil,—never from Me, who do not try any one in this manner.

Whatsoever the devil may put into thy thoughts, leave it to him; neither do thou dispute nor deal with him in anywise.

Be simply, and continue quietly resigned to the divine Will; and, even if, on account of the greatness of thy spiritual desolation, thou appearest not wholly conformed to the divine good pleasure, do not trouble thyself, nor make thyself uneasy; but throw thyself, without anxiety, on My Heart, and repeat: God, my Saviour, Thy Will be done in my regard, in time and in eternity.

It is impossible, My Child, that he, who thus intrusts himself to the divine Will should perish. Sooner shall heaven and earth pass away, than that he be lost, who gives himself up, without reserve, to the divine good pleasure.

For the rest, be of good cheer, Child of My Heart, generously endure this martyrdom, with which the Disciples most dear to My Heart are honored, and which secures an unfading palm and an everlasting crown.

9. *The voice of the Disciple.*—O Jesus! O Thou my last refuge! what shall I say to all this? Behold! comforted, and disconsolate at the same time I cannot give utterance to what I feel: but Thou seest into my heart.

By Thy own supreme desolateness, Lord Jesus, save Thou my soul, for which Thou hast endured torments, so numerous and so excessive.

As much as I am able, I intrust myself wholly to Thee: I surrender myself altogether to the care of Thy Heart: Thy Will be done in my regard in time and in eternity.

CHAPTER XXIV.

THAT JESUS ACCOMPLISHING ALL UPON THE CROSS, TEACHES US TO ACCOMPLISH, IN LIKE MANNER, ALL THINGS UPON THE CROSS.

1. *The voice of Jesus.*—Behold, My Child, at last I completed the work which My Father gave Me to do.

Having come down from the highest heaven to run my way, lo! I have finished My career.

I now finish a life made up of labors, and sorrows, and ceaseless sacrifices: the pains of all these are now brought to a close, but the merits and fruits of them endure forever.

The irreparable ruin of Satan's kingdom is consummated, and he himself, the prince of this world, is despoiled of his dominions and cast out.

My kingdom—which I have acquired by My

own Blood, to which I have given success by the very love of My Heart, which I have strengthened by every means unto a lasting stability and security, so that thereof there shall be no end,—stands firm.

Whatsoever existed from the beginning as types of Me, whatsoever has been written concerning Me, now sees its end: behold! now is the time that transgression may be finished, that sin may receive an end, that iniquity may be abolished, and everlasting justice may be brought.

Naught remains undone, naught remains to be suffered: all is consummated. Now, I will die with My Heart satisfied.

Here pause, My Child, and attend where I have consummated all things. Behold! I persevere upon the cross. Consider, and act according to the model that was showed to thee on the mountain.

2. If now thou hast learnt the sentiments of My Heart, and hast put on the same, thou wilt not desire to live, thou wilt not desire to die, except fastened to the cross.

For no other road than the one whereon I have journeyed is given under heaven to men, to become Saints, and to be saved.

O if thou knewest what good things for the present and the future life thou mightst procure for thyself, by lovingly continuing on the cross; assuredly, like Myself, thou shouldst not be willing, of thyself, to come down therefrom.

It is much safer, it is much better, in every respect, to persevere on the cross, for love of Me, than, of thy own accord, to free thyself from the cross

My Child, if thou didst know the value and the reward of tribulations, thou wouldst deem this life too short for suffering, but eternity long enough to enjoy the recompense.

3. If thou desirest to persevere with ease in afflictions, do not reflect upon the years, the months, nor even the weeks during which they may last: but think of the present day, as if it were to be the last, and, as if thou shouldst have nothing more to suffer, and to merit thereafter.

Blessed they that, amid their tribulations, are more anxious to render themselves alike to Me than to free themselves therefrom! These are they that, by the purest love, perfect themselves in union with Me.

Look at the example of the Saints, who, despising everything that was merely self, sought Me with such purity, were inflamed with such ardor to conform themselves to Me, that they longed, some either to suffer or to die; others, not to die but to suffer.

Nor were they satisfied to suffer those things only which divine Providence meted out to them; but, moved by My Spirit, they assumed voluntary mortifications and labors, and, in their fervor, they were ever urged onward to perfect themselves in Me by love.

4. Examine and try all things, My Child, thou wilt at last be obliged to come back to this truth, that the spiritual, the interior life is reduced to this, that thou do constantly sacrifice the inclination and aversion of nature for love of Me, in order to live by My Spirit.

And this thou must do. so long as life endures.

For, so long as thou livest, thou art man, and therefore, prone and liable to evil; nor canst thou, otherwise than by striving and using thy endeavors, shun what is evil and imperfect, and do what is good and perfect.

Thus, generously to go counter to nature, and to follow grace for love of Me; this is the spirit of the Saints.

5. If thou art wise, My Child, thou wilt desire no other reward in this life for the things which thou sufferest than a greater love for Me, and more abundant grace to suffer for My sake.

Thy afflictions shall never equal Mine: I, however, persevered in them until I consummated My life, that thou mightst learn to continue in thine, so long as it is the Will of the divine good pleasure.

Be ashamed, My Child, for that thou art, sometimes, so silly as even to think of forsaking Me upon the cross.

If thou lovest Me for My own sake, thou wilt under no circumstance depart from Me. But if thou lovest Me for thyself, no wonder that, while trouble besets thee, thou darest to wish for what is to thee more agreeable.

A hireling cares not so much for his master as for his own self: and he finds no difficulty in leaving a master whom he must serve with hard labor, and without an immediate advantage.

Yet thou didst not receive the slavish spirit of a hireling, but a nobler spirit, the spirit of a Child; that where I am, thou also mayst be.

Take heed, lest thou grow degenerate in spirit: persevere with Me, determined rather to die at thy post, than to abandon the same.

6. What shall it avail thee to have suffered much for My sake, unless thou perfect it by perseverance?

If, hitherto, thou hast followed Me amid tribulations, rejoice thou, My Child; yet, at the same time, remember, not he that begins, but he that perseveres, will be saved. A reward is, indeed, promised to them that begin, but it is given to them that persevere.

To stimulate thee to perseverance, frequently place before thy eyes that everlasting reward which awaits thee among the Saints, and which far exceeds all present tribulation.

Pray much, My Child, that thou mayst not be disheartened, nor lose the crown prepared for thee. So long as thou prayest well, thou wilt continue well.

Finally, Child, be ever mindful of My example, and of My presence: daily renew thy resolve, and strengthen thy heart, to abide with Me. Thus thou shalt pass through each successive day, and come, at last, to a final and blissful consummation.

7. *The voice of the Disciple.*—O most sweet Jesus! by the merits of Thy passion, by the merits of all the Saints that clung so faithfully to Thee, grant me to persevere with Thee unto the end.

I am, indeed, desirous and anxious to remain with Thee on the cross, and to consummate all with Thee thereon: but I know and feel that my powers are insufficient for this.

Strengthen and inspire me, therefore, I beseech Thee, with that grace which the Saints have found fully sufficient to accomplish it; that I may perfect myself upon the cross, as a holocaust to Thee for an odor of sweetness, and for the everlasting salvation of my soul.

―――――――

CHAPTER XXV.

THAT JESUS COMMENDING HIS SPIRIT INTO THE HANDS OF HIS FATHER, TEACHES US HOW WE MUST WHOLLY GIVE UP OURSELVES TO HIM.

1. *The voice of Jesus.*—My Children, yet a little while am I with you, until, all things being now consummated, the love itself of My Heart be consummated.

Behold, Child, nothing now is left to Me except My Spirit, for, not only affectively, but also effectively, My Heart has sacrificed all the rest as a holocaust.

Although My soul was ever in the hands of My Father, and voluntarily consecrated to Him from the beginning; now, however, in order to complete the excess of My love, I sacrifice, I lay down the same. No one takes It away from Me, but I of Myself lay It down.

In this consummation of the excess of Its love, My Heart, before It expires, utters Its last words for thee.

And that thou mayst understand of how great an importance they are, I did not now sigh, but I cried out with a loud voice: Father, into Thy hands I commend My Spirit.

This is the uttermost excess of humility and

love, beyond which it is not possible to go in this life; and in this same I die.

In the supreme extremity of every kind of sorrows, behold! I throw Myself, entirely and completely, into the hands of My Father.

Now I do not say to My Father: Not Mine, but Thy Will be done. For My Will is no longer Mine but that of My Father, into whose hands I have delivered the same.

2. My Child, receive thou with a special affection these last words of thy Saviour, dying for love of thee; treasure them up in thy heart, and piously meditate thereon.

For they contain the abridgment and completion of all the things whichsoever I have hitherto taught thee concerning the interior life, concerning virtue and holiness.

In them lie hidden the secrets of My Heart most precious and most useful to thee. Search thou into them, Child: use them: but, above all, study diligently to reduce them to practice.

Wherefore, as I commended My Spirit into the hands of My Father, so do thou intrust thy spirit into My hands.

If thou do this, thou wilt cease altogether to live by thy spirit, and wilt begin so to live by My Spirit, that thy heart, thy mind, thy all, will breathe naught save My Spirit.

Then thy will, now no longer thine, but delivered up to the divine Will, shall be, in some manner, one with Mine.

3. Behold, My Child, the highest degree of sanctity in a life made perfect by virtues, when the soul with a holy indifference toward everything. wills of

her own accord nothing further, but suffers Me to will, to dispose, and to do in her regard, and concerning all besides, as is pleasing to Me; whilst she herself consents to My every Will and ordinance, being, always and everywhere, conformed and united to Me.

Blessed the soul that reaches this degree! in Me she finds repose amidst and above all things: above every feeling, above every virtue, above all salvation, above every good.

In such a soul, I so set in order the purity of charity, I so ravish her with the love of My Heart, that, far above all things visible and invisible, she is wholly Mine and I hers.

When thou wilt have in this manner delivered thyself entirely and completely to My divine good pleasure; then shalt thou, in the most perfect manner, be free from all vain fear and inordinate sadness, from every merely natural wish and desire, finally, from every superfluous care and uneasiness.

Then, as it were, forgetful of thyself and of what may happen in the future, thou wilt look upon this as thy joy, to cause Me joy by doing My good pleasure. Provided My Heart be satisfied, thine will also be contented, regardless whether this be pleasing or displeasing to nature.

4. All the Saints have excelled in this greatest of virtues: and so highly did they esteem the divine good pleasure, and to such a degree did they cherish the same, that, in some manner, forgetting themselves, they preferred it above all things.

Imitate the Saints, My Child, if thou wilt be a Saint, or desirest to reign with the Saints.

This life of the divine good pleasure is an image

of the life in heaven. For, the inhabitants of heaven, being perfectly satisfied, each one with his own beatitude, are, by the same divine good pleasure, all rendered blissful.

Take away this conformity to the divine Will, and behold! the interior life becomes a delusion; neither does there exist any longer a road to sanctity.

5. When thou dost will and not will the same with Me in all things, in great as well as in small, in things spiritual as well as in things temporal, in adversity no less than in prosperity; finally, in life as well as in death; then be glad and rejoice, My Child, because thou art become a Disciple according to My own Heart.

Thou wilt now not only offer, not merely resign thyself, and all that is thine, to Me, that I may use the same; but of thy own accord thou wilt allow, thou wilt desire that I dispose, according to My good pleasure, of thyself and of thine, of all thou art, and of all thou possessest.

Deliver, therefore, My Child, and leave to Me thyself and whatsoever is thine; and continue faithfully, even unto death, in this surrendering, in this abandoning of thyself to the Will and good pleasure of My Heart.

Be persuaded that, if thou hast thus died with Me, thou shalt also live with Me, and reign among the Saints in the life never-ending.

8. *The voice of the Disciple.*—O the sublimity of the sanctity of Thy Heart, Lord Jesus! However, since Thou invitest me so urgently, and callest me so gently thereto, I must courageously strive, and generously make bold to attain thereto.

Wherefore, relying upon the power of Thy grace, and animated by Thy example, behold! I intrust my spirit to Thy hands; to Thee I consign my spirit, that I may live by Thy Spirit alone; to Thee I give up my will that I may move, act, suffer, die by Thy Will alone.

Lo! I am wholly thine; take me, then, and dispose of me always and everywhere according to the good pleasure of Thy Heart.

May I at last, by a perfect likeness to Thee, and a perfect union with Thee, become a perfect Disciple of Thy Heart!

CHAPTER XXVI.

THE HEART OF JESUS, AFTER HIS DEATH OPENED FOR LOVE OF US, IS THE REFUGE AND SOLACE OF ALL.

1. *The voice of the Disciple.*—See Jesus dying upon the cross! O spectacle! O God, behold Thy Son! O Mary, behold thy Jesus! O Angels, look ye and weep!

O saddest sight, such as never was before, never shall be again! Lo! as the Creator expires all creation is moved, all mourns. The heavens are moved, hide their light for grief, and wrap the world in darkness.

The earth wails, and trembles even unto her foundations, and shakes and tears asunder the rocks and stones.

Religion weeps, and, as if for a sign of grief,

rends her garment, when the vail of the temple is rent in two from the top even to the bottom.

Death itself is moved, and as if sorrowing for its deed, suffers the dead to arise. Behold, the tombs are opened, and many bodies come forth.

All nature in a pang, the whole universe laments for Jesus dying upon the cross between heaven and earth.

O spectacle! Jesus, the Son of God, died in torments for love of us! O everlasting memorial of the love of the Heart of Jesus!

2. But, behold! one of the soldiers, with a spear, opened His Side, and immediately there issued forth Blood and water. New miracle of love; manifold mystery!

The Heart of Jesus is opened that thence may be formed His only one, His perfect one, His Virgin Spouse, the Holy Church.

Blood and water issue forth: Blood, that redeems; Water, that cleanses souls. The Water flows, that, by the laver of Baptism, men may be born again into the Church: the Blood flows, that, by the fruit of His Heart, the most Holy Sacrament, they may be perfected in the Church.

Jesus willed that His Heart should be opened, to show us, that, even after the end of His life, He does by no means cease to cherish us; and to convince us, that, even after His death, His Heart is burning with love for us.

Finally, He willed that It should be opened, that we might possess in His Heart a permanent place of refuge, solace, everything necessary and useful.

He willed that His Heart should not merely be

wounded, but that It should be opened and continue open, that there might ever be access, that the door might ever remain unclosed, through which he that enters in shall be saved,—and he shall go in, and go out, and shall find the pastures of life everlasting.

3. Behold, then, through the opening of the Side, the innermost of His Heart is seen: that great mystery of love is revealed: the designs of the mercy of our God are unclosed, whereby He visited us, He the Orient from on high.

Jesus willed to retain forever the visible wound of His Heart, whence the invisible wound of His love is made to appear, that It may be not only the place of refuge for mortals, but likewise the Paradise of the Blessed.

Hence it is that, from this fountain of the Saviour, men, upon earth, draw with joy the living waters of all gifts and graces; and the Angels and Saints, in heaven, obtain with exultation ever-flowing streams of admiration, and praise, and thanksgiving, and never-ending love.

4. O my soul! lift up thy eyes to Jesus; see thy own Beloved; view that Heart wounded by love opened by love.

Behold, the opened breast displays the affections of His Heart; the Wound proves to what an extent that Heart cherishes thee.

The whole appearance shows that Jesus, thy Beloved above all, is truly meek and humble of Heart.

The Heart of thy Jesus, behold! is open; It is opened that thou mayst draw near and enter therein; that to Him thou mayst give and deliver up thy heart.

5. Behold the unfathomable abyss of goodness; who shall measure the same? who shall comprehend its depth and breadth? Neither man nor Angel shall ever comprehend its bounds.

Who among the unfortunate can dread to approach the Heart of Him who died for love of the unfortunate; yea, who even keeps His Heart open, that to all the wretched there may be given a free entrance!

Gaze upon the heart of Jesus, who died for thee, and His evident love, stronger than death, more vigorous than life, all sweetness, will expel fear, will remove distrust, will cast aside faintheartedness, will arouse faith, will strengthen hope, will enkindle love: and thou wilt go to immerse thyself into this ocean of goodness.

If ever thou becomest forgetful of the love of Jesus, or doubtest His affection, turn thyself to Him and hearken: His wounded Heart will cry out, how He loves, how much He cherishes; and will cry out again, that thou shouldst love in return, that thou shouldst requite His affection.

If thou art straitened, if thou art troubled, hasten, run, to this fountain of every grace, to this gushing spring of all consolation.

If thy unfaithfulness frighten thee, let thy confidence and courage be cheered on by the tokens of benignity of the Heart of Jesus, His head bowed down, His arms outstretched, His Breast glowing with love for thee.

In every peril, in every difficulty, throw thyself confidingly upon the Heart of Jesus: cast thy anxieties upon Him, because He has a care of thee.

And if thou hast done any good action, if thou hast gained any merit, hide it safely in the Heart of Jesus, that this Sacred Heart may sanctify the same by Its virtue, may keep it from the thief, vain glory; and from the moth, self love; and may guard it for the day of final retribution.

6. O most precious, O most sweet wound of the Heart of my Jesus, deserving of love above all decorations of honor; O Thou our resort before every other place! if out of Thee I take but one draught of love, I soon forget all my miseries; I feel a disgust for things worldly and earthly, and I relish things spiritual and heavenly,—naught, except Jesus, and Him wounded by love, do I care to know and love.

O most sweet Jesus! draw me to Thee: draw me through the wound of Thy Breast to Thy divine Heart, that now I may no longer live in myself, but may have life in Thee, may live in Thy Heart, the blissful abode of all the Saints.

Grant, I beseech Thee, Oh! do grant that my heart, wholly united with Thee, and possessing in all things one and the same sentiment with Thee, may be forever closed to Thy enemies, dead to myself and the world, ever open to Thee, breathing Thee alone, above all things loving Thee.

O Jesus, Beloved of my soul! forever preserve me in Thy Heart, which is sweeter than every sweetness, and wherein I find all I can desire for true beatitude.

DIRECTORY FOR THE FOURTH BOOK.

1. The purpose of the Fourth Book is, to teach the soul how to unite herself with God her Saviour. This is effected by divine love. Now, this whole Book treats of the divine love, its causes, its effects, its various ways. These things, if looked into at their very source, if considered in the very Heart of Jesus,—loving, that we may return his love; burning that we may melt; uniting Himself with us that we may unite ourselves with Him, must needs ravish our hearts, melt us wholly, so as to become, in some manner, one with Him.

2. This life of divine union, which is the most perfect and the most blissful portion of the interior life, is not to be so understood as if the souls that live this life ought no longer to perform any exercise pertaining to the purificative or the illuminative life. The practices of these three sorts of lives are never, on this earth, altogether separated. So long as you live, to whatsoever degree of the divine union you may have attained, you shall always have something to do, in order to cleanse the heart more perfectly, or to preserve it pure; you shall always have to practice virtue, either by doing or by suffering.

But this life is to be so understood, that the soul,—when duly cleansed, and sufficiently adorned with genuine and solid virtues, acquired by generous acts of self-abnegation, lives in intimacy with Jesus her God,—enjoying a certain holy, mutual, and unspeakable familiarity with Him, relishes what He relishes, wills what He wills, dislikes what He dislikes, occupies herself, meanwhile, for the most part, with those exercises, those acts, by which this union is fostered and consolidated; although, sometimes, through love, rather than any other motive, she performs such things as belong to the purifying of the interior, or the practicing of virtues. In like manner, souls,—that labor for the most part to purify themselves interiorly, or apply themselves, for the most part, to acquire solidly true virtues,—are said to lead the life of purification or of illumination, according as they occupy themselves commonly with the one or the other, even if they perform, at the same time, many practices, which properly belong to other parts of the interior life.

And these things are to be carefully attended to, lest a person fall into a delusion, here particularly full of danger. Wherefore, unless he is willing to be deceived, and to imperil himself, let no mortal ever think that he has not to labor any further; that he has no longer anything to accomplish. Above all, let no one ever believe that he has no longer anything to fear; that he may freely expose himself to danger, under this or the like pretense, that he is not moved by any created object, or that he seeks or wills naught except God. By such a delusion they themselves, who were distinguished

by the name of sanctity, and the glory of martyrdom, and glittered like stars in the firmament, have
shamefully fallen into the abyss. From this same
source of presumption other delusions flow; such
as, to neglect one's duties, or other signs of God's
Will, for the sake of quietly reposing amid the delights of divine favor; to seek rather the gifts of
the Lord than the Lord Himself; to desire things
which are extraordinary.

3. When, therefore, you are in this part, you
ought to direct everything to this, that you do ever
more and more love Jesus, your God and Saviour, and that you do, by the purest love, unite
yourself intimately with Him. Now, this love is
obtained by considering His countless favors, the
ineffable workings of the love of His Heart, His
stupendous and most delightful promises; lastly,
all the good things which He prepares for you in
time. and in eternity: by contemplating His most
lovely and infinite perfections, on account of which
alone He is most worthy of all possible love: finally,
by prayer, by visits in person or in spirit to the
most Blessed Sacrament, by dealing devotedly and
fervently with Him in holy Communion.

4. The method of using this book may be one
of the four laid down before the First and Second
Books. Of these, each one may here follow that
method which he believes more useful for himself,
according to the state of his soul; and which he
will so apply to the matter here proposed, as to
secure the object of this Book.

However, it should be carefully noticed, as in
others, so especially in this part of the interior life,
that it is by no means proper so to adhere to a set-

tled manner or method, that you do not suffer yourself to be guided by heavenly grace, or by the
Spirit of God, who is accustomed frequently,—particularly with regard to souls that, purified and illumined, take pains to unite themselves wholly
with God,—to pass by every mode or method, to
leave off almost all processes of reasoning, to enrapture the heart, to raise it up into His admirable light, and to affect it in an unutterable
manner.

The affections, to which it is here proper to give
yourself up, and the acts which you ought to excite, are chiefly these:

Of gratitude, or of thanksgiving for the gifts and
graces granted to yourself and to others: yea, also,
for the glory, the beatitude, and the perfection of
the Lord our God; as the Church teaches us by
her example, when she says: We thank Thee for
Thy own great glory.

Of joy, on account of His mercy, His liberality,
His love toward yourself, and all other creatures: on
account of His perfections in themselves; on account of His honor, and blissfulness, and joy.

Of confidence in the goodness of His Heart, in
His care, in His Providence.

Of admiration, on account of the magnitude and
the multitude of the blessings bestowed upon yourself and others, the works of divine love, His infinite perfections.

Of praise, so as to extol His marvellous works,
now alone by yourself, now in union with the
Church; again by inviting all creatures, and again
by associating yourself with the Saints and Angels
in heaven.

Of zeal, for his honor and glory, and for the salvation and perfection of souls, for His sake.

Of humility, so as to remember and acknowledge that you are worthless, but that God is generous, since He pours out for you the treasures of His Heart.

Of filial love, whereby you are filled with a holy dread of offending the Lord; whereby you lovingly grieve for the offenses with which His Heart has been saddened by yourself and others.

Of pure love, whereby you give, surrender, and sacrifice yourself and all you possess, to Him; whereby you conform yourself in all things to His Will and good pleasure; whereby, finally, you live uniform, completely united with Him.

But these and other acts, as elsewhere, so especially are they here to be made in such a manner, that, so long as you can usefully occupy yourself with one, you do by no means pass over to another; but continue to entertain yourself sweetly and devoutly with the same, until either the time of prayer is past, or the Spirit of grace leads you to others; but if, whilst you endeavor affectionately and quietly to adhere to one act or affection, you find that you can no longer apply yourself to it, pass over to some other, suggested either by the wants of your soul, your own devotion, or the Spirit of grace.

Lastly, suffer yourself freely to be led by the Spirit of the Lord to whatever is good, whether to meditation, or to contemplation; to deal with Him by means of the affections, or to repose in His presence; to hold converse with Him, or to hearken to Him; to ask or to give. Neither use any efforts to remain actually conscious of your occupations in prayer.

5. The rules, which do properly belong here, for the discernment of spirits, inasmuch as they are quite nice and delicate, must be well learnt and understood, so that they may be applied with profit. The Saints teach us the following:

The first. There is a twofold divine union, with a consummation of the same: the first is called active; the second, passive union.

The active union consists in the perfect uniformity of our will with the divine Will. This is the whole perfection of divine love. Through this union the sentiments of the Heart of Jesus are our sentiments, the Spirit of Jesus is our spirit, the life of Jesus our life. Hence, sweetly united with Jesus, we enjoy Him constantly, and we are truly made blissful.

The passive union, on the other hand, consists in this, that, by the abundance of light and love poured in, the faculties are suspended; so that the memory does not remember, the intellect does not think, the will does not love, except the Lord God; the whole soul being so absorbed by the divine object, that she does not perceive this state of suspension. This union, replenished with marvellous and most delightful gifts, is, generally, each time of short duration, nor is it wont to last an hour. Hence, during the intervals, the soul should be occupied and content with the active union.

Every one may attain to the active union by faithfulness to the grace which is given him; but no human industry—the divine goodness alone—can raise the soul to the passive union.

The consummation of the divine union consists
in this, that the soul united with the Lord, is, in
some manner, so transformed into the divine object
of her love, that, the faculties being neither suspended nor impeded, she herself, habitually, pla-
cidly, and sweetly enjoys her Lord; being wholly,
in a wonderful and delightful manner, absorbed as
it were, in Him, and, nevertheless, exceedingly
well-disposed both to action and to contemplation.

The second. It is a safer way to long and seek
after the active union, rather than the passive, or
the things which are sometimes vouchsafed in the
passive, such as visions, revelations, and similar
communications. It may happen that souls that
live in the active union, have much more merit than
those to whom the passive union is granted; because they do and endure greater and more generous things for the Lord, and they are satisfied, according to the divine good pleasure, to be deprived
of those consolations,—given to others, but not to
themselves, in the present life,—which they will
receive when more sweetly and more abundantly
bestowed in the life to come.

The third. Let the soul, in order to move and incite herself to do and bear great and noble things
for the Lord, acknowledge and confess that she has
received and does receive many and great things
from the Lord; not that she may deem herself better than others, but that she may serve Him
with more generosity and perfection. Wherefore,
let her reject, as coming not from the good but from
the evil spirit, every thought, every emotion, which,
under any pretense whatever, leads her to com-

plaints about her misery, to dejection of heart, or pusillanimousness.

The fourth. Whatsoever outpourings of the divine goodness the soul may receive, howsoever intimately she may be united with God, how much soever she may even be made perfect in the Supreme Good, she ought ever to remember that she is not impeccable, but that she may still perish,—unless she be faithful to the Lord. And, therefore, the more and the greater favors she receives, the more humble it behooves her to be, and the more purely should she love God. Hence, if she be moved to rely upon the long duration of her virtuous life, or the firmness of her good resolves, or the solidity of her virtue, in order to expose herself to dangers, let her know that she is moved by the evil, not the good Spirit.

The fifth. Matters which lead or call you away from the Catholic faith,—such as some instigations and communications,—should be carefully and powerfully rejected, as the effects of the evil spirit. Those, on the contrary, which are consistent with the Catholic faith, and serve to unite the soul with her Lord and God, may be received with humble thankfulness, as fruits of the good Spirit; and they may even be asked humbly and resignedly, with the intention that the soul may increase in the love of God, and become more perfectly united with Him.

The sixth. When it is known that, by means of the communications received, the soul becomes more and more dead to herself, is animated with desire of greater perfection, and advances in the love of God, it is a sign that they come from the good Spirit.   But when it is perceived that, in consequence of these communications, the soul becomes inclined to gratify corrupt nature, or loses the hunger and thirst after greater perfection, or that with a sort of stubbornness she wants to defend or hold the communications as divine, although the director of her conscience does not believe so, or is in doubt about it, it is a sign that they come from the evil spirit.

The seventh.   The soul should not desire visions or revelations, nor place her perfection and sanctity in having them.   Let her remember that, through them, several have been deceived and have fallen into the greatest danger.   If she experiences a longing after them, let her believe, without a doubt, that it has been suggested or excited by the evil spirit, and let her check and expel the same.

The eighth.   The more eagerly extraordinary things of this kind are coveted, the greater danger they present, that the soul may be deluded, and led away from the true path of sanctity, which Jesus—the meek and humble of Heart—has indicated, and which the Saints follow.

St. Ignat.   St. Alphonsus   Blessed Margaret Mary.

THE FOURTH BOOK.

ADMONITIONS HELPFUL TOWARD UNITING ONE'S SELF WITH THE HEART OF JESUS IN BLISS.

CHAPTER I.

THE MOST BLESSED SACRAMENT OF THE EUCHARIST IS AN INVENTION OF THE LOVE OF THE MOST SACRED HEART OF JESUS.

1. *The voice of Jesus.*—I was dead, My Child, and behold I am living for evermore.

I had come forth from the Father, and had come into the world: at last I was leaving the world to return to the Father.

However, the love of My Heart did not allow nor suffer that I should leave them orphans, whom I cherished more than My own life.

The love of My father called and invited Me, that, coming, I might be glorified with Him, with the glory which I had with Him before the world was created.

The love of men also invited and urged Me on, that, staying among them, I might comfort them amidst all the troubles of life.

And behold! My Heart invented a means of satisfying both My love for My Father, and My Love for men.

A mystery, My Child, that going up into heaven I may be seated at the right of the Father, and abide with you even to the consummation of the world.

A mystery, which, unless I Myself had drawn it forth from My Heart, no mortal could ever have imagined: a mystery which transcends all created nature: a mystery, in fine, which exceeds all finite power.

There is need, therefore, of stupendous miracles, to be wrought by divine omnipotence alone. But love triumphs: love, which in My divine Heart found the design, there also found the power of executing the same.

All things are possible, all things are easy, if I will them in My Heart, whose Will is power and execution.

2. As men were not able to bear the sight of My glorified Majesty, and the world could not subsist in the effulgence of such a brightness; regard was to be had to their weakness, lest, alarmed at the splendor of My greatness, they might be kept away. Wherefore, I must needs conceal My dazzling glory, and display naught that might fill them with dread.

Moreover, My Child, since thou hast here no permanent city, but lookest for one to come, it is expedient for thee, that I do abide with thee under another form; lest, forgetting that thou art a pilgrim on earth, thou be willing to make here thy abode, and cling to the things of the present; but that, mindful of thy place of exile, thou mayst aspire to thy country, where thou shalt be able, with face unvailed, to gaze upon My glory.

Lastly, since this life is short, and after it there shall be no longer any time to gain merits, it is good and most useful that I hide My countenance, that thus thou mayst have a greater opportunity of reducing to practice faith, as well as all other virtues.

3. If for so many reasons it is advantageous that I dwell henceforth in another form among men upon earth: from among all possible forms that one should be chosen, which is best suited to My Heart, and most profitable to men.

Now, My Child, since I came down to men, that they might have spiritual life, and since I stay in their midst that they may have it more abundantly; and as the spiritual life bears in every way a resemblance to the material life, which is sustained and strengthened by natural food; they need a supernatural food, whereby the life of the spirit may be preserved, may grow in solidity, and flourish ever more and more.

It is better, therefore, that I remain under the appearance of food, since I am not only the Bread of life, but Life itself. For how much more abundantly will the faithful soul have life, if she be nourished with Life itself?

Besides, Child, My Heart is love: but love is the gift of one's self, and does not rest until it has given and united itself to the object beloved.

Now, as in the life of nature. naught is more intimately united than food and the one that takes it; so also in the spiritual life, by the gift of My love, the greatest and most intimate union occurs between the soul and Myself.

This is that divine and beatific union, whereby I can render every soul blissful: the work of a boundless love.

Finally, I am pleased to stay among men under the form of a banquet, which is a token of the greatest friendship, in order that, even upon earth, the faithful may rejoice in My supernal fellowship, which the Blessed in heaven enjoy; and that they may recall with delight that never-ending bliss, wherein I dispose to you a kingdom, that you may eat and drink at My table, and where, girding Myself and going about, I will minister to you.

This will be the union everlasting, and thrillingly blissful,—the Passover of never-ending joy,—the wine of eternal love, which I will drink with you ever new in the kingdom of My Father.

4. In order that men might gradually be prepared for mysteries so great, I willed that, in many ways, all this should be foreshadowed in the Old Law.

A figure thereof was the fruit of the tree of life planted in Paradise, by the food of which men, in a state of innocence, were to be nourished, and to bloom with life, that they might preserve themselves from death, and thus secure immortality.

A figure thereof was the bread and wine offered by Melchisedech, the priest and king: priest of the Most High, king of Salem, king of peace.

A figure thereof was the Paschal Lamb, the Lamb without blemish, which was both offered and eaten: which was to be consumed neither raw nor cooked, but prepared with fire: and they that eat the same were to have their loins girded, shoes on their feet, staves in their hands, as if in readiness to go on a journey.

A figure thereof was the Manna in the desert, which fell every day from heaven, possessed the pleasantness of every kind of savor, was called the bread of Angels, of which neither he that gathered more than the usual measure had more, nor he that collected less than another possessed less.

A figure thereof was the Ark of the Covenant, wherein the Majesty of God was honored between the Cherubim; and whence He was wont, day and night, to impart to His people propitiation, aid, and comfort.

Lastly, a figure thereof was the bread baked under the ashes, whereby the Prophet was freed from his faintness and depression of spirit; and, endowed with new vigor, walked, on the strength of that food, even to the mountain of God.

5. It was not unknown to Me, my Child, how much this institution would cost Me: how great and how many a sacrifice this My Sacramental life would require.

I know to what humiliations I subject Myself, to how many insults I expose Myself. But all these My Heart deems less than the love, whereby It is borne towards My Father and towards men.

My love is overcome by no obstacles: it triumphs easily over all. Nay more, these very difficulties themselves, it looks upon and displays, as so many proofs of its greatness and generosity.

Behold, then, eminently the great Sacrament of affectionateness, which, conceived by My love before all ages, was realized by My supreme power in time, appeared wonderful to the Angels, was preached to the nations: which has consoled the world, and which by its sweetness has inebriated the hearts of mortals.

6. *The voice of the Disciple.*—O the hight of the wisdom and love of Thy Heart, Jesus, Son of the living God! How marvelous, how stupendous are Its works! How lovely, O Lord, how sweet!

Behold, how Thou didst love us, most loving Jesus! Thou didst annihilate Thyself for love of us, taking upon Thee the form of food, becoming like unto nourishment, and being found under the appearance of bread, but the Bread of life everlasting!

O what power of love did enkindle Thy Heart, when about to pass from this world to the Father, Thou didst institute this most wonderful, this most delightful means of abiding with us, and of abiding in such a manner!

O prodigy of love! O divine institution! wherein Thou Thyself, O most benign Jesus, art at once the banquet and the guest, the offering and the offerer, the joy of Angels, and of men!

7. Thanks to Thee, Lord Jesus, eternal thanks to Thee, for the unutterable goodness of Thy Heart, whereby Thou didst bestow upon us this incomparable blessing.

Would that I were able to return Thee suitable thanks for so great a gift! Come, ye Angels and Saints of God; come ye, all peoples and tribes; give ye thanks with me, to the Lord: let us praise, and exceedingly magnify Him, for this the love of His Heart.

Let us sing a new canticle to the Lord; for that, abiding with us after a new manner, He pours forth upon us from His Heart, blessings ever new.

Let us joyfully sing to God, our Saviour: let us fall down before Him, let us weep for joy and gratitude in His presence.

8. O Jesus, infinite love! who through love didst come into this world, and remainest here through love; nay more, through love art become wholly mine: to Thee, in return, I give and deliver my heart, all my affections, my whole self: grant, I beseech Thee, that, by love, I may be Thine for evermore, that whatsoever I am and possess, may be at the disposal of Thy love and glory.

Take away from me all obstacles to Thy love; extinguish in me every ill-ordered affection, that naught may affect, naught may move me, except what concerns Thyself, or Thy interests.

Thou, O delight of my heart, Thou, O bliss of my soul! do Thou live and reign in me: be Thou henceforth the first and last object of my thoughts and affections: let me be ever occupied with Thee, or for Thee, who art all to me.

CHAPTER II.

OF THE MARVELOUS INSTITUTION OF THE MOST BLESSED SACRAMENT OF THE EUCHARIST.

1. *The voice of Jesus.*—I am the living Bread, that came down from heaven. He that comes to Me shall not hunger, for the Bread which I shall give him is My Flesh for the life of the world.

When I had said these things, My Child, the Jews disputed among themselves, saying: How can this man give us His Flesh to eat?

And, in reply to them, I declared positively: Verily, verily, I say to you, unless ye eat the

Flesh of the Son of man, and drink His Blood, ye shall not have life in you.

For My Flesh is meat indeed, and My Blood is drink indeed.

2. Before the festival day of the Passover, knowing that My hour had come, that I should pass out of this world to the Father, having loved My own who were in the world, I loved them unto the end.

It being now evening, I sat down to the last Supper, and the twelve Disciples with Me: to them, as they were seated around, I said: With desire, I have desired to eat this Passover with you.

And whilst they were at Supper, I took bread, and blessed, and broke, and gave it to My Disciples, saying: Take ye and eat; this is My Body.

And taking the chalice, I gave thanks, and gave to them, saying: Drink ye all of this; this is My Blood.

Do this for a commemoration of Me.

3. *The voice of the Disciple.*—These, then, are Thy words, Lord God, truth eternal, whereby Thou didst solemnly promise beforehand, that Thou wouldst give Thyself to us as the Bread of Life: these are the deeds whereby thou didst afterwards truly fulfil what Thou hadst promised.

Thy Church, taught by these words and deeds, even before they had been recorded, enjoyed this, Thy divine gift; and was doing this, as Thou hadst enjoined, for a commemoration of Thee.

By these words, Thou didst overthrow and thwart the foreseen difficulties of infidels, and the objections of heretics, and the temptations of demons.

For, by them, Thou taughtest, that whatsoever Thou, the infallible truth, utterest, must be believed, even if we do not understand how these things can be.

And through the holy Church, Thy true Spouse, we know the things Thou didst utter; but in what manner the mysteries which Thou didst proclaim by words, are inwardly constituted, or realized, that we do not comprehend, since our limited reason cannot reach those things which transcend all the bounds of reason.

If we do not understand the things which are below ourselves, how shall we understand those which are above us?

That a seed sown in the ground, after it has decayed, grows up into a new stalk, and produces much fruit, we believe, because we perceive it outwardly; but how these things happen intrinsically, although they belong to the natural order, we are unable to penetrate.

Should he not deservedly be regarded as unsound in mind, who, whilst, by means of the senses, he perceives that there are mysteries of nature, would not be willing to admit them, because he does not comprehend how they do exist?

Now, even by means of the senses, we perceive that there are mysteries of religion revealed by Thee; because faith comes by hearing: and, moreover, by reason itself, we see that those mysteries are true; because it is evident to reason, that it is impossible that Thou, the essential truth, shouldst utter what is false.

The submission, therefore, of all them that faithfully believe in Thee, is reasonable. But they that refuse to believe Thee, thinking themselves wise, have become fools, and altogether unreasonable.

And it proceeds from a secret pride, instigated by the cunning of the devil, that they are unwilling to subject to Thee, its Author, the noblest gift, their reason; and to honor Thee, by the submission of the same.

But all they that at any time have been humble children of the Church,—how greatly soever they were distinguished for their genius,—have brought their intellect under subjection, to obey Thee by faith.

By this Thou showest that Thou art the Lord of all, good towards all, no respecter of persons: and that from all, from the learned, as well as from the unlearned, Thou desirest the obedience of a subdued intellect and a submissive will.

4. Lord God, my Creator and Redeemer, I prostrate myself before Thee, and submit my reason wholly to Thee: ay, my whole intellect and will, my body, and all my senses, in obedience to faith, for Thy glory.

But it is also my glory and advantage that I may return to Thee, their beginning and end, all the gifts of soul and body which I have received from Thee; and that, by means of whatsoever I have received, in the order of nature, I may freely co-operate with Thy grace for the supernatural order, and, consequently, for my own everlasting honor, my never-ending bliss.

Reason and faith are both Thy gifts, Lord; the former a natural, the latter a supernatural gift: both ever assist each other, are never contrary: both given for truth, each one in its own order.

If I believe, because my natural reason moves me thereto, my faith is a natural one,—neither supernatural nor saving. If I believe, because a supernatural motive impels me, my faith is supernatural and salutary.

Blessed are they who have not seen and have believed. And, certainly, how can the senses perceive what does not fall under the senses? or, how can reason comprehend what does not lie within the grasp of reason? Or, how can the cold utterance of man explain that which the exceeding love of Thy Heart has effected?

5. In the spirit, therefore, of Thy Church, I do firmly believe that Thou, O Lord Jesus Christ, true God and man, art truly and substantially contained in the most Blessed Sacrament, under the appearance of things visible, bread and wine.

I do firmly believe that Thou art wholly and entirely present under each species, and under every part of each species, if they be separated.

I do firmly believe that Thou, there present in Thy glorified state, art the same, whom, at Thy entrance into the world, the Angels adored, whom Mary and Joseph, the Shepherds and the Magi, worshipped under the form of a Child, who, meek and humble of Heart, didst go about doing good; who, having died for us, didst rise again; who, having gone up to heaven, art seated in glory at the right of God the Father.

I do not, as the Jews, ask for signs, nor search into the manner; I do not desire, like the unbelievers, to understand reasons intrinsically concealed. I do not require, like heretics, that my individual judgment be gratified: for me the testimony of Thy infallible Spouse, the holy Church, which is the ground of the truth, is sufficient.

I reject whatsoever is opposed to her doctrine: this is my security, my faith.

6. O Lord God of infinite Majesty, Thou the Saint of the Saints! who art so marvelously and so lovingly hidden in this mystery, Thee I adore, Thee I worship devotedly.

Humbly prostrate, with body and soul, in Thy presence, I profess before heaven and earth that Thou art my God and my Saviour; to Thee do I pay the supreme worship, due to Thy Majesty.

I offer to Thee also the adorations, honors, and homage which the Angels, and the Saints, and Thy whole Church pay to Thee.

O that all men would acknowledge Thee, would adore Thee, would show Thee homage and reverence!

But, since so many fail in their duty, I, O Lord, uniting myself with Thy Saints and Angels, and all faithful souls, do adore and venerate Thee, in their stead: and I desire, in this manner, to make amends for the negligence of all unfaithful souls

7. O Jesus! whatsoever I may be able to do for Thee, is as nothing in comparison of what I owe to Thee.

In this most delightful Sacrament, by the pure love of Thy Heart, Thou hast given me whatever Thou possessest, Thy Body and Soul, Thy Humanity and Divinity, with all their treasures. I owe, therefore, to Thee, as much as Thou art worth, Thou who art infinite.

I give to Thee, in return, my body and soul,

whatsoever I have, whatsoever I am: but behold! after I have given all this, my debt remains infinite.

It is good for me, Lord Jesus, that I am thus indebted to Thee, that I may be moved and impelled to love without bounds the infinite goodness of Thy Heart.

Mindful of Thy pure and boundless love, O Jesus, I love Thee, in return, with my whole heart, and I long to be able to satisfy Thee by an unlimited love.

8. Help me, O most loving Jesus, that I may love Thee with that affection, that tenderness, that reverence, which love alone can inspire.

Grant that, henceforth, I may live by pure love for Thee, who by infinite love livest for me in the most holy Tabernacle.

By Thy most Sacred Heart, thus made a captive, thus detained by love, I beg and implore Thee, so bind my heart to Thine, that it may be a captive of Thy love, and be never dissevered nor separated therefrom.

CHAPTER III.

WITH HOW LIVELY A FAITH THE CHURCH HAS ALWAYS AND EVERYWHERE MANIFESTED HER DEVOTION TO THE MOST BLESSED SACRAMENT.

1. *The voice of Jesus.*—My Child, the Church exults at this most excellent favor of My Heart, and venerates this supreme miracle of My love with every demonstration of devotedness.

Enraptured at the excess of the goodness of My Heart, she melts with love for Me, she rejoices securely in the possession of My most delightful presence, and continues to rejoice, whilst generations pass by, whilst the face of the earth is changed, and ages speed away.

Behold! in every age of the past, from the East and the West, from the North and the South, the children of the Church have arisen and have called their Mother blessed, on account of so great a love of My Heart, which abides with her all days even to the consummation of the world.

In this presence, uninterrupted, and full of mutual love, I celebrate the great Supper, the divine festival of My spiritual nuptials, with My immaculate Spouse, the holy Church.

To these the faithful are invited and called, be they poor, and weak, and blind, and lame, that the house may be filled with guests, and that their joy may be full.

2. *The voice of the Disciple.*—Hear ye this, O mortals, and come ye clothed with the nuptial garment. Here taste ye, and see how sweet is the Lord.

To this sacred banquet, at which the Angels minister, all the truly faithful do, always and everywhere, come adorned with this festive garment, that, being pleasing to the Lord, they may, whilst they are nourished and refreshed, rejoice with Him.

But they that are without this garment, being defiled, do rightly "abstain," because they deservedly fear, "lest they eat and drink judgment to themselves;" or "because they do not confess that the Eucharist is the Body of our Saviour, Jesus Christ, which suffered for our sins, and which the Father raised to life." (I Cor. 11, St. Ignat. Mart., Cent. I.)

But we "have been taught that the Eucharist is the Body and Blood of Jesus Christ, who became incarnate." (St. Justin, Mart., Cent. II.)

How great a gift is, therefore, bestowed not only upon our soul, "but also upon our body, which is nourished with the Body and Blood of the Lord!" (St. Iren., Cent. II.)

Hence, how great a reverence is required! "Ye know, ye who are accustomed to assist at the divine mysteries, how, when ye receive the Body of the Lord, ye watch with all care and reverence, that nothing, be it ever so little, fall down, that naught of the consecrated gift slip off: for ye believe yourselves guilty, if, through carelessness, anything do fall. So great is the precaution ye use, and deservedly so." (Origen, Cent. III.)

No sooner had the Church emerged from the persecution of three hundred years, than, rejoicing and crowned with laurels, she, in her first general Council,—her sons having been assembled from every part of the world,—regulated the manner in which the divine Sacrament should be dispensed throughout the world, in order that so sacred a mystery might everywhere be handled with holy awe.

She does not bring forward new things, but, faithful guardian of her deposit, she recalls and inculcates the ancient practices. "Neither the Rule," says this watchful Mother, "nor custom has handed it down, that they, who have not the power of offering the Sacrifice, should present the Body of Christ to them that offer the same. Let them receive according to their rank the Holy Communion from the Bishop or the priest, after the clergy." (1st Nic. Counc., Cent. IV.)

Behold the most Holy Communion! behold the Sacrament of the Lord! "For under the appearance of bread, He gives us His Body, under the appearance of wine He gives us His Blood, that, when you have received the same, you taste the Body and Blood of Christ, having become partakers of His Body and Blood: for thus we become *Christiferi,* that is, bearing Christ in our bodies: thus, according to the blessed Peter, we are made partakers of the divine nature." (S. Cyril of Jerus., Cent. IV.)

"Bread, indeed, it is before the sacramental words: but when the Consecration has been pronounced thereon, of bread it becomes the Body of Christ. By which words then, and by whose language is the Consecration made? By the words of Christ the Lord. Therefore, the Word of Christ affects this Sacrament. Which Word of Christ? The one, whereby all things were made. The Lord commanded, and the heavens were made: the Lord commanded, and the earth was made: the Lord commanded, and every creature was produced. You see, then, how effective is the Word of Christ. If, then, there is so great a power in the word of the Lord Jesus, that things, which were not, began to exist, how much the more effective is it to change into another that which did already exist? He spoke, and it was done." (S. Ambros., Cent. IV.)

" O Sacrament of godliness! O sign of unity! O bond of charity! He that desires to live has where he may live, whereby he may live. Let him become incorporate that he may receive life. Let him not be a decayed member, which deserves to be cut off; let him not be a misshapen one, of which he is ashamed. Let him be fair, fit, sound: let him cleave to the body: let him live of God for God." (S. August., Cent. V.)

"As many of us, therefore, as become partakers of this Body, let us reflect that we taste Him, who is seated above, who is adored by the Angels. That which the Angels dare not freely gaze upon, by reason of the dazzling splendor, by that we are here nourished, to that we are united, with that we became one body. In order, therefore, that we may not only become this by charity, let us also in very deed be blended with that body: for this is effected by the food which He has granted to us. Let us, then, go away from that table, like lions breathing fire, having become an object of dread to the devil." (S. Chrysost., Cent. V.)

"How goodly is that Bread which nourishes the Angels by its outward appearance, that they may be sated therewith in the land of bliss; and us by faith, that we may not faint on the way. That man might eat the Bread of Angels, the Creator of Angels became man, nourishing both, and remaining whole and entire." (St. Fulgent., Cent. VI.)

4. "They, however, that live wickedly, and do not cease to communicate, thinking, that, by such a Communion, they are cleansed, let them learn that they make no progress toward a cleansing, but toward condemnation. For the body of Christ is the food of Saints." (St. Isid. of Seville, Cent. VII.)

Prepare ye, therefore, your heart. "For the Eucharist is a Communion, whereby we have fellowship with Christ, and receive His Humanity and Divinity, and unite ourselves between us." (St. John Damasc., Cent. VIII.)

"Let them hear, then, who wish to weaken this word of the Body, as if it were not the true Body of Christ which is now celebrated in the Sacrament by the Church, nor His real Blood. They seem desirous to approve or invent something new, as if it were merely a certain virtue of Christ's Body or Blood, so that the Lord is made to speak falsely, when Truth itself says: This is My Body. He did not then say, when He broke and gave the bread, This is, or in this mystery is, a certain virtue or figure of My Body, but He said plainly: This is My Body: and, therefore, it is what He said, not that which any one may imagine. No one has as yet openly gainsaid that, which the whole world believes and confesses." (St. Paschas., Ab., Cent. IX.)

5. "In churches, the Eucharist is always accessible: which custom the ancient churches have preserved." (Luitprand., Cent. X.)

Wherefore, "Christ cannot be accused of forgetfulness: Christ does not enjoin things contrary to His commands. He is the Bread that came down from heaven, which is daily brought to the table of the Church, as a heavenly food, which is broken for the forgiveness of sins, which feeds and nourishes unto life everlasting them that eat the same." (St. Peter Damian., Cent. XI.)

"Neither need we pretend that to this our age is denied, either that apparition, which was vouchsafed to the Fathers of the ancient Covenant; or that presence of His Body, which was exhibited to the Apostles. Since, to them that consider faithfully, neither the one nor the other can be wanting. Surely, it cannot in the least be doubted that, in the Sacrament, we have even now present with us the true substance of His Body. We have revelations, but in spirit and in power, so that it is proved that naught is wanting in any kind of grace." (St. Bern., Cent. XII.)

6. "The delightfulness of this Sacrament none can adequately express, whereby spiritual sweetness is tasted in its very source: and the remembrance of that most excellent charity which He manifested in His Passion is recalled to mind. Wherefore, that the immensity of this love might be the more intimately imprinted in the hearts of the faithful, at the last Supper, when, after He had celebrated the Passover with His Disciples, He was about to pass from this world to the Father, He instituted this Sacrament, as an everlasting memorial of His Passion, the fulfillment of the ancient figures, the greatest of the miracles wrought by Him, and the exceeding comfort of those that were saddened by His absence." (St. Thom. Aq., Cent. XIII.)

"A spiritual and interior person finds in the partaking of the Body of Christ Jesus twelve excellent fruits: Fortitude, to forsake easily things earthly and perishable: Progress, in the things relating to salvation: Elevation of the soul above whatever is outside of God: Strength to practice good: Enlightenment of the understanding more perfectly to know God, and all things which are seen in the mirror of eternity: Fervor of love for God: Fulfillment of those things which beget hap-

piness: a Treasure of wealth: a constant Cheerfulness of spirit: a certain secure Firmness; perfect Peace: Union of the soul with God." (Thauler,
Cent. XIV.)

"O precious, magnificent, saving banquet, replete
with every delight! By this, sins are cleansed
away, virtues increased, the mind is enriched with
the abundance of all graces." (St. Antonin., Cent.
XV.)

7. Wherefore, delivering her doctrine concerning this august and divine Sacrament—which the
Catholic Church, instructed by Jesus Christ our
Lord Himself, and by His Apostles, and taught by
the Holy Spirit, who always inspires her with every
truth,—has ever retained and will preserve to the
end of the world,—she teaches, and openly and
simply professes that, in the bountiful Sacrament of
the Eucharist, after the Consecration of the bread
and wine, our Lord Jesus Christ, true God and
man, is truly, really, and substantially contained
under the appearance of those visible elements.

She warns, exhorts, prays, and entreats, through
the tender mercy of our God, that all and each one
of those that bear the name of Christian, do meet
and agree, in this sign of unity, this bond of charity, this symbol of concord,—mindful of so great a
Majesty, and so eminent a love of Jesus Christ our
Lord, who, as the price of our salvation, laid down
His beloved life, and gave us His Flesh to eat:—
that they do believe and revere these sacred mysteries of His Body and Blood, with constancy and
firmness of faith, with devotedness, and piety and
worship of spirit, so that they may be enabled frequently to receive this supersubstantial bread, and

that this may truly be to them everlasting life and health of the soul.

That, being invigorated by the strength thereof, they may be enabled, from the journey of this weary pilgrimage, to come to the heavenly country, there to eat unvailed the same Bread of Angels, that now they eat hidden beneath the sacramental vails. (Council of Trent, Sess. 13, Cent. XVI.)

8. O Lord God! how did the faithful, through all ages, burn to honor Thee in this Sacrament of Thy love! with what piety did they strive here to exhibit for Thee the utmost reverence! How they did exert themselves to show due gratefulness to Thy Heart, and to compensate by love for the love of Thy Heart!

And, therefore, too, should we be blamed, we, the heirs of the faith once delivered to the Saints, we, the children of the Saints, were we to grow lukewarm in this devotion of devotions, in this chief point of our Religion; whilst so long a succession of ages calls forth our lively faith, when so great a multitude of the faithful of all times and places throughout the world stimulate us by their example; and since so great a goodness of Thy Heart excites our hearts.

Enliven our faith, most loving Jesus, and, when enlivened, increase it unceasingly. Strengthen our hope and confidence. Enkindle and inflame our love.

Grant, O Lord, that we may ever be enabled to worship in the spirit of faith, to venerate devotedly this most sacred and most sweet Mystery, and to partake worthily thereof.

CHAPTER IV.

THAT THE MOST SACRED HEART OF JESUS, IN THE
SACRAMENT OF HIS LOVE, IS PERFECTLY BLISS-
FUL.

1. *The voice of Jesus.*—That for which My Heart
longed, that which It sought through every excess
of love, this It now enjoys contented in the holy
Sacrament of the Eucharist.

Behold! now not only the justice of My heavenly Father, but also the love of My Heart is
satisfied. Herein rejoices and exults My Heart,
that nothing is now wanting to Its wished-for bliss.

Rejoice with Me, My Child; because here is the
joy, the delight, the blessedness of My Heart.

Here is the new heaven, wrought and adorned
by skill divine, where My Heart is well pleased
and blissful all days.

Yet behold! Child, My Heart does not here enjoy those things wherein the world by its vain
struggles seeks for happiness. It possesses not the
display of earthly wealth, nor the pleasures of the
senses, nor those objects which flatter the passions.

All these I willingly do without: nay, frequently
even I am wont to be surrounded with what the
world shuns and abhors. Yet My Heart is completely contented and blissful.

2. Why should not My Heart be happy here,
since in this Paradise of supernatural delights It
overflows with a torrent of divine joys and supreme
sweetness?

I am perfectly happy in Heart by possessing

those things which as the Son I have by inheritance from the Father, and which, as the Saviour of
the world, I have acquired at the price of My life.

But thou, My Child, wherein dost thou seek thy
felicity? is it also in the divine union, in supernal
communing, in the sweet consolation of the divine
good pleasure?

Dost thou not sometimes lose the joy or even the
peace of thy heart, because thou hast not that which
gratifies nature? Art thou also, according to the
divine Will, gladly deprived thereof?

Look thou attentively, Child, and be persuaded
that thy heart, like Mine, cannot be made happy
by the love and enjoyment of things sensible, of
objects created, but of those which are supernatural
and divine.

3. Here, moreover, is My Heart blissful, by
reason of the happiness which the faithful draw
from this fountain of blessings, whereof they partake with Me.

As a good father experiences happiness when he
finds himself among his beloved children; so do I in
the midst of My people.

Here the faithful, as children most dear to My
Heart, are trained and formed by Me; they banquet, they entertain themselves with Me: they drink
in the generosity and fortitude of My Heart: they
are incited to emulate My virtues: yea, they learn
to glorify and delight in the same things with Me.

For this is My Heart glad indeed, as It deems
Itself happy whensoever It has made others happy.

Rejoice with Me, My Child, seeing that thy happiness is not only an object of care, but also of joy
to My Heart.

4. O if thou knewest, how great a bliss My Heart does, over and above, enjoy here, on account of the tenderness, the devotedness of the love of so many souls, that, in every state and condition of life, are wholly consecrated to Me, and live, with every affection of their heart, for Me alone!

Here, My Child, here is Benjamin with Me in ecstasy of mind. Here are pure souls enraptured with heavenly delights, wherewith the Angels themselves are inebriated.

Here those generous souls, although weak by nature, form great and noble designs for Me, and, by affection and deed, make compensation for the sacrifices of My love, consecrate themselves wholly to My interests.

And should not I be delighted with a love so great, so tender, so chaste? Should I not pour forth My whole Heart upon them? shall I suffer Myself to be overcome by tenderness and generosity of love?

My delight is to be with the children of men: the hight of My delight to enjoy the love of pure souls, and, in return, to make them taste the sweets of My love.

5. Here, therefore, is My Heart in various ways, and perfectly replenished with bliss; yet if there be any who are ungrateful or degenerate, and who are insensible to My love, or act unjustly towards My Heart, they only can make themselves wretched, but cannot render Me unhappy.

For, since I am risen to a life of glory, I die no more; neither am I affected by sorrow. My joy, My beatitude, is perfect and complete: none shall take it away from My Heart, none shall lessen the same.

As My Heart is personally united to the Divinity, It is blissful with the beatitude of the very Divinity.

And therefore, in order that My Heart may be perfectly blissful, It needs no external means; for, whether these be present or absent, It will ever be most blessed.

No less blissful in the hut with the dying poor, than in the palace of the nobleman or king; as blissful in the Tabernacle of the altar, as upon the throne in heaven.

For the reason of My beatitude is within; whence it is ever the very same in every place, at all times, under all circumstances.

This is the inner recess, where I have placed My abode, where I dwell in light inaccessible, where I enjoy a full and unchangeable beatitude.

6. The Angels that throng around Me are filled with wonder, and prostrate they worship, and exulting they exclaim: Let us be glad, and give glory to our God!

And much more are they rejoiced at My bliss than at their own; for, rapt in Me, and forgetful of themselves, in their exceeding love for Me, they exult with Me amid joys unutterable.

In like manner, do many faithful souls,—although still in the body they experience the miseries of this mortal life,—rejoice exceedingly, because I am what I am: and they derive the highest happiness from this, that they know that I am supremely blessed.

And thou also, My Child, if thou lovest **Me** truly, wilt surely rejoice for that I am blissful, not only in the enjoyment of the highest glory at the right of God the Father, but also in this Sacrament of the love of My Heart.

7. *The voice of the Disciple.*—Thou art My witness, most sweet Jesus, and knowest that, through love for Thee, I rejoice at Thy perfect beatitude in the most delightful Sacrament of Thy Heart.

Yea, Lord, my heart and my whole soul rejoice in Thee, because Thy Heart is blessed, and is confirmed in blissfulness forever and ever.

O how truly must the highest joy overwhelm me, because, Thy Passion being now over, Thy glory and bliss are full, and placed beyond every change!

It is true that, since I still have to endure the hardships of my banishment, the time has not yet come to rejoice at my own glory and bliss everlasting: but, meanwhile, it is enough for me that Thou my God, my Saviour and Father, rejoicest to the utmost fullness, in glory and beatitude supreme.

This is for me a reason to rejoice, and to rejoice with my whole heart, even while I abide and weep in my captivity, and call to mind my everlasting inheritance in heaven, which, as God, Thou hast prepared for me, which, when lost, as Saviour, Thou hast repurchased for me, which, as Father, Thou bequeathest to me.

And because it is meet and just that I do love Thee more than myself, and whatsoever is my own; so, in like manner, it is right and wholesome that I do rejoice more at Thy beatitude than at my own happiness, either present or future.

And in reality, Lord Jesus, I do rejoice more intensely on account of Thy glory and blessedness than on account of any honor or exaltation of my own,—on account of any joy or consolation whatever.

But I also rejoice, with all my heart, at the very joy wherewith Thy Heart is replenished by the happiness, the devotedness, the love of so many souls, throughout the earth, consecrated to Thee.

8. Grant, O most kind Jesus, that I, too, may be of the number of those who in return love Thee, their pure and generous Lover, with so great a purity and generosity.

I ask not for the singular and marvelous favors granted to them so frequently and so abundantly: Thee, O my Jesus, Thyself do I ask, as a reward of my labors and sorrows, if I have endured any for Thy sake, and as my sole happiness in all things.

Not the riches or the pleasures of this world, not the things which flatter nature, not even merely sensible consolations, can render me happy. My bliss is, O most sweet Jesus, to repose on Thy Heart, to enjoy Thee.

Hard, indeed, is all rest which aoes not recline on Thy Heart: Vain are all things which are not referred to Thee: meaningless, whatsoever is not in harmony with the sentiments of Thy Heart: tasteless, whatsoever is not seasoned with the unction of Thy love.

Grant me only, that, by divine union, I may possess Thee, love Thee as purely, as generously as I am able; and I willingly abandon all the rest to others: by this gift alone I shall be most blissful with Thee.

CHAPTER V.

THE MOST SACRED HEART OF JESUS IS THE HEART
OF HIS HOLY CHURCH.

1. *The voice of Jesus.*—My Heart, Child, which
lives in the Sacrament, is the heart of My Church,
which is My mystical Body.

This, My Body, is a living one, endowed with a
soul. That soul is the principle of the supernatural life, which the Body lives.

This principle of life proceeds from My divine
Heart: for out of My Heart the Church was made;—
which is evidently to be understood, not of the
members, not of the Body, but of the soul.

Many members, indeed, but one Body, which, by
the divine principle, My Heart animates, and fos-
ters, that My life may be made manifest in the
Body.

The Church, therefore, consisting of a Body,
which is its human element, and a soul, which is
the divine element, subsists as a moral individual-
ity in the oneness of person, and in the participation of the human and divine nature.

As the vine, by its influence, communicates the
life-giving sap to the branches when properly disposed, so do I, to the properly disposed members
of the Church, communicate the divine principle of
Life.

And as the vine and the branches are one, so am
I and the Church, in a manner, one.

Truly, then, am I and the Church intimately

united, not only by a moral, but also by a substantial union; not by a sensible, but a spiritual union; not by an hypostatic, but nevertheless by a personal union, in this sense, that I am so united to the Church, that she constitutes with Me one moral personality, receiving from Me her principal part, her soul, the divine principle of supernatural Life, and having, at the same time, members, each of them personalities, in another respect, which subsist by and for themselves, truly distinct and merely human personalities.

2. Thus united to Me, thus animated by a divine principle, the Church lives, in some manner, a divine Life, a supernatural Life, a Life of merits worthy of everlasting beatitude.

Nay more, it is from the same source that man is enabled to begin to be a member of the Church, when, in Baptism, he is regenerated by the water and the Spirit of My Heart, as the Scripture says: We were all baptized into one body, whether Jews or Gentiles, whether bondmen or free.

For this did the water flow from My opened Side, the symbol of Baptism, which is the laver of regeneration.

By the same principle, likewise, are the members of the Church intimately united. The faithful are, indeed, gently and happily bound together among themselves by many links; but in the Sacrament of the love of My Heart, they become, as it were, incorporated with Me and endowed with My Spirit, and thus they become incomparably more closely, more sweetly, and more perfectly united together.

And this is the mystery of love, whereof the

Apostle speaks, when he says: Although many, we are one body, who partake of one Bread. One body and one spirit.

What wonder, then, if the faithful should possess but one heart, My Heart, of whose fullness all receive the Spirit of Life?

For, as in the natural body the blood, with its life-giving power, starts from the heart, and diffuses itself through all, even the most remote and the least, parts which present no obstruction; so the principle of the supernatural Life proceeds from My Heart, and is imparted to all, and every one of the members of My mystical Body, that present no obstacle.

3. By this divine power not only does the Church live, but at the same time that her members are intimately united, by this she is nourished, endowed with vigor, and preserved in the perpetual bloom of youth.

Yea, if any member is weak, or even, by the abuse of his free will, has hindered or cast aside My life-giving influence and communication, so as to become supernaturally dead; so long as he cleaves to the Body of the Church, he can recover life itself and supernatural health from My Heart, if, by the Sacrament of Penance, he cleanses himself in the bath of the life-restoring and purifying Blood of My Heart, and thus removes the obstacle or hindrance.

But the living members of the Church, as they are animated by My Spirit, as they are constantly nourished by the influence of My Heart, as, lastly, they abide in Me and I in them, bring forth much fruit, true and permanent fruit, fruit of life everlasting.

All false religions and sects,—as they neither do nor can receive Life from My divine Heart,—since they are altogether cut off from My mystical Body,—are soulless beings, destitute of the principle of the supernatural Life; and, therefore, they cannot bear genuine and saving fruit. For, as the branch of the vine cannot bear fruit of itself, unless it abide in the vine, so neither can men, unless they abide in Me.

Do not then wonder, if the sects and false religions, like branches lopped off, wither, decay, and finally perish altogether.

4. If these things, whereby the Church thus lives, flourishes, and brings forth fruit, are marvelous and sweet, still more wonderful and sweeter far are those other favors which I impart to her, and whereby she has a resemblance to Myself.

For, whatsoever I have by nature, the Church according to her capacity, has of Me by grace.

And, since I, who am the Holy One, animate the Church with the divine principle of Life, and have her so united to Me, that we are, as it were, one, she is necessarily holy, not only outwardly, by her origin, by her end, and the means she employs to attain to eternal bliss, but also inwardly, by her very soul, wherein, properly speaking, holiness resides.

By the perpetual union and influence of My Heart, I perfect her in holiness, that I may exhibit her as a Church, glorious, without blemish, or wrinkle, or aught of the kind.

I cannot err: therefore neither can the Church. Should she err, I Myself should err: but I am the infallible truth, whence also she herself is infallible.

The words which the Father gave Me, I gave to her: and I unfolded their meaning, that, under the guidance of My Holy Spirit, she might understand and keep them.

The Church, which is My Body, dies not, because I die no more; but so she remains, until I come, in glory, at the end of the world.

I Jesus yesterday, and to-day: the same also forever: and, therefore, My Heart, which vivifies and preserves the Church, nurses and fills her with vigor, sanctifies her by Its holiness, and consolidates her by Its truth; endows her also with Its own perpetual Life, and imparts to her a bright immortality.

5. Learn hence, My Child, how worthy of thy veneration, how worthy of thy love is the Church, who is so intimately united to Me, and represents My Own Self so completely, that she may justly say: He that sees Me, sees also Christ.

Be glad, Child, rejoice with all thy heart, because thou art a member of this My mystical Body, than which there is naught seen on earth more beauteous, more noble, more marvelous.

If thou lovest Me, love also My Church, for which I gave Myself up, and than which, of all the things that are made, in heaven and in earth, there is nothing dearer to My Heart.

Above all, in the most Holy Sacrament of My love, thou wilt be more closely united in Me to the Church, and there wilt thou better learn of My Heart her spirit.

Whosoever wishes to know the spirit of the Church, must learn the Spirit of My Heart; because the Spirit of both is one and the same.

The Church must be considered in the same spirit wherewith she is animated: and her manner of acting must be viewed, not in a worldly sense, but in that spiritual sense by which she is moved when acting.

O! if all knew the sentiments of the Church—which far surpass the sentiments of the best of mothers, since hers are the very sentiments of My Heart;—how fondly would they love the Church! how completely would they approve all her works!

Do thou pray, My Child, that all may know and love the Church, that they may be worthy members of this Body, animated with the Spirit of Life: members by whom I may be honored and glorified.

Do thou pray, much and frequently, that all may be invigorated with the sentiments of My Heart and increase throughout therein, until they all meet into a perfect Body, and be joined in fellowship with the Angels and Saints, who, in heaven, are confirmed in union with My Heart.

6. Meanwhile, My Child, have a special care, that thou abide in Me, not by faith, hope, and charity alone, but also by means of the Sacrament, by a perfect union.

This is the one, the necessary thing for thee, that thou be united with Me. From this union arise for thee life, and vigor, and perfection, and holiness.

The more closely thou art united with Me, and the better disposed thou keepest thyself, the more copious streams of graces, and supernal blessings, thou wilt draw upon thyself from My Heart, at all times, indeed, but, chiefly, in holy Communion.

Hence thou wilt bear much fruit of holiness

whereby thou wilt show forth the divine power of My Heart, and promote Its true glory.

7. *The voice of the Disciple.*—O Lord, our God! how wonderful, how lovely is Thy Heart! Who should not be astonished at the depth of the mysteries of Its power! who should not be moved by the boundless tokens of Its love!

The taking upon Thyself of our nature, was indeed a great and marvelous work of Thy love; but O, how much greater, how much more marvelous was the giving of Thyself in the Sacrament!

In the Incarnation Thou didst assume our humanity: but in the Communion Thou bountifully givest us Thy own Divinity, and grantest us Thy own Humanity.

By assuming our nature, Thou didst come down to us, and live a mortal life; but, by communicating Thyself to us in the Sacrament, Thou raisest us up to Thyself, and impartest to us a divine Life.

When Thou becamest man, Thou didst redeem and gather us together: by becoming the food of our life, Thou unitest us to Thyself, that we may be perfected in Thee and through Thee.

O Lord! how prodigious, how delightful is the love of Thy Heart for us, for whom Thou workest such mighty things!

Would that all might know and love these wonders so stupendous, so deserving of love! Would that I possessed the hearts of all, that I might consecrate them to Thy love.

8. O Jesus, the life and delight of my soul! how unutterable is the love wherewith Thou didst love me!

For, how great a condescension of Thy love was it, that, by nature, Thou didst create me in Thy image! But how incomparably greater was that love whereby, through grace, Thou didst raise me to Thy likeness! What shall I say, what shall I think of that, whereby Thou didst elevate me to an intimate union with Thyself! Who am I, and who art Thou, that Thou dealest in this manner with me!

O love incomprehensible! O most sweet Jesus, lovely above all things lovely! How shall I not die, if I love thee not! how shall I live, if I live not for Thee!

O Lord, the principle, the support, the end of my life! grant, I beseech Thee, grant that I may live united with Thee, that I may live through Thee, that I may live for Thee, to the glory and joy of Thy Heart, whereby Thou effectest such marvelous, such delightful things.*

----

* The things whereof the author speaks in this Chapter are very useful and consoling. But, although there is nothing in them which cannot be understood, yet it may be of use to give some explanation, and to develop that which, in the matter here treated, may be asserted upon theological grounds.

The Head of the mystical Body of Christ, or of the Church, is Christ; its members are the faithful. But between the Head and the members, as the author concisely says, there exists a union:

1. *Substantial*, not simply moral, such as exists, for example, between the head and the citizens of a commonwealth.

2. *Spiritual*, in this sense, that it is not a physical union, namely, effected by a cohesion or a mingling of the material parts or molecules, except during the time that the sacred species of the Eucharist continue in a person. But it is, on this account, no less a substantial union; for the cohesion

CHAPTER VI.

THE MOST SACRED HEART OF JESUS UNITES THE
CHURCH MILITANT ON EARTH WITH THE CHURCH
TRIUMPHANT IN HEAVEN.

1. *The voice of Jesus.*—My Child, I am established Head over the whole Church, the glorious
part whereof triumphs with Me in heaven.

This part, this Church Triumphant, to which
the rest will one day exultingly ascend, is the

---

and mingling of material entities is in the end nothing but
accident. It is in this union, of which we are speaking, that
the Spirit of Christ informs the living members.

3. *Personal,* in some manner. For this whole mystical Body
forms one person. And Christ, as the Head, gives that which
is the principal in this personality. He, indeed, is not the
whole and sole person, since the person is effected by the
whole subject, for which the members also are to be taken
into account; but He is that whence the members have
spiritual life, and whereby they are informed and governed.
This, however, is not an *hypostatic* union, which is also called
personal. For, in the *hypostatic* union, the Person of the
Word so assumed the human nature, that in this nature, in
no respect any personality obtains, and that there is in every
respect only one Person, that of the Word; but in the union
of which we are speaking, every member is already a subject or person; not, indeed, in as much as he is a member of
Christ's mystical Body, but in as much as this member can,
in another respect, exist for himself, and can be the *principle
which,* as the Schoolmen say, of actions. But the human nature in Christ is only the *principle by which* of actions, and can
be, in no respect, the *principle which* of the same: therefore,
this union is *hypostatic* and personal. On the other hand, the
members of Christ's mystical Body are, indeed, the *principle
by which* of actions, for as much as they are considered as

society of all the Angels and Saints, illustrious for victories, crowned with laurels everlasting, wholly and immutably devoted to My glory and love, by far the most pleasing and most dear to My Heart.

What wonder, then, if My Heart was carried away with this glorious portion into the land of the living, into the kingdom of everduring bliss? But behold! at the same time, by a prodigy of love, It was retained in the Sacrament with the Church Militant.

In this manner, therefore, It is present with both,

---

members of the mystical Body; but they can exist and be considered as *so many principles which* of actions, for as much as they are considered single or individual subjects. Hence it is quite manifest that the *hypostatic* union is greater, more intimate, and more admirable than the one of which we speak.

We are, however, truly members of Christ, and we can be said to be: "Flesh of His Flesh" (according to St. Paul), just as the soul, which is the principal in man, can say of the members of her body: This is my member; I inform such and such other member: whence it is truly her member. Whence also Christ calls us rightly His true members, His flesh, etc.

That which principally constitutes or unites this mystical Body, according to some, is the Holy Eucharist. According to this, they deem, that these words of Christ are explained best and in the most obvious meaning: "Unless ye eat the Flesh of the Son of man . . . ye shall not have life in you." And those others: "He that eats My Flesh . . . *abides* in Me and I in him."

The life of which there is here treated, whereby Christ informs the members of His mystical Body, is not animal life, as is plain, but supernatural life, as the author says. Whence such members as are corrupted by mortal sin, are indeed members of this mystical Body, but dried up and dead; and, if they do not return to life, to be one day wholly cut off from the Body. (P. J. A. Cens.)

and joining both by Itself and in Itself, It makes the two one.

2. Both have in Me the same victim: the Triumphant, indeed, has the Lamb standing as if slain, a victim which is not now immolated, but, being immolated formerly, is adored: and the Church Militant possesses the same Lamb of God that takes away the sins of the world, a continued Sacrifice, which is offered in every place—a clean Oblation.

Both, likewise, use the same table: the one, in heaven, is filled without mystery with the Bread of Angels, for which, as they eat thereof, they are ever longing, and wherewith they are at the same time, ever satiated: the other, on earth, enjoys the same food, under the vail of mystery, in a manner adapted to her present condition.

Lastly, both are refreshed at the same fountain: for the one that reigns above, is inebriated with perpetual delights, from the torrent of divine pleasure, springing up from My Heart into everlasting life: the other, that struggles here below, draws, with gladness, from the same gushing spring, the waters of grace, of consolation, and of blessedness.

3. Making, in this manner, both parts one, My Heart brings it to pass, in the sacred Tabernacle, that there exists between them a continued and never-ceasing communication and fellowship.

For, wherever I am in the most Holy Sacrament, the Angels are continually descending from heaven, to minister to Me, to adore, to love, to praise Me.

And astonished at the love that forces Me, so marvelously and so gently, to abide with men, they, as in heaven before the throne of My glory, so upon earth before the Sacrament of My love, with unceasing voice cry out: Holy, holy, holy, Lord God Omnipotent! all the earth is full of Thy glory.

And when they depart, behold! they mount up into heaven, having golden vials, full of odors, which are the prayers of the Saints,—of the faithful worshiping Me in spirit, with truth and holiness: these they offer up before the throne of the divine Majesty, and expose the wants of their companions, who are combating upon earth.

At the intercession of the Angels and Saints, and at My Heart's own desire, mercy and grace descend to console and refresh mortals, and fill them with gladness from above.

And thus, Child, whilst the inhabitants of heaven fully enjoy everlasting bliss, the faithful here are unceasingly being prepared by the most Holy Sacrament for the same blessedness: and they that are prepared are constantly entering the heavenly tabernacles.

4. Therefore, in My Heart is the Church, the one in heaven as well as the one upon earth, united. Itself is the principle, by which the whole becomes one, and the parts have a mutual and continual intercourse.

For it pleased Me to join together therein all things, whether in heaven or on earth; so that all, being rooted and strengthened in the same, may abound through My Heart.

It was necessary that this should be done, My Child: for, unless I had liberally bestowed the grace of My Heart, that men, fortified, yea, elevated thereby, might attain to the heavenly fellowship, they could never, by the powers of their own nature, have reached that supernatural beatitude.

In this manner, then, didst thou draw nigh to the City of the living God, the heavenly Jerusalem, to the fellowship of many thousands of Angels, and to the Church of the first-born, who are written in the heavens.

5. Admire thou, My Child, these sublime dispensations: revere these mysteries of love: take advantage, for the advancement of thy soul, of so great a goodness of My Heart, which grants thee, although a weak mortal, to hold intimate communion with the Saints and Angels, and from the same treasure with them to draw forth blissfulness.

See, how the Church Militant, enraptured with this love of My Heart, vies, by her praises and manifestations of gratefulness, to emulate the Church Triumphant.

For, as the Church in heaven has no rest, but without end praises Me, forever glorifies Me: so the Church on earth ceases not to honor, to celebrate Me.

Let not thy sentiments, My Child, be different from the sentiments of the Church, thy Mother: but have thou the same sentiments that she entertains.

When thou appearest before My beloved Tabernacle, expand thy heart, give thyself up to devotion, give glory to the Lord thy God.

Unite thyself with the Church Militant; join thyself also to the Church Triumphant: thus, associated with the faithful, and with the Spirits above, praise thy Saviour-God with the joyful exultation of mouth and heart.

Fall prostrate with veneration, adore, entreat, enjoy My presence.

6. *The voice of the Disciple* —O most loving Jesus! how admirable is the love of Thy Heart, whereby, to cheer and console me on earth, Thou didst cause me, in some manner, to enjoy here below the bliss and companionship of heaven!

Thus, O love incomprehensible! thus Thou didst soothe, in a wonderful way, the bitterness of my banishment; yea, didst change it into heavenly sweetness.

And should I not love Thee after this? should I not praise Thee? should not Thy love be ever in my heart, Thy praise upon my lips?

Yea, I will love, I will praise Thee, O Lord: I will love and praise Thee as much as I can, and I wish that I were able as much as I ought.

I invite heaven and earth to join me in loving and praising Thee.

Enravished with love for Thee, let the Angels and Saints, all the just and the faithful praise Thee in the most sweet Sacrament! Let the Triumphant together with the Militant Church, cause heaven and earth to resound with hymns of love and praise!

Nay, let all things created, visible and invisible, animate and inanimate, that do Thy bidding, not cease day nor night to praise and glorify Thee, because Thou art worthy of every praise, of every glory, world without end.

7. O Thou most charming of friends, Jesus, Thou the bliss of all the Angels and Saints! Where on earth shall I seek for happiness, if I do not seek for it here!

Here I become the companion of the Saints, here I dwell in the midst of Angels, here I find the very delights of heaven.

O ineffable goodness! O infinite sweetness! **Thou** who drawest to thyself from above the heavenly Spirits, draw me also unto Thee; that here I may rest, here, amid the Angels, gaze upon Thee, adore Thee, praise Thee, supplicate Thee.

Whenever I am elsewhere detained, O do Thou draw hither my heart and mind; that, in spirit at least, I may be here with Thee; that, by frequent thought and affection, I may converse with Thee, may be occupied with Thee.

What can I desire better or sweeter in this world than here to enjoy Thee? Here is the new earthly Paradise, where I long and resolve to live, until I am transported hence into Thy heavenly kingdom, and triumph forever with the Angels and Saints.

CHAPTER VII.

THE MOST SACRED HEART OF JESUS UNITES TO-GETHER THE CHURCH, THAT SUFFERS IN PURGA-TORY, WITH THE MILITANT AND TRIUMPHANT CHURCH.

1. *The voice of Jesus* —My Child, none shall enter the kingdom of heaven, the Church Triumphant, unless he is holy, stainless. For nothing defiled shall enter therein.

Whosoever leaves this world, defiled with sin which may be forgiven in the world to come, shall be saved, yet so as by fire.

In this fire, My Child, is the Suffering Church, a multitude of souls, that formerly, beneath My standard, fought for My sake against the flesh, the world, and the devil, but in the battle were, in one way or another, wanting in their duty, and, during life, did not repair their shortcomings

They suffer, My Child, and the more vehemently, since, as they now understand things more fully, they also long the more ardently to be with Me in the triumph of the heavenly kingdom.

Relying on this certain hope of bliss, they experience on this very account more violent sufferings: for hope delayed afflicts the soul.

And, although the soul is glad to be there cleansed, and would not go thence uncleansed, she, however, finds no rest, but, impelled by an excessive longing, she cries out: When shall I come, oh when shall I come and appear before the face of my God!

2. These souls I cherish, My Child, because in life they loved Me, and did not unto the end leave My standard.

Their names are written in the Book of Life, and their rewards are safely laid up in My Heart.

Meanwhile, the grace of My Heart informs them, the virtue of My Heart relieves them, the boundless love of My Heart comforts them.

Thus, through My Heart, is the Church Suffering vivified, as well as the Church Militant, and the Triumphant: and in My Heart these three are one.

Animated by the supernatural life of My Heart, the one that is glorified in heaven, the one that is being cleansed in Purgatory, the one that combats upon earth, all concur in one and the same end, which is lasting triumph for the unending glory of the divine Majesty.

3. And, since all receive life out of My Heart, and return the fruit of this life to My Heart, all good things become common among them in My Heart; the charity whereof, penetrating into heaven, the earth, and Purgatory, distributes them to all the members, to the advantage of each and all.

But as the souls in Purgatory can no longer gain any merit for themselves, and cannot be assisted by men, except through their suffrages, My Heart drew out of Its love a means to help them in the most bountiful manner.

For It willed that the Eucharistic Sacrifice should be applicable to them, in view whereof, the divine Majesty either sets them free, or, certainly, shortens or lessens their sufferings.

It is, then, owing to My Heart that those souls are in this manner relieved and purified by the virtue of My Blood, which is applied to them through the Holy Sacrifice.

Thus, My Child, Purgatory is emptied, heaven filled; and to those sojourning on earth the sweetest consolation is given, in regard to them that have departed this life.

4. Behold, therefore, how beautiful is the whole Church, all the parts whereof are perpetually communicating with each other in My Heart.

The Militant part, adorned with the victories already obtained, and marching onward in pursuit of new ones, rejoices with those that rejoice in the Triumphant, and weeps with them that weep in the Suffering Church.

Love, compassion, joy, prayers are ever passing to and fro through every part.

Rejoice, My Child, that thou art not of the number

or them that have no hope beyond the tomb, but of those whom,—united as they are in My Heart,—neither the distance of places, nor the empire of death can separate.

5. Take to thyself the Spirit of My Heart: as often as thou art present at the most Holy Sacrifice, humbly remember the faithful departed: for whilst the sacred and adorable victim lies before thee, it is especially a wholesome thought, a most religious practice, to pray for the dead, that they may be loosed from sins.

In the same Spirit also, if thou gainest any indulgence, which may be beneficial to them, apply the same for their relief and consolation.

And when thou art united to Me in Holy Communion, then, above all, do thou commend to My Heart those whom thou didst hold dear in this world, as well as the rest, for whom it is proper that thou shouldst pray.

Call to mind, Child, with how great a feeling of gratefulness and love, these souls will endeavor to repay thee, whom, by thy prayers and suffrages, thou didst introduce into heavenly bliss.

This devotion, this charity toward the souls suffering in Purgatory, is a peculiar characteristic of the Disciples of My Heart; who, after Its example, transcend the bounds of this world, and whomsoever they find capable of being helped, they comfort by their charity.

6. *The voice of the Disciple.*—O most sweet Jesus! what a Heart is Thine! how admirable! how bountiful!

For, behold! in Thy Heart, I find even those whom I had lost out of this life; and I am once more united with them, whom in this life I cherished.

Here I hold with them an intercourse full of sweetness: here I can solace both them and myself.

Making use with thankfulness of this most consoling means, through Thy very Heart, I present to Thee, for the relief of the souls of the faithful departed, the fruit of every Holy Sacrifice of the Mass wheresoever offered.

And, in union therewith, I offer up whatsoever good works, through Thy holy grace, I do possess, that Thou mayst deign to wash away all the defilements of those souls, and thus make them worthy of the fellowship of the Church Triumphant.

I also offer to Thee my prayers and supplications, especially for my departed parents, brothers, sisters, friends; for all, in fine, who have done good to me, whether in things temporal or spiritual.

Those souls also do I specially commend, of whose sufferings I may, in any manner, have been the cause.

But particularly do I pray for those departed, who, in the present life, have been devoted Disciples of Thy most Sacred Heart.

Finally, I do humbly entreat Thee for them all; that, released from sufferings, they may enter into everlasting joys, and there be mindful of me.

7. O Jesus, Thou who consolest all Thine, and renewest all things! when I am here with Thee before Thy sacred Tabernacle, the world of sense seems to vanish away: for here the spiritual world is thrown open to me: and oh! how vast, how marvelous! with what mighty and countless wonders does it appear filled!

Here I hold communion with the Church Triumphant in heaven, and with the Church that is purified in Purgatory: here I converse, in freedom and holiness, with the Angels and all the inhabitants of heaven: here I deal with my kindred and friends who dwell in the invisible world.

And to whom am I indebted for all this, if not to Thy Heart? Here, therefore, here is the place of my choice, the place of peace and repose, the place of joy and consolation.

O how good it is for me to be here, most bountiful Jesus, source of every good! Let others go whither they prefer; let them be entertained by the objects wherein they delight: I, so often as Thy Will may grant it to me, I will constantly repair hither; here will I entertain myself with Thy own; here will I treat with Thee, heart to Heart, in the plenitude of thy sweetness.

CHAPTER VIII.

OF THE INEFFABLE OCCUPATIONS OF THE MOST SACRED HEART OF JESUS, IN THE SACRAMENT, WITH RESPECT TO HIS FATHER.

1. *The voice of the Disciple.*—If the works of Thy Sacred Heart, Lord Jesus, in regard to every portion of Thy Church, are so wonderful, so sublime, of which kind, I pray, are Its occupations with respect to Thy Father, by whom Thou art

loved infinitely, and whom Thou also lovest infinitely?

These, indeed, are mysteries so great, that, were any one, in order to unfold them, to speak the language of men and Angels, he should still be as a child that knows not how to speak.

Yea, Lord, these are secrets which it is not given to man to utter.

Do Thou Thyself, therefore, reveal them to us, so much as Thou knowest them to be useful for Thy glory and our good; that we may be enabled to worship and love Thee worthily in Thy most Holy sacrament.

2. *The voice of Jesus.*—Listen reverently, My Child, attend religiously: and I will unfold to thee the divine secrets.

Here, in My innermost retreat, in the light uncreated, I contemplate, with Heart enraptured, the divine Essence, and am infinitely delighted in Its perfections.

Hence, My Heart is inundated with unutterable joys: and It is now the more abundantly and the more delightfully overflowed with these, the more It was, during Its mortal life, filled with bitterness.

Amid these splendors, amid these divine ecstasies, the Father is in Me and I in the Father; and, without the sound of words, the Father speaks to Me and I to Him.

Here the Father communicates to Me the eternal counsels of His Wisdom, the decrees of His supreme Omnipotence, the most lovely good pleasure of His Goodness.

These My Heart embraces in return, and finds Its pleasure therein.

3. For My Heart loves the Father supremely, and with such a love for Him does It burn, that It never grows cool, nor loses aught of Its ardor.

Behold, My Child, a love with which no other heart can love the Father, since every other heart is only referred and united to Him as the heart of a son, not by nature, as is My Heart, but solely by adoption.

In this, then, My Heart is alone and unrivaled. Therefore, also, the Father is delighted, above the love of all the Saints and Angels, with the love of My Heart, because it is the love of the Heart of His only-begotten Son.

4. As I am the son of God the Father, and as all things which the Father has are Mine, I enjoy them all, I use them all in the Holy Spirit.

Whatsoever things the Father does, these I also do: I create, preserve, perfect all the same things with the Father and the Holy Spirit.

But as the Son of Man, I, in some manner, annihilate Myself before the presence of the Father, and pour forth, before Him, perpetual adorations.

Here I worship His divine Wisdom, Goodness, Power, and other perfections, in such a manner that neither the Cherubim, nor Seraphim, nor any other created beings can so glorify the same.

5. But, whilst, in this mystical and sublime solitude of the divine Sacrament, I am thus alone treating with the Father in the Holy Spirit, My Heart is not unfaithful, so as to forget the work of Its predilection among the children of men.

For them My Heart does unceasingly offer to the Father Its manifold and stupendous sacrifices.

If any there are infirm or drooping in spirit, or

dead, here It prays for them with unspeakable groanings.

And It pours Itself out, with all Its affections before the Father, that he who is just, may be justified still, and he that is holy may be still sanctified.

Nor do I cease with My Heart to offer prayers and supplications for all, whom I am not ashamed to call brethren before the Father:

Saying, that all may be one; as Thou, Father, in Me, and I in Thee, so they also may be one in Us.

I in them and Thou in Me; that they may be made perfect in one: that the world may know that Thou hast sent Me, and hast loved them, as Thou also hast loved Me.

I pray not that thou wouldst take them out of the world, but that Thou wouldst keep them from evil. Sanctify them in the truth.

Father, I will that where I am, they also whom Thou hast given Me, may be with Me; that they may see My glory which Thou hast given Me.

6. Behold, My Child, the occupations in regard to the Father, which, here in the holy Tabernacle, My Heart uninterruptedly continues.

Do thou endeavor, when here thou appearest in My presence, to imitate these occupations of My Heart.

Raise thy heart above all sensible objects: and with the Church, thy Mother, who, as the symbol of her faith, keeps a constant light burning before the most Holy Sacrament, contemplate, by the light of Faith, thy God, thy Saviour, present to thee.

In silence, with deep reverence, and pious affection, meditate on all those things, wherewith My Heart is here employed.

Hither do thou frequently resort, My Child, here pour out thy heart: here do thou love: here delight in My Heart.

7. *The voice of the Disciple.*—O how marvelous, O how divine Thy occupations, my Jesus, in the sacred Tabernacle !

These, Lord, these, if they are pondered, if they are understood, teach that which neither books can show, nor talents make known.

O divine solitude of Jesus in the Sacrament! here is the fountain of heavenly secrets: this is the school of contemplation, where souls are taught to rise above things sensible, to go to the Father, and the Son, and the Holy Ghost; to gaze upon the wonderful works of God, to pray with mind and heart; to speculate on things mystical and divine.

The eye has not seen, the ear has not heard, no sense has perceived—by faith alone it is descried, by pure love it is tasted—how great a felicity, how great a sweetness, how great an abundance of all good things lies here concealed.

Here, Lord Jesus, is the retreat, wherein, at rest Thyself, Thou puttest all things to rest; wherein Thou Thyself occupied, occupiest us; wherein, Holy Thyself, Thou sanctifiest us.

Here is the spot which the Angels surround: wherein pure souls long to make their abode.

Here, most sweet Jesus, here will I ever seek Thee; here, I implore Thee, let me deserve, in Thy light, to behold the light wherein Thou dwellest; to be occupied with Thee, to be delighted with the wonders which Thou workest with the Father, and the Holy Ghost; to be absorbed by the flood of divine fire, which bursts forth from Thy Heart; in fine, to be transformed in Thee by love.

Bring me, I beseech Thee, into the very secrets of Thy Heart, and keep me with Thee in this divine repose, where all merely human emotion ceases, where everything that moves, springs from the Godhead, and tends to the Godhead.

If I have found favor in Thy eyes, O Lord, give me admittance, I entreat Thee; unite me with Thee by the indissoluble bond of love; fill all my faculties within and without, that I may live of Thee and for Thee.

CHAPTER IX.

THE MOST SACRED HEART OF JESUS, IN THE BLESSED SACRAMENT, HONORS HIS FATHER INFINITELY.

1. *The voice of Jesus.*—Now, dearly beloved, is the Son of man glorified, and God is glorified in Him.

How much, thinkest thou, is the Father glorified, how much is he honored by the Son; who, for the honor and glory of the Father, is not now seen on earth, but hidden in the Sacrament?

The Father is worthy of all worship, praise, and homage: and, therefore, do I, in this sacred mystery, exhibit the same to Him, by the boundless humiliations to which I here subject Myself.

So much the more is the Majesty of God the

Father exalted, the more the Son, made man, humbles Himself, that He may honor the Father.

Measure, if thou canst, the depth of humility, into which I here descended for the glory of God the Father. Into a deep abyss I certainly did go down by My Incarnation; into a deeper one I sank during My lifetime: into the very deepest I lowered Myself by My death. But here, I have sunk beneath all those depths: here I exceed all those excesses, and continue to do the same.

Endeavor as much as thou canst, struggle as much as thou wilt; thou mayst wonder, thou mayst be astounded, but never shalt thou be able to grasp or understand neither the depth, nor the breadth of the abyss, into which My Heart here lowers Itself.

The very Angels are amazed, when, struck with awe, they gaze upon Me, whom they acknowledge and worship as their Lord, humbling Myself more deeply than they themselves could possibly do.

Powerfully, indeed, are they thereby enkindled and stimulated to glorify the divine Majesty, whose infinite grandeur they cannot comprehend, but whom they thus more clearly perceive, by My example, as worthy of infinite honor.

2. If the state itself, My Child, wherein I have here placed Myself, honors the divine Majesty so exceedingly, how much glory do all the things which I perform for Him, in this condition, give to Him!

Judge not by the outward appearance: things divine are not to be estimated in a human sense.

All My acts, in this Sacrament, since they are the acts of a Person of infinite dignity, unseen though they be, and displaying no splendor to strike the senses of men, are of infinite value.

Wherefore, My Child, the least motion of My Heart for the glory of My Father glorifies Him incomparably more than all things whatsoever done by mere creatures.

Call to mind the great exploits, the illustrious actions, and immortal deeds, which men have achieved for the world, and whereby they have spread their renown over the earth: behold, all these, compared with a single act of My Heart, what are they except smoke, compared to a blazing fire?

Nay more, add together the virtues, the sufferings, the heroic actions, whereby all the Saints, from Abel even to the last of the just, have rendered themselves truly distinguished: these also, My Child, though pleasing and honorable to God, are infinitely below one single sacrifice, whereby My Heart here honors God.

What more? Great, indeed, and glorious are the praises and thanksgivings, which the Spirits above, the inhabitants of heaven, offer to the divine Majesty: yet, greater, and more glorious beyond comparison, are those which My Heart, by one single immolation of Itself upon the altar, presents to Him.

3. Rightly, therefore, does the holy Church rejoice, for that she has for her Bridegroom the Son of God, who honors for her the divine Majesty, as much as He deserves to be honored: and gives Him thanks such as are due to Him.

This she daily acknowledges with grateful feeling, when, through Me, she draws nigh to the

Father, and says to Him: Through Him, and with Him, and in Him is to Thee, God, almighty Father, in the unity of the Holy Ghost, all honor and glory.

Formed by this divine institution, and united to Me, she dares, without fear of refusal, pray the Father and thank Him, through Me, Christ the Lord.

And, since she knows that only through Me her acts are supernaturally acceptable to God, whatsoever she does, whatsoever she offers, she performs it all in union with Me, for the praise and glory of the divine Majesty, as well as for her own advantage unto life everlasting.

4. Blessed those souls, My Child, that, moved by the spirit of their holy Mother, the Church, with ...er unite themselves to My Heart in the Sacrament; and thus strive to pay to God the honor and thanksgiving, which they owe to Him, but which, of themselves, they are unable to render.

Remember, Child, how much thou owest to My heavenly Father, who so cherished thee that, in so marvelous and sweet a manner, He gave thee His only-begotten Son: who so loves thee, that He imparts to thee, in so great an abundance, the gifts of the Spirit the Comforter sent in My name.

How sweet a debt is gratefulness, if thou hast a noble heart! And what can be so sweet, if thou hast the heart of a son, as to display a grateful mind toward the best of Fathers?

And, if thou desirest to be thankful to God, like a son to his father, honor Him: for He says: If I am a Father, where is My honor?

5. *The voice of the Disciple.*—O eternal Father! from whom, as from their highest source, I have

received all things; nay, what infinitely surpasses all, Thy only Son Himself, with all His merits and ineffable favors, the Holy Spirit likewise, and His graces and multiform gifts: what return shall I make to Thee, for blessings so great, so numerous?

If there must be a certain proportion between gifts and the thankfulness for them, behold! I am, every way, powerless to repay the gratitude I owe to Thee, since there is no comparison between Thy infinite gifts and my imperfect gratefulness.

When, besides, I consider that all the divine perfections are infinite, and that these infinite perfections, even if Thou hadst never bestowed any favor upon me, are, for their own sake to be worshiped in a limitless manner, I am overwhelmed by the weight of my debt to which, I acknowledge, I am of myself forever unequal.

But behold! Jesus, Thy only and most beloved Son, who, for Thy love and mine, abides with me upon earth, makes good what I owe to Thee, but am unable to repay.

Through Him, therefore, who knows all Thy blessings bestowed upon me, and fully comprehends Thy perfections, I do here, in union with the love of His Heart, avow the obedience of My dependence, and render to Thee a worship ever most acceptable in Him, in whom Thou art always well-pleased.

6. With all my heart do I rejoice, for that Thou art infinitely perfect, as well as liberal to me; and that, in the Heart of Jesus, Thy well-beloved Son, I possess wherewith I am able to return Thee due honor and gratitude.

Wherefore, I offer to Thee all the virtues of the

most Sacred Heart of Jesus, Thy Son, and all the acts which He ceases not to perform, for the honor of Thy Majesty, and the salvation of the whole world, in the most Blessed Sacrament of His love.

Whatsoever I am able to do, is as nothing in comparison of what I owe to Thee: and this is itself a part of Thy praise, that what Thou deservest, is above every power of mine.

But, look upon the face of Jesus, Thy Son, who is the image of Thy Goodness and of Thy every perfection; and, for Thy glory, do Thou receive all the fullness of the Holiness of His Heart.

Deign, I beseech Thee, Holy Father, to accept the merits, satisfactions, and praises of Thy only-begotten Son, as an atonement for all the insults with which I myself and others have, at times, dishonored Thee.

For which insults I would gladly, were I able, make amends with my blood and with every other sacrifice: but, since whatsoever I may do, is, of itself, by no means sufficient for this, I unite it all with the infinite merits of the Heart of Jesus, Thy Son, and thus present it to Thee.

7. Through the same Heart of Thy Beloved Son—through which I pay Thee a tribute of honor, and render Thee thanks for all the blessings bestowed upon me—I humbly implore new graces for Thy glory.

Above all, grant me, I entreat Thee, a great, a generous, a tender love for Thy Son, the Beloved of my soul, the most sweet Jesus, who stays here so lovingly with me.

Grant that, animated with the sentiments of His

Heart, and united thereto, I may live by Him—through whom alone I am able to come to Thee.

Give me for this, I beseech Thee, the fullness of the Holy Spirit, who ever animated and guided the Heart of Jesus.

Let that divine Spirit replenish my whole heart, inflame it with love for Jesus, and stimulate it ever with hunger and thirst for His most delicious Sacrament.

CHAPTER X.

THE MOST SACRED HEART OF JESUS, BY ITS SELF-OFFERINGS IN THE MOST HOLY SACRAMENT, APPEASES THE DIVINE JUSTICE, AND PROCURES FOR US MEASURELESS GRACES.

1. *The voice of Jesus.*—My Child, thus says the Lord: In every place there is sacrificed and offered to My Name a clean Oblation; for great is My Name among the nations.

This, My Child, is that Victim of salvation, which, once offered on the Holy Mountain for the Redemption of all, is offered daily throughout the world to apply My merits to each one in particular unto the forgiveness of sins, which are daily committed.

For, knowing that the nature of them that were to believe in Me, would be such, that they should all offend in many things; moved by the love of My Heart, I instituted a Sacrifice, not only of supreme worship and thanksgiving, but also of atonement and impetration: by the offering of which, God, being appeased, after granting the grace and gift of repentance, would also pardon crimes and offenses, and liberally bestow His favors.

The same Sacrifice, that I formerly offered upon the cross, I now offer upon the altar,—not indeed in a bloody manner as then, but with the same love of Heart.

As often, therefore, as this ever-enduring Sacrifice is offered, as often as the remembrance of this Victim is celebrated, the work of man's Redemption is renewed.

Upon this Oblation the Almighty Father ever deigns to look with a propitious and favorable eye, and He holds the same more acceptable than the holy sacrifice, the spotless offering which the High-priest, Melchisedech, presented to Him.

Whence also the Church, full of confidence, prays God the Father, that hereby the faithful may be freed from all evils, past, present, and future; and that, assisted by the help of the divine mercy, they may be free from sin, and secure from all disturbance.

For, what can the eternal Father refuse, when He beholds Me, His only Son, through zeal for His honor and love for men, immolated upon the altar and lying there the victim of His glory; whilst My Heart and My very Blood cry out and intercede for My brethren?

2. Most assuredly this Oblation, so pre-eminently clean,—presented by the ministry of priests, through Myself, with the infinite affection of My Heart, to the Heavenly Father,—is ever pleasing to Him, is ever regarded for its dignity.

Thus, indeed, many others are made priests, because death suffered them not to remain, and because this Victim is offered in every place: but I, since I endure forever, possess an everlasting priesthood. Whence also I can save, forever, those that, through Me, draw nigh to God.

The earth, therefore, is, as it were, uninterruptedly crimsoned by the offering of this most sacred Victim; and its fragrance, blending with the virtues and merits of My Heart, is unceasingly ascending to the Father for an odor of sweetness.

If the many sins of men do much offend the divine Majesty, and provoke His justice, this holy Sacrifice does incomparably more to honor and appease the same; since His only-begotten Son pleases Him infinitely more than all sinners displease Him.

What land on earth is not, in some manner, dyed with the blood of My Heart, or what spot is excluded from Its prayers and protection? What region, then, in this world, can God smite, without striking a place defended by the Heart of His Son?

Behold! sinners have sinned, and they were not, according to their deserts, cast into the pool of fire everlasting: yea, they are even suffered to live, not indeed that they may continue to sin, but that they may save themselves.

For I place Myself between God My Father and the sinners; for them I offer Myself, and make intercession: Look Thou, holy and righteous Father, behold My hands, and My Side: see how much they have cost Thy Son! by the love, wherewith Thou lovest Me, spare, Father, spare Thy people.

3. My Child, ought not the sinner to yield to so great a goodness, whereby I keep hell shut, lest he be swallowed up therein; whereby I restrain the demons, lest they carry him off; whereby I stay the arm of the Almighty, lest the bolts of divine justice destroy him?

Thou shouldst indeed wonder, didst thou see all the secret means which My Heart here employs to save souls; which, unless I turned away the divine wrath from them, should soon be deservedly devoured.

If now, as of old, sudden and immutable punishment is not inflicted upon the wicked; they should remember that it is owing to the Sacrifice of My Heart, whereby the whole world is preserved.

Lo, Child, how My Heart loves, everywhere mindful of men, even of the most wretched; everywhere promoting the salvation of souls.

4. With what sentiments, then, is it befitting that thou shouldst approach this mystery, whence thou mayst obtain remedies so great! Whence thou mayst secure graces and favors of every kind: for it is of infinite value.

But, although this Sacrifice is of infinite value, the fruit thereof is, however, applied to man in a limited manner, according to the liveliness of the faith and devotedness, the disposition of the soul of him that assists thereat, or for whom it is offered up; as the Church, taught by the Holy Spirit, insinuates, when, during the Sacrifice, she prays God to remember His servants, and all the bystanders, whose faith is acknowledged, and whose devotedness is known by Him.

Wherefore, My Child, do thou celebrate or hear

Mass with a lively faith, a true devotion, a holy disposition; that thou mayst deserve to obtain the greatest fruit of the Sacrifice, and secure all the graces for which thou prayest.

For the divine Clemency grants, without doubt, to them that are rightly disposed, whatsoever favors they ask during the Mass; nay, frequently bestows liberally blessings for which they did not petition.

Remember this, Child, that piously to hear Mass is a most wholesome means to keep thyself from dangers, to preserve thyself from an unforeseen death, and to follow the path of righteousness.

If thou wilt lay up merits, so often as it is permitted, be thou present at the Sacrifice of the Mass, for, by the devout hearing of one Mass, thou meritest far more than if, through devotion, thou didst macerate thyself for a long time by fasts and austerities, or didst undertake a distant pilgrimage.

Lastly, if thou desirest to make thyself agreeable to My Heart, assist at Mass as frequently and as devoutly as possible; for this Sacrifice glorifies the most Holy Trinity, rejoices the Angels and Saints, enriches the just with grace, helps sinners for their conversion, relieves the souls detained in purgatory, in fine, cheers and comforts the whole Church on earth.

5. *The voice of the Disciple.*—O most sweet Jesus! how great the mercy! how disinterested the love! how resistless the kindness! how astounding the goodness of Thy Heart!

Even for them who, as much as in them lies, sadden Thy Heart, Thou ceasest not to immolate Thyself; that Thou mayst stay the weight of the divine anger, whilst they betake themselves in safety beneath the protection of Thy Heart.

And I, for I will confess it, although so plentifully blessed with the gifts of Thy Heart, I, most ungrateful of men, have grieved Thy Heart.

To the great mercy, to the infinite goodness of Thy Heart it is owing, that I am not destroyed, that I still remain unharmed.

6. O Heart of Jesus! Heart full of sweetness and delight! most loving Heart, every way poured out through an excess of love! how can I possess a heart worthy of the name of a human heart, if I do not love Thee in return?

Who, O Lord, who can resist Thy love, when he considers, how, in the most Holy Eucharist, Thou shelterest us in Thy Heart, and offerest Thyself to Thy Father for us!

O my Jesus! what would happen shouldst Thou cast away the sinner from the protection of Thy Heart! how dreadfully would the thunderbolts of divine justice hurl him into the lowest depths of hell!

Far, O Lord, far be it from me, that, by provoking Thy Heart, through ingratitude, through sin, I should expose myself to so great a danger!

7. Grant, O my Saviour! that I may be more eager to please Thee, who art so solicitous for me; that I may love Thee more fervently; that, through gratitude and love, I may visit Thee more frequently, and assist oftener or more devoutly at Thy holy Sacrifice.

O how little do I love Thee, if I do not daily come hither, to be present at Mass; here to meditate, to converse with Thee, to beg much of Thee.

How considerable a time of the day do I give to worldly occupations! how much to rest and to recreate myself! and cannot I spend here with Thee half an hour for the affair of my everlasting salvation, and for the divine glory; the more as I should take hence Thy grace and blessing, whereby my affairs themselves, and all the rest, would be made holy and prosperous?

Yea, O Lord, daily will I be here with Thee. And, if I am necessarily hindered from being bodily present, even then I will be here in spirit with Thee.

CHAPTER XI.

THE MOST SACRED HEART OF JESUS, IN THE SACRAMENT OF HIS LOVE, IS OUR GREATEST CONSOLATION ON EARTH.

1. *The voice of Jesus.*—My Child, behold My Tabernacle with men! behold here I dwell with them. Here I Myself console them that come, and I wipe away every tear from their eyes.

And, as there is no place on earth, where affliction does not sometimes shed tears, My Heart multiplies Its miracles, that It may everywhere multiply consolations.

Hence, thou mayst learn, My Child, that the mercy of My Heart is greater than man's misery can be.

If any remedy, if any comfort is required in misfortune, here it is found in My Heart; here it is drawn with gladness from the same.

Behold! here I make all things new: things

heavy I change into light, things tasteless I make to be savory: bitterness I turn into sweetness, mourning into joy of heart.

Nay, more, this vale of tears I transform into a Paradise; earth into heaven before its time. For here is the plentifulness of all the good things of heaven, here is the fountain of peace and gladness; here are the Angels, here am I Myself, here is bliss ever-enduring.

2. These are the wonders of love, Child, which My Heart works for thee, that thou mayst not be cast down amid the tribulations of life; but that, attracted by the goodness of My Heart, thou mayst come to this overflowing fountain of all consolation.

If thou hast once duly tasted Its sweetness, thou wilt soon forget every affliction of the past, or wilt even deem it all joy.

When, here before the Tabernacle, thou pourest forth thy heart; above all, when, after holy Communion, thou speakest to Me heart to Heart, and resignest thyself wholly to Me; then wilt thou perceive that affliction yields to consolation, fear to confidence, lukewarmness to fervor of heart.

If, overlooking Me, thou runnest elsewhere to find some one to relieve and help thee in thy dejection, thou shalt often be able to say: I sought some one to comfort me, but I found none.

But hither thou shalt never come in vain: hence thou shalt never depart without relief.

Hither, then, do thou ever fly, that thou mayst receive a remedy for thy troubles; and turn thy sufferings into consoling merits.

3. If misfortune, if loss of possessions or even

if want fill thy heart with groanings and thy eyes
with tears, so as to render thy soul weary of life;
here, My Child, thou shalt find what no mortal can
give thee; here thou shalt obtain a soothing of thy
grief. If thou lookest upon My example, thy
heart shall be comforted: My promise of permanent possessions, which thou shalt receive by sharing My inheritance, after having passed a few days
here below, will cheer up thy spirit: lastly, the,
secret grace of My Heart will not rarely turn the
tears of grief into tears of consolation.

If the world hates thee, if men slight, oppose, or
oppress thee; here, O My Child, here in this mystery of love thou shalt be abundantly comforted:
when thou possessest Me, yea, when thou pressest
Me to thy heart, Me thy Saviour, thy faithful
Friend, thy best and dearest Father, thou wilt be
contented enough to be hidden, to be humbled with
Me, that thou mayst be the more alike and pleasing to My Heart, in order to be forever exalted by
Me among My elect.

And, if thou art afflicted or tormented with pains
of the body and anguish of soul; behold, Child,
behold here is thy solace, which alone can reach
the innermost recesses of the ailing heart, and
which none can hinder, except thyself—by heark-
ening rather to thy own thoughts than to My
whisperings.

Thou shalt also experience that which has been
felt by thousands of faithful souls that came hither
in sorrow, and with an aching heart; and soon, refreshed by the sweetness of the love of My Heart,
went away their hearts dilated with bliss.

If annoyed by temptations, if worn down by

desolateness; hasten hither, My Child. Behold! My Heart invites and awaits thee thus tempted and rendered desolate. It will receive thee with gladness; It will strengthen thee by Its own fortitude; It will fill thee with the sweetness of Its unction.

Shouldst thou even commit a fault, arise quickly, and run thou hither. Here thou shalt easily repair all: here thou shalt recover peace and joy of heart.

O if thou knewest, My Child, with how great a longing to console every one, My Heart watches here at all times,—consoling Itself whenever It comforts some one in his affliction;—thou wouldst then understand whence it is that none, in what trouble soever he may find himself, can come hither well-disposed to My Heart, without receiving consolation.

4. For, in the sacred Tabernacle, thou now possessest Me, the same Saviour, that, whilom, when I lived a mortal life, comforted all: the very same Heart, that, whilst placed in the manger, gave peace to the Shepherds, and filled the Magi with heavenly delight: that, in childhood rejoiced them that came to Me: that, throughout life was the refuge and solace of all.

Thou knowest, My Child, how all the sick and the weak, the blind and the lame, the deaf and the dumb, the wretched and the disconsolate were wont to appeal to My Heart, and implore Its compassion and help.

Was ever one of these disappointed in his hope, by what suffering soever he was bowed down; at what time soever of the day or of the night he came to me?

Did not every one, in whatsoever hour he had recourse to the goodness of My Heart, go away more consoled than he had dared to hope?

And, My Child, all these wonders, all these consolations, My Heart does here ceaselessly renew; but in a manner all the more perfect and useful, the more spiritual it is, and the better adapted to everlasting life.

There, indeed, It healed the diseases of the body: here It cures the ailments, the infirmities and miseries of the soul.

There It freed them that were possessed by the devil, or tormented by him; here It does more, since It guards the faithful against the demon.

There It cleansed those afflicted with leprosy: here It purifies souls, and makes them clean and whiter than snow.

There, by a miracle, It sated thousands of men with a natural food: here It nourishes all the faithful with the Bread of Angels.

There It restored the dead to life: here, what is better beyond comparison, It preserves souls from death.

And as then My Heart, full of compassion, mercy, goodness, was accessible to all; so now It is open to every one, even to the most wretched and afflicted.

Believe not, My Child, even should a spirit suggest the thought, that My Heart does now possess a different feeling, either in respect to God, or with regard to men.

Take heed lest thou deem My Heart, that abides here to comfort thee, different from My Heart, that erewhile, in Its mortal life, so marvelously, so sweetly relieved men, and filled them with every consolation. For every spirit, that thus severs or divides My Heart, is not of God.

6. Dilate thy heart, My Child, and understand, as much as thou art able, what comfort, here, as from a perennial fountain, flows down upon thee from My Heart.

Behold all the consolations, admirable and delightful,—which, during Its mortal life, It imparted to many and various persons,—It bestows in Its Sacramental life upon thee alone.

How much happier, then, art thou, than they that were living at the time of My mortal life! Neither did these, like thyself, uninterruptedly enjoy My presence: neither were they in the same manner, as thou, possessed of Me: nor, lastly, did they receive or enjoy Me, as thyself, O Child of My Heart.

Lo, then, to what a degree My Heart favors thee. In every necessity, therefore in every difficulty whether interior or exterior, do thou fly hither. Here, if thou art guilty, thou shalt obtain pardon, if sick, healing; if downhearted, courage and fortitude; if afflicted, relief and help; if in danger, protection and safety; a remedy for all miseries; always a true and sanctifying consolation.

7. *The voice of the Disciple.*—O Jesus, my love! how delightful are the designs of Thy Heart, whereby, to soothe the bitterness of this life, Thou journeyest, in some manner, with me in my banishment, nay, changest my very exile into a Paradise!

Shall I speak, O Lord, or be silent about what I conceive of the exceeding love of Thy Heart for us

men? Yet, for the glory of Thy Heart, I will not
be silent: Thus, O Jesus! thus Thou didst nowhere
deal with the Angels themselves; thus Thou never
gavest Thyself to them to enjoy!

O my Jesus! infinite sweetness, how immensely
hast Thou loved me! how givest Thou Thyself to
me! how dost Thou wholly become my consolation!

Whence, O most loving God, so great a goodness
toward an ungrateful Child, not worthy of the name
of Child!

Thus, O ineffable love! Thou displayest the
greatness of Thy goodness, since Thou regardest not
Thy Majesty and my abjectness, but kindly followest the goodness of Thy Heart, moved by my in-
digence and Thy charity.

8. O Lord Jesus, Father of mercies, and God of
all consolation! with how great a gladness do I
come to Thee, full of courage and confidence in
Thy pure goodness!

Many, indeed, and great are my miseries: yet,
confidingly and cheerfully do I draw nigh, attracted
by the sweetness of Thy love.

For now I know that, although Thou art incapable of pain, Thou art not without feeling; that,
although my sorrows do not cause Thee any suffering, Thou art not indifferent to them.

Now I understand, that Thou art able and willing to feel compassion for my infirmities; and that
my great and numerous miseries are the objects of
Thy infinite mercy.

If, hitherto, I languished miserable and disconsolate, I myself was in fault; because I neglected to
come to the ever-open source of mercy and comfort.

But, henceforth, whenever I shall be afflicted, I

will arise and go to this fountain of all blessings, where I shall find more remedies than I need; where I shall have greater consolations than I can contain in my heart.

CHAPTER XII.

THE MOST SACRED HEART OF JESUS, IN ITS SACRA- MENTAL, AS FORMERLY IN ITS MORTAL LIFE, WHILST INSTRUCTING MEN, DOES NOT CEASE TO TEACH THAT HE IS MEEK AND HUMBLE.

1. *The voice of Jesus.*—Come ye, sons of men, and give ear.

Behold how I am here with you all days! here at all times, here learn ye of Me, how meek and humble of Heart I am.

Marvelous, indeed, did the humility of My Heart and Its charity appear during Its mortal life: yet, here, in My Sacramental life, far more admirable is the abyss of Its humility, the excess of Its charity.

This whole mystery is humility, all charity. Here not only is My Divinity, but even My Humanity, hidden from the sight of mortals. Here is charity, not unto death only, not unto the end of the world, but unto every excess of love.

What eye has seen, what ear has heard, what heart has conceived, to how great a degree the humility of My Heart does here descend, to what extent love is exceeding?

2. If thou art astonished, My Child, if thou art enraptured at the excess of love, whereby, whilom, during My mortal life, I showed Myself meek and

humble of Heart: what must be thy sentiments, when thou considerest attentively, how meek and humble of Heart I am now, in My Sacramental life!

So long as I was seen on earth and dwelled with men; at no time, in no place, did I cease to exhibit to all and every one the true and efficacious humility and meekness of My Heart.

Recall to mind, My Child, with how great a humility and charity of Heart I was wont to treat My Disciples; the ignorant and unmannerly people; the unhappy and the distressed; the wretched sinners; finally, My enemies themselves.

What was ever able to obstruct or check the fountain of this humble and exhaustless charity? Neither the faults, nor the ignorance, nor the importunateness, nor the obstinacy, nor the abjectness, nor the perverseness itself of men. Naught of all this could ever make Me show Myself, even toward one mortal, otherwise than meek and humble of Heart.

Witness all the people so hard to please; witness the heathen, who, attracted by the sweetness of My Heart, came running toward Me, saying: "We wish to see Jesus:" witness the woman of Canaan, and all the disconsolate: witness the Magdalen, and every sin-laden soul that had recourse to Me: witness the Pharisees, men that persecuted Me unto death. All these bear witness to the deeds of My meek and humble Heart, during My mortal life.

3. But behold! Child, in My Sacramental life, I continue such deeds: yea, amid these, I show Myself meek and humble of Heart in a more sweet and marvelous manner.

For consider, how men here deport themselves toward Me, not only with rudeness and irreverence, but even with contempt; and see how I endure this behavior.

Consider, how many souls, cherished by Me in a special manner, when presented with a small share of My cross,—a most precious pledge of My love,—bring and return to Me here, instead of praise and love, complaints and repinings: and observe, with how great a goodness of Heart, I do not only endure them, but encourage and stimulate them to better sentiments.

Consider, how many ungrateful souls, laden with My favors, depart hence, and, whilst they enjoy My benefactions, forget and slight Me, their Benefactor: how many others, who, after having abused the graces I have already so often bestowed upon them, present themselves without shame before Me, and clamor for new favors: and see, with how great a meekness I bear with them, with what generosity I suffer them, with how gentle, and, at the same time, how firm a charity, I excite and help them to faithfulness and fervor.

Consider, how the wicked make use of My very gifts and favors to oppose, to offend Me, to wound My very Heart: and watch, with what disposition of Heart I do not return them evil for evil, but overcome evil with good.

Consider, in fine, how often the enemies, the persecutors of My Heart, come hither to insult Me: and with how divine a charity of My humble Heart, I receive even them into My presence, and offer them mercy, and pardon, and peace.

Thus, My Child, at every hour, at every moment

of the day, and of the night, in season and out of season, the good and the wicked, the grateful and the thankless, friends and enemies, all come and go, and each one behaves toward Me according to his disposition: but, see, by the light of faith, how I deal with all and every one; with how lowly, unwearied, exhaustless a benignity and sweetness of charity!

4. These wonders of the love of My Heart, thou canst not understand, My Child, unless thou lookest at them with a lively faith, and meditatest thereon with a devoted heart.

For the depth of the humility, which My Heart does here practice, must be gazed upon with the light from above, must be entered into by pious meditation, must be learnt in silence by prayer.

And the sweetness of the charity, which My Heart here displays, must be sought in like manner, must be relished by making use thereof, must be tested by experience.

Look, My Child, and see in what manner thou hast hitherto done all this: how thou hast until now profited by this continued example of My Heart.

Cheer up, and renew thy courage, learn by deed and in truth, what I cease not to teach here, that I am meek and humble of Heart.

5. *The voice of the Disciple.*—How good, O Jesus! how good Thou art! who, to teach all generations the more gently and the more efficaciously Thy Spirit, abidest so humble, so meek, in this most sweet mystery!

Here truly and supremely humble and meek of Heart, Thou alone art the teacher of humility and charity, doing and teaching from generation to generation.

Yea, all things that surround Thee, cease not to proclaim, that Thou art meek and humble of Heart.

The deep and tranquil solitude wherein Thou art hidden, proclaims it: the solemn silence, in which the prostrate and enraptured Angels adore Thee, proclaims it: the tender devotedness of the pious faithful proclaims how meek and humble of Heart Thou art, O Lord.

O Jesus! who can still be proud? who can still be hardhearted? Can there be any one that does not rejoice to humble himself? Can there be any one that does not burn with love?

Alas, O Lord! what faith, what hope, what love have they, that do not yield to Thee here? O souls full of pride and bitterness! in the midst of you there stands One whom ye know not, whom ye heed not.

6. Attend thou, my soul, and learn, who thy beloved is, how sweet, how wholly desirable, how wholly worthy of love.

Enter into the place of the marvelous Tabernacle, even into the abode of thy divine Saviour: and contemplate the God of Majesty, the Maker of heaven and earth, the Joy of the Saints and Angels, thus humbled for love of thee,—thus made a captive by love for thee!

Here learn to humble thyself through love: here learn to cherish in purity thy Bridegroom, who loves with so wonderful a purity.

Hearken thou, to what so great and so admirable an example of His, speaks within thee to thy heart; be thou attentive to Him who teaches thee so gently by His own example, and confirms so powerfully His teaching by unceasing miracles.

7. O prodigy of humility, Jesus, Son of the living God! O miracle of love! I love Thee, I cherish Thee, with my whole heart; O Thou my meek and humble Beloved, most sweet and most pure Bridegroom of my soul!

Thee alone I desire to love, to cherish; farewell to all beside: Thy love alone I desire: for the sole love of Thee, I long to live and die amidst sacrifices, the practices and proofs of love.

For, the example of Thy Heart has taught me these things: the unction of Thy love has rendered them pleasant to me.

O Jesus, of all the most bountiful! preserve Thou this disposition of my heart: and kindly grant that, by approaching Thee here frequently, I may ever learn better to love Thee purely, and, for love of Thee, to show myself toward all meek and humble of heart.

CHAPTER XIII.

THE MOST SACRED HEART OF JESUS WILLED THAT THE MOST HOLY EUCHARIST SHOULD BE AN ENDURING REMEMBRANCE OF HIS PASSION, AND AN EVERLASTING MEMORIAL OF HIS LOVE DISPLAYED THEREIN.

1. *The voice of Jesus.*—As often as ye shall eat this Bread, and drink the chalice; ye shall proclaim the death of the Lord, until He come.

This I enjoin, My Child, to remind all men of that excess of the love of My Heart, whereby I loved them, in some manner, more than Myself;

since I suffered death in order that they might have life.

I glory in that death, whereby, whilst the love of My Heart triumphed, the Eternal Father was appeased and exceedingly honored; whereby men were set free and saved; whence arose for Me the glory of the Resurrection, and Ascension, and of My everlasting reign over all things.

And, therefore, I willed that there should be, always and everywhere, a remembrance of My Passion; and that they who reaped the fruits thereof, whether in heaven or on earth, should ever thankfully remember so great a condescension.

2. And, assuredly, in their heavenly bliss, the Elect are ever mindful of My Passion, knowing that to the same they owe their salvation and glory: and they worship forever the Lamb of God, as it were slain, having five wounds, more splendid and dazzling than the sun.

On earth, the Church,—acknowledging that she was brought forth by My Heart when It expired upon the holy Mountain, and that, from that same fountain, all good things flow down upon her,—does not cease to commemorate with every feeling of gratitude My death, all days, until I come to take her up with Me into glory. For the Sacrifice which she offers daily, has Me present as the Victim, and, by the separate Consecration of the Body and Blood, exhibits Me as it were dead.

Besides, in every soul that partakes of the most Blessed Sacrament, there is made some representation and commemoration of My death. For, as upon the bed of the Cross, through the Passion, I lost My mortal life, so, through Communion, I lose My Sacramental life in the heart of the faithful.

Nay more, My Child, the state itself wherein I here continue is a certain image of My Passion For, in My Passion, the splendor of My Divinity, and the very beauty of My Humanity was in some manner vailed: and are not the lowly and gentle species of the Sacrament an evident representation of this vailing?

3. The Sacrifice of the life of My Heart, My death, is the centre of time. Whatever had gone before, sacrifices, ceremonies, and everything else belonging to Religion, had reference to it: thence they derived all their power and efficaciousness.

In like manner, whatever follows it, Oblation, Sacraments, and the rest, all have relation to the same, and possess thence their virtue and efficacy.

Behold, then, the Sacrifice offered up from the beginning of the world in types, upon the cross in truth, continued, substantially, in the Church even to the end of ages.

Such, My Child, is the unfathomableness of the designs of My Heart: such is the extent of My love!

Hence, My whole career on this earth, from the beginning even to the end of the world, whether through My promised presence, My mortal life, or My Sacramental abiding, and whatsoever I effect by these means, is one whole, one perfect work of infinite Goodness; to be completed only then, when, at the end of time, with the Church, I shall mount on high, to enjoy an everlasting triumph.

4. What wonder, then, My Child, if the mystery

appears to thee ever new, ever equally worthy of veneration, when thou receivest the holy Communion, when thou hearest or celebratest the holy Mass?

For, when thou receivest the holy Eucharist, thou shouldst ever be present with the same disposition of heart, with the same affection, as if thou wert at the last Supper, and didst sit down to the same, to receive from Myself the Bread of life.

It is in reality the same Supper: and the same death, that I foreshowed in the Supper-room, thou showest in the Sacrament.

By the action itself, Child, when thou celebratest Mass, or takest the holy Communion, thou proclaimest My death; since the manner of either, as well of the offering of the Sacrifice, as the consuming of the Sacrament, proclaims the same death.

5. But when thou art engaged in mysteries so great, which My Heart by Its death merited for thee, thou must also, on thy part, do that, whereby thou mayst be enabled to commemorate it in an appropriate manner.

As, therefore, in My Passion, I offered Myself to God the Father for a perfect holocaust; so thou also shouldst offer thyself to Me in holy Communion as a clean and entire victim.

Yea, even whilst visiting Me, it is proper that, with great feeling of piety, thou do commemorate the sacrifices of My once suffering life: which thou wilt do, if thou meditatest with devotedness, if thou resignest thyself to Me in every affliction; if thou givest thyself wholly to Me, in the presence of the sacred Tabernacle; where all thou perceivest around thee serves to put thee in mind of those sacrificings of My Heart.

Thus, Child, thou wilt better feel the greatness of that charity, whereby, from a life of labor and sorrow, I advanced through many and great sacrifices, to that last and supreme sacrifice, even to death, and to this captivity of love, wherein I continue an abiding Victim of love.

By affectionately calling this to mind, wilt thou not be excited to gratefulness, to a requital of love, to imitation; so as to show forth in thyself the effect of My example, not only in thy heart but also in thy works?

Thus, whilst, in a practical manner, thou commemoratest My Passion more profitably to thyself, thou wilt learn not to be cast down or troubled by humiliations; but rather, in a supernatural manner, to glory and rejoice therein.

This active remembrance of My death will be perfect, My Child, if as often as thou approachest the sacred mysteries, thou dost ever more and more die to thyself and to creatures, in order that thou mayst live for Me, as I, after having died for thee here live for thee.

6. But alas! although there are many who wish to be refreshed by this heavenly food, and to be thence replenished with the delights of the Angels; how few there are willing actively to recall My Passion, to imitate it in practice!

Therefore also, My Child, many are and continue ever the same, ever imperfect, although they do not unfrequently approach the sacred Table.

For, since they do not correspond to the end of its divine institution and to grace granted therein, they remain deprived of much fruit.

Would that this were understood by those souls,

that are more anxious about the number of their Communions, whereby they may show or feel devotion, than about the fruit of them, whereby they may be sanctified and raised to greater perfection!

Thou, Child, be thou wiser and more faithful. So recall My Passion, so express My death in thy conduct, that, whenever thou receivest the holy Communion, thou dost always obtain its fruits of sanctification.

7. *The voice of the Disciple.*—O most bountiful, most sweet Jesus! Thou didst die for love of me, and here livest for me by love: and oh! how dost Thou here live for me!

Truly, Lord, truly he deserves death, who refuses to die to self, that he may live for Thee.

If Thou, Lord God, thus sacrificest Thyself for love of me, how is it anything great, how is it wonderful, if I, wretched creature, sacrifice myself for love of Thee!

And yet, I blush to say it, sometimes I hesitate to sacrifice, not myself, but a trifle, some pride, some aversion, or inclination of corrupt nature.

Woe is me! whilst in words I make profession of loving and following Thee, I show in my deeds, how little I cherish Thee, how far I am from a practical remembrance of Thy Passion, from a true Imitation of Thy Heart.

And can I complain or wonder, that my Communions produce so little fruit for me?

One Communion can make a person, that is well-disposed and co-operates with Thy grace, a Saint. And, after so many Communions, alas! who and what am I?

I myself, O Lord, I myself, I own it, am in

fault: for in so many Communions I have received grace enough to sanctify a thousand souls; but I have neglected to co-operate therewith. For I acted as if grace alone, without my co-operation, ought to sanctify me: and, meanwhile, I have continued to live for nature, not for grace, for myself, not for Thee.

I acknowledge that, in Thy sight, I have become unworthy of life, since, abusing Thy infinite love, I have neglected to live for Thee.

But spare, Lord Jesus, spare, I beseech Thee, my past negligence, of which, for Thy love, I repent exceedingly.

Henceforth, I will be more faithful: co-operating with the grace of the Sacrament, I will die to the things of this world, to the ill-ordered inclinations of nature, that I may live for Thee.

Assist me, most kind Jesus, that I may thus prove my love for Thee in deed, and may ever derive, from holy Communion, abundant fruit of sanctification.

CHAPTER XIV.

THE MOST SACRED HEART OF JESUS DISPLAYS IN THIS WONDERFUL SACRAMENT THE SUM AND SUBSTANCE OF ALL DIVINE MYSTERIES.

1. *The voice of Jesus.*—Being merciful and gracious, the love of My Heart has made a remembrance of Its wonderful works.

This It has chiefly done in the Sacrament, where

It has gathered together Its astounding prodigies, where It incloses even the profound mysteries of God.

And because these things were done, not for the Angels but for men, it was proper that it should be under visible symbols, that, by the sight of things seen, they might be put in mind of the unseen, and that their sensitive heart might be worked upon by sensitive proofs of the divine love.

Such things, therefore, did the love of My Heart do: and It saw that all It had done was exceedingly good, and It was delighted with Its works.

All Its works are perfect and full of sweetness, whereby It has poured out, as it were, the riches of Its goodness toward men, in this mystery,— wherein the plenitude of the Divinity corporally dwells.

2. Hence, My Child, this divine Sacrament possesses, by concomitance, and ever recalls to the minds of the faithful, the sublimest of mysteries, that of the Trinity.

For I and the Father are one: and he that sees Me, sees also the Father; but where the Father and the Son are acknowledged, the love of the two, which is the Holy Ghost, is certainly not unknown.

But to know this mystery the better, to love it the more, to adore it the more worthily, grace is here given to the faithful, that, aided and enlightened thereby, they may believe it more firmly, love it with purer affection, and venerate it with a more perfect worship.

Guided by this light from above, and strengthened by this assistance, they proceed from one mystery to another.

3. For behold! the most sweet mystery of the Incarnation is also contained in the holy Eucharist, and extended in a marvelous manner.

Indeed, what is the mystery of the Incarnation? The Word, and a Soul, and the Body come together in one Person: and these three are one Jesus, the God-man.

Now, in the most Blessed Sacrament, the Word, that is Eternal and God; the Soul, which was created when it was infused; the Body, which, by the divine operation, was taken without blemish of the Immaculate Virgin; these three abide: but they abide in the unity of Person.

Moreover, here there is an extension of this mystery, marvelous and overflowing with every delight. For I, the same who, by the Incarnation, dwelled in the bosom of the Virgin, dwell by the Communion in the heart of each one of the faithful communicants.

Astounding, indeed, and awe-inspiring is the depth and breadth of this mystery; but it is all the more worthy of love, it should be relished with the more delight, devotion, and tenderness.

4. Besides, all the mysteries, so full of consolation, of My whole life are also contained in this divine Sacrament.

For although the time, when these began and took place, has passed away, yet, by reason of My personal presence, these continue in their effects and are present.

Therefore, also, the Church ever views and celebrates them as present: and, in meditating on them and commemorating them, she is ever animated with her first sentiments, ever burns with her first fervor.

Look, on the other hand, at heresies and sects which deny My perpetual presence in the Eucharist: how in them all things spiritual languish: how dead their ways as well as themselves, when they attempt to recall My actions by means of festivals!

It is not so with My Beloved, My holy Church. When the time returns, she hastens to the Cave of My Nativity; there prostrate, she gazes upon Me, lying in the manger; she adores, rejoices, sheds tears—through tenderness of devotion.

5. Here is the Bethlehem where faithful souls find Me more sweetly and more easily than they whom heaven called formerly to the Stable: where they enkindle their fervor, nourish their piety, sanctify themselves: where they pour out their hearts, and consecrate them to Me: where, in return, they are inebriated and rendered blissful with the sweetness of My love: where the Angels do not promise peace to men of good will, but where I Myself bestow it upon them with a lavish Heart.

Here is the Sanctuary, wherein I am presented to God the Father, and devoted to the salvation of men; wherein I so give Myself to the faithful, that they may not only take Me into their arms, like Simeon, and caress Me as did Anna, but receive Me into their very hearts, and enjoy Me intimately, by a favor granted neither to Simeon nor to the blessed Anna.

Here is the exile of Egypt: a banishment, not, as formerly, of seven years, but of all ages: a banishment, among men likewise given to idolatry,—who worship pleasures, riches, honors as their deities: a banishment wherein I am unknown, except to a few, and looked upon and slighted by many as a stranger.

Here is the Temple, wherein I continue to be occupied in what concerns My Father: where, in the midst of the listening doctors, I utter My Spirit, instruct souls, communicate the hidden things of the spiritual life: where they that love Me, seek Me, and, like Mary and Joseph, rejoicing find Me.

Here is Nazareth, where I lead a life hidden in God: where, being made subject, I am occupied in ceaseless actions, which do not indeed strike the senses of men, but excite the admiration of Angels: where, a pattern of the interior life, I live with interior souls in a manner known to them alone.

6. Nay more, My Child, in this Sacrament are seen the mysteries of My Evangelical life. Behold here truly the field of My labors, the place of the well-doings of My Heart.

For here I am the *Saviour*, who seek that which was lost; who, amid My labors, seat Myself near the Well; where I give, from the fountain of My Heart, to every Samaritan—every soul that thirsts, the living water, which quenches the thirst for earthly things, and springs up into life everlasting; who, when the labors of the day are over, pass the night in the prayer of God.

Here I am the *Good Shepherd:* I go in search of the lost sheep, and, when found, I carry it, and warm it in My bosom: I love My flock, and feed the same with My own substance: I guard all, watching over them with My Heart, by day and by night.

Here I am the kind *Father*, who with gladness

embrace my prodigal son, when he returns; who, having clothed him with his first garment, restore and entertain him with a heavenly banquet: and who, according to their capacity, share all things with My faithful children.

Here I am the divine *Physician*, since I soothe and alleviate, with the unction of My Heart, the sorrows of the suffering: since I cure the souls that are ill, healing every ailment and infirmity: since I do also take away the deformity caused by the sickness of sin, and restore former beauty.

Here I am a *Teacher*. For I teach by the whisperings of My Heart, as well as by My example: Blessed are the poor in spirit: blessed the meek: blessed they that mourn for sin: blessed they that hunger and thirst after justice: blessed the merciful: blessed the clean of heart: blessed the peacemakers: blessed they that suffer persecution for justice's sake: blessed, in fine, they that do the divine Will; because they are My brethren and sisters, and co-heirs of the kingdom of heaven.

Here I am a *Friend*, who style the faithful, that, by grace, lead a supernatural life, no more My servants, but My friends: a Friend, such as there is none other, more sincere, more sweet, more faithful than all, in prosperity and in adversity, in life and in death: a Friend that under no circumstances is wanting, yea, accompanying and consoling even in eternity.

Here I am the *Bridegroom:* yea, My Child; the divine Bridegroom of virginal and chaste souls, whom I have chosen and espoused to Myself, that, always and everywhere, they may follow Me as My companions; them I here honor and enrich, and render blissful, in a manner which fills the very Angels with wonder, and yet is merely a prelude to that which I reserve for them in the kingdom of My glory.

7. Here, lastly, are also the mysteries of the rest of My life. For, is not here the Supper-room. where I eat the Passover with My Disciples; where I pour out My Heart to them; where I leave them My peace?

Is not here Gethsemane, Jerusalem, the theatre of My sorrows? Remember, Child, the Holy Week, how the faithful come hither, as to the spectacle of My Sufferings; how they weep, as if before their eyes they beheld Me in suffering.

Is not here, too, the mystery of the Resurrection? See how the Church, when celebrating this solemnity of solemnities, returns, as it were, with Me to life, and how, like other Marys, at the first dawn, pious souls hasten to My glorious Sepulchre, and behold Me, by faith, in My glory; embrace Me, by hope, enjoy Me, by love. And is this not lawfully so? is it not rightly? is it not sacredly? for, here I am truly present with the same qualities with which I rose again: with a heavenly beauty, with a glorious brightness, with an incomprehensible subtility, with a perfect impassibility, adorned and blissful with immortality.

Thus, My Child, the Church accompanies Me through every mystery, puts on in each of them the feelings of My Heart, and celebrates each with similar affections.

8. From the mysteries here celebrated before Me, the Church, mindful that I am reigning in the glory of heaven, gazes forward into eternity: she con-

templates with rapture, she anticipates in affection, those most joyous mysteries of the life in heaven, those ever-enduring festivals prepared for her, promised to her.

O Jesus! she exclaims in her ardor, may that soon be for which I long so exceedingly, that, beholding Thee with face unvailed, I may be blessed with the sight of Thy glory.

Thus, Child, glows the Church, enkindled with the fire of My Heart here present: thus has she all things present to herself: thus is she filled with every consolation.

Take the sun away out of this world; what will this earth be, except a dark, cold, and dreary place? In like manner, if My living and life-giving Heart, if My Sacramental presence were taken away from the Church, all the mysteries of Religion, now so full of splendor, so soul-stirring, so consoling,— how different should they then appear.

9. Taught by the example of thy holy Mother, apply thyself, My Child, to celebrate the festivals of Religion with the same feelings; to recall to mind the mysteries which I display here in the Sacrament; in fine, to draw for thyself, from all these sources, the plenitude of all graces.

For this end do thou animate the fervor of thy heart: a fervor, I say, not necessarily sensible, but vigorous with the liveliness of faith, the confidence of hope, the generosity of love.

If thou art destitute of this fervor, thou wilt do everything without affection, without relish, without much fruit: that which enraptures fervent souls, stirs up the Angels themselves, will not affect, will not move thee.

But this fervor thou wilt awaken and foster in thyself by prayer, by devout meditation, by pious reading, by mortifying and denying thyself in some things; and, especially, by frequently visiting this divine Sacrament, and by religiously partaking thereof; since here there is fire enough to inflame the whole world.

6. *The voice of the Disciple.*—O Lord Jesus! how boundless are the excesses of the love of Thy Heart! how many wonders dost Thou here present to me! how many good things! how sweet! how desirable!

What wonder if I am allured, if I am gently and powerfully drawn hither! what wonder if here is the place of my heart's delights!

Here, amidst the Angels, I can find Thee in every mystery; I can behold Thee in every condition of Thy life, as my necessities, my profit, or my comfort may require.

Yea, here I can now be with Thee and enjoy Thy favors; here again, if I lift myself up, I may contemplate Thee in Thy glory, view the wonders of Thy kingdom, and rejoice beforehand in what Thou hast there prepared for me.

How easy, O Beloved of my soul! how easy and sweet it is, to meditate here, to occupy the mind and the heart with Thee here, to enjoy Thee here! for this I need no skill, no book, no labor. Here, present before Thee, I need only gaze upon Thee by faith in every mystery, hearken to Thee, watch Thy actions, implore Thee, love Thee.

O how delightful is this place! how lovely the company! how sweet the employment! how holy the intercourse!

Who does not wish to be here with Thee forever? Here certainly I will be present at Thy feet, among the heavenly spirits, as often as I can.

O that I could spend here all my time! But Thy Will, which is my sole comfort, requires that I be often absent in person, that I comply with the obligations of my state, that I fulfill the duties of my office, that I provide for the needs of nature, that I even use an innocent relaxation.

Yet, amidst all these, I will frequently turn in affection to Thee, I will occupy my heart with Thee: for wherever is the object of my love, thither also tends my heart: wheresoever my treasure is, there also will be my heart.

CHAPTER XV.

THE MOST SACRED HEART OF JESUS, IN THE MOST BLESSED SACRAMENT OF THE EUCHARIST, LEADS US TO THE DIVINE PERFECTIONS.

1. *The voice of Jesus.*—Attend, My Child, and here, in the Sacrament, I will show thee a still higher way, whereby thou mayst ascend in contemplation even to the very perfections of the Deity.

Be thou prepared, that thou mayst enter into the divine secrets, and that, with all the Saints, thou mayst contemplate the height, and breadth, and depth of those oceans, whence in heaven the Angels and Blessed, and, on earth, pure and interior souls draw, and are inebriated.

Behold what My Heart makes known to thee here in this most sacred mystery: and, following the divine Spirit, from what is here made known, go thou forward into the plenitude of things.

But do all this in such a manner, My Child, that thou becomest more and more established in humility, that thou ever glowest with a purer love, so that, being introduced by My sacred Humanity, by My Heart Itself thou mayst cling—as forming but one and the same Spirit—to the Deity, as perfectly as thou art able.

2. Look into and ponder the divine *Wisdom* which My Heart displays in this adorable Sacrament.

Here It shows forth those marvelous inventions, whereby It reconciled those things which appeared contrary; so that, at one and the same time, I should reign amidst glorious triumphs in heaven, and abide upon earth the everlasting Comforter of men; whereby I might be enabled to give Myself not only to the human race, but to every individual as well: whereby, in fine, through the most simple means, such as those of the Sacramental species, I might obtain the most sublime ends.

Hence do thou mount higher, and contemplate this infinite Wisdom, which reaches all things from eternity to eternity: which beholds all present, the past and the future, things existing and things possible.

This, by its eternal counsels, ordained, in a manner so marvelous, all the stupendous works of the Creation and Restoration, of nature and grace, of sanctification and glory.

This divine perfection is like an infinite light,

which penetrates all; which completely surveys thee and thy whole interior; from which thou canst not recede, which thou art unable to grasp.

In this light do thou rejoice, My Child: herein live thou cheerfully for thy God.

3. Observe the divine *Goodness*, which is made manifest in this most sweet Sacrament, and is resplendent with such flames of love.

Nowhere on earth does the divine Goodness shine forth with so wonderful a profusion, with so great a sweetness: for here it does, as it were, pour out and exhaust itself: here it gives all things and itself over and above. Elsewhere, are the rays of divine love, here is its focus. Elsewhere, there are some good things, here is the fountain of them all.

From this, proceed thou to the contemplation of this abyss of Goodness. Look into its depth, survey eternity itself; thou shalt find no bounds.

From this infinite Goodness everything that is good, whether in heaven or on earth, derives its goodness: everything that lives, its life: everything that moves, its vigor: everything that understands, its intelligence: everything that is happy, its bliss.

This divine attribute is, as it were, a boundless ocean, whence arises as a cloud, the plenitude of all things good· into which, while the Blessed and Elect are immersed, they rejoice in supreme delight.

My Child, plunge thyself also into the same: taste how sweet is the Goodness of thy God: therein do thou rejoice, love, praise.

4. Behold the *Almighty Power*, which is re-

vealed in the venerable mystery of the Eucharist, in which alone it works more and greater wonders than in all the world beside: in which it ceases not to renew these astonishing prodigies.

After having reverently viewed these things, lift thyself up to a general contemplation of this stupendous Omnipotence; which, without labor, at its mere pleasure, made all things that have existence: which produces countless and unutterable objects of every kind, all things, in short, if it only wills: which, again, by its simple nod, is able to destroy the whole world, and bring all things to naught.

Contemplate the efficacy of this infinite Power, which can overthrow all the attempts of its opponents, and bring it to pass that all things warring against it,—not only those which are indifferent, but even such as are evil,—do, unconsciously, and even in spite of themselves, concur to its own holy ends.

By this Omnipotence, not only are creatures preserved in being, but they receive besides power to effect whatsoever they do: men receive the divine concurrence to use the faculties of body and soul: animals their efficiency: the stars their force of rolling and glittering in space: the earth its vigor to produce fruits: the winds and storms their might and impetuosity: in fine, all things their excellence.

This divine perfection, in its manifestation, is like the atmosphere, which, when it is gently stirred, refreshes and invigorates the life of creatures: when it moves with violence, lays prostrate and scatters whatever opposes, but to whatever yields, gives a new impulse, and helps it to go forward.

Rejoice, My Child, at so great a Power of thy God: place thy trust therein; and, by prayer, have frequently recourse to the same.

5. Consider the divine *Justice*, of which My Heart reminds thee in this most Blessed Sacrament.

Behold! My sacred Humanity, which is here present for thee, is the sign of the divine Justice; for I assumed it, to make satisfaction to the same. And does not the Sacrifice, which My Heart here offers daily, through the ministry of the priests, put thee in mind of the divine Justice? Nay more, do I not display an adorable Justice in the Communion, when I give there to every one according to his works, according to his disposition?

Contemplate thence the perfection of this divine Justice, whether in heaven,—whence it hurled, like lightning, the wickedly rebellious spirits; and wherein it recompenses forever with a condign reward all, even the least, good deeds of the Angels and Saints:—or whether on earth, where, through My Heart, it is allied to the divine mercy, and reaches those only who are unwilling to embrace mercy; where, also, when it is justly incensed, it is mindful of mercy:—or whether in hell, where, for My sake, it punishes below the full desert of the reprobate, and so adapts punishment to the number and grievousness of sins, that it forces the condemned themselves to confess that the divine Justice is good.

Consider the consolation of this divine attribute which will one day justify, in the presence of all, them that are now oppressed by unmerited detraction, by reproaches, or by calumnies; and which will not only restore reputation, and honor, and glory, and whatsoever else has been taken away, but will exalt all things the more, the lower they have been depressed; which will make good, by an ever-enduring reward, all deeds of virtue, even those which men slighted; which, in fine, estimates and repays the merits of works, not according to their outward success, as does the world, but according to the inward disposition of him that performs them.

This divine perfection is like fire, which, according as objects are disposed, by the same action, consumes these, cheers those; hardens some, softens others.

Admire this attribute of the Deity, My Child; exalt it with a holy fear; but cherish it more.

6. Direct thy mind to the divine *Mercy*, which My Heart displays in the most Holy Sacrament, in ways as sweet as they are wonderful.

Is not this whole mystery a marvel of infinite Mercy? Who is there alive, that does not endure misery? but what unfortunate one has come hither with proper dispositions, and has not found mercy? Boundless is here the kindness of My Heart, and there is no end to Its compassion.

When thou hast devoutly meditated hereon, proceed to the consideration of the infinite Mercy visible everywhere: in heaven, which the divine Mercy fills with Saints, whom formerly it freed from sin and now crowns with bliss: on earth, where it hovers over all the works of God, and refreshes them by remedy, and assistance, and consolation: finally, in hell itself, where, on account of the merits of My Heart, it punishes less than what is due, and is acknowledged by the reprobate themselves.

Contemplate the vastness of this divine Mercy toward men; which embraces all, excludes none, casts off nobody; which waits for the very sinners so long as they live, and offers them grace sufficient for their conversion and pardon; which, in fine, extends itself to all miseries of whatsoever kind, and finds naught in this world, how wretched soever it may be, which it is not willing to relieve, and, in a direct or indirect manner, to turn into a means of salvation.

Behold, a divine perfection, like an infinite abyss, which no magnitude of miseries cast into it, can fill up; which no multiplicity of necessities which draw therefrom, can exhaust.

Use thou, My Child, but do not abuse so sweet an attribute of thy God: widen thy heart: be thankful: fly to this abyss of mercy with faith, with hope, with love.

7. Observe the *Sanctity* which shines forth in this Holy of Holies; which by its splendor throws the Angels themselves into an ecstasy.

With deep piety look thou into this Sacrament, the mirror of the divine Sanctity. Here, everything is perfect purity: here, My Body is itself as a Spirit; here, all breathes holiness.

Hence, thou mayst contemplate infinite Sanctity, which, absolutely perfect in itself, is the cause, the standard, the end of all created holiness, of all purity, of all beauty; which is such that nothing can be added thereto, nothing be taken therefrom.

Gaze upon this divine perfection; captivated by

the purest beauty of which, the inhabitants of heaven are overspread with a beatific joy: by the similitude of which, when the souls of mortals are adorned, they become supremely ennobled: on account of the majesty of which, the demons tremble even in the lowest hell.

From the brightness of this perfection, whatsoever is beautiful, whatsoever is lovely, whatsoever is excellent, borrows its every beauty, its every loveliness, its every excellence.

This divine attribute is like the sun in the firmament; which imparts to objects the brightness of color, elegance, cheerfulness: which, shining upon things clean and unclean, is ever equally pure, ever equally beautiful.

Rejoice thou, My Child, at so great a beauty and loveliness; so great and varied an excellence of the sanctity of thy God: affectionately revere the same, imitate it according to thy ability.

8. Behold the divine *Immensity*, which this Sacrament of My Heart represents.

For here I am wholly in the whole Consecrated Host, and wholly in every particle of the Host when divided. And by the multiplication or replication of My presence in all the Hosts, all over the earth, do I not display a certain representation of immensity? Finally, in every place, where I abide sacramentally, do I not so deal with each one as if I there abode for him alone?

By conceiving these things with a lively faith, thou wilt assuredly be led to the contemplation of the divine immensity, which contains all things, whether existing or whether merely possible, and is contained by none: whereby the Deity is wholly in the whole universe, and wholly in every part of the universe.

Contemplate this universal presence of the Divinity, together with His infinite Wisdom, and Goodness and Power, and Justice, and Mercy, and Sanctity, and infinite Perfection of every kind: and remember that in Him thou art, thou livest, thou movest.

Whithersoever thou mayst turn thyself, thou perceivest the Deity present in every object, and so caring for the same, as if He were there for it alone. Behold the birds of the air: they neither sow nor reap, and yet He that is present everywhere, feeds them. Consider the lilies of the field: they labor not, neither do they spin; and yet, not even Solomon in all his glory was arrayed as one of these.

To this divine Providence, therefore, do thou intrust thyself: rest thou in the same, as in the bosom of a Father supremely perfect: abandon thyself wholly to Him, for He has a care of thee. Behold the very hairs of thy head are all numbered, neither does one fall without His Will. Fear not then, neither be thou troubled, nor uneasy: but live resigned to Him, and blissful in Him.

9. *The voice of the Disciple.*—Truly full of consolation is all this, O Lord God, but how sublime! Of my own accord, I neither dare nor can essay things so exalted.

If, however, Thy divine Spirit guide me, reverently indeed and conscious of my own weakness, I will follow Thee with joy and security, and having entered, through Thy most sacred Humanity, into the wonderful works of the Divinity, I will contemplate the things which surpass all understanding.

Send, therefore, I beseech Thee, Thy Holy Spirit
to lead me so far into this contemplation as Thou
wilt kindly deem it conducive to my sanctification
and Thy glory.

Grant me, I humbly implore Thee, this divine
Spirit, with His seven-fold gifts, that He may guide
me both in contemplation and in action.

The Spirit of wisdom, who may so dispose me
wholly, that I do find all things of earth distasteful,
and those of God full of delight; that I do rightly
judge and feel concerning all; that I seek with
affection after whatsoever serves for my sanctification.

The Spirit of understanding, to remove and dis-
perse darkness of mind, illusions of heart; that,
with a calm mind and clean heart, I may view all
that infinite Goodness has made, things seen and
unseen; and that I may ever understand what the
divine Will, infinitely good, requires of me.

The Spirit of counsel, to remind me ever of my
own weakness,—whereby I am unable to do aught
for my salvation,—and to induce me efficaciously to
have recourse to the help of divine Omnipotence,
by whose aid I can do all things.

The Spirit of fortitude, that He may move me
to exert all my strength, to co-operate faithfully
with the help of divine grace; that thus I may, by
generous efforts, aspire after perfect justice, without
caring for the judgments of men, regarding Thee
alone, the just Judge.

The Spirit of knowledge, that He may teach me
discernment, whereby I may, practically, distinguish
between things natural and supernatural; so that
my every prayer and action may always begin from

Thee, and be perfected through Thee; and whereby I may so devote myself to praying and acting, that, for the sweetness of contemplation, I do neither neglect the works of corporal and spiritual mercy toward my neighbor, nor, for the sake of works of mercy toward others, overlook mercy toward my own soul.

The Spirit of piety, who, by fostering in me a tender devotion, may stimulate me gently and strongly to holiness; and may cause me to conduct myself as a compassionate parent toward inferiors, as an affectionate brother toward equals, as a dutiful son toward Superiors.

The Spirit of a loving fear, of a filial, pure love; whereby I may, everywhere, supremely revere Thee, my God, and joyfully fulfill, with a holy affection, Thy every Will.

CHAPTER XVI.

HOW GREAT A REVERENCE, BOTH OUTWARD AND INWARD, THE HEART OF JESUS WILLS US TO HAVE FOR THE MOST BLESSED SACRAMENT.

1. *The voice of Jesus.*—My Child, if the heavens were thrown open before thee, and if thy eyes beheld there My glory; how thou wouldst be affected by this sight! how thou wouldst tremble with holy awe! with what reverence thou wouldst fall prostrate!

For, before My throne, sending forth the splendors of glory, like blazing flames and lightnings, thou shouldst behold thousands of thousands of

Angels praising Me with all veneration; and, standing around the throne, ten thousand times a hundred thousand ministering to Me.

Thou shouldst, also, behold the mighty throng of Saints, whom thou couldst not count, falling upon their faces in sight of the throne, adoring, and melting with love.

Thou shouldst behold how everything is aglow in My presence: at one time thou shouldst perceive how, by reason of the greatness of the all-pervading reverence, there reigns a deep silence throughout heaven; at another, how the whole place resounds with the voice of its inhabitants, bursting forth and singing in unison: Amen: blessing, and glory, and wisdom and thanksgiving, and honor, and power, and strength, to our God forever and ever.

Now, My Child, I the same, who in heaven am worshiped with such a manifestation of honor and praise, am here present in the most Blessed Sacrament, surrounded by a multitude of heavenly Spirits.

See, therefore, and consider, how mortals ought to conduct themselves toward Me. If the very pillars of heaven tremble with awe, what should the dust of the earth do?

2. Here, I desire reverence, here I claim honor, here I exact due worship.

By the free choice of My Heart, I was born in a stable, and I so passed My mortal life, that I had not where to recline My head; but, when I was about to institute this most Holy Sacrament, I ordered to be prepared a large Supper-room furnished, to show how much I wished to be respected and honored, and worshiped in My Sacramental life.

Taught by this, the Church has ever loved the beauty of My house, and erected, to the best of her power, magnificent temples: she has called to her aid nature, that by richness, and art, that by genius, they might adorn My chosen dwelling-places: ever full of solicitude, she has taken care that, according to the desire of My Heart, she may honor Me every way in this most august mystery, and thus testify her own love for Me.

If thou lovest Me, My Child, yea, if thou hast faith, and by its supernal light, viewest My Majesty here vailed, and all that visibly and invisibly surrounds Me, thou wilt surely ever exhibit here supreme reverence.

Thou wilt not here appear before Me among the Angels, except inwardly and outwardly full of recollection and veneration; thou wilt show interiorly and exteriorly naught save piety and devotedness, reverential awe, and love.

3. *The voice of the Disciple.*—Truly, O Lord Jesus, Thou, the love and beatitude of all the Angels and Saints! truly, Thou art here to be worshiped with every regard, with every sanctity of love. Holiness becomes Thy very Tabernacle, Thy very house.

For Thou art the Holy of Holies, and dwellest in Holiness, where the Angelic Spirits themselves appear trembling with awe, and admire the unapproachable splendors of sanctity.

How, then, shall a mortal man, if he considers Thy infinite Majesty, and his own utter unworthiness, dare to present himself before Thee?

Assuredly, didst Thou Thyself not invite me to draw near, and did not the well-known goodness of

Thy Heart calm the vehemence of my dread; frightened, I would depart from Thee, because I am a sinful person; neither should I dare to come to Thee, lest, perhaps, I might be guilty of Thy offended Majesty.

But behold! that very kindness of Thy Heart, which calls on me so mercifully, and breathes confidence into me with so fatherly an affection, is a new cause for reverence.

For if, through want of reverence, I misuse this grace, I become the more guilty, since I am bad, because Thou art good.

4. O Christ Jesus, my God, All-knowing and All-powerful! how awe-inspiring is this place, wherein Thou art truly present!

How shall I demean myself, in a manner worthy of Thy presence in this most Holy Sacrament; where all that I behold around me, warns me that the highest respect must be shown!

This ever-burning light tells me that, through a lively faith, I should be mindful where, and in whose presence I am.

The secluded Sanctuary warns me, that the place of Thy abode is holy with no ordinary sanctity.

The lofty Tabernacle reminds me how lowly and full of reverential feeling I ought to appear in Thy sight.

The brightness of the sacred vessels teaches me how great an inward and outward purity is required.

Every soul, here rapt in thought, busied with Thy love, admonishes me, with how great a devotion, with how tender an affection, it behooves me to deal with Thee.

5. O Jesus, God of all sanctity! Thou teachest me how perfect a reverence must here be shown to Thee; since Thou art not willing that any one should be near to Thee here, or dwell beneath the same roof with Thee, except heavenly Spirits, and those angels of earth, religious persons, and Thy priests; who are to be so clean of heart that they may deserve to see God, so chaste in body that they may embrace purity itself!

With what dispositions of body and soul ought I, therefore, to come hither, since I am associated with so pure, so holy a company!

If Daniel, if Tobias, if John, the beloved Disciple, if other Saints, in the presence of one Angel, were so struck with his aspect, and seized with so great a reverence, that they fell prostrate upon the ground; with what sentiments should I be animated here, where I am in the presence of so many Angels; yea, even before Thyself, the Lord of all the Angels!

Surely, no unbefitting thought, no inferior affection ought to occupy me here. Nay more, as often as I repair hither, I must not only keep myself free from every evil, but also honor Thee by holy acts of virtue.

6. Of how great a wrath of Thy indignation, of how great a punishment of Thy justice should I be deserving, if, in Thy presence, I should busy my heart with unlawful thoughts or evil affections; if thus I dared here to appear unholy among angelic Spirits, and insult Thee to Thy face with so great a disrespect, so offensive to Thy Heart!

O did I but follow faith, I should doubtless neither suffer my thoughts to stray, nor my affections to be poured out elsewhere, nor myself to be turned in any-wise away from Thee, as if Thou, O supreme bliss of all! wert not sufficient for me, and worthy of my attention!

O Lord God! I tremble when I think on the greatness of the irreverence whereof I render myself guilty, when I appear to honor Thee with my lips, whilst my heart is far away from Thee, engaged with things which it either inordinately loves or fears, or with objects of dissipation which it cares not to remove.

Alas! my very exterior proves by how great a distraction my heart is dissipated; in how great a desolateness it languishes, even when here before Thee I partake of a heavenly fellowship.

7. And yet, my outward deference ought not to be less than the inward; since Thou requirest equally the homage of the body and of the soul in this most august Sacrament, where Thou, my God, art Thyself present with Body and Soul.

It is befitting, therefore, that the greatest modesty do here appear, and be made known to all men, because Thou, O Lord, art so near.

Here no idle word should find a place: no inquisitive, no wandering look; no position, no motion of the body in the least disrespectful.

O Jesus, life and sweetness of my soul! although there is naught on earth which delights me more than the most Holy Sacrament of the love of Thy Heart, there is, at the same time, naught that fills me more with dread.

For, if I use it rightly and reverently, I find in it all things desirable. If, on the contrary, I use it wrongfully and irreverently, what dreadful evils do I draw upon myself!

8. But, O if I loved Thee sufficiently, if my heart were inflamed with that divine fire with which Thy Heart is here burning, there would be no need of such an amount of reasons to induce me to exhibit to Thee a due regard.

For, then I would not only most studiously avoid every irreverence, but I would demean myself before Thee in that manner which love alone understands; with that delicate attentiveness which the purity alone of love can teach.

Then, how sweet would it be for me to spend in Thy presence a happy and joyous time, rapt in love of Thee, forgetful of all beside:

Then, how eagerly would I desire to visit Thee in Thy most lovely Tabernacle, and prove to Thee my love.

Then, with how holy and delicious a hunger and thirst would I be urged forward, to resort frequently to the heavenly banquet, which Thou hast here prepared with so great a sweetness:

9. Grant me, therefore, most loving and amiable Jesus; grant me love for Thee; a love which may soften and expand my hard heart, and fill it with the unction of piety.

Inflame me wholly with that love, wherewith the Angelic Spirits, and so many pure souls, are here burning in Thy presence, and whereby they honor Thee so perfectly.

O Lord! have pity on me, and forgive me every negligence in Thy regard; every distraction of mind, every dissipation of heart, whatsoever, in fine, I have done contrary to that reverence which is due to Thee:

And kindly grant that, as Thy favors to me are

ever increasing, and being heaped up, so also my love for Thee may be augmented and redoubled.

CHAPTER XVII.

THAT WE SHOULD ENDEAVOR BY EVERY MEANS TO ATONE FOR THE INSULTS WHICH ARE OFFERED TO THE MOST SACRED HEART OF JESUS, IN THE SACRAMENT OF HIS LOVE.

1. *The voice of Jesus.*—My Child, they repaid Me evil for good, and returned Me hatred for My love.

Whatever is best and most precious in heaven, whatever on earth is most useful and wholesome to men, whatever is most sacred and consoling in Religion, I placed, by the disinterested generosity of My Heart, by the most pure love, in this Sacrament.

Are not these things so great, My Child, that if the hearts of all should be consumed with love; if the tongues of all mortals should together be employed to return just thanks; if the whole world should sacrifice itself as a victim of praise; all this should be still so far from what is deserved, as things divine surpass those which are human, as the finite is below the infinite?

Heaven itself stands astounded at the boundless grandeur of this gift: and the Angelic Spirits exclaim, in admiration: Behold our God! behold the marvels He has wrought upon earth!

Thinkest thou, then, that, on earth, there can be found a person, who is insensible or indifferent to this gift of gifts?

And yet, My Child, there are souls without feeling, without affection, thankless creatures that, so far from loving Me, the generous donor of a treasure of such blessings; on the contrary, do use these very blessings to load My Heart with bitter insults.

2. Behold! very many run whithersoever their interest or passion impels them; but, in order to visit Me, they are unwilling to leave their house, or to turn ever so little aside from their way.

So little do they esteem My gifts, so cold-hearted do they feel toward Me, that they are unwilling to undergo the least inconvenience of nature to come hither, to ask for the good things I have prepared, or to testify their love for Me, who, for love of them, came down from heaven through every inconvenience, and abide here for their sake.

To how many can I truly say: So long a time have I been with you, and ye have not known Me!

To them I am as a stranger; and, as an alien, I am neglected by them. So little do they think of Me: so little do they care for Me!

3. And even among them that frequently resort to My Tabernacle, how many there are who do indeed come, but place an abomination in the holy place! For, how many present themselves before My eyes, in My sacred temple as idols, to lead men astray from devotional love for Me, and to turn away their mind and attention toward themselves!

Not a few resolve in their mind things execrable.

cherish in their heart things detestable; and, by their will, commit sins in My very sight, thus shamefully insulting Me.

How many, also, who by look, or gesture, or by their very dress sadden the Angels, and exasperate Me!

How many there are who would rightly blush, to demean themselves toward a mortal with so much insolence, so much irreverence, as they here exhibit toward Me!

4. Nowhere, My Child, are more cruel affronts heaped upon Me than in this divine mystery. Where abounds the goodness of My Heart, there also abounds the wickedness of men.

For, how many heretics do impiously deny Me! how many unbelievers do horribly blaspheme Me, whom they know not!

But, My Child, although these things are most grievous, they are, however, less painful to My Heart than the horrifying profanations of them that receive Me sacrilegiously through Communion.

O how great an insult! how abominable an attempt, when men, even the dispensers of My mysteries, approach Me, whilst they possess the devil within themselves; and, after sacrilegiously receiving Me, cast Me, their God, at the feet of Satan, who sits enthroned in their heart.

5. *The voice of the Disciple.*—How long, O Lord God, how long shall sinners do such things with impunity? Arise, O Thou All-powerful One, scatter those monsters! place the sacrilegious wretches like stubble before the face of the raging fire: for this they have deserved.

The voice of Jesus—Not so, My Child, not so as

yet, although they deserve, even at present, the extreme of punishment: I wish to show that the love of My Heart is greater than the malice of the heart of men.

My mind, therefore, is disposed to give them still grace, that they may yet be able to save themselves. For if, co-operating with the same, they reform, it will be the triumph, the joy, the exultation of My Heart, at the salvation of these souls, for which I did not hesitate to lay down My life.

And if they are unwilling to be converted, and to love Me in return, I have time sufficient to satisfy My justice, since everlasting ages are Mine.

Meanwhile, Child, lo! I will continue to bear those insults for love of thee, for the love of the Elect; whom I love more than I am offended by sinners, and for whom I gladly continue to reside here.

6. Thou, My Child, wilt not be insensible, I trust, to this singular excess of love, by which My Heart, during so many ages, endures such indignities from the wicked, in order that It may bestow upon thee all the good things which It has stored up in this Sacrament.

If thou lovest Me, thou wilt cheerfully do whatsoever thou canst to make amends for sacrifices so numerous and so great, which My Heart here makes; and to repair My honor, which is here injured in so many unworthy ways.

Indeed, it is one of the chief ends of the devotion to My Heart, to atone, so far as possible, for the insults which My Heart receives from every side in this most holy Sacrament.

Do not believe thyself a true Disciple of My

Heart, if thou dost not burn with zeal for Its honor.

7. Here, then, before My Tabernacle, do thou frequently pour forth the ardent affections of thy heart,—affections of thankfulness, of generosity, of self-offering, of manifold love, whereby My Heart may be comforted.

Let thy devotion be fervent, when here thou prayest, or worshipest, or busiest thyself in any manner; so that, as much as thou canst, thou make up for the indifference of the lukewarm, and awake in them an incentive to shake off their sluggishness.

Exhibit everywhere a sincere, not a fictitious veneration for the most Blessed Sacrament, that thou mayst in some sort make amends to My honor; and, whilst edifying others, induce them to reverence Me, and thus lighten the burden laid upon My Heart.

Frequently offer up thy good works, thy sufferings, and all the meritorious deeds which are performed in the Church throughout the world, to honor Me in the holy Eucharist.

For the same end offer up the virtues and merits of all the Angels and Saints: all the praise, and honor, and whatsoever else is done in heaven.

As often as thou hearest or celebratest Mass, or receivest holy Communion, among others, have this intention, to atone, by this holy action, for the insults, which at any time have here been offered, by thyself or by others, to My Heart.

Nay more, My Child, imitating My Heart, pray for those who behave so unworthily towards Me; that the patience of My Heart in waiting for them, and Its readiness in pardoning them, when returning, may triumph, to Its own great joy, and to their everlasting happiness.

Lastly, whether interiorly or exteriorly, endeavor to do everything thou art able, that, insults being set aside, all may show Me honor and love, in this holy Sacrament.

8. *The voice of the Disciple.*—O most sweet Jesus! how greatly didst Thou honor us! how much didst Thou love us! Lo! for love of us Thou camest down from heaven upon earth: and, to lead us from earth to heaven, Thou didst not cease to labor and suffer.

Thou didst sacrifice all Thy interests, and shed even Thy blood, to redeem us when dead: Thou didst suffer death to give us life: Thou wast willing that Thy Heart, wounded by love, should remain open, that Thou mightst thence bestow upon us all blessings: Thou didst condescend to be wholly ours, always and everywhere.

In Thy mortal life, Thou gavest Thyself to us as the price of salvation, the fountain of life, the pattern of perfection, the way and guide to heaven.

In Thy Sacramental life, Thou givest Thyself over and above to us as the food of life, the sanctification of soul and body, the solace of our pilgrimage, the abundance of all things good.

In Thy glorious life itself, Thou givest Thyself to us as the Advocate with the Father, as the giver of the Spirit the Comforter, as an everlasting reward.

What more, O most loving Jesus! what more could Thy Heart invent, what more could It do, which It did not invent and accomplish for us?

How great a thankfulness, then, how great a love, how great a fidelity hadst Thou a right to expect!

But alas! Lord, alas! instead of gratitude, of love, of fidelity, oh! behold, affronts, profanations, sacrileges, and every most cruel misdeed!

Was it this, O good Jesus! was it this,—which moves the Angels themselves to shed tears,—was it this Thou hadst to expect from us for all Thou didst do, and endure, and bestow, and prepare for us.

9. Would, O Lord, that, with my blood, I could wash away things so horrible! Would that I were able, at the cost of my own honor and life, to atone for indignities so great, insults so cruel!

But, since I can only desire these things: I offer to Thee, as a compensation for all the injuries ever done to Thy Heart, as an atonement for Thy honor,—in whatsoever manner it may have been wounded by myself and others,—all my thoughts, words, actions, all that I may do or suffer.

For the same end, I offer to Thee my whole self, to undergo all the humiliations, to suffer all the insults, to endure whatsoever Thy divine good pleasure may will.

I offer to Thee, also, all the pious affections, the holy desires, the meritorious works of all the faithful who are pleasing to Thee, throughout the world: all the Sacrifices of the Mass, the holy Communions, in short, whatsoever is done for Thee in the whole Church.

I, likewise, offer to Thee the praises, and thanksgivings, and blessings, and all the testimonials of love of all the heavenly Spirits, and of the Saints who reign in heaven.

Accept, I beseech Thee, O most kind Jesus, these offerings in union with the merits of Thy most Sacred Heart: receive them through the Immaculate Heart of Thy Virgin Mother, through which I dare to present all this to Thee.

Through that innocent Heart: guilty as I am, I yet do confidingly draw near to Thy Heart; and implore mercy and grace for myself and for all other miserable sinners.

Spare, O Lord, spare us sinners: forgive the evils we have done: forget the insults we have offered to Thy Heart.

Grant that, by purity of life, we may repair the past; that, by the fervor of our affections, we may return Thy love; and, that, by a persevering fidelity, we may delight Thy Heart.

CHAPTER XVIII.

THAT WE MUST PROVE OURSELVES BEFORE WE APPROACH THE HOLY SACRAMENT OF THE EUCHARIST.

1. *The voice of Jesus.*—My Child, let a man prove himself, and so let him eat of that Bread, and drink of the Cup. For he that eats and drinks unworthily, eats and drinks judgment to himself, not discerning the Body of his Lord.

No small punishment threatens him, that receives the Lord his God unworthily. Behold! My Blood shall be upon him, and shall cause a curse to fall upon his body and soul.

Consider, Child, how indignant thou art at the conduct of Judas, the betrayer. But, he surpasses in audaciousness, ingratitude, and wickedness this faithless Disciple, who,—not restrained by the most lamentable fate of Judas, and abusing My forewarnings, as well as My favors,—whilst at this most sacred banquet he reclines on My very Heart, betrays Me by a sacrilegious Communion.

How dreadful, then, how terrible the expectation of judgment! how fearful a punishment awaits him who betrays, who persecutes Me by so cruel a baseness!

If they, who misused the ancient types of this divine Sacrament, were punished so severely: if the sons of Heli, because they had behaved in an unbecoming manner in the Sanctuary of old; if Oza, because he had irreverently touched the Ark of the Covenant; if Balthassar, because he had used the sacred vessels for an unholy purpose; if all these, in punishment of their crimes, were overtaken by death, what does that sacrilegious wretch deserve, who, so far as in him lies, tramples under foot and spurns God Himself, his Creator and Saviour?

Would not the earth open and swallow him alive, did not My Heart prevent it, in order that It may still offer him a chance of salvation?

O crime! O enormity! how horrible it is, for one guilty of so great an impiety, to fall into the hands of an Almighty God!

2. *The voice of the Disciple.*—Lord! Lord! I shudder with horror when I reflect on the heinousness of such an abominable crime!

Prostrate in the dust before Thee, I beg and beseech Thee: preserve me from an unworthy Communion of Thy Body and Blood.

By Thy Heart Itself, I implore Thee, Lord God, make me understand what it is to eat this Bread and drink this Cup unworthily, that knowing it, I may sedulously be on my guard, lest I draw upon myself a most frightful condemnation.

The voice of Jesus.—It is, My Child, to receive the holy Sacrament of the Eucharist, whilst the consciousness of a grievous sin burdens him that receives.

Lest, therefore, he take so great a mystery unworthily, and consequently death and condemnation, let a person prove his conscience.

And this proving is necessary, so that no one, self-conscious of a mortal sin, how contrite soever he may appear to himself, should approach the holy Eucharist, without previous sacramental Confession.

3. *The voice of the Disciple.*—Forgive me, I beseech Thee, O Lord, if I appear not to understand fully what is said; for I am dull of comprehension.

Pardon me, also, if I ask things which seem less appropriate; for I am uneasy in heart.

Not that I am not willing to make a greater preparation for so great a Sacrament than that which is required not to receive unworthily; but because the enemy of my salvation, sometimes, suggests that, even after I have done what I could, I should be guilty of the Body and Blood of the Lord, were I to approach the holy Communion.

Thus, when darkness covers my interior, and the enemy roars in the obscurity, so that I cannot clearly discern objects, nor distinctly hear Thy voice within me; I either approach with reluctance and with danger, *or*, deceived by the wiles of the devil, I abstain from the best remedy for all my miseries.

Show me, therefore, I entreat Thee, what signifies to be conscious of mortal sin. For, this being well understood, I shall more easily avoid the snares of the devil, and guard more effectually against an unworthy Communion.

4. *The voice of Jesus.*—My Child, he is self-conscious of mortal sin who knows in his heart that he is in a state of mortal sin. For he is conscious of a thing, who has the consciousness of it. Now, consciousness is certain knowledge.

Knowledge, however, is not to be sought in the same way in all things, but in every matter according to its own manner: absolute in matters absolute, physical in things physical, moral in what belongs to morality.

Wherefore, Child, they that are wont to sin voluntarily, if they doubt, whether, when solicited to a sin, they did commit that sin, are morally certain, from what commonly happens to them, that they are guilty of that sin.

On the contrary, when thou strivest sincerely to cling to Me, or so long as thou art habitually in dread of being deprived of divine grace; if thou knowest not, if thou hast no certain knowledge, that, in grievous matters, thou didst voluntarily consent to the temptations of the enemy, or didst, in any way, lose the state of grace; if thou receivest the Sacrament, thou dost not receive it unworthily.

5. Let these truths, My Child, ever console thee, let them encourage, let them guide thee; especially, when serenity does not reign within—when the noise of the foe fills thy heart.

Thou wilt, however, do rightly, if thou ever makest as perfect an act of contrition as thou art able for all, even thy hidden transgressions, such as they are in the sight of God; that, being thus better disposed, thou mayst, amid the Angels, approach the divine mystery.

It will, likewise, prove useful, if, when thou art about to approach the sacred table, thou provest thyself even in slighter sins; and, by an ardent love, purifiest thyself from them and all inordinate affections; so that, entering with a stainless wedding-garment, thou mayst sit down with Me to the heavenly banquet.

If then, Child, thou dost not consent to mortal sins, although thou feelest thyself tempted thereto; if thou dost not voluntarily commit venial ones; if thou strugglest to go against nature when it opposes itself to the divine good pleasure; behold with the permission of the director of thy conscience, it is lawful for thee to approach holy Communion, whensoever thou art willing.

And, although this purity is infinitely below that divine purity, which is received in the most Blessed Sacrament; yet, it suffices for man, in order to frequent with humble confidence and affection this sacred and sanctifying mystery, and to be thereby more perfectly purified.

For this divine Sacrament is not instituted for creatures that are by nature Angels, who cannot sin, but for men who are angels by desire, and are not willing to sin; so that by it they may attain to the perfection of purity and sanctity, which is rather the fruit of Communion than a preparation for it.

6. It belongs peculiarly to the demon, to turn away from frequent Communion souls that are sufficiently well-disposed; and every one among men who does so, whether directly or indirectly, imitates the demon, and does the devil's work.

Undoubtedly, I require reverence; but I desire love more: and thou wilt show the one and the other better by frequent than by infrequent Communion.

I, indeed, do not desire, My Child, that thou shouldst often approach holy Communion, and at the same time continue to sin, although only venially, or follow the ill-ordered likings or dislikings of nature; but this I will, that, with a fixed will thou be determined to abstain both from committing even the least sin, and from following the inordinate inclinations of nature, and that thou frequently approach thus the holy Sacrament, in spite of what they may think who, in this matter, defend the part of the evil spirit.

If, in consequence of this determination, thou art wont to lead a pure life, then, Child, even if, through frailty, thou fall occasionally into some defect, do not on that account omit thy usual Communion; but, after having made the requisite proving, come to it with a more intense preparation.

Consider, Child, and remember, how greatly My Heart is honored and delighted by a pious and holy Communion, with how great a joy heaven is filled, with how much comfort the faithful departed are helped, with how many gifts and graces a well-disposed soul is replenished, to secure her salvation the better, and to attain to sanctity.

Are all these results not such that they do not

only counterbalance, but infinitely outweigh, the labor or effort required for the proving and cleansing of thyself?

7. There is no one who cannot in this manner prove himself, cleanse himself, in fine, dispose himself; since to all grace is given for this purpose.

Nor can any one attribute the lack of disposition to nature, or to his condition in life; since neither nature nor condition in life, but an ill-regulated will, or carelessness, renders the soul indisposed.

Excite thy fervor, My Child, stir up thy heart for a matter of such importance, that, in this life, there can be naught greater, naught more useful for thee.

Here every one receives the reward of the labor which he has employed in preparation, and, in proportion as he draws nigh purified and disposed, he departs laden with graces and favors.

8. *The voice of the Disciple.*—Thanks to Thee, most kind Jesus, for that, in so weighty a matter, Thou instructest me so clearly, so distinctly; and, with so great a benignity of Heart, invitest and pressest me, although so poor and wretched, to a frequent participation of the divine banquet.

Henceforth, I will come with more security and cheerfulness to this sacred Table; since I know, how I must prove and dispose myself, as well to be acceptable to Thee, as to partake with fruit of this heavenly food.

I ardently desire, Thou knowest it, O Lord, and I most firmly resolve, to live free from every voluntary sin whatsoever, and from every inordinate affection; that, without hindrance, I may, as frequently as possible, receive Thee in holy Communion.

Whatsoever may be wanting to me, poor and destitute as I am, do Thou, I beseech Thee, good and merciful Jesus, supply from the treasury of Thy Heart: clothe me with the white robe of innocence: adorn me with the beauty of faith, hope, charity, and of all virtues, that I may deserve to appear among the holy Angels, and banquet with Thee, unto Thy joy and honor, and my consolation and sanctification.

CHAPTER XIX.

HOW WE OUGHT TO PREPARE OURSELVES FOR HOLY COMMUNION.

1. *The voice of Jesus.*—My Child, My time is near at hand; do thou await Me: behold! I will come, and will enter with thee, and I will make My abode with thee.

And when I come, I shall not be alone, but many Angels with Me; nor shall I come with empty hands, but bring along riches, and honors, and happiness, that I may enrich and ennoble thee; that I may make thee contented and blissful.

Prepare, therefore, a place for Me, in which there is not only no stain, but wherein also everything is becomingly adorned.

If thou considerest well, whom thou art about to receive, thou wilt, indeed, acknowledge that, even if thou didst possess the innocence of Angels, thou oughtest still to prepare thyself with the utmost care.

For, with how great a purity, how great a holiness should his body and soul be glittering and adorned, who does not merely approach and embrace purity itself, sanctity itself; but receives the same, is incorporated with the same!

Do, then, whatsoever thou canst, to prepare thyself in body and soul for this grand work.

2. Grand, indeed, is this work: for thou preparest a dwelling-place not for a superior or a prince, but for thy Saviour-God: neither dost thou labor for perishable things, but for everlasting possessions.

Wherefore, some time before the day previous to My coming, begin to dispose and prepare thyself remotely, according to thy condition, by some acts of self-denial and other virtues.

Direct thy good works, yea, even those which are indifferent, thy words, and thoughts also, to this object; and offer them all, that they may be as so many ornaments, pleasing in My sight, of the place which thou art exerting thyself to prepare for Me.

3. Excite and cherish a living desire of the happiness which thou art about to enjoy in the holy Communion. This will stir up and animate all the rest.

And why shouldst thou not be goaded on by this desire, if thou considerest in how manifold ways thou standest in need of Me? Why shouldst thou not experience an ardent longing, if thou givest heed to the great blessings which thou art about to receive? Why, in fine, shouldst thou not be wholly inflamed, if thou meditatest, how eagerly My Heart desires to bestow Itself upon thee?

In correspondence with this desire of My Heart let thy heart, in return, long for Me; and let it, from time to time, renew and inflame its eagerness to be dissolved by love, and be with Me.

Now address the Angels: Have ye seen whom my soul loves? I adjure you that ye tell Him that I languish with love.

Then call upon the Saints: I entreat you, Brethren, by our Lord and by His Heart, assist me with your prayers.

Again, express to Me thy longing desire: O my Beloved! my chosen one among all others, show me where Thou feedest among the lilies. Who will grant me that I may find Thee, that I may embrace Thee, that I may lead Thee into the dwelling of my heart! Bid, O bid me experience how good Thou art to them that seek Thee; how sweet to them that find, how ineffable to them that possess Thee! Come, Lord, and do not delay.

With these, and other affections suited to the state of thy soul, entertain thy fervor; excite a spiritual hunger after the most wholesome Sacrament of the Eucharist, which demands a hungry soul, and fills and satiates the hungry soul with good things.

4. Make, besides, a pure and holy intention, and cause the same to bear on the various ends, particular as well as general, which thou hast proposed to thyself.

Beware, My Child, lest thou approach the holy Communion for form's sake, or through custom, as it were without any purpose: nor be thou less on thy guard, lest thou go to it in order that thou mayst appear devout, or, on the contrary, that thou mayst avoid reproach; or, lastly, that thou mayst experience sensible consolation.

Proceed with straightforwardness, follow after things pure and holy, according to the divine good pleasure, from which thou oughtest for no consideration whatsoever to turn aside. For, whatsoever is foreign thereto, is of no value, how good soever it may appear.

Thus it will happen, that, when about to approach the holy Sacrament, after a careful preparation, if thou dost not feel, according to thy desire, the fervor and relish of devotion, thou wilt bear it in peace and with profit, resigned to My divine Will, which thou wilt deem the greatest of all consolations.

And if thou dost experience the ardor or sweetness of devotion, thou wilt receive it with a humble and grateful mind, and relish it in thy innermost heart; knowing that it is not an effect of thy own seeking, but a gift of the goodness of My Heart.

5. When the time is now near at hand, that I am about to come, think that thou hearest thy Guardian Angel, who says to thee: Behold, the Bridegroom comes: go thou forth to meet Him.

Arise thou quickly, and, having with thee thy lamp lighted with sanctifying grace, hasten to My holy Tabernacle, watch there, and make the immediate preparation for My coming.

Let thy heart be dilated, let all the powers of thy soul exult: let the present felicity replenish thee wholly inwardly and outwardly.

Imagine that now thou art no longer on earth, but amidst the Angels, who invisibly surround thee.

6. And whilst I tarry in the Tabernacle, adore Me with a lively faith, cherish a great hope, renew thy love for thy neighbor. Apply thyself diligently to this: insist on this with much affection.

Then, occupy thyself with acts of those virtues which are peculiarly pleasing to My Heart, and which I Myself practiced in a marvelous manner in the Supper-room, before I instituted this Sacrament; thus giving thee an example, that as I did in My Heart, so thou shouldst also do before holy Communion.

For, how deeply did I there humble Myself, when I cast Myself at My Disciples' feet, and washed and wiped them!

Taught by such an example, humble thyself, as much as thou art able, with thy whole heart, with thy whole mind, with all thy strength.

And, when thou hast done all thou oughtest and canst, acknowledge that thou art unworthy to receive Me, to enter into divine companionship with Me.

What more do I ask than a soul truly humble, in which My Soul finds its delight, upon which My Heart may pour out the abundance of Its graces, and which My pure love may pervade, ravish, transform?

By love, My Child, by love was this most delightful Sacrament instituted: by love it must be received.

As the love of My Heart in this mystery is exceeding, and pours itself out without measure, without restriction: so, Child, when thou becomest a partaker of the same, give thyself wholly up, without limit, without terms, to divine love.

This living love, this pure affection, this entire surrendering of thyself, is the highest preparation for holy Communion; because it is the nearest disposition to the divine union.

Here, therefore, do thou linger: here act with thy whole heart; ask, give, according as the Spirit of grace will interiorly teach or direct thee.

7. If thou lovest Me purely, My Child, thou wilt perceive that it is not in thy power to love Me sufficiently: and thou wilt feel, that whatsoever thou dost or art able to do, is as nothing compared to what thou seest is befitting to receive Me in thy heart.

Wherefore, be not satisfied with those adornings of virtue which thou thyself makest ready or possessest; but borrow from the Angels, the Saints, and all the good, whatsoever ornaments they have, for the solemn occasion, when thou art going to receive Me.

And this thou canst do, My Child, if, with a sincere and fervent heart, thou desirest, and offerest to Me, for thyself, all and each one of the merits and virtues of the Angels and Saints; that by these thou mayst be pleasing to Me, and receive Me in a more worthy and perfect manner:

If, for the same end, thou wishest efficaciously to receive Me with that purity, faith, hope, charity: with that humility, love, and holiness, with which all the just and virtuous, yea, My Immaculate Virgin-Mother herself, have ever received Me in the Sacrament.

Holy affections of this kind, Child, if they flow from a pure love for Me, are so pleasing to Me that I am not less delighted with these pure and burning desires, than if thou didst thyself possess the things desired.

But, My Child, seek thou after still better things: perfect the adornment of thy heart with the very virtues of My Heart.

Finally, when I come out of the Tabernacle, when thou hearest the words: Behold the Lamb of God! inwardly and outwardly collected, and full of reliance upon the goodness of My Heart, come thou amidst the Angels, come forth to meet Me.

At this supreme moment, forget in some manner thyself, and, intent on Me alone, receive Me with all thy affections, and enter with Me into thy heart.

8. Behold here the manner, My Child, in which it behooves thee to prepare thyself for holy Communion. If, as is befitting in a Disciple of My Heart, thou drawest these preparatory acts out of thy own heart, instead of reading them out of a book, thou shalt find this method, as it were, ever new.

For thou wilt elicit these acts, now in one way, then in another; according as thy wants, or thy devotion, or the inward unction of the spirit shall move thee.

But, if thou canst not yet act interiorly in this manner, make use of a book; but use it so as to learn by degrees to converse with Me in thy heart, and to be able, at last, to make thy immediate preparation without a book.

Retain, therefore, the method, but vary the manner of following it; shorten one act, lengthen another, according to the present state of thy soul.

Attend not to the form of the acts, but to the

sincerity of the affections: bring forward, in a simple and affectionate manner, the sentiments of thy heart; but, above all, follow the spirit.

Thus it will come to pass, My Child, that thou wilt prepare thyself every time in some new way, adapted to thy present circumstances, and also with new fervor.

For this it will help thee much, to dispose thyself, and to approach holy Communion in such a manner, as if it were to be the last of thy life.

And, in truth, Child, thou knowest not whether thy next Communion shall not be the last: but this thou knowest, that some one unknown to thee shall be the last.

It is, therefore, a prudent and pious counsel to go to every Communion with such a disposition and such an intention, that, if it be the last, it may be thy *viaticum* unto life everlasting.

9. *The voice of the Disciple.*—How great and wonderful is the goodness of Thy Heart, Lord Jesus, that Thou dost so instruct me, and teach me a method so holy and so sweet, to prepare myself for holy Communion!

With thankfulness do I embrace, O Lord, and faithfully will I follow the method Thou givest me; which I own,—as it is so simple and varied,—will be easy and ever new.

But behold! when I shall have performed whatsoever I can, to prepare myself for Thy reception within my heart: what is it all compared with Thy dignity? Or what is it in comparison with the bliss which I am to enjoy?

In that most delightful hour, when Thou wilt enter into my innermost heart, what shall be want ing to my felicity? Shall I not find in Thee whatsoever I can desire?

For Thou, O unfailing fountain of all good! Thou art my life and joy; Thou art my virtue and sanctification, Thou my wealth and honor, Thou my rest and sweetness, and every bliss.

O Jesus, the most beloved of all the beloved! how I long for Thee! how I stand in need of Thee! O when wilt Thou come? When wilt Thou admit me, miserable, weak, ignorant, hungry, and lonely!

For Thou, O my Jesus! Thou art my Saviour, my Physician, my Leader; Thou art my Shepherd, my Friend, the Beloved of my soul.

O Lamb of God! Thou who takest away the sins of the world, I am not worthy that Thou shouldst enter beneath my roof; but have pity on me, follow the goodness of Thy Heart, come.

O my Beloved, O Thou the Bridegroom of my soul, sweeter than honey and the honey-comb; fair with the beauty of innocence, blushing with the purity of love, draw me to Thee, make me like to Thee.

Assist me to prepare myself, in holiness, for Thy coming: grant that I may keep my lamp trimmed and lighted; that I may neither sleep nor be sluggish; but that I may so watch for Thee in prayer that I may so glow with piety, that, when Thou comest out, I may go forth to meet Thee with my soul prepared, and be found worthy to enter with Thee.

CHAPTER XX.

WHAT WE MUST DO AFTER WE HAVE RECEIVED THE BLESSED SACRAMENT.

1. *The voice of Jesus.*—My Child, so soon as, through holy Communion, thou hast received Me, setting aside all other care, be thou wholly Mine, as I am thine.

Behold! then surrounding and prostrate Angels adore, worship with reverential awe, marvel in astonishment, burn with love: canst thou, in the midst of all this, remain indifferent?

Everything within and without is holiness and devotedness, peace and joy, and pouring out of favors and gifts, sweetness and felicity. Partake thou of the same, My Child: enjoy all these blessings in Me, whom thou possessest.

For lo! in thy innermost heart I Myself am present, thy God, thy all. Stay with Me, My Child, nor leave Me alone, by wandering away with thy mind, thy heart, or thy senses.

Having closed the doors of every avenue, spend with Me that time, than which none can be better, more pleasant, more precious for thee.

Blessed art thou, if thou knowest how to employ this time, on which the principal fruit of Communion, the chief progress of thy soul, depends!

How many things thou hast to do in this most joyous hour! how much to pray and to ask for! how many wants to make known to Me! how much, also, hast thou to hear from Me! how many sacrifices to make: how much, in fine, to receive for thyself and for others!

Wherefore, do not neglect the time of my visitation: but have a care, that not the least part of so good a gift overpass thee.

2. First, then, in sincerity of heart, return the greatest thanks to Me, thy Saviour-God, for that I have deigned so mercifully and so lovingly to visit thee.

And, since thou art unable to return worthy thanks for an infinite favor, call upon the Angels, who are attending unseen: invite all the heavenly Spirits and the Saints; nay more, invite everything that breathes, every created being, great and small, that, with thee and for thee, they may praise together, and extol exceedingly the Beloved of thy soul, so loving and so lovely.

But, because all these are below the greatness of the divine well-doing, offer up all the thanksgivings, the praises, the acts of love, which the Angels and the Saints, and all the just have ever offered, and will offer forever.

Offer all this, united with the merits of My Heart; which, since they are infinite, are equal to the infinite gift.

3. Then, make acts of the most profound adoration, freely submitting for a holocaust, all the powers of thy soul, and the senses of thy body, as a homage of faith due to Me.

This holocaust, containing as it does the greatest humility, and as it immolates thee wholly to Me, pleases and honors Me supremely.

After this, what is there for which thou mayst not hope from My Heart, so lavish of Its gifts.

Hope boldly, My Child: form great and strong acts of firm hope. Now cherish an assured hope that whatsoever thou mayst ask will be given thee. Again cast thyself upon My Heart, as a child upon the bosom of its parent, trusting that here thou shalt find what thou desirest, hoping that here thou shalt be safe.

And will not, meanwhile, thy heart be burning in thee, when so great a kindness is shown thee, so undue a condescension, so disinterested a love?

Here be persevering, My Child: give thyself altogether to the divine love; cease not to make acts of love, until thou hast satisfied thy devotion, or the Spirit of grace directs thee to other matters.

For, while the divine love is working in thy heart, and exercises its power, then is the acceptable time,—if, through human frailty or in any other manner, thou hast done things which may be displeasing to My Heart,—both to grieve, out of pure love of God, for having committed them, and to resolve to commit them now no more.

The living heat of divine love, if thou co-operatest with it, pursues sin like dry stubble, burns and consumes it.

4. Then, that thou mayst not fall again, pray earnestly to be cured of thy evil passions, if thou have any; to be freed from inordinate affections, whereby thou either lovest or shunnest unsuitably created objects; to be delivered from miseries, to which thou art subject; lastly, to be preserved from sins and defects, especially from those to which experience teaches thee that thou art more inclined.

Nay more, in order that thou mayst become more

solid and perfect, as well as more alike and dear to My Heart, do thou beg earnestly for virtues or an increase of them.

Ask for a more lively faith, a more firm hope, a more fervent love, a greater affection for holy poverty, a more Angelic purity, a more perfect obedience, a more eminent humility and meekness, conformity to My divine Will, an intimate and abiding union with Me: other virtues, in fine, which thy state requires, and which are befitting in a Disciple of My Heart.

Proceed still further, and implore a special help, whereby, for love of Me, thou mayst perform cheerfully and meritoriously those sacrifices in particular which grace asks and desires of thee.

Devote thyself wholly, with all thou art and hast, as a living victim to My honor and to My love.

5. Lastly, My Child, exercise the zeal of love: pray much and fervently for others, to the greater glory and joy of My Heart.

Through the merits of the Saints and Angels, through the Heart of My Immaculate Virgin Mother, through My Heart Itself, pray humbly for the universal Church; that she may enjoy peace, increase in holiness, and be spread throughout the world.

For the Supreme Pontiff, My Vicegerent, and for all My Ministers; that they may be good laborers in My Vineyard, may possess rightness of intention, purity of life, the pursuit of perfection, the fervor of zeal.

For Religious; that they may preserve their first spirit, make constant progress in virtue, edify the world, console the Church.

For all the faithful people; that every one, in the vocation to which he was chosen, serving Me in a worthy and laudable manner, may strive to make his calling sure.

Pour forth, likewise, thy prayers and supplications for the conversion of infidels, of heretics, of all sinners; that, freed from the errors of the mind and the vices of the heart, they may direct their steps into the way of salvation and peace.

For thy kindred, benefactors, friends, and expressly for thy enemies; that they may be assisted with help from above, be sanctified, and that they may obtain all things necessary and useful to them.

For all the just, the afflicted, those in danger, those who are in their death-struggle; that they may obtain perseverance, comfort, protection, and a happy end.

Finally, for the faithful departed, for those especially for whom thou mayst, in any manner, be obliged to pray; that they may deserve to enter heaven, and be able to intercede for thee before the throne of the divine mercy.

6. Do all these things faithfully, My Child, and endeavor to perform them in a gentle and efficacious manner, according to the spirit.

However, if I whisper or communicate anything to thee, or occupy thee in any-wise, or deal with thee, leave off all beside, and hearken to Me with docility and reverence.

If I chide thee for anything, receive My rebuke with a submissive heart: if I exhort, if I press aught upon thee, resolve, decide: if I grant or promise aught, be liberal in return: if I bestow any comfort, receive it humbly, allow thyself to be replenished with the sweetness of consolation, remembering that I am good, that My mercy endures forever.

And, if it happen that the love bursting forth from My Heart suddenly takes possession of thee, fills thee with rapture, yield thou, My Child, and suffer thyself to be carried whithersoever it wills.

Conceal thou outwardly, as much as thou canst, that which grace does inwardly,—lest some may attribute to thee what is exclusively due to Me,— and suffer love to be excessive, and to carry thee through all its transports: permit thyself to be enkindled with the divine fire, to be melted, to be dissolved.

Such things, through Its exceeding love, does My Heart sometimes effect, in regard to My true Disciples, in order to reward them for their toils and troubles, lovingly endured for My sake, or for sacrifices which they have generously made for Me: or to make them taste, with a full heart, how delightful It is in the Sacrament, and how great a sweetness It reserves for them in heaven: or, yet, that, when disposed, It may, by a wonderful power of love, transform them into Me.

But, Child, if after piously and devoutly receiving Communion, thou dost not experience the sensible effects of grace, the motions of divine love, be not uneasy, be not troubled. The fruit may not be less, without the feeling of these gifts.

And even if, by straining thyself, thou do excite this feeling, thou shalt derive no profit from this emotion of nature; but, on the contrary, thou wilt foster self-love, nourish vanity, and expose thyself to delusions.

But continue thou humbly and quietly in My presence, exercising ordinary acts of virtues: and thus endeavor to carry with thee a greater humility, a more perfect conformity to the divine good pleasure, if thou do not feel the ardor and sweetness of love.

This, My Child, is the common way of the Saints, who rested contented wheresoever they were placed: if not at My Side with Thomas, nor on My Breast with John, they remained with Mary at My feet, continuing faithful to the present grace, and thankful therefor: and, whether prostrate at My knees, or admitted to My embrace, under either circumstance, they profited according to the measure of grace granted to them.

7. In this manner, therefore, wilt thou act, My Child, after thou hast received the most Blessed Sacrament. And this method, although ever the same, will ever appear new: for thou wilt each time use it differently and variedly, according to the state of thy soul, and the motion of the spirit.

For I wish that, after Communion, thou sufferest thy heart to pour itself out before Me; to speak and deal with Me, according as it is affected or able.

If thou readest certain forms of prayers, even the most pious, thou dost not so much give utterance to what is thy own, as rehearse what belongs to another; thou dost not communicate to Me thy heart, but, with or without feeling, thou recitest in My presence, what another heart has said. Shall I praise thee? herein I do not praise.

Thinkest thou that, in this manner, thou canst become a truly interior person? that thou can't discern the secrets which I am wont inwardly to suggest to the soul? or enjoy My intimate communications?

Wherefore, Child, accustom thyself to converse with Me, heart to Heart, to unfold to Me thy sentiments, to receive Mine for thyself, to give what thou hast, and take, in return, what I liberally bestow.

If, however, by reason of thy want of skill, or some desolateness which presses upon thee, thou canst do nothing, unless thou readest some forms of prayer; read, but read little and slowly and attentively, and, pausing now and then, endeavor to draw something from thy heart and communicate it to Me. Thus thou wilt make progress; thus thou wilt acquire, by degrees, the science of the Saints, the art of inwardly conversing and dealing with Me.

8. When it is now time to return to thy own, forget not the remote thanksgiving.

Entreat the holy Angels, to continue, in thy stead, their praises before Me: and, together with their praises, offer to Me whatsoever thou art about to do or suffer.

Then, go whithersoever the divine Will calls thee: but outwardly and inwardly give heed to thyself: shun unnecessary occasions of distraction and dissipation: take care lest thou pour forth thy heart in things worldly or useless.

Make for Me in thy innermost heart a sanctuary, where thou mayst keep Me ever present; pray to Me frequently, consult Me, and communicate to Me all thy concerns.

According to thy ability, prove by deed that thou art mindful of the divine favor thou didst receive: exercise some virtue in a more perfect manner: show a greater charity to them that are ill-affected toward thee; or, on the other hand, to those against whom thou feelest some bitterness: exhibit a deeper humility, a gentler meekness, and other virtues, whereby thou dost manifest to Me thy gratefulness and love; and, at the same time, edify thy neighbor to be zealous for better things, and delight My Heart.

9. *The voice of the Disciple.*—O most kind, O most sweet Jesus! from my heart of hearts do I return thanks to Thee, for that Thou didst condescend to instruct me so perfectly, so lovingly, so gently.

If, henceforth, after holy Communion, I do not spend my time well, if I do not act rightly, I confess myself inexcusable.

Hadst Thou not spoken to me, hadst Thou not thus taught me, my imperfect manner of acting, the little fruit derived from my Communions, might, perhaps, to a certain extent, have found an excuse before Thee: but now I have no excuse.

O Jesus, infinite goodness! excite me to fervor: assist me with Thy grace, that I may reduce to practice the sweet and holy things, which Thou hast drawn out of Thy Heart, and delivered to me, and which I desire with all my affections.

For what is there sweeter in life? what is there happier in this world? what is there better or holier?

O my love, Jesus, divine Bridegroom of my soul, Thou ever-enduring delight of the Angels and Saints! when I enjoy Thee, what can I desire beyond?

Grant, I beseech Thee, that then I may be wholly

Thine, and Thou wholly mine; that I may deal
with Thee according to the good pleasure of Thy
Heart; that I be and remain wholly resigned, and
united to Thee.

CHAPTER XXI.

THE MOST SACRED HEART OF JESUS, IN THE BOUNTIFUL SACRAMENT OF THE EUCHARIST, GIVES US A REMEDY, WHEREBY WE ARE FREED FROM VENIAL, AND PRESERVED FROM MORTAL SINS.

1. *The voice of Jesus.*—My Child, this is the
Bread which comes down from heaven; so that if
any one eat of it, he may not die.

The first substantial and enduring fruit, that the
soul gathers from My Heart, in holy Communion,
is that she is freed from defects, is strengthened in
good, and preserved from spiritual death.

That this, so consoling an effect of Communion,
might be made known, this life-giving Sacrament
was instituted under the appearance of food. For
nourishment keeps the body from weakness, increases its strength, continues its life.

What natural food does in the body, that, but in
a much more perfect and marvelous manner, this
supernatural nourishment, this Bread of Angels,
effects in the soul.

If the fruit of the tree of life, placed in Paradise, could save the human body from death, and
preserve it in an everlasting youthfulness; how
much more will this food, which comes down from

heaven, be able to guard the soul against death and keep her in permanent vigor?

Yea, My Child, the fruit of the Sacrament, this heavenly nourishment does, sometimes, for the soul what neither the fruit of the tree of life, nor any terrestrial food can effect for the body. For should it happen that some one, after a sincere proving of himself, after a sincere examination of his conscience, should invincibly, and, therefore, inculpably, be ignorant of a mortal sin, and so in good faith eat of this living Bread, he would obtain, at the same time, the life of sanctifying grace and the remission of his hidden sin.

2. This divine Sacrament supplies, not only great strength to turn away from evil, but even hinders or lessens the very causes of evil.

Does not water extinguish fire? But the divine Eucharist extinguishes, much more effectually, the heat of the passions. For it contains every virtue, and, therefore, it checks every passion.

What wonder, My Child, if this heavenly mystery renders all vices and unlawful pleasures unpleasant and distasteful, since it gives to men to drink the wine whose fruit are virgins, and offers to them the delights of Angels?

Am not I the Bread of the life of bliss, the fountain of everlasting sweetness? He that comes to Me shall no longer hunger or thirst after the forbidden and dangerous aliments of the world: for, him I satiate with the good things of God, which, by their deliciousness, have the power of causing all that is prohibited, all that is of earth, to appear bitter and distasteful.

3. When I am Sacramentally present, the ene-

mies of salvation flee far away from the soul, which, through holy Communion, has become terrible to them.

If, at any time, they venture to assail her, they approach her full of dread, and make their attacks from afar.

And these assaults themselves,—since the passions of the soul have become more subdued and tranquilized,—affect her less, and expose her less to danger.

For, when she perceives herself tempted to sin, if she thinks that she has received God in her heart, or that she is about to receive God therein, will not this mere thought suffice to repel the temptation? will it not be an inducement to exert her strength, that she may preserve her heart unsullied, and that she may remain faithful?

How many souls have there been in this world, that,—although at first they were the slaves of baneful passions, yet, by the pious and frequent use of this saving Sacrament,—were not only, in a short time, happily delivered from them, but overcame, with ease, the attacks of demons, and continued ever faithful.

And, indeed, if during My mortal life, when I dwelled with men, a virtue went forth from Me, and healed all infirmities; how much more now, in My Sacramental life, does the virtue issuing from My Heart, heal and strengthen the souls united to Me by Communion?

4. Moreover My Child, when I come to the soul, through the holy Sacrament, I bring with Me all the sentiments of My Heart, and, according to the disposition of her heart, I share these with

her: the love of humility, the love of charity, the love of holy poverty, the love of purity, the love of obedience, in fine, of all virtues which remove the sources of vice, that they themselves may occupy their place.

This love, which is the soul of all virtues, and which My Heart communicates through the Sacrament, is strong as death. This, unless thou hinder it, will render thee invincible.

Call to mind the primitive Church: how great a fortitude of love My Heart was wont to impart through holy Communion, so that the faithful,—even they that were weakest by nature, children and tender maidens,—were victorious over all the enemies of salvation, and stronger than death itself.

Whatever allurement the pride of life possessed, whatever the lust of the eyes could effect, whatever effort the concupiscence of the flesh could make, was not able, in the least, to captivate hearts, that,—fortified with this food of the strong, replenished with the sweetness of My love,—longed for naught save to persevere in love for Me, and feared nothing except to be deprived of My love.

What could separate these from My love? not tribulation, not distress, not persecution, not death in any shape.

5. That which this Sacrament of the love of My Heart did formerly work so visibly, the same it does even now.

For, whence, except from My Heart in this divine mystery, among so many of the faithful, so great an abhorrence of whatsoever the world and self-love pursue? whence, among so many youths and maidens, so great a love of innocence, that they spurn and trample under foot all things contrary thereto, how charming soever they may appear to nature; that they seek, and embrace with joy, every safeguard of their beloved virtue although disagreeable to nature? Whence, in many, that generousness of heart, even to loving the cross for My sake, even to making sacrifices with gladness for love of Me? Whence, in fine, in very many, of every condition in life, so great a fortitude, that, although they own themselves weak, they withstand, unconquered, every opposition of the world, all the assaults of hell, yea, overcome them triumphantly?

Behold here marvelous things, My Child; behold, how this divine Bread, which the love of My Heart bestows, gives life and preserves it from death and even from decay.

6. *The voice of the Disciple.*—O living and life-giving Sacrament! whence I have the Bread of life, whereby I may live and be strong in spirit. I beseech Thee, O Lord, give me always this Bread: but so that I may not grow sick nor die.

For how many examples have we heard, and how many have our fathers related to us, of them that have eaten this Bread of life, and died!

Nay, we have seen and known, and trembled with fear, that even of them that frequently or even daily banqueted with Thee, and ought therefore to have lived like Angels, some have shamefully gone away, and filled themselves with the husks of swine, and wallowed in the mire, despising grace, despising heaven, despising the dread of hell itself!

The voice of Jesus.—Behold, My Child, men who, when they were in honor, did not understand, but have become like to senseless beasts!

But judge thou rightly: if thou perceivest that even they, who here banqueted in purple, have sought their delight in filthiness, ascribe it solely to their senseless, evil will.

For, this saving Sacrament, although of itself it preserves from death, does not however deprive man, if he be unwilling to live, of the power of causing death to himself.

By weakening the passions and the foe, it strengthens and assists, in a wonderful manner, the freedom of the will, but it places no necessity upon the same.

Wherefore, a person often and duly strengthened by this divine nourishment, will live and not die, although he may do so, if he misuses, for the purpose of causing death, what is given for the purpose of life.

When, therefore, thou hearest the examples of them that have fallen, reflect on thyself, and say: He that stands, let him take heed lest he fall.

And be thou so much the more on thy guard, lest by voluntary defects and lukewarmness, thou hinder holy Communion from producing its saving and divine effects.

7. *The voice of the Disciple.*—O Jesus! O life! through which I live, without which I die: bid me ever live by this life: bid me ever enjoy vigorousness of spirit.

O my beatitude, O Lord! whom I possess through holy Communion, I ask no sensible consolations, but that love, by which I may be so strong, that I do never grow weak; by which I may be so replenished, that whatsoever the world offers me, may cause me disgust, never any relish.

Grant me, I beseech Thee, to watch more cautiously over all the senses of my body, to guard more attentively every faculty of my soul, so that no fault do hinder the fruit of Communion.

Drive, and keep far from me, all occasions of sin; protect me powerfully, and preserve me unharmed amidst the dangers to which, for the sake of Thy service, I must be exposed.

But, more than all, keep me from all sin, and grant that I may never be separated from Thee, who art my only true and blissful life.

8. How good it is to be with Thee, O Jesus, sweetness of my heart, sole felicity of my soul! O do not suffer me to depart from Thee, nor do Thou Thyself, I implore Thee, withdraw from me.

Stay with me, I entreat Thee, lest darkness seize me, lest dangers encompass me, lest, destitute of courage and strength, I perish: for Thou art my true light, Thou my place of refuge, Thou my strength and salvation.

By the love of Thy Heart, I beg and implore Thee, abide with me, O most kind and sweet Jesus: without Thee, nothing is well, nothing is pleasing. Without Thee, O how miserable am I! but O how blissful with Thee!

Stay, therefore, with me, and rather deprive me of the possession of all else, of the love of all creatures, than permit that I should be deprived of the possession and the love of Thee.

CHAPTER XXII.

BY HOLY COMMUNION THE MOST SACRED HEART OF JESUS UNITES US WITH HIMSELF, AND MAKES US LIVE THROUGH AND FOR HIM.

1. *The voice of Jesus.*—My Child, he that eateth Me, the same shall live by Me.

Why should he not also live for Me, since he is so united with Me that he is incorporated with Me, and animated by Me?

For behold! if ever, it is assuredly in Communion thou art become a member of My Body, of My Flesh, of My Blood. Wilt thou, then, taking a member of Christ the Lord thy God, make it a member of the world or of iniquity? God forbid.

But, rendered living and holy by My very Body and Blood, thou wilt show thyself living of Me, holy, pleasing to Me in all things.

As the body does, in some manner, put on the qualities of the food wherewith it is wont to be nourished; so that he who, being properly disposed, nourishes himself with strong and solid aliments, becomes himself strong and robust: thus, My Child, thou shalt find by experience, if thou feedest often and properly on Me, the principle of all purity and sanctity, that thou also shalt become pure and holy.

Thy soul cleaving to Me, will now no longer crawl with her mind among earthly and perishable things, will no longer with her heart find delight among the low and vain pleasures of the world but will seek the things which are above and enduring; she will relish that which is supernal and good.

Principles foreign to Me shall animate thee no more: merely natural sentiments shall no longer exercise an influence over thy life; but because I live, thou shalt also live.

This true, supernatural, holy life, which thou wilt live as effected by Me, which thou wilt live hidden in Me, thou wilt also live for Me.

2. If, in this thy life, thou dost any good works, if thou practicest any virtues, if thou performest any exercises of piety; all these will be for Me.

If any one ask thee, why thou thinkest, why thou speakest, why thou actest, why thou sufferest in this manner, thou wilt be able to answer: It is all for the sake of Him who loved me, and gave Himself to me.

Marvelous intercourse of My Heart, secret and divine communing with a pure and faithful heart, in this Sacrament of love! The world understands not these things.

And who can comprehend it, save the innocent in body and the clean of heart? The same shall know, he shall experience, he, in fine, being admitted to higher and more interior things, shall live for Me in a still more marvelous manner.

3. For, being continually nourished of Me, and completely united with Me, he will at last not live save of Me: he will not breathe save by My breath, he will not love except by My love.

Yea, as the living Father has sent Me, and I live through the Father: so he that eats My Flesh, the same shall in like manner live through Me.

Attend, My Child, and understand all the sublimity of this. As I receive of the Father, and unceasingly have in the Father, divine being, life, and perfection: so he that is rightly disposed, receives of Me, through holy Communion, and possesses uninterruptedly in Me a holy being, a holy life, a holy perfection.

I am holy because My Father is holy: and he that is here incorporated with Me, partakes of My sanctity.

4. My Child, does not fire communicate its heat and color to the iron or wood which is put into it? But in the Sacrament there is a far more wonderful and more perfect communication between Me and the soul which is rightly prepared.

She communicates herself wholly to Me, and, if disposed, she receives in return the communication not only of My Humanity, but also of My Divinity; which, when My Humanity ceases to exist and act in her, continues to operate in her, like a supersubstantial food, which not merely preserves, but even increases and perfects her spiritual, her holy life.

Yea, it causes My Spirit to flow perpetually into that blissful soul, and the love of My Heart to urge her on gently and strongly; incited by which she allows herself to be guided by My Spirit: nay more, whithersoever she is guided by My Spirit, she cheerfully concurs with the same, living always and everywhere in Me.

In this wise, therefore, does a well-disposed soul, through holy Communion, live through Me and for Me. Being often refreshed sacramentally, she becomes, at last, so assimilated to Me, that she manifests My life in herself.

Take courage, Child, be zealous of these things, and strive diligently to attain to what is so consoling, so advantageous, and so glorious to Me and to thee forever.

5. *The voice of the Disciple.*—O Lord Jesus Thou knowest how I long, how I yearn for these things.

By Thy most Sacred Heart, I entreat Thee, O Thou the beginning and end of my life, do Thou frequently, in this Sacrament, nourish with Thyself me, whom by Thy grace Thou hast begotten, that I may live for Thee.

Behold, O Lord, it is by Thy gift that I live. but for what do I live, if I live not for Thee?

O Jesus, fountain of life, never-failing bliss free me from every inordinate disposition, that I may be wholly replenished with Thee, that I may wholly live for Thee.

So often as, through holy Communion, Thou comest to me, if Thou findest in me aught that is worldly, aught that is foreign to Thy Spirit, aught that is opposed to the good pleasure of Thy Heart; do Thou root it out, I beseech Thee, that it may yield its place to Thee, to the Spirit and love of Thy Heart.

Free me altogether from every obstacle: with the divine fire of Thy Heart, do Thou consume whatsoever hinders me from being sacredly and perfectly united with Thee, so that, being no longer mine but Thine, I may altogether live for Thee.

6. Renew, sanctify my body and soul, that, being consecrated to Thee, and animated by Thee, they may be solely occupied with Thee, and for Thee.

Grant, I entreat Thee, that I may undertake and perform every employment for Thee; and that, during the same, so far as is allowed, I may often entertain myself with Thee.

Grant, that, when I am free from my occupations, I may forthwith, with mind and heart, turn myself to Thee, as the weight, when the obstacle is removed, hastens to its centre.

Be Thou alone, henceforth, the beginning and the end of all I do or suffer, whether inwardly or outwardly.

Ah, Lord Jesus! although nourished by Thee and for Thee, how long, how often, have I labored and endured not for Thee, but for the enemies of Thy honor and glory,—for self-love, for a vain pride!

Forgive me, I implore Thee, this perverseness, this injustice, this great ingratitude.

Give me efficacious grace, that, as is most just and worthy, living of Thee, I may likewise live for Thee.

7. O Jesus, most loving and most amiable Bridegroom of my soul! enlighten me, enkindle me, that I may more perfectly know, more fervently love Thee, my only blissful life.

I acknowledge and confess, O Lord, that I am not worthy that Thou shouldst raise me to the sublimity of Thy life, which Thou art wont to communicate, in the Sacrament, to Thy Saints: but Thou, Lord, art most worthy to be served, for the glory and joy of Thy Heart, in a holy manner— even by me.

This grace, therefore, do Thou grant to me, that, through a frequent and devout Communion, I may attain to this, that I may live, as **Thou** also livest.

Yea, live Thou, O Jesus, infinite sweetness, my everlasting happiness! live Thou, reign Thou, triumph Thou in me, unto Thy honor, unto everything that can be pleasing to Thy Heart.

May everything I possess, may all I am, be immolated, be sacrificed to Thee by purest love: Thou alone, most sweet Jesus, art my life: Thou alone art everything to me.

CHAPTER XXIII.

THE MOST SACRED HEART OF JESUS, THROUGH HOLY COMMUNION, PERFECTS HIS UNION WITH US, AND TRANSFORMS US INTO HIMSELF.

1. *The voice of Jesus.*—My Child, he that eats My Flesh, and drinks My Blood, abides in Me, and I in him.

Behold here a perfect union, whereby I, a divine Person, am found with Body and Soul in thee; and thou, a human person, art found with body and soul in Me.

This union is, therefore, true and substantial. For no one is in Me, unless I be in him.

If some one pours melted wax into other melted wax, the one must necessarily commingle with the other: in like manner, when thou receivest My Body and Blood, thou art so united with Me, that thou art in Me, and I am truly and intimately in thee.

Is not this, My Child, a mystery of love? Verily, it is even an excess of love; for the force and power of love over My Heart are such that thereby it is given to man, not only to be completely made one with My Body, but also with My Soul and My very Divinity, and that he sweetly enjoy the same.

How the Angels wonder at this! how they stand astonished! how blissful they pronounce thee.

2. In this holy intercourse, My Heart pours forth that delicious and precious grace, whereby this consummate union becomes enduring, so that I abide in thee and thou in Me.

For, even after the Sacramental species are consumed, I, as God, abide personally in thee, not only as living in a living temple, adorned with habitual grace, but also as the perpetual principle of supernatural sanctity, elevating thy life by the continual influence of sanctifying grace, and by the frequent infusion of actual grace! and thus thou, in return, abidest, in a peculiar manner, in Me.

Hence it is, My Child, that thou art enabled to live a life truly holy, a life, in some manner, divine: since thou possessest ever, both in thy body and soul, My Divinity, whence thou mayst draw life.

And this abiding union between Me and thee will be perfect, whensoever there shall exist between Me and thee a true similarity, a true uniformity: for things dissimilar and different are difficultly and imperfectly united with each other.

Blessed perfection of abiding union! Blessed thou, My Child, if, through frequent and devout Communion, if, through manifold grace thence received, if, through a generous fidelity, if, through constant fervor of love, thou disposest thyself to this perfect union!

3. For what springs from a perfect union, if not oneness? Therefore, we shall now be no longer two, but, in some manner, one.

This marvelous, delightful, beatific oneness is above all distinguished—and excels all others, which are blended together from created objects—by this, that it arises, not from the combining or putting together of us both, but from the transformation of the one into the other.

Thou wilt not, however, change Me into thee, like natural food: but thou shalt be changed into Me.

Then, My Child, the affections of thy heart shall no longer be thine, thy desires shall be thine no more, thy joy thine no more.

And, whatever natural inclinations thou shalt possess, and whatever other affections according to man, these, for this transformed life, shall be as if they were not; since thou shalt not live by them.

But in this new life, thou shalt live My life: the affections and inclinations of My Heart shall now be thy affections and inclinations: the love, the desires, the joy of My Heart, shall now be thy love thy desires, thy joy.

The aversion of My Heart to evil, to the world, to everything vain, will pervade and replenish thy heart.

The boundless zeal, wherewith My Heart is burning, for the honor and glory of God, for the salvation and perfection of souls, will inflame thy heart.

Whatsoever is bitter, thou shalt find sweet; what is distasteful, thou shalt deem delicious; what is difficult, thou shalt account easy in Him in whom thou livest and art able to do all things.

Thou shalt think of everything as I think; thou shalt will as I will; thou shalt live as I live: yea, thou shalt live, thyself no more, but I in thee.

4. Behold, My Child, the hight to which the faithful soul is raised through holy Communion! Who, except one that has experienced it, can understand all the holy, all the delightful, all the marvelous things of a soul thus transformed into Me!

Many are called to this supernatural transformation, but few are chosen: not that I am unwilling to choose them that are called, but because they do not dispose themselves, by means of the grace imparted to them.

For, how many there are, who, even though they frequent the holy Sacrament, do yet continue, in almost everything, to follow nature!

How many, also, there are, who strive indeed to keep themselves in a state of grace, but who, satisfied with this, so serve nature that they perform their actions from natural aversion or inclination!

How many, in fine, who, although they make profession of a pious or even a religious life, and have spent several years therein, have not yet learnt to pass beyond nature!

What wonder, then, if these remain always imperfect, always miserable, ever unprepared for that divine and perfect union!

5. But they who, being disposed, have reached this state of transformation, how great a happiness

do they possess! how holy a liberty do they enjoy! with what purity do they taste My sweetness!

Hence, they despise all things that perish, they forget themselves; made perfect and blissful, they abide in Me.

The greatest bliss, My Child, the greatest hight, the greatest perfection, to which a person can be raised in this mortal life, is this, that he abide transformed and consummated in Me.

Marvelous, yea, unspeakable state, wherein Mine are and remain thine, and thine Mine, and wherein oneness and fellowship between Me and thee are perpetually strengthened!

Come, then, My Child, do not lose the hope of so great a perfection, but, after having heard the blissfulness of such a state, be more courageous, more generous, more faithful: thus, at the proper time, I will lift thee up unto Myself.

6. *The voice of the Disciple.*—O Jesus, my love, most pure Bridegroom, most holy God! with how great a sweetness dost Thou deal with me, who comest so often and so kindly to me in this most delicious Sacrament, in order to unite me, miserable creature, with Thyself, with Thy most sacred Humanity, with Thy adorable Divinity!

By the love of Thy Heart, whereby Thou deemest me worthy of such a favor, I beg and beseech Thee, consume Thou whatsoever there is in me contrary to the perfection of this union; and enkindle within me a great fervor; that, generous and faithful to every motion of grace, I may transcend all merely natural things, and practice pure virtues.

Thou knowest, O Lord, how great a desire,

through Thy goodness, possesses me of disposing myself ever more and more to this perfect and permanent union with Thee.

Behold! I offer, I deliver up to Thee, whatsoever I am: I give Thee my heart, that it may be united with Thine: I give Thee my spirit, that it may be absorbed by Thine: I give Thee my whole self, that, by the efficacious grace of Thy Sacrament, I may be made of one likeness and form with Thee.

Receive me, O Jesus! accept me: unite me wholly with Thee: absorb me altogether: transform me into Thyself.

7. O how great and wonderful is the power of Thy love, whereby Thou changest the soul into Thyself! how great the condescension of Thy goodness! how great, likewise, the dignity and excellence of the soul transformed into Thee!

O Lord my God! lo, shall it ever be given me thus to enjoy Thee? O let it be so, I beseech Thee! all the honor and glory of so blissful, of so disinterested a favor shall belong to Thy Heart, the fountain of all blessings.

Let me cease to be what I am, that I may begin to be what Thou art, Lord Jesus: live Thou alone in me with Thy love, with Thy Spirit, with all Thy Heart's inclinations and dispositions, with Thy good pleasure for time and for eternity.

CHAPTER XXIV.

THROUGH HOLY COMMUNION THE MOST SACRED HEART OF JESUS BESTOWS UPON US THE GIFT OF PERSEVERANCE.

1. *The voice of Jesus.*—My Child, he that eats this Bread shall live forever.

And why should he not lead an immortal life? for, he has within him an enduring, an ever-living principle, whereby he may continue upon earth the life of grace, until he arrive at the life of glory in heaven.

Thou wilt understand the price of this saving fruit of the holy Communion, and burn with love for the same, if thou attendest to the magnitude of the gift, whereby perseverance in the life of grace is secured.

Perseverance, My Child, is the consummation of virtue, the guardian of merit, the last and permanent triumph, the secure reward of labors and sufferings, the crown of everlasting glory.

Without perseverance, all other things, whatsoever they be, are devoid of their everlasting fruit and reward: perseverance alone crowns all.

And therefore were all the Saints so particularly anxious about this great gift, that, since they could not condignly merit the same, they might, at least, put no hindrance to it, and might, through the means given, carefully prepare themselves therefor.

Do thou, in like manner, diligently dispose thyself, My Child, by the removal of every obstacle.

and, as they did, so wilt thou also, through holy Communion, obtain this most excellent gift of perseverance.

2. This have I determined in My Heart, Child, that the greatest Sacrament, the holy Eucharist, should impart the greatest grace—perseverance.

And, indeed, since in the Sacrament I give Myself to thee, whereby the Majesty of the Divinity may seem to be debased; why should I not give perseverance, whereby the glory of the Divinity is exalted?

Wherefore, although of thyself thou art weak and hast many miseries, here thou wilt receive for thyself such strength from My Heart that thou wilt be enabled to reach the goal in safety.

For, if the Prophet, in the strength of the food, which was only a figure of the Sacrament, reached the mountain of God, how much more shalt thou be enabled, by the strength of the truly life-giving, of the truly divine food, to reach the hights of the everlasting hills?

Lift up thy eyes, and see how many, of themselves not less weak, not less feeble than thyself, have safely reached there even now. Take courage, and proceed thou cheerfully.

3. My Child, yield to no immoderate fear: united with Me, thou canst efficaciously and easily guard against falling.

Whence arises the beginning of ruin if not from lukewarmness? For, when the soul languishes with lukewarmness, things spiritual must needs become unsavory and unpleasant, and nature desire and seek its own.

Then man, by the propensity of his nature, be-

gins to neglect watchfulness over the powers of his
soul and the senses of his body; yea, in order to entertain his failing heart, he gives a freer scope to
them, and occasionally exposes them to the allurements of sin; at first, not without some dread, but,
by degrees, in a bolder manner.

And hence, by three steps, he falls into destruction.   At the first, he acts carelessly, until he finds
himself in the proximate danger of sin: at the second, he does not strive to pray earnestly, and implore the divine grace that he may escape the danger, that he may not be overcome by sin; at the
third, alone and defenseless, in the midst of enemies, from within and from without, conspiring
against him, he plays, and he amuses himself, as it
were, with the charming monster, when, behold! he
is overpowered, and rolls headlong into the abyss.

4. By what other means, My Child, canst thou
more securely and more easily avert such evils, than
by the saving Sacrament, which unites thee with
Me, binds thee with the chain of love, and makes
thee a partaker of My own strength?

What is there so well suited to drive lukewarmness away from thy soul, as frequent and devout
Communion; through which the fervor of divine
love enters, and takes wholly possession of thee?

Yea, if, during the time intervening between
Communion, any beginning of lukewarmness make
its appearance, a new and devout receiving of the
Sacrament removes it, and restores the first fervor.
For heat and cold, fervor and tepidity, cannot dwell
together in the heart.

Nay more, My Child, a holy Communion recalls
the whole man to interior things, and brings to-

gether all the powers of his soul and the senses of his body, to celebrate with Me, in peace and gladness, the sacred banquet.

But the propensity of corrupt nature does not lead to this; for it is itself also curbed in the divine mystery, which soothes the passions of the soul and tranquilizes the ill-regulated motions of the body.

Here, heavenly delights, whilst they satiate, awaken a longing for them: and worldly pleasures, if any were tasted before, produce such a loathing that the desire of them appears base and unworthy.

Wherefore, being frequently renewed in spirit through Communion, and self-collected in Me, taught by the experience of thy own heart, thou wilt understand how much thou art obliged, and of how great an importance it is to thee, to be faithful.

On this account, during the intervals of thy Communions, thou wilt endeavor to be on thy guard, and not expose thyself, of thy own accord, to danger. And, if at any time thou findest thyself in a necessary or unforeseen danger; by reason of thy wonted intimacy with Me, which thou hast learnt in Communion, and cherished all along, thou wilt forthwith have recourse to Me, and strive, by prayer and supplication, by distrust in thyself and reliance upon Me, to flee, as soon as possible, from the danger, and to unite thyself more closely with Me.

By so doing, My Child, thou shalt walk upon the asp and the basilisk, and thou shalt trample under foot the lion and the dragon, and avoid every monster of sin, and, at last, reach thy end safe and unharmed

5. Wherefore, unless thou art often nourished

with My Body and Blood, in the Sacrament; and unless thou dost sufficiently co-operate with the grace of the Sacrament, thou shalt not persevere in the supernatural life.

This co-operation is, however, made sweet and easy through Communion, by reason of the peculiar grace given for this end in the Sacrament, and on account of the special love infused from My Heart, whereby everything is alleviated and sweetened.

Behold, then, how thou mayst secure for thyself, through a frequent, devout, and holy Communion, the gift of gifts, final perseverance.

Come then, My Child; it is a matter of supreme importance to thee: be brave and magnanimous, as is befitting a Disciple of My Heart. Faithfully employ the means: keep thyself constantly united with Me: thus thou shalt attain to those boundless and precious blessings, which now accompany holy perseverance, and will follow it throughout eternity.

6. *The voice of the Disciple*—How limitless, how precious, Lord Jesus, are those blessings! They are so great, that, for them, Thy Saints gave up willingly everything, and that, when tasting them, they frequently shed tears in the excess of their blissfulness.

How, then, could I be willing to exchange things so full of bliss for the miseries of sin? how could I abandon charity, love of Thee, for the love of the enemy of my happiness?

For, I shall not lose those things which are the effect and fruit of charity, unless I first abandon, unless I first expel charity itself from my heart. For, of itself, charity never falls away.

Thou didst love me first, O most kind Jesus. Thou camest first: but behold! Thou wilt not be the first to withdraw: Thou wilt not forsake me first, unless I myself first forsake Thee. So kind is the goodness of Thy Heart!

O Jesus! suffer me not to leave Thee. Without Thee, what is there for me but darkness, and grief, and anguish, and bitterness, and misery, and never-ending death.

Oh! allow not evils so great to befall me. Grant, O Lord, grant, I beseech Thee, that, united with Thee, I may rather die any death of the body whatsoever, than lose Thee, the life of my soul, the fountain of all blessings.

By Thy Heart, by the Heart of Thy Virgin-Mother, by whatever is pleasing to Thee in heaven and on earth, I beg and entreat Thee, grant me perseverance; bestow grace, add courage, that I may efficaciously employ the means Thou hast given.

7. I am, indeed, weak and infirm, O Lord; but Thou art all-powerful and good. Assist me, therefore, and strengthen me. Be Thou unto me a Saviour-God, and Thy Heart a house of refuge to save me.

O Jesus, good Shepherd! for Thy Name's sake, do Thou lead me, and nourish me with Thyself, do Thou refresh me with the living waters gushing out of Thy Heart, that I may cheerfully continue to follow Thee.

O Jesus, heavenly Physician! have pity on me, heal my frequent infirmities, repair my shortcomings, restore my vigor, that I may not grow faint on the way.

O Jesus, my Teacher! teach me to do Thy Will: guide my way even unto the end.

O Jesus, my Beloved! entertain Thou me, comfort me in my afflictions, help me in my difficulties, incite me, urge me on to proceed and to persevere.

O Jesus, divine Bridegroom of my soul! hold me closer to Thee: draw me after Thee: behold! being willingly drawn, I will run by Thy strength: I will run unwearied to the secure and everlasting possession of Thee.

CHAPTER XXV.

THROUGH HOLY COMMUNION THE MOST SACRED HEART OF JESUS GIVES US A PLEDGE OF FUTURE GLORY.

1. *The voice of Jesus.*—He that eats My Flesh, and drinks My Blood, has everlasting life: and I will raise him up on the last day.

Behold, My Child, a great mystery, but a great mystery of love, a great mystery of consolation.

For, here in the most holy Sacrament, thou receivest both the medicine of immortality, and the symbol of resurrection.

Hence, not only the soul, vivified and sanctified through Me, attains to the life forever blissful, but even the body, corruptible and obscure, united and incorporated with My life-giving and glorious Body obtains never-ending glory and immortality.

Wherefore, not merely on account of sanctifying

grace, but also for a new reason, for the sake of the holy Communion, will I make thy soul forever joyous and blissful, reform thy body, render it like unto My Body, and adorn it, in a peculiar manner, with glorious properties.

Lo, My Child, the most delightful and most marvelous fruit of Communion—which completes and crowns all the others.

2. My Child, when the goodness of My Heart wishes to display all Its magnificence, behold! all Its other qualities and virtues are at hand, and concur and vie to ennoble and perfect the object.

Now, in the holy Sacrament of the Eucharist, the love of My Heart has decreed, so to manifest the grandeur of Its munificence, that Its most glorious fruits should endure for all eternity.

Do not then marvel, if this mystery overflows with prodigies so great and numberless, if it possesses so rich an abundance of blessings; if the whole is sublime, holy, delightful, replenished with consolation.

A very great miracle, indeed, is here promised to thee, that thou shalt live not merely in soul, but also in body, through all eternity; but this is less than that which has already been done for thee. For it is, assuredly, less that a person should live in eternity, than that God should die in time; it is less, that man should be raised up unto a glorious life in heaven, than that God should be lowered unto a hidden life in the Sacrament.

And why should not the member rise again, when the Head is risen? And why should not he live forever, who possesses in himself everlasting life?

Wherefore, when I, thy Life, shall appear, then thou also shalt appear with Me in glory.

3. Behold, My Child, in the Sacrament thou hast the pledge of this ever-enduring glory, a pledge not of an ordinary kind, but one which is equivalent to the promise.

See, therefore, how great an assurance of thy future blissfulness, My heavenly Father, on His part, has given to thee, when He gave, in so wonderful a manner, His only-begotten Son as a hostage!

And what must wholly complete thy joy and consolation, is that, in this pledge itself, thou hast wherewith, on thy part, thou mayst not render uncertain that most delightful assurance.

What then remains, My Child, except to be thankful and faithful, to rejoice in the goodness of My Heart, to delight in the blessings poured out upon thee, and, as often as thou receivest Me, to call to mind, with gladness, that everlasting beatitude of which thou possessest the pledge, which thou enjoyest by anticipation?

When that which is promised shall come, the use of the Sacrament shall cease; and thou shalt not now have an anticipated partaking of bliss, but thou shalt possess the plenitude itself of bliss—thou shalt enter into it, and be penetrated by the same.

Then, faith shall yield to sight, hope to complete fruition: and abiding charity shall burst forth into never-ending joys. In that beatitude of thine, thou shalt breathe naught save love, thou shalt speak naught save love, thou shalt do naught but love: for thou shalt be in the pure realm of love.

4. The Sacrament of love leads to the realm of love: the more love has been nourished here, and the more perfectly it has been kindled in thy heart in time; the more will it there enrapture thee, and the more gloriously will it shine in thee during all eternity.

Wherefore, My Child, live thou resigned by love, until the shadows of mortality decline, and the day of immortality dawn: advance thou peacefully by pure love.

Whatsoever thou beholdest around thee, whether things prosperous or adverse, view them with the same eye of pure love, being, amidst them all, solely intent upon Me, in whom thou possessest life, and resurrection, and beatitude.

If thou feelest this mortal life heavy with miseries, know that thou wilt all the more relish thy future bliss, the more thou hast experienced the miseries of the present life; and that thou wilt repose the more sweetly upon My Breast in heaven, the more hardships thou hast endured, for love of Me, upon earth.

Meanwhile, Child, be cheerful and valiant: repair thy strength and courage by the life-giving Sacrament; for love of Me, remain conformed to My good pleasure, in life and in death.

5. *The voice of the Disciple.*—O excess of good· ness! O Jesus! who can comprehend, in this life, what a Heart Thou hast!

Behold! Thou givest Thyself to me in the Sacrament, to procure for me in abundance all things desirable in time, and, together with this, Thou givest Thyself to me as the pledge of the everlasting bliss, which, by a gratuitous liberality, Thou hast promised to me.

Thanks to Thee, most kind Jesus, endless thanks to Thee, for so great a charity of Thy Heart.

With all my heart do I rejoice at so great, so precious a gift, so gently and so lovingly bestowed, whereby Thou givest me the sweetest confidence of my everlasting salvation.

I beg, O Lord, my God, I humbly beg of Thee, that Thou wouldst grant me efficacious grace, that my election to the glory of heaven, so certainly and so divinely pledged on Thy part, may not be made void; but that, on my part, through my faithfulness, good works, and true merits, it may, in like manner, become certain.

6. O most sweet Jesus! with how much fervor and cheerfulness ought I to serve Thee: with how great a courage to walk the roughest roads; with how great a love to cling to Thee; that I may reach those unspeakable joys whereof I have here a foretaste, and whereof I possess here so sweet a pledge?

Ah, Jesus, my Beloved, purest Bridegroom of my soul! if it is so delightful to enjoy Thee in my exile, what shall it be in my own true country? if Thy consolations are so sweet in the Sacrament, what shall they be in Thy kingdom? if, whilst Thou art here vailed, Thy embraces so enrapture the heart, what shall they do when I behold Thee face to face, when I recline upon Thy Heart, when I am satiated and inebriated from the torrent of Thy delights?

O my God! when I think on this, whatsoever I find upon earth becomes burdensome and wearisome to me.

Life itself loses all pleasure, since naught therein can wholly satisfy, or completely satiate me.

Nay, even Thy consolations themselves and Thy very sweetness afflict me with a marvelous and unutterable pain; because they cause me to know Thee more distinctly, and to thirst with more eagerness after Thee, the fountain of all consolations, and of every delight.

After Thee, O my Jesus! after Thee do I thirst: Thee do I wish to behold unvailed: upon Thee in Thy glory I desire to gaze: Thee, with all the ardor of my soul, do I long to enjoy by everlasting love.

Come then, O my love, come Thou: burn me: wholly consume me: dissolve me, that I may be with Thee, O Thou my sole desire, my only good!

CHAPTER XXVI.

RECAPITULATION.

THE MOST SACRED HEART OF JESUS IS OUR ALL.

1. *The voice of Jesus.*—My Child, My Heart, which thou possessest in the most Blessed Sacrament as the pledge of future glory, and which in heaven will be thy beatitude, is meanwhile, so long as thou sojournest on earth, all things to thee.

For It is wholly, with all It possesses, delivered up to thee, for thy use and enjoyment.

Now this Heart, as It consists of a human nature, is indeed human, and can, therefore, feel for thee in a human manner; but, as It is hypostatically united with the divine Nature, It is, at the same time, divine,—is the Heart of a divine Person, and, consequently, possesses that which is divine and infinite.

Behold, then, the fountain of all blessings, always accessible, always gushing, whence thou canst ever draw, but which thou canst never drain.

Here, My Child, here shalt thou find whatsoever is necessary, whatsoever is useful to thee.

If at any time thou growest cool in spirit, here thou shalt be kindled again, here thou shalt be renewed interiorly, here thou shalt recover inward vigor.

If thou hast offended, here thou shalt find mercy, here thou shalt obtain forgiveness, here thou shalt regain peace.

If thou art languishing through weakness, here thou shalt be restored, here thou shalt be strengthened, here thou shalt be invigorated with a divine power.

If thou needest counsel, or courage, or assistance, here thou shalt obtain it in abundance.

If thou desirest some divine grace, some useful favor, some genuine comfort, here thou shalt find the same.

Whatsoever, finally, is conducive to thy real happiness, thou shalt here secure, at any time and in any place, in health and in sickness, in life and in death.

2. Moreover, My Child, in the Sacrament, My Heart is, likewise, a pattern of every virtue and of all sanctity.

Contemplate with the eyes of faith, love, and imitate the virtues of My Heart all reduced to unity, and yet remaining separate. One and the same love combines, ennobles, and displays them all.

See here the gentleness of the love of My Heart, Its humble charity. Behold here truly the Heart of a hidden God, who emptied Himself: but to what an extent did He empty Himself! the more deeply thou shalt meditate hereon, the deeper thou shalt find the abyss of that humility, and the better thou shalt perceive the magnitude of that kindness, whereby My Heart, ever gentle, ever meek toward all, undergoes and endures so much for love of thee.

Look at Its piety. Consider how It devotes Itself to the service of God Its Father: how It consecrates Itself to His interests: how It is ever busy with the things that belong to His good pleasure.

Look at Its poverty. Look into the innermost of this Heart, what are Its sentiments in regard to the possessions of this world. See how It uses them. See how It is destitute of what is suitable. Behold here the model of holy poverty.

See Its purity. Yea, My Child, behold and observe, how It possesses a Body, made in some manner spiritual, like the ray of the sun, pure always and everywhere: behold and observe in what manner It employs Its senses: behold and observe how holy are all Its affections. Lo, the mirror of purity.

See Its obedience. Behold and be astonished, My Child. Lo! at the voice of a simple creature, at the word of the priest, I am ready, with My Heart prepared for everything: and even if the priest speak for the sake of sordid gain, yea, even if he be wicked, as soon as he has uttered the words of holy Consecration, I am present, with My Heart disposed to all things. In what place soever I may be put, there I rest, with My Heart resigned. In what manner soever I am treated, although I am not insensible, I yet am and remain full of bliss. This, My Child, is the pattern of perfect obedience.

See Its prudence. Examine devoutly, how great a prudence It teaches thee, in the sacred Tabernacle, by Its example, in devoting and applying the means to the end: how great a prudence in the choice of companions, since It dwells ever among Angels; how great a prudence in manifesting affections, whether of liking or dislike.

See Its justice. Contemplate, how It refers Its Sacramental life, and Its every occupation to God, to whom all is due. Examine and observe, with how great a fidelity It directs all things, great and small, to the divine glory.

See Its fortitude. Mark Its virtue, in enduring, with an even and unconquered mind, every hardship, as well from the faithful, from sinners, from the lukewarm, and from all the ungrateful, as from the places wherein It is left, or neglected, or even treated with indignity: in persevering in the undertakings of divine love, in spite of every opposition and contrariety: in making use of things adverse themselves to manifest a purer love for God and for man.

See Its moderation or discretion. It distinguishes between the person who sins and the sin of the person. Knowing that man is the work of God, but sin the work of man, It desires and seeks, with

unwearied patience, to destroy the sin and to save
the man. It distinguishes between nature and
grace, between the appearance of things and the
reality. It distinguishes between good and good,
and approves of that as better, which the divine
Will actually requires or prefers.

See Its zeal. It burns here with the desire of
saving souls, seizes every opportunity, and labors
in a marvelous manner. For this object, It pours
forth prayers, night and day: for this, It shows
an example of forbearance, of mercy, of every
virtue: for this, It speaks to souls in many and
various ways: for this, at one time It inspires and
moves; at another, It presses and urges. Thus It
teaches a zeal possible for all, easy for them that
love.

See Its generosity. Behold what It gives, and
with how great a cheerfulness: lo! It gives not
only gladly what It has, but even what It is; not
only Its graces, but also Its merits; and—more
than all—Its very Self. See what It sacrifices, and
with what nobleness of love. See what consolation It feels, when, for the divine glory, It comforts the heart of man.

See Its perseverance. Here, in holiness, It
spends year after year, nay, age after age. Compare with this the time of thy perseverance, during
the short space of a lifetime. It perseveres, not
like thyself—now growing lukewarm then again
fervent,—but ever with the same fervor. It perseveres with gladness, because It perseveres out of
love.

Behold, My Child, the crown of sanctity, the
crown of the twelve constellations,—which embrace

all the stars of virtue,—wherewith My Heart is adorned, and in each of which love is twinkling and glittering.

For it is the love of My Heart that is humble, that is meek, that is pious, that is poor, that is pure, that is obedient, that is prudent, that is just, that is long-suffering, that is discreet, that by its zeal promotes faith, hope, charity; that is generous and ennobles all things, that is ever persevering.

3. Lastly, My Child, My Heart is the Way, the Guide, and the Gate of heaven.

The most safe Way, by following which thou canst not err: the shortest Way, because the straightest: the most pleasant and most easy Way, because the Way of love: the Way, in fine, wherein all My Saints have walked, and whosoever walks therein will become a Saint.

The Guide, who will protect thee on every occasion, and ward off all danger from thee: who will assist thee with manifold grace, and reinvigorate thee with the very Bread of Angels: who will entertain and sanctify thee with the display of mysteries, through which he will lead thee, and by which he will keep thy mind and heart occupied in a pleasant and holy manner,—advancing from mystery to mystery, from virtue to virtue, from one degree of holiness to another,—until thou reachest the kingdom of heaven.

The Gate, beside which there is none other, through which thou canst be admitted into heaven: the Gate, through which alone entrance is given: the Gate, through which, if any one do enter, he shall be saved and blissful forever.

Beware, therefore, My Child, lest thou hearken

to them that say, that there is a higher and better road for more perfect souls; a way, not of My Heart, but of the mere Godhead, a way, which,—setting aside or overlooking My Humanity,—can lead thee in a sublime manner to thy end, through the Divinity alone.

Whosoever says this to thee, be he a man or an Angel, believe him not, trust him not.

For, through My Humanity, I came to men: and, through this same Humanity, must men come to Me.

Whosoever tries another road will go astray: he shall wander about amid dryness of mind and dryness of heart: frequently, destitute of inward occupation and entertainment, he shall become exhausted; yea, he shall be in danger, at last, of falling away altogether.

But thou, My Child, be thou mindful of My Heart, wherein thou shalt find all things. Here do thou frequently resort to Me: here be often in My presence: here pray, give thanks, praise, hearken to My words, meditate on My Heart: gaze upon Me abiding with thee, offering thee all things.

Come then, My Child, yet a little while, and thou shalt repose secure upon My Heart forever. Meanwhile, occupy thyself with Me, and I will occupy Myself with thee.

Hold thyself in readiness: for coming I will come, and take thee up with Me into My everlasting kingdom.

4. *The voice of the Disciple.*—Yea, most loving and most lovely Jesus, until Thou comest, I will ever be mindful of Thy Heart; in It will I live, in

It will I busy myself with Thee, in It will I hold myself in readiness.

How could I ever forget that Heart, to which I owe everything, and in which I find all things?

Behold, O infinite sweetness! henceforth, Thy Heart shall be my rest, my true bliss.

Here will I repose the more safely, and securely and pleasantly, O Lord my God, the wiser, the more powerful, the more delightful Thou art.

If the world lays snares, if the devil tempts, my heart shall not be troubled; for its abode is in peace, since it dwells in the aid of the Most High, in Thy very Heart Itself.

O my soul: how intimately shalt thou be united with thy God in the Heart of Jesus! how perfectly present to Him! There shalt thou be ever with Him: thou shalt live blissful in Him, gazing upon Him not in figure, but infused into thee; loving Him not as appearing to thee, but working in thee; possessing Him not as holding Him, but as possessed by Him.

In this Paradise of most pure delights, thou shalt overflow with uninterrupted bliss, ceaselessly enjoying the good things of the Heart of Jesus, the Lord thy God.

O Heart of my Jesus! Heart of my God! true heaven, everlasting repose of all the Elect! be it but granted to me, that I may always dwell in Thee, enjoy Thee; naught on earth shall be wanting to my bliss.

For Thou art the safeguard and security of them that dwell in Thee: Thou art the reward and glory of them that persevere in Thee: Thou art the joy and delight of them that enjoy Thee.

In Thee is the light of the mind, the fortitude of the heart, the salvation of the soul, the perfection of sanctity, the completion of beatitude.

O Heart of my Beloved: in which there are infinitely more and better things than the mind can understand, or the heart can grasp; why should I seek for aught that is good outside of Thee? Behold! in Thee are all blessings.

5. Wherefore, most kind Jesus, in Thy Heart is for me the life of bliss: and O may death not find me except in Thy Heart! Oh! that there I may, at last, give up my soul!

Yea, may Thy love grant, that, henceforth, I may live, in Thy Heart, a life as it were dead, such as thou livest in the Sacrament!

What death can be more blissful than this? what rest is there comparable to this? Behold! this is my repose in that death, whereby I desire to be disengaged from everything, and, by pure love, to live in Thee and for Thee alone.

O Jesus, my life and my every good: being thus perfectly dead, may I live for Thee so purely, that, when comes the end of mortal life, nothing remains for me, except calmly upon Thy Heart to breathe my last!

Let my last sigh be the sigh of Thy own expiring Heart: the sigh of pure love resigned: let me die by love, as also Thou didst die! let me die a holocaust of pure love, consumed in Thy Heart!

Will not this death, O Lord my God, be a blissful repose, a sweet slumber, whereby I fall asleep upon Thy Heart in the land of my banishment, to awake upon Thy Heart in the kingdom of glory, to rest secure and rejoice for evermore?

Thus, O thus, my Jesus and my God! thus I wish: thus let it be, I implore Thee, O Thou my sole desire, my Good supreme!

6. O Heart of Jesus! Thou canst not be named, without enkindling: nor thought of, without consoling: nor seen represented, without cheering: what, then, shall it be to gaze upon Thee unvailed, to embrace Thee in truth, to be satiated with Thy everlasting joys?

O beatitude incomprehensible, most blissful life, life without end, without change; life free from all discomfort, replenished with all blessings! how I delight in the remembrance of thee! how I burn with longing for thee!

Appear Thou, O do appear, O Jesus, consummate blissfulness! bid me enter into Thy joys, O Lord! let me join in fellowship with the choirs of all the Angels and Saints, and begin, with them, the ever-enduring canticle of the love of Thy Heart!

O beatitude above every beatitude: forever and evermore, may I gaze upon Thee, may I love Thee, may I enjoy Thee, for the honor and joy of Thy Heart, O Jesus, O my God and my all!

MEMENTO.

WHOSOEVER you are, Christian soul, remember, how greatly Jesus Himself has recommended the devotion to His most Sacred Heart. For, appearing to the Blessed Margaret Mary, He said: "Recommend this devotion to ecclesiastics and religious, as an efficacious means of attaining to sanctity, the perfection of their state: recommend it to those that labor for the salvation of souls as a sure help to move even the most obdurate hearts: recommend it, in fine to all the faithful, as a most solid devotion, one best calculated to overcome their passions, to secure peace, to root out defects, to obtain a fervent love of God, and to reach in a short time a high perfection. My Heart will abundantly pour out Its riches upon all that devote themselves to the same." (Month of the S. H. of J., with the approb. of Abp Paris.)

"This devotion," says St Alphonsus, "consists wholly in the practical love for Jesus. Now, this love is the devotion of devotions. It is truly to be lamented, that many Christians perform various exercises of piety, but neglect this devotion; it is deservedly to be regretted, that there are many preachers and confessors, who inculcate many practices of piety; and never, or almost never, mention this devotion, which yet ought to be the chief one of every Christian. From this neglect it comes that souls make so little progress in virtue, continue to live in the same defects, and relapse even into grievous sins." (Introd. Noven. S. H J.)

Justly, therefore, does that Spouse of the Sacred Heart exclaim: "Why cannot I make known to the whole world those treasures of graces, which are stored up in the Heart of Jesus, and which He is willing to pour out so plentifully, upon them that are devoted to Him! By means of this devotion, He intends to preserve souls from destruction, and to establish in them the reign of *His love, which will suffer no one of those consecrated to It to perish.*" (Blessed Margaret Mary.)

EPILOGUE.

1. Behold, O Lord Jesus, by a new favor of
Thine, which Thou hast added to numberless others, I have accomplished, what, at death's door.
I had vowed to Thy Heart: but Thou knowest
how imperfectly I have performed it, Thou who
art a perfect judge of Thy gifts, and a perfect
witness of my ungratefulness. O Jesus, meek
and humble of Heart! by that very goodness of
Thy Heart, whereby Thou hast bestowed upon
me unworthy, such blessings, I beg and implore
Thee, do Thou vouchsafe to forgive all my shortcomings and my ingratitude.

2. Relying upon the known kindness of Thy
Heart, I offer to Thee, O most benign Jesus, this
debt of mine, this little work every way so imperfect; and I earnestly entreat Thee, to accept and
bless the same, and to pour into it the holy unction of Thy Heart; that thus it may become a rel-
ishable and efficacious means of attracting hearts
to Thee, of purifying them, of adorning them with
Thy virtues, and of perfecting them by Thy sanctity, of uniting them with Thee, of consummat-
ing them in Thee, for Thy everlasting glory.

3. Prostrate before Thee, O Lord my God, I

earnestly pray for all those that shall use this little work. I ask special and abundant graces for them that they may be truly Disciples and Apostles of Thy Heart, meek and humble of heart, and that before Thee they may remember me,—who am not worthy to be called a Disciple, much less an Apostle of Thy Heart,—that they may pray for me, so that I may save and sanctify my poor soul, through the Imitation of Thy most Sacred Heart.

4. This grace, O Lord Jesus, I myself do urgently request. For, of what avail is it to know, that Thou art meek and humble of Heart, if I myself am not meek and humble of heart? Of what use is it to point out to others the easy and certain path of salvation and holiness, if I myself become a castaway?

5. Wherefore, most loving and most lovely Jesus! I pray and beseech Thee, by the Immaculate Heart of Thy Virgin Mother, and by Thy own Heart, crown Thou Thy gifts so gratuitously, so sweetly bestowed upon me. Grant me this choice gift that, united with Thee by the bond of love, I may never be separated from Thee: give me this perfect gift, that I may love Thee perseveringly; love Thee with that purity, with which the holy virgins love Thee; with that fidelity, with which the holy Confessors love Thee; with that fervor, with which the Martyrs love Thee; with that zeal, with which the Apostles love Thee; finally, with that love, with which the Angels love Thee; that I may repay its every love to the love of Thy Heart; that, in every way, may atone for the insults ever offered to Thy

Heart, that, having perfectly put on the sentiments of Thy Heart, I may live out of sole love for Thee, until I be admitted into the endless kingdom of Thy love. Amen.

APPENDIX.

All of the following prayers are found *verbatim* in the writings of Blessed Margaret Mary.

MORNING PRAYERS.

ADORATION AND THANKSGIVING.

O MY GOD! with a most lively faith and profound veneration I adore Thee, and thank Thee for all the graces I have received from Thy bounty, especially for the grace of my creation, redemption, and preservation, for the gift of the true faith, and for having preserved me during the past night from sudden death.

OFFERING AND INTENTION.

O SACRED HEART! I give and consecrate myself entirely to Thee: my heart, my memory, and my will, in order that everything I shall do and suffer be done for Thy honor and for love of Thee; that I may love Thee in all I see and hear; that all my words may be so many acts of adoration, love, and praise of Thy infinite Majesty; that every movement of my lips be an act of contrition for the sins which I have committed, and for the omissions of which I was guilty. Most amiable, divine Heart, would that I could draw me to Thee as often as I breathe; that

I could offer Thee to the Eternal Father as often as
I respire, in thanksgiving for all Thy benefits.

Trusting in Thy infinite mercy, I also form the
intention of gaining all the holy indulgences to be
gained to-day, and I implore These to let them aid
the salvation of my soul.   I moreover unite in all the
prayers, good works, and holy intentions of the
Church militant, suffering, and triumphant.   Thus
submitting my whole being to the dispositions of Thy
most holy will, I implore Thee, O Lord, for Thy holy
blessing.

PRAYER TO THE BLESSED VIRGIN MARY.

HAIL, most amiable Mistress, O holy Mother of my
God! I venerate thee with all my heart, and resign
into thy hands my liberty, imploring thee to be the
guide of my steps, the mistress of my life, and the
rule of all my intentions, desires, and actions.   Most
holy Virgin, be thou my star in the ocean of life, the
secure ha.en of my eternal salvation.   Obtain for
me, together with thy protection and blessing, the
grace to live and die like thee.

TO THE GUARDIAN ANGEL AND HOLY PATRONS.

HOLY Guardian Angel, and ye, my holy Patrons,
hail! Grant me, I pray, your mighty protection and
help.   Amen.

INVOCATION.

DIVINE Heart of Jesus, living in the heart of Mary!
I implore Thee to live and reign in the hearts of all
men, and to enkindle in them the flames of Thy pure
love.

EVENING PRAYERS.

ADORATION AND INVOCATION.

Most sacred and divine Heart of Jesus! convinced of my unworthiness, I prostrate myself before Thee to do Thee homage, to adore, love, and praise Thee as much as is in my power. O Jesus, my most sincere Friend! I expose to Thee all my wants, I discover to Thee all my miseries, my weakness, my tepidity and sloth—in a word, all the wounds of my soul, and fervently implore Thee to let Thyself be moved to pity by them, and that Thou wouldst come to my aid according to the magnitude of Thy mercies.

(Examine your conscience.)

ACT OF CONTRITION.

O Sacred Heart of my Jesus! by that ardent love which consumed thee on the cross, a Victim of love and of suffering, and induced Thee to continue this sacrifice on our altars to the end of time, I, Thy miserable, sinful child, beseech Thee to grant me pardon for all the sins and outrages which I committed against Thee, for all ingratitude and infidelity of which I was guilty, and for my forgetfulness of Thee. Pardon all the sins of my life. I hate them, because Thou dost hate them; I detest them, because Thou dost detest them. For love of Thee I am sorry for having committed them, and should feel the greatest compunction for them even if there were neither heaven nor hell, solely because they offended

Thee, Who art infinite goodness and worthy to be
loved above all things. I would rather die a thousand times than offend Thee again, Whom I love
above my life.

COMMENDATION TO THE SACRED HEART.

O most amiable Heart of Jesus! let me, my
relations, and friends, and all that have commended
themselves to my prayer, and for whom I am bound
to pray, experience Thy most powerful aid. Assist
them individually in their necessities. O Heart full
of mercies! convert all hardened hearts, console the
souls in purgatory, be a refuge of the dying, the
consolation of all distressed and suffering. Above
all, be the refuge of my soul at the hour of death,
and receive it into the bosom of Thy mercy.

In it I sleep securely and rest in peace.

Our Father, Hail Mary, Glory be to the Father,
etc.

PRAYER.

Most sacred Heart! I select Thee as my resting-
place, that Thou mayst be my strength in combat,
my support in weakness, my light and guide in darkness, the expiation of my faults, and the sanctification of my intentions and actions, which I unite with
Thine. Amen.

DEVOTIONS FOR HOLY MASS.

AT THE INTROIT.

O MY GOD! I offer Thee the infinite merits of this holy Sacrifice of the precious body and blood of my Redeemer in satisfaction for my sins: to implore Thee to cause Thy grace to become efficacious in me, and that Thou mayest make me persevere in good works; that thou mayest fulfill Thy holy will in me, and grant me the grace to mortify my own will, together with a lively faith, a steadfast hope, and an ardent love; and that at the end of my life I may have true contrition and a happy death. Be pleased, also, to accept this sacrifice in union with all the desires, sentiments, affections, and beatings of the Sacred Heart. Again I offer Thee, O my God, this holy Mass for the exaltation of holy Church, for our holy Father, the Pope, for our country and its needs, for all those in spiritual fellowship with me, for all ecclesiastical Orders, and for this community, the care of whose spiritual and temporal welfare I commend to Thee. Give us, O Lord, the spirit of true charity and humility.

I beseech Thee also for the conversion of sinners and infidels, for the destruction of heresies, and for the release of the souls in purgatory, the consolation of the afflicted and suffering, and the assistance of the dying. O my God! whilst I unite myself with all the holy intentions Thou didst have when instituting this holy Sacrifice I implore Thee to distribute the merits of this holy Mass, and of all the holy

Masses celebrated to-day according to these intentions; for I wish in all my prayers only that Thy
divine will be fulfilled, and that the fulness of Thy
grace descend upon us.

FROM THE GLORIA TILL AFTER THE EPISTLE.

ETERNAL FATHER, receive, I beseech Thee, the
offering that I make of the Heart of Jesus Christ,
Thy well-beloved Son, as He offers Himself to Thee
in sacrifice. Be pleased to receive this offering for
me, with all the desires, all the sentiments, all the
affections, all the pulsations, all the actions of this
sacred Heart. They are all mine, since He immolates Himself for me; and I desire for the future
never to have any other intentions but His. Receive
them in satisfaction for my sins, and in thanksgiving
for all Thy benefits. Receive, them and grant me,
through their merits, all the graces I stand in need
of, and particularly the grace of final perseverance.
Receive them as so many acts of love, adoration, and
praise, which I offer to Thy divine Majesty, since
it is by Him alone that Thou art worthily honored
and glorified. Amen.

AT THE GOSPEL.

MY Jesus was obedient unto death, even unto the
death of the cross. (*Rising, and signing forehead,
lips, and breast with the sign of the cross:*) O God! be
Thou in my thoughts, on my lips, and in my heart,
that I may worthily receive Thy holy gospel!

O Sacred Heart of Jesus! to Thee I devote and
offer up my life, thoughts, words, actions, pains.

and sufferings. My entire being shall henceforward only be employed in loving, serving, honoring, and glorifying Thee. Be Thou, O most sacred Heart, the sole object of my love, the Protector of my life, the Pledge of my salvation, and my secure refuge at the hour of death. Be Thou also, O most bountiful heart, my justification at the throne of God, and screen me from his anger, which I have so justly merited. In Thee I place all my confidence, and, convinced as I am of my own weakness, I rely entirely on Thy compassionate mercy. Annihilate in me all that is displeasing and offensive to Thy pure eyes. Imprint Thyself like a divine seal on my heart, that I may ever remember my obligations and never be separated from Thee. May my name also, I beseech Thee by Thy tender goodness, ever be fixed and engraven on Thee, O Book of Life, and may I be a victim consecrated to Thy glory ever burning with the flames of Thy pure love, both in time and in eternity. In this I place all my happiness; this is all my desire, to live and to die in no other quality but that of Thy devoted servant. Amen.

FROM THE CREDO TO THE SANCTUS.

O MOST sacred, most divine, most adorable Heart of Jesus! I adore Thy supreme Majesty with all the powers of my soul; and because of Thine infinite goodness I will, through a feeling of fear and respect, keep myself continually attentive not to offend Thee. O Heart most holy, I love Thee, and I desire to love Thee supremely above all things, detesting sin with my whole strength and power: and as I belong wholly to Thee, having received life from Thee amidst such bitter sorrows on the cross, I hope that Thou wilt have pity on my weakness and misery, and wilt not permit me to be lost eternally. I offer myself, then, wholly to Thee, O Heart of love, and desire that my whole being, my life, and my sufferings should all tend to love, honor, and glorify Thee in time and eternity. O Heart most amiable, I love Thee as my sovereign good; in Thee I find all my happiness and all my joy, for Thou alone art worthy of the love of all hearts. Would that my heart might be worthy to be consumed through the vehemence of that love which causes me to renew with my whole heart all the promises I have ever made unto Thee! Preserve me from offending Thee, and make me ever do that which is most agreeable to Thee! O Heart, the source of pure love, why am I not all heart with which to love Thee, and all spirit with which to adore Thee! Grant me at least this grace, namely, that I may love only Thee, and all else in Thee, through Thee, and for Thee; that my memory may only be occupied by Thee; that I may henceforth have no understanding but to know Thee, no will or affection but to love Thee, no tongue but to make known Thy praises, no eyes but to see Thee, no hands but to serve Thee, no feet but to seek Thee, so that one day I may love Thee without the fear of ever losing Thee. Amen.

DURING THE CANON.

Thirty-three Salutations to the Sacred Heart of Jesus.

HAIL, Heart of my Jesus—save me!

Hail, Heart of my Saviour—deliver me!

Hail, Heart of my Judge—pardon me!

Hail, Heart of my Spouse—love me!

Hail, Heart of my Master—teach me!

Hail, Heart of my King—crown me!

Hail, Heart of my Benefactor—enrich me!

Hail, Heart of my Pastor—keep me!

Hail, Heart of my Friend—caress me!

Hail, Heart of the Infant Jesus—attract me!

Hail, Heart of Jesus dying on the cross—atone for me!

Hail, Heart of Jesus in all its conditions—give Thyself to me!

Hail, Heart of my Brother—remain with me!

Hail, Heart of incomparable goodness—forgive me!

Hail, Heart most glorious—shine forth in me!

Hail, Heart most amiable—inflame me!

Hail, Heart most charitable—work in me!

Hail, Heart most merciful—answer for me!

Hail, Heart most humble—repose in me!

Hail, Heart most patient—bear with me!

Hail, Heart most faithful—make satisfaction for me!

Hail, Heart most adorable and most worthy—bless me!

Hail, Heart most peaceful—calm me!

Hail, Heart most desirable and most beautiful—delight me!

Hail, Heart most illustrious and most perfect—ennoble me!

Hail, Heart most holy, Balm most precious—preserve and sanctify me!

Hail, Heart most holy and most salutary—reform me!

Hail, Heart most blessed, true Physician and Remedy for all our ills—heal me!

Hail, Heart of Jesus, Consolation of the afflicted—comfort me!

Hail, Heart most loving, ardent Furnace burning with love—consume me!

Hail, Heart of Jesus, Model of perfection—enlighten me!

Hail, Divine Heart, Source of all happiness—strengthen me!

Hail, Heart of eternal benediction—call me to Thee!

AT THE ELEVATION OF THE SACRED HOST.

O MY Saviour! with sincere humility I adore Thee, and offer Thee up, by the hands of the priest, to Thy heavenly Father in reparation for my sins and for the sins of the whole world.

AT THE ELEVATION OF THE CHALICE.

Most precious Blood, flow on my soul and sanctify it! May the love through which Thou wast shed for me be enkindled in my heart, and purify it!

AFTER THE CONSECRATION.

O SWEETEST JESUS! I unite my soul with Thine. I unite my heart, my spirit, my life, and my intentions with Thy Heart, Thy Spirit, Thy Life, and Thy intentions, and present them thus united to Thy heavenly Father.

Receive me, O Eternal Father, through the merits of Thy divine Son, which I offer up to Thee with the priest and the entire Church. Hidden in His wounds, covered with His blood, and adorned with His merits I appear before Thee. Cast me not away from Thy countenance, but receive me into the arms of Thy paternal goodness, and grant me the grace of salvation. O my God! I thank Thee for all Thy benefits, for Thy sacred Passion, and for the institution of the holy sacraments, especially for the Most Holy Eucharist.

(Say the *Pater Noster*.)

AFTER THE PATER NOSTER.

HUMBLY prostrate before Thee, O Sacred Heart, I adore Thee, I praise Thee, I bless Thee, and I love Thee with all the strength and all the love of which my heart is capable; but I beseech Thee to increase its capacity and augment my love so that I may love Thee still more, and that this love may make me forever all Thine. This favor I ask for all hearts that are capable of loving Thee, but particularly for my own cold, rebellious, and unfaithful heart which has so long abused Thy graces, and ever resists and offends Thee. I am so lukewarm in Thy service that, were it not for Thy infinite mercy

Thou wouldst long since have vomited me forth and cast me from Thee as an object of horror and disgust, deserving to suffer eternally all the rigors of Thy just anger. But I conjure Thee, O Sacred Heart of my Jesus! by that burning charity which consumed Thee as a Victim of love and suffering upon the cross, and which will retain Thee as a Victim upon our altars until the end of time, to grant me, a poor miserable sinner, the pardon of all the sins which I have committed through ingratitude, forgetfulness, or want of fidelity, and all the other injuries which I have heaped upon Thee, and for which I repent from the bottom of my heart. I ask pardon for them with all the grief and regret of which I am capable. I would that I could shed my blood by means of all the torments imaginable, and thus satisfy Thy divine justice, and repair the outrages which I have committed against Thee. I accept beforehand all the sufferings with which Thou wilt be pleased to chastise me in this life, with the exception of being abandoned to myself and to sin, and of being thus deprived of Thy love. O most amiable Saviour, do not give me over to such a dread shame as that of not loving Thee! Rather let me be tormented by all the pains of hell than be one moment without loving Thee. O Divine Heart, source of all love and goodness! do not forget Thy mercies and condemn to eternal privation of Thy love a heart which desires to live only for Thee, and to breathe and aspire only for Thy love in time and eternity! O most loving heart of my Lord Jesus Christ, graciously hear my humble petition, and grant me the grace I most earnestly ask of Thee, namely, that of my true conversion. I have such a detestation and horror for the past, that I would rather be plunged into the abyss of hell than return and continue as before; but, my Jesus, if Thou wilt condemn me to the flames, let them be those of Thy pure love. Yes, cast me into this burning furnace, to remove every vestige of my past offences. And if the excess of Thy goodness prompt Thee to accord me still another grace, I ask of Thee nothing less than the most sweet torment of love. Grant, I beseech Thee, that I may be consumed thereby and entirely transformed into Thee. In revenge for my not having loved Thee, and for my inordinate self-love, pierce, O Jesus, my ungrateful heart through and through with the dart of Thy pure love, in such a manner that henceforth it may be incapable of containing any earthly or human affection, but solely the plenitude of Thy pure love, which shall leave me no other liberty but that of loving Thee in suffering and in the accomplishment of Thy most holy will in all things.

These, then, most sacred Heart, are the graces which I humbly beseech Thee to grant unto me, and to all those hearts which are capable of loving Thee; and I ask for them and for myself the grace of living and dying in this same holy love. Amen.

SPIRITUAL COMMUNION.

ETERNAL FATHER! I offer up to Thee my intellect, that it may learn to know Thee alone.

Sweetest Jesus! I offer up to Thee my memory, that it may remember Thee alone.

Holy Ghost, Spirit of charity! I offer up to Thee my will, that Thou mayest enkindle and warm it by Thy divine love. Adorn my soul with Thy seven gifts, and let me become Thy pure temple. Fill me with Thy grace, and prepare my heart to receive spiritually my God.

Jesus, my God! as my sins render me unworthy to receive Thee into my heart, do Thou receive me into Thine, and unite me so perfectly with It that nothing may ever be able to separate me even for a moment from Thee. Engulf my misery and my nothingness in the abyss of Thy mercy, that I, changed into Thee, may henceforth live only for Thee, by Thee, and in Thee. Come, therefore, Thou, my only satisfaction, come to take possession of this heart, which belongs to Thee, and cannot live one moment without Thee.

AFTER COMMUNION.

I THANK Thee, O my Saviour, that Thou wast pleased to unite Thyself spiritually with me. I offer up myself totally and without reserve to Thee, that it may please Thee to fulfil in me all Thou dost desire to accomplish. Destroy in me the spirit of self-love, humble in me whatever proudly asserts itself, and destroy whatever is opposed to Thee.

CONCLUSION.

Consecration to the Sacred Heart.

LORD JESUS, holy and sweet Love of our souls, Who didst promise that where two or three are gathered together in Thy name there wilt Thou be in their midst: behold our hearts united with one accord to adore, praise, love, and please Thy most holy

and sacred Heart, to which we dedicate and consecrate ours for time and eternity, renouncing forever
all love and affection which are not in the love
and dependence of Thy adorable Heart, desiring
that all the wishes, aspirations, and affections of
our hearts may be always conformable to the good
pleasure of Thine, which we wish to satisfy as much
as we are able. But as we can do no good of ourselves, we beseech Thee, O most adorable Jesus,
by the infinite goodness and sweetness of Thy most
sacred Heart, to support ours by confirming them
in the resolution we have made to love and serve
Thee, so that nothing may ever separate or detach us
from Thee, but that we may be faithful and constant
in this resolution, sacrificing to the love of Thy sacred
Heart whatever may give vain pleasure to our hearts,
or amuse them idly with the things of this world.
We confess that all is vanity and affliction of spirit,
except loving and serving Thee, our God and Saviour;
we desire henceforth no other glory than that of belonging to Thee, as slaves of Thy pure love; no
other aim or motive than that of pleasing and satisfying Thee in everything, even at the expense of
our own lives.

And since, O holy Mary, thou art all-powerful
with this sacred Heart, obtain for us that Jesus may
receive and accept this consecration that we now
make of ourselves in thy presence and through thy
hands, protesting that we will be faithful to His
sacred Heart, being assisted by His grace and thy
prayers, which we entreat thee never to deny us.
Amen.

DEVOTIONS FOR CONFESSION

Before Confession.

PRAYER.

Most merciful Father, behold me, Thy prodigal child, who sinned against Thee by squandering away the spiritual goods with which Thou hadst enriched me. Reject me not, but remember Thy mercy, and exercise it towards my soul, unworthy as it is. Permit it not to perish before Thy eyes after Thy sacred Heart has suffered so great pain to bring it to life.

Grant, O Sacred Heart, that I know and avoid everything that might offend Thee. Remove from me, I beseech Thee, everything that might be an obstacle to Thy love; for I detest and abhor whatever prevents me from loving and serving Thee perfectly.

(Examination of conscience.)

ACT OF CONTRITION.

Most sacred and adorable Heart of Jesus! humbly and with contrite heart I prostrate myself before Thee, bitterly bewailing that I was remiss in Thy love and have offended Thee by my ingratitude and unfaithfulness, thereby becoming unworthy of the manifestations of Thy love. Filled with confusion and fear, I can but say, "I have sinned against Thee, I have sinned!"

Most amiable and divine Heart, have mercy on me, though I do not deserve mercy. Reject me not.

but reveal, rather, I beseech Thee, the excess of Thy mercy by granting me, a poor sinner, who appears before Thee in the abyss of his nothingness and misery, pardon for my sins.

PRAYER FOR PARDON AND GRACE.

O DIVINE REDEEMER! humbly prostrate at the foot of Thy cross, I call upon Thee to incline Thy sacred Heart to pardon me.

Jesus, misjudged and despised—have mercy on me!

Jesus, calumniated and persecuted—have mercy on me!

Jesus, abandoned by men and tempted in the desert—have mercy on me!

Jesus, betrayed and sold—have mercy on me!

Jesus, insulted, accused, and unjustly condemned —have mercy on me!

Jesus, clothed in a robe of ignominy and contempt—have mercy on me!

Jesus, mocked and scoffed at—have mercy on me!

Jesus, bound with cords and led through the streets—have mercy on me!

Jesus, treated as a fool and classed with malefactors—have mercy on me!

Jesus, cruelly scourged—have mercy on me!

Jesus, held inferior to Barabbas—have mercy on me!

Jesus, despoiled of Thy garments—have mercy on me!

Jesus, crowned with thorns and reviled—have mercy on me!

Jesus, bearing the cross amid the maledictions of the people—have mercy on me!

Jesus, bowed down by ignominies, pain, and humiliations—have mercy on me!

Jesus, crucified between thieves—have mercy on me!

Jesus, dying for my sins amid all kinds of suffering—have mercy on me!

LET US PRAY!

SACRED HEART of Jesus, my Redeemer! exercise, I beseech Thee, Thy office of mediator with me, and permit not that Thy sufferings and cruel death be in vain for my salvation, but let them bring forth, for Thy glory, fruits of salvation in me, that my heart may love, praise, and glorify Thee for ever and ever. Amen.

IMMEDIATELY BEFORE CONFESSION.

GRANT pardon, O Sacred Heart, grant pardon to this my sorrowful heart, that places all its confidence and hope in Thee. Do Thou now take my case in hand, and absolve me of my sins and of the punishment due to them. Do Thou, my true Friend, defend me and satisfy the judgment against me.

O Sacred Heart, be my refuge and help now and at the hour of my death.

AFTER CONFESSION.

PRAYER.

O HEART most mild! how thankful must I be to Thee for having borne with my ingratitude so long! At an auspicious moment has my poor, inconstant heart experienced Thy merciful pardon. O Sacred Heart of Jesus! I now give and bequeath to Thee irrevocably, but filled with confusion for having so long withheld from Thee Thine own, my heart and my love. O Sacred Heart! Thou didst deign to give me a proof of Thy infinite love by giving me opportunity to serve Thee, but how little did I improve it! What confusion for me! Amend my faithless heart, O Heart of Jesus, and grant that henceforth it join its love to Thine, and draw near to Thee in future as in the past it withdrew from Thee. And as Thou hast given it its being, I fervently implore Thee to call it one day to life everlasting. Amen.

(Now perform your penance, if possible.)

COMMENDATION TO THE SACRED HEART.

O LORD, I elect Thy sacred Heart my abiding-place. May it be my strength in combat, my support in weakness, my light and guide in darkness; may it supply for my defects and sanctify all my intentions and actions. In union with Thine own I offer them up that I may be prepared to receive Thee.

Strengthen and support, O most sacred Heart, the purpose and desire of loving and serving Thee with which Thou didst inspire me, and grant that I perform all the good that according to Thy will I should.

Be Thou, O God, my strength; do Thou support and defend me, for I am and intend to be forever Thine.

DEVOTIONS FOR HOLY COMMUNION.

BEFORE COMMUNION.

ACT OF ADORATION AND HUMILITY.

O GREAT GOD, Whom I adore in these humble species, is it possible that Thou didst thus conceal Thyself in order to come and remain substantially with me? Though the heavens are the throne of Thy Majesty, Thou art satisfied with these humble species to be with me always!

O incomprehensible bounty! could I believe such a miracle if Thou didst not Thyself assure me of it? And how would I dare to think that Thou shouldst humble Thyself to pass my lips, to rest on my tongue, and to dwell in my heart? Nevertheless, it is Thy will. and to incite me Thou dost promise innumerable graces if I heed Thy invitation.

O God of infinite majesty and ineffable love! why am I not all intelligence to conceive such mercy, all heart to be sensible of it, and all tongue to proclaim it? Thou, O God of my heart, hast created me to be the object of Thy love and ineffable bounty. The angels weary not beholding Thee; they long for Thee even whilst enjoying Thy presence; and could I be able to withstand the desire of possessing Thee? Therefore, because it is Thy wish, most amiable Saviour, and because my necessities compel whilst Thy goodness permits me to desire Thee, I open my lips and heart to receive Thee.

ACT OF DESIRE AND PETITION.

COME, O Divine Sun! For, behold, I dwell in the horrible darkness of sin and ignorance. Come and dispel this darkness, and enlighten my intellect with a ray of divine light!

Come, most amiable Saviour! Thou hast given Thyself to save me from hell, but I relapsed into the servitude of sin: come and disrupt the bonds that bind me, and liberate me!

Come, amiable Physician of my soul! Thou hast prepared for me a bath in Thy blood, and hast given me in Baptism more salvation and welfare than I deserved; but through my own fault I fell into countless mortal illnesses, that weaken my courage, corrupt my heart, and bring death to my soul. Come, then, O divine Physician! for I have more need of Thy help than the paralytic whom Thou didst ask if he wished to be healed. Indeed, O my God! I wish it from all my heart. But as Thou knowest how tepid this my desire is, do Thou animate it by enkindling in me the flames of Thy love.

Come, most faithful, most kind, most amiable and most sweet of all friends, come into my heart! The soul Thou lovest languishes in fatal infirmity; and if hitherto I was insensible of my misfortune and reckless in danger, Thou, O Searcher of hearts! knowest that with the help of Thy grace I have reformed, and sorrowfully call on Thee for help. By Thy incomparable friendship, by Thy word, I conjure Thee to assist me. Come, then, and do not permit that I ever cause Thee to depart from me.

Come, O life of my heart, soul of my life, and only support of my being, Bread of Angels made man for love of me, given in ransom for me and become the food of my soul!   Come, to nourish me, to support me, to give me increase, and to let me live by and in Thee, my sole good and my life!   Were a body bereft of its soul, how would it seek and call for it!   Do I know Thee and myself so little that I should not know what I am without Thee?   Come, then, O my God and my all, impart life to my soul languishing for Him Who is the crown of its beauty, the source of its power, and the fountain of its life.

Most bountiful Jesus! grant that my heart rest not until it has found Thee, its centre, its love, and its happiness.

AFTER COMMUNION.

ACTS OF ADORATION AND THANKSGIVING.

O DIVINE and most amiable Heart of Jesus! humbly prostrate before Thee, I adore, praise, honor, and glorify Thee; I proclaim Thee my supreme Ruler, to Whose service I am bound forever, and Whose right to my love and fidelity I openly acknowledge.

Sustain me, O Sacred Heart, because I belong entirely to Thee, despite all attacks of my enemies. Reject me not, but acknowledge that I am Thine, sustain and defend me as Thy possession.   Support my weakness, and grant me the graces necessary to accomplish fully the desire of my heart to love and please Thee, and to pray, labor, and suffer in the purity of Thy love.

ASPIRATIONS.

O JESUS, my sole love, I beseech Thee to draw all my thoughts to Thee. Through the power of Thy love, which is more effective than fire and sweeter than honey, disengage my heart from all created things. Let me die for love of Thee, as Thou didst die for love of me. O Lord, wound my heart in such a manner, and transfix it so thoroughly, that henceforth it may no longer affect things merely human.

O loving Heart of Our Lord Jesus Christ, Who art able to soften a heart of stone and melt a heart of ice, Who transformest the innermost recesses of the soul, change my heart, and wound it with the wounds of Thy most holy body, and inebriate my soul in the chalice of Thy most precious blood, that, wherever I turn I see nothing but my crucified God, and whatever I see appears to me bathed in Thy blood.

O divine Heart of the Friend of my heart! behold, the soul Thou lovest is ill: visit me and heal me. Because Thou dost love me, Thou canst not possibly let me perish in my misery.

ACT OF CONSECRATION.

O HEART of love! I consecrate myself entirely to Thee. I offer Thee my life, my sufferings, and my whole being in order to honor, love, and glorify Thee now and forever.

O most amiable Heart! I love Thee because Thou art my Supreme Good, my happiness, and my only joy, alone worthy of the love of every heart. Oh, that my heart were reduced to ashes by the intensity of the flame of this love, with which I now renew all consecrations of myself I ever made. Permit not that I ever become an object of Thy displeasure, but let me ever accomplish what is most pleasing to Thee.

O Source of pure love! why am I not all heart to love, not all spirit to adore Thee? Grant that I love Thee alone, and all else in Thee, through Thee, and for Thy sake; that my memory recollect, my intellect contemplate, Thy love; that my will and desires aspire to it; that my tongue praise Thee, my eyes behold Thee, my hands serve Thee, my feet follow Thee alone; so that I one day may love Thee in the glory of heaven without fear of ever losing Thee. Amen.

EJACULATIONS.

O GOOD SHEPHERD! withdraw me from all earthly things and from myself, that I may become more and more united with Thee.

Let Thy voice, O Lord, be heard in my heart, and draw it to Thy love in such a manner that it may no longer be able to resist Thee.

My heart belongs to Thee, O Lord! Permit it not to attach itself to anything but Thee, Who Thyself art the reward of all my victories, and the sole support of my misery.

PRAYER TO THE HEAVENLY FATHER.

O MY GOD! I offer up to Thee Thy well-beloved Son, in return for all Thou dost desire of me. Receive Him as my adoration and gift-offering, as my love, my petition and purpose of amendment, my thanksgiving for all Thy benefits. Accept Him, Eternal Father, for I have nothing worthy of Thee except Him Whom Thou permittest me so affectionately to receive.

Visit to the Blessed Sacrament.

ACT OF REPARATION.

O DIVINE Heart of Jesus, boundless source of love and goodness! how much do I regret that I have forgotten Thee so often and loved Thee so little! O Sacred Heart! Thou dost merit the love and devotion of all those hearts which Thou hast infinitely loved and cherished, and Thou dost receive nothing but coldness and ingratitude from them, and particularly from my own ungrateful heart, which justly deserves Thy indignation. But since Thou art a Heart of love, Thou art also a Heart of infinite goodness, from which I hope pardon and reconciliation. Alas, O Divine Heart! it is with profound grief that I acknowledge myself guilty of so much tepidity, and that I consider the unjust proceedings of my wicked heart, which has so unworthily deprived Thee of the love which was Thy due, and has applied it to itself or to some other transitory object. O Heart most gentle, if the grief and shame of a heart which sees its error is capable of satisfying Thee, pardon my poor heart; for this is the state into which its want of love and fidelity has plunged it. Alas! what could it expect but hatred and punishment, if it did not hope all from Thy mercy? O Heart of my God, Heart most holy, Heart to which alone belongs the pardon of sinners, have mercy, I beseech Thee, upon this miserable heart of mine. All its powers are united to make Thee, in all humility, a reparation of honor for all its wanderings and infidelities. Ah, how could I have refused so long to give my heart to Thee, since Thou alone art its rightful possessor! I regret from the bottom of my heart that I have wandered so far from Thee and Thy love, from the source of all good, in a word, from the Heart of my Jesus, Who, without having any need of me, sought me and loved me first. O most adorable Heart, how could I have treated Thee thus,—Thee on Whose love and goodness I am entirely dependent; and if Thou wert to withdraw but for one instant either the one or the other I should be reduced to the most abject misery or utterly annihilated. How infinite has been Thy goodness, O Heart of love! to have supported my ingratitude so long; it remains only for Thy mercy to pardon my poor inconstant heart. O Heart of my Jesus! I now consecrate and give to Thee all my love and my heart; I give Thee both irrevocably, although with a deep feeling of confusion for having so long refused Thee that which was Thine own. O Divine Heart! Thou wouldst testify to me the excess of Thy love, by rendering me capable of loving Thee, and, alas! I have profited so ill by this opportunity of meriting Thy favors! I am truly grieved, and I most humbly beseech Thee, O Heart of my Jesus, to renew my heart, which was hitherto so faithless.

Grant that henceforth it may be bound to Thee by the bonds of love, and that it approach so much nearer to Thee as it has hitherto wandered far from Thee; and since Thou art my Creator, be also, I beseech Thee, my eternal reward.   Amen.

ACT OF CONFIDENCE.

It is out of the abyss of my nothingness that I prostrate myself before Thee, O most sacred and divine Heart of Jesus, in order to render Thee all the homage of love, adoration, and praise of which I am capable; to lay before Thee all my wants, by revealing to Thee, as to my best friend, all my miseries, my poverty, and my lukewarmness, in a word, all the wounds of my soul: beseeching Thee to have pity and compassion on me, and to help me according to the greatness of Thy mercies.   O Heart of charity, I beseech Thee, by all that is capable of moving Thee, to accord me this grace, that I may save my soul, and that the souls of all those who, like myself, are in danger of being lost eternally, may be saved.   O Heart most merciful, let me not perish in the deluge of my iniquities.   Do with me what Thou wilt, provided only that I love Thee for all eternity.   In Thee I have placed all my trust; reject me not forever.   I call upon Thee, I invoke Thee as the sovereign remedy of all my ills, of which the greatest is sin.   I beseech Thee to destroy it in me, and to grant me pardon for all the sins which I have committed in my life, and of which I repent from the bottom of my heart.   O Sacred Heart, make me and all those hearts which are capable of loving Thee to feel and experience Thy sovereign power; I ask this grace for my parents, friends, and for all those who have been recommended to my prayers, or who pray for me, and for whom I have a special obligation to pray. I beseech thee to help them according to their several necessities. O most loving Heart! soften hardened sinners, and relieve the souls in purgatory; be the sure refuge of the agonizing and the consolation of the afflicted and of those who are in need. Finally, O Heart of love! be my All in all; but particularly at the hour of my death be the haven of rest for my longing soul, and receive me at that moment into the bosom of Thy mercy. Amen.

DEVOTIONS TO THE SACRED HEART.

THE FIRST FRIDAY OF THE MONTH.

It was the special desire of our Lord Jesus Christ, revealed to Blessed Margaret Mary, that the first Friday of each month be consecrated to the devotion to and adoration of His most sacred Heart. In order to better prepare for it, it would be well to read, the evening before, some book treating of this devotion, or of the Passion of Our Lord, and to make a short visit to the Blessed Sacrament. On the day itself we should, on awaking, offer and consecrate ourselves, with all our thoughts, words, and actions, to Jesus, that His sacred Heart may be thereby honored and glorified. We should visit some church as early as possible; and as we kneel before Jesus, truly present in the tabernacle, let us endeavor to awaken in our soul a deep sorrow at the thought of the innumerable offences continually heaped upon His most sacred Heart in this sacrament of His love; and surely we cannot find this difficult if we have the least degree of love for Jesus. Should we, however, find our love to be cold or lukewarm, let us consider earnestly the many reasons we have for giving our hearts to Jesus. After this we must acknowledge with sorrow the faults of which we have been guilty through our want of respect in presence of the Blessed Sacrament, or through our negligence in visiting and receiving Our Lord in holy Communion.

The Communion of this day should be offered by the adorers of the Sacred Heart with the intention of making some satisfaction for all the ingratitude which Jesus receives in the Most Holy Sacrament, and the same spirit should animate all our actions during the day.

As the object of this devotion is to inflame our hearts with an ardent love for Jesus, and to repair thereby, as far as lies in our power, all the outrages which are daily committed against the Most Holy Sacrament of the Altar, it is evident that these exercises are not confined to any particular day. Jesus is equally deserving of our love at all times; and as this most loving Saviour is daily and hourly loaded with insults and cruelly treated by His creatures, it is but just that we should strive each day to make all the reparation in our power. Those, therefore, who are prevented from practising this devotion on the first Friday can do so on any other day during the month. In the same manner they may offer the first Communion of each month for this intention, consecrating the whole day to the honor and glory of the Sacred Heart, and performing in the same spirit all the pious exercises they were unable to accomplish on the first Friday.

Moreover, Our Lord suggested another feature in this consoling devotion of the first Friday, by the faithful practice of which he led Blessed Margaret Mary to expect the grace of final perseverance, and that of receiving the sacraments of the Church before dying, in favor of those who should observe it. This was to make a novena of Communions in honor of the Sacred Heart on the first Friday of the month for nine successive months.

THE MONTH OF THE SACRED HEART.

Interior Practices.

1. AT the beginning of this month examine yourself, and see what is your predominant passion, or the fault which you most frequently commit, and the best means of overcoming it. Having discovered this fault, make a firm purpose to use the means to overcome it, commending your resolution with a childlike confidence to the Sacred Heart. Choose some short ejaculatory prayer which you will repeat often each day during the month, in order to remind you of your resolution, and to implore the grace of God to help you to fulfil it.

2. Each morning, offer all the actions of the day to the Sacred Heart of Jesus, and renew the resolution you took at the beginning of the month, humbly praying for grace to keep it during the day.

3. Take for your subject of meditation the Sacred Heart of Jesus, for which end the consideration of Its many virtues and attributes is recommended.

4. Make the resolution made at the beginning of the month the subject of your particular examination of conscience morning and evening, thanking the Sacred Heart for the good you may have done, and begging pardon for the faults you have committed.

Exterior Practices.

1. IN a convenient situation, place a picture or statue, suitably adorned, of the Sacred Heart; for

Our Lord has promised to bless the houses in which a representation of His Heart is set up for honor.

2. Recite every day a special prayer in honor of the Sacred Heart. Be particular to repeat often during the day some ejaculation.

3. Endeavor to assist at holy Mass every day, and if you possibly can, make a visit every evening to your divine Saviour in the sacrament of His love.

4. Endeavor with prudence and discretion to lead and encourage others to honor the Sacred Heart of Jesus. This may often be done by the distribution of books, pictures, prayers, medals, etc.

FEAST OF THE SACRED HEART.

THE feast of the Sacred Heart is the feast of the love of Jesus towards men. The intention of Our Lord in instituting this feast was to move our cold hearts to love Him. In order to more easily obtain this end, He offers us for the object of our devotion His divine Heart—that Heart which gave the most evident proof of love for us. This day should, therefore be consecrated in a special manner to the adoration of this most sacred Heart, bearing in mind the intention which is the object of this devotion, namely, to make some return for the love which Jesus bears to us, by giving Him all the affection of our heart, and by making every reparation and satisfaction in our power, for the ingratitude of mankind towards a God so infinitely worthy of all love, and who, notwithstanding, is loved by so few of His creatures.

In the morning, therefore, offer your heart and your whole being as a holocaust to the Heart of Jesus, and renew this offering often during the day, which ought to be entirely consecrated, in silence and recollection, to the love of your Saviour. Strive to perform all your actions in the spirit which should animate this feast. Let your visits to the Blessed Sacrament be frequent, and remain in conversation with Jesus as long as your health and the duties of your state of life permit you. Prepare your heart with diligent care to receive Jesus worthily in holy Communion, and offer your Communion to God the Father in satisfaction for the unworthy Communions of so many Christians, testifying at the same time your gratitude and love to Jesus.

If you have enjoyed this book, consider making your next selection from among the following . . .

If you have enjoyed this book, consider making your next selection from among the following . . .